FUELING CHANGE

How We Created Climate Change
One Fuel at a Time

Twyla Dell, Ph.D.

and
David W. Jackson

LAST LAP PRESS
overland park, kansas

2020

Dell, Twyla J. (1938-); Jackson, David W. (1969-)
 Fueling Change: How We Created Climate Change One Fuel at a Time.
 432 p.   cm.
 Includes bibliographical references, illustrations, and index.

ISBN-13: 978-1-7335017-1-2   (Last Lap Press)

Earth Day Edition, April 2020.

1. Force and Energy—United States—History. 2. Energy Development—Social Aspects. 3. Energy Development—History. 4. Energy Consumption—United States. 5. Power Resources—History. 6. Kansas City (Mo.)—History. I. Dell, Twyla J. (1938-). II. Jackson, David W. (1969-). III. Title.

Cover design by Lee Zuvanich, Elizabeth Bailey, and David W. Jackson.

For more information on how you can proceed at the dawn of the 21st century Solar Age, consult *Fueling Change*'s practical, companion guide, ***The Gasoline Diet***.

Published in the United States by:
Last Lap Press
Overland Park, Kansas
TDell@twyladell.com
twyladell.com

Testimonials

I was a captive reader from the moment I read the Introduction's title: "Fueling Change Means Changing Fuel." As a leadership professor who teaches managers how to lead change, I am well aware of the challenges of organizational and societal change initiatives.

Fueling Change is a clarion call to urgent change. It also presents the challenge in a simple call to action by laying out a 10-year plan to reduce gasoline usage (i.e., carbon emissions). Rather than being overwhelmed by pending environmental disasters, this plan provides a concrete, hope-filled way to prevent them.

While the book is a fact-filled, historical text on the evolution of energy, it contains beautiful art, pertinent photos, and lots of tables and graphs to make the data manageable. The chapters are short, and the pace is lively which helps to make the plethora of information in this book absorbable.

Near the end of the book the authors' purport that, "cities, not states, are becoming the engines of change." I would reduce the level of agency further. We are ALL the agents of environmental change.

Fueling Change provides a look backward and a map forward. I highly recommend it.

Charlotte Shelton, Ph.D.
Executive Associate Professor & Senior Scholar
Helzberg School of Management
Rockhurst University, Kansas City, Missouri

Fueling Change tells the story of energy and people through time.

This impressive collection of insights pulls together documents, artifacts and bountiful visuals to provide snapshots of how one city, Kansas City, has experienced transitions and variations in its energy supply.

Dell's hard work in *Fueling Change* offers a promising example that others might consult to tell a city's story through the energy that makes it go.

Brian C. Black, Ph.D., Head, Division of Arts and Humanities
Distinguished Professor of History and Environmental Studies
Editor, Energy and Society book series with WVUP
Penn State, Altoona, Pennsylvania

Once I read Part 4, I changed the way I move in the world.

Kay Laurent, Overland Park, Kansas

Dell's work is thorough, easy to read, and engaging. I've learned a lot about the history of Kansas City and feel richer for it.

Tom Jacobs, Mid-America Regional Council, Kansas City, Missouri

Fueling Change is an encyclopedia of facts and history that reads like a good novel.

Bob Painter, energy expert, Kansas City, Missouri

How We Changed as Our Fuel Changed

The Wood Age

Follow these four figures through 200 years of history as they experienced three fuel transitions. Join them at the dawn of the Solar Age as we face what can only be called a gasoline diet as we transition to alternative and renewable fuels.

The wagon wheel represents the Wood Age; animals provided power. The fire and candle were their only source of heat and light. What tasks sustained life on the frontier for our ancestors? Judging from this mural, what conditions could only exist in the Wood Age? What can you say about men's roles? What were women's responsibilities?

The Coal Age

Here the wooden wheel has become iron. When the railroad united East and West in 1869 with the Hannibal Bridge over the Missouri River in the background, The Coal Age introduced the superior fuel. It brought heat, light, electricity, and the ability to fire furnaces of great size, like iron bridges and the iron horse to roll over them. Which characters' lives changed the most? The least?

The Oil Age

Oil amazed us and changed our world with its many uses from lubrication to light to travel. Oil's quantity, power, and versatility surprised and delighted everyone. How did this marvelous fuel change our ancestors' lives?

Our ancestors' lives changed dramatically with the introduction of oil into all parts of the economy. How did they change? Whose changed the least? Have women's lives improved? The woman holds a spoon in her hand. Using the spoon as a clue, what did the use of coal as fuel for manufacturing provide her for the first time in history? Notice the railroad wheel is left behind for the automobile wheel. How did that change the face of America...the world? How does the Oil Age shape your life?

The Solar Age

As the Solar Age emerges, how shall we power everything in our world? What inventions, solutions and bridges to the next scenario will amaze us? Looking forward to technologies that may tantalize us, we need to remember to balance present and future fuel needs. *The way we will live using the fuel available is our fuelture.*™ The automobile wheel must now be replaced by the bicycle wheel in the 21st century. Not until we declare burning gasoline as intolerable because of the CO_2 it emits will we enter the Solar Age. These four characters, the current and future generations, have a new kind of world to build. What might it look like? Where would you place these four on a timeline of the 21st century? What are these characters' roles now? Have duties and jobs changed with what we might call "fuel liberation?" Only the fuelture™ will tell.

Fueling Change

The use of the city of Kansas City as a model is innovative, and the reader anywhere in the developed world can relate to the examples Dell provides. Dell uses storytelling combined with history, science, and technology in a compelling narrative that takes the reader to a provocative yet practical answer.

Nancy Cramer, retired teacher, author, Retreat to Victory

What could be timelier than a new book about how fuel and energy have and do continue to shape our lives and our planet to this very minute? Twyla Dell has taken a complex subject, the history of a major city in America's heartland, and turned it into a saga of city change and expansion through the use of three fuels.

Tom Marsh, author
To the Promised Land: A History of Government and Politics in Oregon

Twyla Dell has produced a lovely book that underscores how national energy transitions shape local history. Kansas City, Missouri produced amazing innovations in their society when faced with the possibilities and limits of energy sources, and seeing the history depicted as energy history brings an entirely new interpretation to a familiar story.

Alesia Maltz, Ph.D., Core Faculty, Department of Environmental Studies
Director, Program in Interdisciplinary Studies
Antioch University, Keene, New Hampshire

Fueling Change is a readable history of the impact of fuel transitions on the settlement of Kansas City and its growth as a trade center. I recommend that libraries (public and high school) provide access to the book.

Dolores Furtado, Ph.D.,
Professor Emerita, Medical Microbiology, University of Kansas

The illustrations and data charts kept me reading what is very interesting history. Thank you!

Fran Hess, Leawood, Kansas

I found *Fueling Change* fascinating, thoroughly enjoyable, and informative about the ways in which gasoline has been "the sculptress of our ways and means." I'm very interested in history and especially the history of the Kansas City region. Even though I have held positions on local and state historic societies, I learned a lot from *Fueling Change*.

You can't change what you don't understand, and the history Dell has shared about the evolution of the country and the Kansas City community, specifically through the lens of energy, is the perfect way to equip us and inform our decisions to make the changes that are required if we care about the future of Kansas City…and the planet. I found the social and economic forces (such as food in low-energy systems, or slavery as an energy source) being directly connected with our energy choices—from the Osage and early settlers to contemporary citizens—very interesting and informative.

Bob Berkebile, Fellow, American Institute of Architects
Principal Emeritus, Kansas City, Missouri

Contents

Introduction

How We Created Climate Change One Fuel at a Time

When humans began burning wood maybe a million years ago, each fire left a little cloud of smoke we now know as carbon dioxide. No problem when fires are few. When they multiply in number, intensity and type of fuel? Big problem.

Early humans saw in fuel something they had to own and master. The concentration, discipline, and organization they used to hunt was now applied to a different outcome. The more fuel they found, the more they burned. The more they burned the better their lives became. The better their lives the more CO_2 collected in the sky, the overhead vault. Our history hangs in particles above us. It holds our triumphs and failures . . . a ledger of spent resources in pursuit of human progress. We made a date then with today's climate-change crisis.

Fuels are the tectonic plates of civilization under the feet of humanity. When they move, things change. *Fueling Change* is about three different fuels seismically shifting in the 19th century around the world and certainly in the United States of America. *Fueling Change* uses one Midwestern city to unpack this story. As Kansas City and the rest of the globe faces another tectonic movement of changing fuel, this history instructs us on our road forward.

This city's transition from one fuel (wood) to another (coal) and then another (oil) and soon a fourth (renewables) in less than 100 years is a street-level story—the way changing fuels changed lives. Kansas City's history seen through the lens of fuel and energy gives us a rare look into this historic phenomenon. The town sprang from nowhere to a powerful entity in the heart of the country in the last gasp of Wood-Age conquest. Landscapes of "inexhaustible forests" fell before the settler's ax and saw. The town derived its energy from the hordes of opportunity seekers passing through it, and from those who stayed and settled.

Kansas City was a place of simultaneous arrivals and departures, all going west. It lay at the very Western edge of the known world at a moment when Eastern knowability would soon overtake it. Wagon trains would be replaced by railroads in a 20-year span. Horses, the Wood-Age's best offer for transportation, would be replaced by the Coal Age's unbeatable takeover of 250 trains a day in the 1890s (page 179). By then, passengers could ride in style in all directions. Moving tectonic plates at work forced the city's residents to change fuels hand over hand, pipe over pipe, reins to steering wheel, all the while building a fine city of boulevards, parks, and fountains.

That story can be divided into parts as the process of introducing and amplifying a fuel's impact on a city forces it to grow and change. First, a local supply of fuel satisfies basic needs in the "Discovery and Development" phase of a delivery system. Soon that local supply plays out and the community needs to create a larger "Systems Organization" to reach new supplies of that, or another fuel. If that works, then the heavy lifting of supplying a population with fuel requires "Expansion and Defense." Quite often several supplies of fuel or varieties of fuel will compete and defend themselves in the marketplace. Finally, supplies tend to thin or die out, and one or more goes into "Niche and Decline." This is a process through which all fuels travel, sometimes quickly in a few decades, and sometimes over a century or two.

All young cities go through these transitions and have their own unique narratives. Kansas City is a microcosm of the great fuel and energy transitions of the 19th century. Rarely does a community history acknowledge fuel as its executive producer. *Fueling Change* does.

Part 1 lays out life in the last moments of the Wood Age. River towns competed with one another. Small businesses outfitted people with wagons and livestock and organized wagon trains to trade with the towns in western territories. Crowds of hopeful fortune seekers rushed into the great unknown. Native Americans like the Osage were displaced from their ancient hunting lands. Missouri's statehood led to the opening of virgin prairies to farming.

What makes the founding and growth of Kansas City memorable is its unique moment and placement in 19th century American history. A sparse human population over eons exploded into a city of more than 320,000 in the 20th century. The lifeway of a successful aboriginal culture of at least 600 years at this site would be replaced in a few decades by the pioneering inroads of a foreign culture—Euro-American settlers. Upward, onward, forward expansion of human appetite to transform "Indian land" into a white man's city became a bustling landscape of soul satisfaction. Bringing in coal and displacing wood changed hearth to stove. For the first time in history women could stand up to cook.

Still held captive by the Wood-Age animal infrastructure, enterprising businessman Francis X. Aubrey doubled, then tripled his trade from Kansas City to Santa Fe in 1853. By pressing horses beyond their expected limits, by stationing a fresh horse at intervals along the way, and by sleeping in the saddle, he dared the software of brute animal power to elevate him to new profit taking. Aubrey covered 800 miles in five days. He "understood the business of speed" and left two weeks before the other wagons from Kansas City to Santa Fe. His methods were then copied by Alexander Majors who created the Pony Express in that model. Squeezing the last drops of power out of that old fuel ensemble—they didn't call them "hayburners" for nothing-- marked the last decades of the Wood Age. Then the intercontinental railroad changed travel forever. Coal created the speed that had eluded the Wood Age. Trains sprang like jack rabbits over the tracks and collapsed a 5-month arduous trip to a 10-day cruise across the prairies. The Coal Age created the speed that had eluded the Wood Age.

Whole populations moved from candle to kerosene lamp to electric light in 20 years. From wood lot to coal train to oil pipeline. From woodpile to internal-combustion engine. From horse to horseless to auto-mobilizing one's life. New fuels created amazing changes. Each fuel offered its own characteristics and required new kinds of combustion housing, new fuel delivery systems, new products, new labor forces, new management, new investment. Fortunes were made. Humanity's boat floated on new fuels.

Part 2 introduces the superiority of coal even as forests still fell to build cities and navies from the east coast to the Missouri River. The slow and steady accumulation of CO_2 from burning wood accrued in the atmosphere until the Industrial Revolution of the 18th and 19th centuries stepped up the pace. The availability of coal as fuel with its increased heat value

10

almost double that of wood created the volume and intensity of fire that led to rapid manufacture.

Coal blackened skies like wood could never do. Within a generation, a Sears Roebuck catalogue of over 1,000 pages showed the miracle of coal at work, sullied the skies in the name of consumer goods. The catalogue pages held the fruits of this energy transition: the beginning of the consumer revolution made on assembly lines. These were fed by coal mined from underground resources. Demand for quantities of fuel forced greater volume than dragging logs from the forest straight into the forge. These autonomous enterprises would quickly disappear as coal and the Bessemer process created steel on an industrial scale in huge factories (page 187).

All that changed with the spark of the American Civil War. The South fought from the position of the last decade of the Wood Age, while the North fought from the first decade of the Coal Age. Same decade. Different fuel sources. Coal won. The North won. The North traded up to new mechanical processes while the South protected its traditional framework. That was always the South's position. They clung to slaves and their only machine, the cotton gin, and defended the cotton market. Coal forced the arguments about the superiority of coal into a contact sport. The screams of 4 million energy units (the number of slaves in the South, according to the 1860 Census on page 113) split the air, and the Civil War began.

Enter oil in Part 3. Even before the Civil War, oil appeared on the scene in 1859. Wood and coal both burned at full capacity. Wood was an old source but reinvigorated by its position as an active, machine-moving fuel. And coal felt mighty because it was at the beginning of a long run and the mine owners were betting on it. Now comes another fuel so different, dynamic, plentiful and scalable, it blows the other two away.

Oil may be the planet's greatest gift as fuel yet. Oil is there for the drilling, endless amounts rising to the surface. Oil is a liquid capable of being sluiced around the planet in a vast circulatory system. From well to pipeline . . . to ship to refinery . . . to be shaken like a cocktail mix and sent out in different recipes to supply the needs small and large of a vast fuel network. Oil is *better* than any dream we might ever have had.

If people had been asked the day before the first oil well strike in 1859, What oil might yield, what their ideal use of this burbling, oozy liquid would be, they might have answered, "Better lamp light." Lighting was everything since no engines sat idle waiting for a fuel to turn their moving parts. Oil exploded onto an unready population. Oil in its plenitude was beyond their imagination to sketch such a way to power the world. Gushing, bountiful liquidity in such indescribable generosity was the unimaginable element. Extracting all fuels is an act of brute struggle. But little thinking went into welcoming into their lives oil, a liquid fuel of such proportion and versatility.

Oil ran everywhere—into gullies, and hastily forged pits. Having spent the eons of human effort collecting so little that only 1 or 2 ounces could be sold in small bottles as "snake oil," no one had any idea that a fuel as magnificent as oil could leap from the ground in a 100-foot spout and rumble and roar its announcement to life (page 133). The forecast of the end of whaling that produced a small but valuable amount of the finest oil had scared the marketplace.

Fueling Change

What could replace it? Whale oil was already dear. The Titusville, Pennsylvania, discovery of "rock oil" as compared to whale oil, quite literally "saved the whales."

Oil was then refined into gasoline. What a fuel! Part 3 includes a first-ever, comprehensive timeline of gasoline intimately tying its influence to 20th century culture. The love affair started with a slow burn. Then, when engines powered by gasoline were developed, humankind advanced to an entirely new way of life.

All this "fueling up" comes with a price we have just begun to fully realize. This is the message of Part 4. CO_2 in the atmosphere—50% more than 100 years ago—is no longer just a thoughtless, invisible discard, but a depressing reality. We can't recycle CO_2. We can't wash it away. Only healthy, growing plants can clean the air. Still, increasingly, we burn the plant canopy, too. We add megatons of CO_2 particles to the sky every day even as we enjoy the fruits of the burn.

The planetary burn in which we are engaged, to which we add immeasurable amounts of fuel every day—personal and industrial—is a thing unto itself. Burning that amount of fuel creates a platform for self-fulfillment and indulgence for our human population beyond anything our forebears could have imagined. We burn with the willful ignorance of enjoying a bountiful level of fuel support while living in a closed system.

We identified this "greenhouse" problem over 100 years ago. Some of us cautiously accepted it more recently. All of us understand if you light a fire in your house and don't allow the smoke to escape, it will accrue in unpleasant ways making it hard to breathe and even see. We quickly traded the term "energy transition" of the 1990s to the sweatier "greenhouse effect" to a more abstract "global warming," which has given way to the reluctantly accepted but abstract reality of "climate change," and then on to the frightening scope of the "climate crisis' and now to "climate shock." The whole planet now experiences the consequences of the planetary burn and witnesses its creeping effect. The overhead vault—the sky above—is now the lid on the pressure cooker, and the more CO_2 we send up the more it turns up the heat.

In 2020, we can stop climate change in 10 years if we literally put on the brakes.

The challenge of weaning ourselves off gasoline finishes this story in Part 4. Granted this would mean a screech of those brakes of the status quo, and an enthusiastic embrace of the next step: Hybrid. A concentrated push to the brink of the Solar Age and an overwhelming lunge to the revolution of renewable living.

But what choice do we have?

We can't just drive around in our 20th century paradigm while the planet begs us to embrace 21st century imperatives.

The only way to stop climate change is to stop driving 20th-century cars.

We need to cut back burning gasoline by at least 50% if we want to inhabit a place that still looks, feels, smells like a world we would like to live in.

We simply have to stop sending CO_2 ash into the overhead vault, or read our fate in those accumulating, darkening clouds.

History is simpler than we think: It's all about fuel all the time. The kind and amount of fuel defines our human civilization. That was true 10,000 years ago. It is true now. It will be true in our fuelture.™

How Our Fuel Sources Have Changed Over the Last 200 Years

-1820	1820-1870	1870-1920	1920-1970	1970-2020	2020-2050
Wood 3 Coal 1	Wood 3 Coal 2 Oil 1	Wood 4 Coal 3 Oil 2	Coal 3 Oil 2	Coal 4 Oil 3 Alternatives 1	Oil 4 Alternates 2

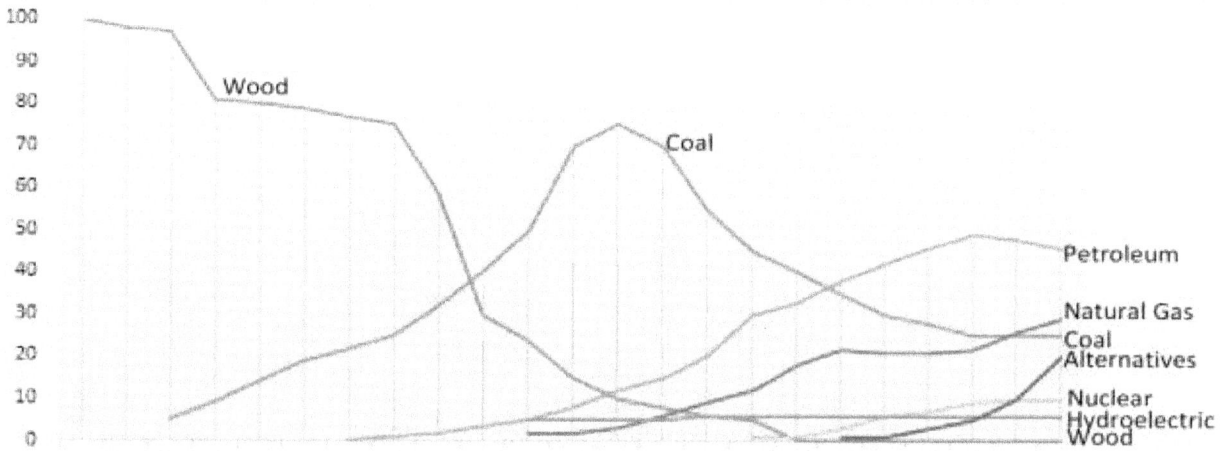

Kansas City, Missouri's History and Population, 1820–2020

Chart labels (left to right along timeline):

- Osage and French trade at Kawsmouth; Lewis & Clark 1804-06
- Missouri Statehood / Santa Fe Trail- 1821 — 1820
- Osage Treaty at Fort Osage-1822; Jackson County created-1826 — 1830
- Town of Kansas founded-1835; Missouri River steamboats — 1840: 300 (1845)
- Water powered grist mills — 1850: 478 (1855);
- Westward wagon trains — 3,224 (1857)
- Civil War, 1861-65; Emancipation — 1860: 4,418; 15,064 (1857)
- Railroads/Coal production/distribution; Hannibal Bridge-1869 — 1870: 32,268
- Electricity; Union Depot — 1880: 55,785
- Steel; Cable cars / Streetcars — 1890: 132,716
- First automobile on KC streets-1899 — 1900: 163,752
- Standard Oil refiners in KC; Oil wells at Unity Village — 1910: 248,381
- Union Station; World War I, 1914-1918 — 1920: 324,410
- Harry Truman's Jackson County Public Works Program-1930-1940 — 1930: 399,746
- World War II-1941-45; Muscle cars and smog — 1940: 399,178
- Demise of KC's streetcars,-1957 — 1950: 456,622
- EPA founded-1970 — 1960: 475,539
- Clean Air Act-1970; Oil embargo-1973 — 1970: 507,330
- Alternative Motor Fuels Act-1988; Exxon Valdez- 1989 — 1980: 448,078
- EPA's Energy Star Program-1992 — 1990: 435,146
- Renewable Fuel Standards Program-2006 — 2000: 441,545
- KC Power and Light's electric car initiative-2015 — 2010: 459,787
- Streetcars return to KC -2016 — 2020:

Created by David W. Jackson, 2018. Data: Dell; Whitney (1908); Schurr and Netschert (1960); mcdc.org; eia.gov

Fueling Change

Expansion
& Defense

Systems
Organization

Discovery &
Development

Niche &
Decline

4 Stages of Energy Transitions

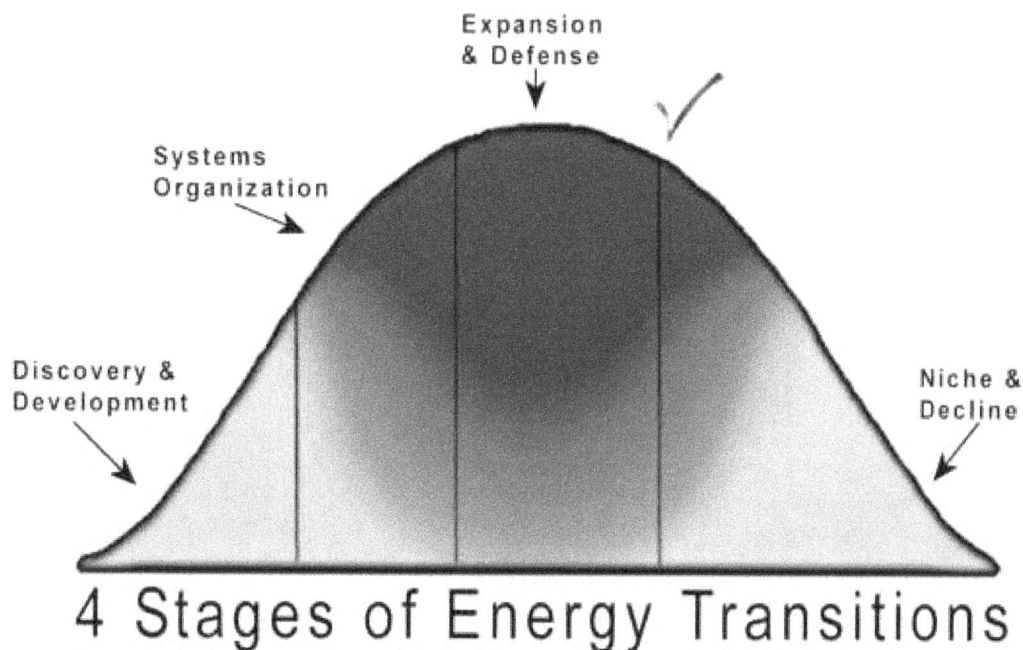

This simple bell curve shows the rise and eventual fall of all fuel sources whether local or worldwide. Every fuel use goes through the same process.

In Discovery and Development stage the site of the fuel—forest, mine or well is discovered and first used. A decision is made whether to exploit this source for fuel and energy.

If the fuel is bountiful enough, the quality good enough, the situation surrounding the fuel site from labor to politics secure enough, Systems of Organization form: removal, transportation and use with accompanying financial means are added to transform raw resource to marketplace commodity.

As the greatest amount of that resource is made available by the previous two stages, that fuel gains a part of the marketplace. Expansion and Defense take over: Other sources of the same fuel or other fuels make room for it as a marketable supply expands to accept more fuel. As the source of the supply dwindles, that fuel becomes scarce. The checkmark at the third division shows where we may be in the 21st century in terms of fuel and supply.

Niche and Decline are inevitable: Some fuels become a niche fuel like coal retreating from home heating to specialize in industrial and electrical heating; others die out like wood as it is replaced by a new fuel.

This unique view of the four stages of energy transitions shows both an abstract concept and a local community proving that concept. Twyla Dell has studied energy transitions for the past 10+years and now offers this unique view of a local community interacting with the world through its fuel supply as citizens grapple with gains and losses as they move from building the town with wood, the city with coal and the suburbs with gasoline.

A New Fuel and Energy Vocabulary

In discussing a city in terms of fuel and energy it is important to clarify terminology:

Culture: The sum of human custom, mores, technology and artifacts defined by kind, amount and quality of fuel available.

Energy: Invisible, may or may not be combustible; available in potential from sun/eco-system, may be converted to muscle and mechanical power; produced by interaction between humans and eco/econo-systems; follows bell curve of life and health of ecosystems from which fuel is also derived; ability to do work; is reduced by the amount of work done; derived from burning fuel; output measured by calories, horsepower, watts, kilowatts, joules.

Energy component: subset or one of many parts of the energy suite (like waterways and ecosystems) as well as individual technologies and energy suppliers of the energy suite (like wagon trains, slavery, railroads, automobiles/highways, telephones/communications); what would indicate the kind of fuel that is used to create it, or to support the use of that component as it is used in that population/culture.

Energy intensity: A measure of a nation's energy efficiency calculated as units of energy per unit of GDP. High energy intensity means there is a high price or cost of converting energy into GDP; low energy intensity the opposite.

Energy suite: a matched set of natural and man-made components with a common fuel denominator and the resultant energy generated by all available means in that suite. Each of the major fuels—wood, coal, oil—create and made possible individual energy suites identifiable by the kinds and numbers of dwellings, cultural artifacts, transportation means, technologies and extraction methods for fuel, including the size, types and materials used to make wheels. These suites are commonly identified by the names Wood Age (really, the Age of Wood and Muscle); Coal Age, Oil Age, and Solar Age.

Energy system: complete interaction of man participating in an eco/econo-system and includes whichever fuels are being used. An energy system is comprised of these parts: 1) work, 2) process heat—powering machines, making metals, and 3) space heat.

Fueling Change

Energy transition: An exchange of quantities, qualities and kinds of energy generated by various fuels. In common use the point at which a dominant fuel takes the place of a waning fuel creating a shift in energy availability, generation and intensity.

Fuel: Combustible, measurable, usually visible finite amount available from abundance to scarcity, a result of human gathering/harvesting/mining/drilling/converting; the ability to heat; output measured by BTUs and calories; follows bell curve of fuel use through four stages; converts energy through fire to heat, light, power machines to exert energy to do work; is reduced by the amount of fuel burned; inefficiently used and profligately wasted. When fuel is burned, it produces heat and light; when burned in a machine, it produces energy; the combination of fuel/conversion/energy and animal or machine produces power. The same may be said for animal and manpower, they being the "machines" in question. Fuel is a tool to express the values of a human culture using fire.

Fuel chain: The total production, technological, financial, regulatory activity of fuel extracted, delivered, used and disposed of for a particular fuel. A system that manages and stores fuel for use and delivers it as needed. Plural, the total of all fuels and their activities.

Fuel transition: An exchange of one exclusive or predominant fuel for another in a particular human population.

Fuelture™ (Or, fuel future): A viable future on planet Earth depends on the kind and amount of fuel available to supply comfort, safety, equality and opportunity for all species. *In other words, the way we will live using the fuel available is our fuelture.*™

Hierarchy: component, system, suite; components from wind to wagons create the system of organized fuel and energy that creates the suite defined by technology and artifacts that evolve from the dominant fuel that create the culture of a population.

Overlap: An overlap occurs when one fuel starts to come onto the commercial scene, another loses ground and the two energy suites overlap processes, technologies and uses as they pass each other over a particular time frame. In other words, there is a crossover of different components as one fuel succeeds and the other recedes. Technologies adapt to the needs of each fuel and evolve from one suite to another.

Power: the result of access to energy in various forms that can be measured in mechanical output, physical and political strength, might, force, control and command.

System: The interaction of organized parts that function as a whole to deliver an outcome, for example, wood harvest and delivery along rivers to supply steamboats.

18

How to Map a Fuel Transition

The following grids contain six qualities that each fuel must have to be commercially successful. The second feature is the four stages that any population goes through as they use each fuel. The essential six requisites were written by the coal industry in the 1850s and reinterpreted here from Carmen Di Riccio, *Coal and Coke in Pennsylvania,* to serve as a guide to *any* fuel's life span, and economic and ecologic demands.

What Happens When We Move from One Fuel to Another

Essential Requisites	Stage 1: Discovery and Development	Stage 2: Systems Organization	Stage 3: Expansion and Defense	Stage 4: Niche and Decline
1. Good quality of fuel	Discovery, early development	Finance through corporations	New technologies, products, maintenance of supply	Dealing with fuel supply, new markets and/or steady decline
2. A sufficient quantity of fuel	New fuel site technologies	Delivery technology	Increasing efficiencies	Finding a niche for fuel source
3. Cheapness and regularity of production	Labor supply necessary for production	Workers become skilled; delivery systems evolve; Labor expands	Increased labor supply; changes in labor market, more sophisticated needs	Restructuring finances; laying off workers, closing sites
4. Cheapness of transportation	Initial technology	Organizing delivery systems	Competing in price, position, and demand.	Disposing of infrastructure
5. A sufficiency of transportation	Fuel for transportation	Technology for transportation	Expansion and efficiencies of system	Retooling for new delivery
6. A good market i.e. end users	Education for use with available or new technology	Waste, pollution safety concerns	Environmental laws competing with expanding markets and abundance of goods	Dealing with decline of primary fuel source and all waste sites and disposal

This is a protype of the way the four stages play out with each fuel scenario covered in *Fueling Change.* Each fuel (wood, coal, and oil) has its own chart in the appropriate section.

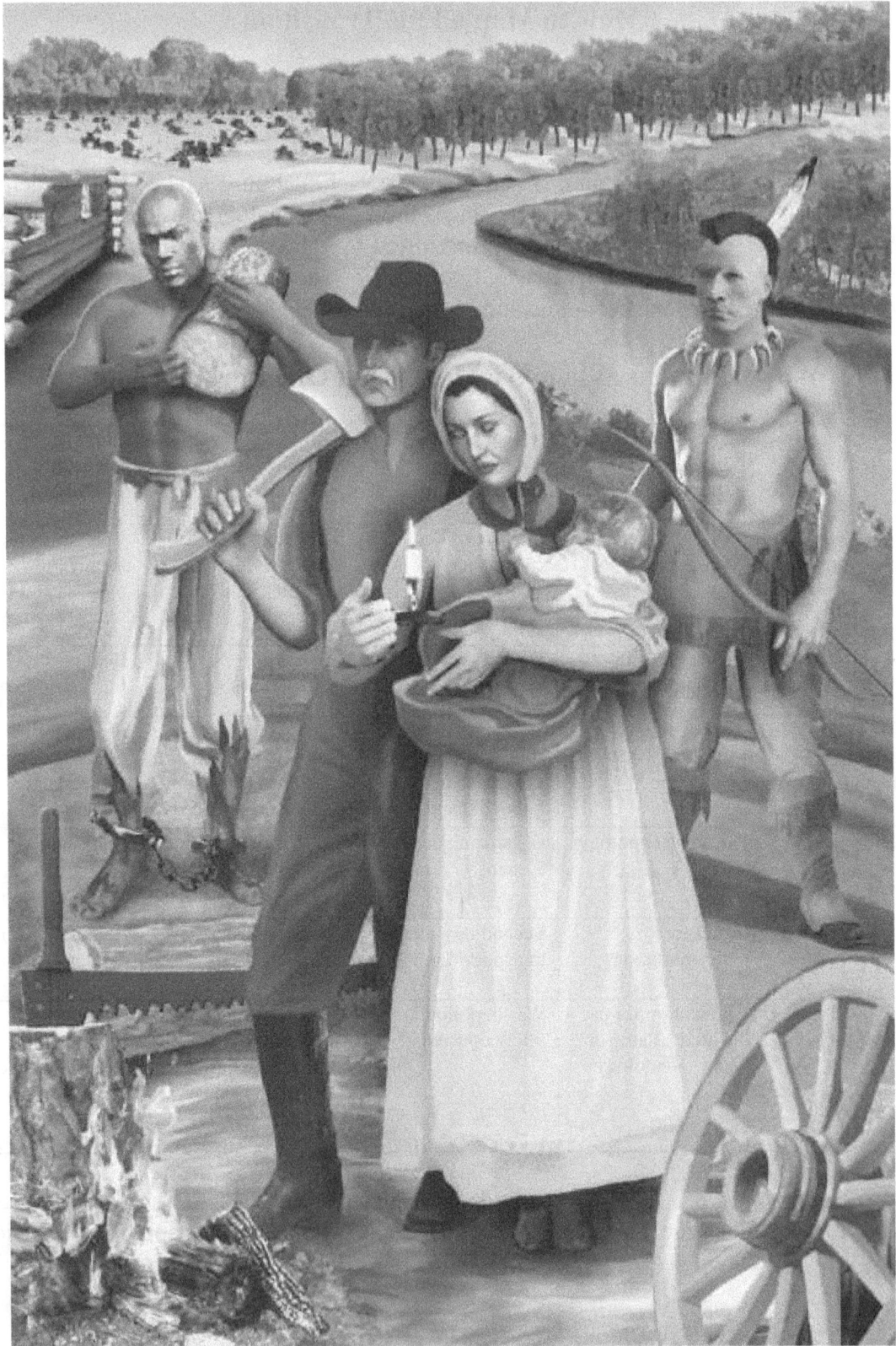

Part 1

Hello to The Wood Age in America, 1620-1890

*The amounts and types of energy employed condition man's way of life materially
and set somewhat predictable limits on what he can do and on how society will be organized.
The influence of energy is seen to be ubiquitous, with economic, political, social,
psychological, and ethical consequences intermeshed.*[1]
--Fred Cottrell, *Energy and Society* (1955)

In two hundred years the exchange of wood for coal, oil and natural gas would completely reverse the ratio of fuel to energy so that "heavy lifting" would seldom be done by human or animal and most all mechanical work would be done by machines. The first hundred years would transform one little outpost in the middle of the American wilderness that would be caught up in the same world-wide transformation.

Most of the inventions of the Wood Age had been made in earlier eras. Little new technology lay on the horizon for wood—except for wood's greatest expression, to move from heating and lighting to motive power for machines—from passive to active fuel, but no one yet thought in those terms.

In the long reign of wood as both fuel and building material, humanity grew from filling its most basic needs for fuel for today to its most sophisticated desires for building long-lasting empires. By the time America's shores were breached in the 17th century by the incoming tides of immigrants, the world's populations had together reached a mature stage of wood use expressed in low- and high-energy intensity. The amounts of energy available depended on the technology developed to use the wood available. Generally, those with little technology lived free of permanent structures and tools while those with high-energy intensity based on the same wood fuel lived in a world of permanent buildings, domesticated animals, agricultural food production, technology and artifacts.

From 1607 onward, when British colonists first established a permanent colony at Jamestown, Virginia, and, indeed, for eons before, humanity used wood nearly 100% of the time for fuel. Coming to America only meant perpetuating that practice with new forests. But this chapter begins at the *end* of this long era (see graph on page 22). By the time permanent Euro-American settlement arrived on the shores of the Missouri River in 1821, the Coal Age had been going on for years in England, had already arrived in Philadelphia, New York, and Boston in the late 1700s, and would by the 1850s arrive at the Missouri River town that became Kansas City.

WOOD

Essential Requisites for Fuel Use	Stage I: Discovery and Development	Stage II: Systems Organization	Stage III: Expansion and Defense	Stage IV: Niche and Decline
Dates:	**1607**	**Early 1700s**	**Until 1885**	**1920s**
1. Good Quality of Fuel for Use	Mature timber available in America and easily accessible	Cities and towns enlarge wood gathering and selling	Technology allowed wood replacement by coal—RRs and stoves	Revival of wood during WWI because of coal shortages
2. Sufficient Quantity of Fuel	Fields cleared for farming provided building materials and farmland	Large cities like Boston and New York search farther and farther afield for wood supply	Erie Canal provides access to northwestern wood supply for coastal cities	Remaining quantity becomes more and more irrelevant for heating and manufacturing
3. Cheapness and Regularity of Production	Much more fine timber and lumber available than ever thought of in Europe	Wood plantations prominent in 18th and 19th centuries for iron works	Wood hawks sold kindling door to door. Frontier markets started with wood	Local suppliers only, small markets
4. Cheapness of Transportation	Waterways and horse-drawn sleds, wagons provided transportation; Sometimes coastal ships	"Wooding up" always a local process, catch as catch can; Labor was cheap and wood vital.	Steamboats devoured loads along inland waterways; $1.50 cord/ wood, $.75 bushel/coal	Still many horse-drawn wagons because roads were poor for trucks
5. Sufficiency of Transportation	Short supply avoided by branching-out to more remote resources, mostly water	Waterways and wagons	Steamboats burned what they found along river banks	As available locally with enterprising wood cutters
6. Good Market, (i.e., End-Users)	No shortage of end users eager for heat, cooking, and fuel for manu-facturing and building materials	Wood selling in a larger area not easy; stove technology increases efficiency	Populations still burning wood away from river delivery or coal piles	Dept of Ag issued a booklet on how to cut a tree and prepare wood for fire for coal consumers during WWI

CHAPTER 1

A Land of Rough Terrain

The native inhabitants of Missouri, the Osage Indians, lived in a low-energy-intensive culture among the plants and animals typical of the Midwest.

The area that became Kansas City showed the Midwest at its best, a mixture of timber and prairie, colorful groves, open meadows, rolling hills—and limestone cliffs overlooking the Missouri River. Bears roamed, eventually to provide "bear bacon" to settlers. Unlike the open prairie beyond the river, this westernmost stretch of Missouri grew a profusion of thick stands of white oak, black oak, hackberry, mulberry, box elder, walnut, ash, sycamore and cottonwoods. Some white oaks measured seventy-nine inches and some walnut trunks sixty inches in diameter and served as witness trees for John C. Sullivan, one of the government men who surveyed the area from 1818 onward as statehood was conferred.[1]

Fueling Change

To look at the beginning of settlement by the Euro-Americans in a land already occupied by the Osage Indian tribe is to create an opportunity to rethink that history in terms of fuel and energy use. Seen through this lens, life before the first steamboat arrived is a complete *energy suite* of people, animals, wagons and wagon wheels, horses and bridles, wind and waterpower working together to produce a certain standard of living with wood as fuel. Both cultures lived in a resource-rich but technology-poor environment. Unknown to them were deposits of coal and oil beneath their feet, the "underground forest" or "underground reservation," as those resources would later be called.[2]

In settling an area dense with forest, the Euro-Americans felled their own trees and chopped their own wood or had slaves do it, in what may be called a pre-commercial use of fuel.[3]

The populations of both Osage and Euro-American cultures found and burned their wood without the exchange of money or trade of goods in any kind of formalized marketplace. None existed for fuel wood on the frontier, nor was one needed. Both cultures lived with plenty of fuel wood in this central Midwest location. However, there was a scarcity of the energy resource of technology. Within those constraints one group lived at the height of the settled Euro-American agricultural version of the Wood Age, while the other group lived at the height of a semi-nomadic, hunter-gatherer version, which could only exist in the Wood Age.[4] This chapter looks at both cultures through the lens of wood as fuel, and the energy available.

A Garden of Eden

Even before the surveyors arrived, Euro-American explorers had reported on the area. In 1804, the Lewis and Clark expedition noted coal deposits on the riverbanks on June 25. Within a week they arrived at the future Kansas City site on July 4. But coal was not used as fuel in an area thick with trees.[5] The natural abundance of the land promised good support to Euro-American emigrants: good soil for crops, plentiful rivers for carrying their harvest to market, thick woods for building houses, bountiful game to eat. The new frontier of the 19th century beckoned with virgin timber and rivers were used as its transport.

Outcrops of layered limestone testified to the geologic history of ancient sea beds as "abundant outcrops of rather heavy beds of limestone accentuate the roughness. The larger streams that drain the high upland plains are also bordered by belts of rough country," wrote William Z. Hickman in his 1920 history of Jackson County, Missouri.[6] The limestone bluffs on the south side of the Missouri River forced the current to deposit its load of good silt instead in Clay and Ray counties on the north bank of the river, the reason Francois Chouteau chose those banks for his first trading post.

He would snag each canoe as it came 'round the bend to unload its catch of furs from distances and places known only by their fur yield. This same current left exposed the natural limestone pier on the south side that would make a good steamboat landing later. On this site would rise the future village of Kanzas, as it would first be spelled. Within a hundred years it would blossom into a robust Kansas City.[7]

Beaver lived abundantly along the many streams; elk and bear flourished, and buffalo ranged here but most abundantly on the western plains, along with a profusion of white-tailed deer.

"Their tracks are as plenty as Hogs about a farm," William Clark wrote on June 26, 1804, a few days after the expedition's stop at the limestone promontory overlooking the confluence of the Kaw and Missouri Rivers.

Brown bears, wild turkey, raccoons, a stunning array of wildflowers, *"rasberreis perple, ripe and abundant,"* tall sweet grass, and all manner of birds from eagles to hawks— not to mention snakes and insects, *"Mosquitos, Ticks and Knats verry troublesome."*

They also saw, "emince number of Deer on both Sides of the river . . . and great quantities of Bear Signs where they had passed in all Directions thro the bottoms in Serch of Mulberries, which were in great numbers in all bottoms thro which our party passed." As for the cliffs, "Hills on the L.S. this evening higher than usial about 160 or 180 feet." In other words (and all misspellings aside), here was a land rich in food, water, cover and fuel, available for the taking.[8]

Meriwether Lewis

William Clark

Neither Lewis and Clark in 1804, nor the first Euro-American settlers, namely French fur trader Francois Chouteau in 1821, encountered a settlement at the site that would become Kansas City, though the larger territory was occupied by a nation of around 5,400 Native Americans known as the Wah-Sha-She, Wazhazhe or Ouazhagi, later pronounced in English as Osage.[9] They were part of an estimated, though unsubstantiated population of some 378,000 Native Americans in the Midwest alone. A white traveler such as Daniel Boone in 1798, however, rode from Kentucky through Illinois to western Missouri without meeting a soul in two months. The Native American numbers, thinned by disease and guarded by their natural wariness, kept out of sight.[10]

Handle Them as Tactfully as Possible

The Osage Indians dominated the "middle waters" of Missouri and Arkansas. Their force could not be ignored then, nor should their story be ignored now. They were fine warriors whose highest goal in life was to die in battle, so visitors soon learned to avoid provocation.

Approaching them meant being particularly sensitive to their strength and prowess, hence the directive to handle them carefully.[11] The Osage enjoyed a hunter-gatherer life of efficiency and long endurance whose meat diet was augmented by small vegetable gardens. They lived in symmetrical, semi-permanent villages, with few tools, and one domesticated animal—the dog. Relatives of the Dhegiha Siouans along the Ohio River, they gradually moved west into Missouri.[12]

Once involved with the French in fur trading in the 17th century, they expanded as far west as the Rockies and as far south as the future states of eastern Oklahoma, Kansas and Arkansas.[13] Strong in both stature and belief in themselves, they occupied a strategic position in the Midwest that made them a formidable presence for any neighbor or interloper. With the simplest technology they were in command of their territories.

The European-Americans arrived with an agricultural system embedded in their psyches imported from the old country. To make the system work required, shall we say, a full wagon: horses, oxen, mules, wagons full of possessions, axes, plows, a few machines such as corn and coffee grinders, and even sometimes a small population of slaves. On the bend of the Missouri River before it turned north, at the western edge of a newly defined political boundary, they intended to build a settlement that would look exactly like those they had left behind either in Europe or the east coast.

These settlers would go about creating their lives there in exactly the

Le Soldat Du Chene
"Soldier of the Oak"
Second Chief of the Little Osage Nation

same way with plow to till the land and gun to ward off danger, with "talking leaves" of paper, as the Cherokee called them, full of promises to the local Indian tribes to give them land farther West.[14] The site that would become Kansas City straddled the edge of East and West. In the settler's eyes, they perched along the border between "Indian Territory" and "civilization."[15]

The pioneers made wood into implements like gears for water wheels and mills as well as all tools from lathes to axes to kitchen tools with just the smallest cutting edge made from iron or steel because each metal piece had to be shaped individually at the forge.[16] Because they had metal cutting tools like axes, saws, lathes and knives, the Euro-Americans used wood as building material if it was at all available. They made only their most prominent buildings in stone, or by using wood-fired furnaces to make brick. Family housing was made with logs or cut wood. They carved wood into furniture and decorative pieces; they paneled walls and ceilings, installed plank floors and covered the sides of their houses with it. Every ship and wagon came from wood sources.

The Osage Indians had no metal tools, no wheeled conveyances, no beasts of burden, no permanent structures and few possessions. They moved with the seasons following game and planting small gardens of vegetables, while the settlers lived in the same place in spite of the seasons, having the tools to keep warm in winter and cleared land to grow sufficient produce to diversify their diets. Euro-American settlers always intended to build at least a village if not towns and cities of permanent dwellings, streets, churches, schools and other accoutrements resulting from their implementation of the Wood Age.

Both the Spanish and the French knew about the Osage and their touchy temperament: "The Osages are the worst two tribes that we have on the Missouri and at the same time the strongest, the more so if they unite," wrote one Spanish official to another in 1790. "For this reason, it is necessary to temporize with them to some extent, handle them as tactfully as possible in order to restrain their excesses, as the few forces in the country do not permit anything else."[17]

The Great Osages, as they called themselves, lived in one village on the Osage River some seventy miles south of that limestone pier. Soon after Lewis and Clark's visit, the federal government-built Fort Osage, some 25 miles east of Kansas City on the Missouri River as an outpost to trade fur for goods with the Osage and as a military force to protect white settlers. No more than a few Euro-American families settled at that time farther downstream where the fur trading post was located. The Osage hunted along the Osage, Gasconade and Neosho Rivers south of the Missouri River to the headwaters of the St. Francis and White Rivers and on into Arkansas. They were estimated in 1825 to have a population of about 1,200 people at this site.

Another branch of the Great Osages lived about 140 miles southwest of Fort Osage in one village on the Neosho River. Their numbers were estimated to be about 400 in population with a hundred or so warriors. The Little Osage, as they named themselves, lived another hundred miles or so south on the Neosho River in three villages along with the remaining members of the tribe called Missouris, who had been folded into their numbers after small pox had destroyed their tribe a century before.

This population was estimated at about a thousand. George Champlin Sibley, Factor at Fort Osage, estimated the numbers of the Indians with whom he traded at the fort. The fort, built in 1808, acted as both a military outpost and a government trading post for the Indians to bring in their furs to exchange for knives, shirts, beads and other trade goods. It was the hope of the United States government that peaceful trade with the Osage would avert attacks on white settlers.[18] Though an exact census of the Indian populations of the continental United States was never made, these numbers were taken at the time as a good estimate.

1 Natchitoches, 1713–1822
2 Arkansas Post, 1686–1808
3 Kaskaskia, 1700–
4 Cahokia, 1699–
5 Los Adaes, 1721–73
6 Pecos Pueblo, ca. 1450–1838
7 Nassonite Post, 1719–62
8 Ft. De Chartres, 1720–64
9 Ft. Cavagnolle, 1739–64
10 Ft. La Reine, 1738–63
11 Lake Nipigon Post, 1684–1791

Map 3. Tribal Locations and Trading Establishments, Southern Plains, 1740, and Central–Northern Plains, 1750

Indian Nations borders in this map suggest territory known by landmarks and geography, rather than the straight lines in pen and ink records of the white man.

The ancestors of the Osage Indians and those of the Euro-American settlers had lived in separate hemispheres up to the 16th century when their cultures began to merge. Each had survived and prospered at different levels of energy use while burning the same fuel. The Osage had developed exquisitely balanced skills to live in the undeveloped world of the Western Hemisphere in a thinly sheltered existence very unlike their Old-World cousins.

They lived *in the woods*, on the ground, outdoors and knew that they themselves needed the same cover, food and water as did the animals they hunted for food. In spite of the large population of Native Americans occupying the continent for thousands of years and using and modifying its resources, great forests still stood, enormous numbers of game ranged, huge catfish swam in the rivers, flocks of birds beyond counting flew overhead.[19] A land of plenty that boggled the imagination of newly arrived settlers had somehow endured eons of use by indigenous populations at a level impressive to Europeans.

Fueling Change

The American Indians of necessity built their energy system on the values of perpetuating their landscape rather than consuming it. Their values, beliefs, mores, actions and artifacts, in other words, their culture, supported that understanding. As Native Americans everywhere had learned, "Over time they acquired a comprehensive understanding of the life-giving uses of resources around them and harvested little more than they consumed or traded for other like items."[20]

This mode of living is what we would call in the 21st century *sustainable*. It was reachable then because the demand on resources was small enough that they could replenish themselves almost every season, in other words *resilient*. That form of living fell to the energy-intensive wave of settlers to come.

Chapter 2

Making Fire: Women's Work or Men's Work?

Women's work is kitchen work no matter where and how they work!

The Osage indigenous women built the fires. They kept the fires going by borrowing fire from the chief's lodge from which all other fires were taken. Women tended the daily cooking fires.[1] Men hunted; women prepared. Men protected the village; women planted gardens, built the housing, made clothing and blankets from animal skins and cared for the children. Gathering and transporting firewood was women's work.[2]

The Native American approach to firewood contrasted with that of the white settlers. Native women gathered driftwood, twigs and branches. With a sprig of fire taken from the main lodge, they cooked over small fires and heated the confines of their teepees in winter or lodges in summer.[3]

Women used no hacking, sawing or cutting to gather their daily load. Those tribes who may have captured slaves sent them out on the onerous task of bringing home firewood, a journey that, toward the end of a population's stay in an area, might take them several miles in a day.[4]

The Osage lived along the banks of rivers not just for ready access to water, but for the driftwood that would wash up on the banks as well. Paul Wilhelm, Duke of Wurttemberg in his *Travels in North America, 1822-1824,* remarks several times about the "driftwood heaped against the bank," which suggests a steady delivery of wood to a nearby tribe.

Once an area had been picked clean of firewood, the village would have to move, or else longer journeys to new gathering sites would become part of the women's daily pattern, perhaps one of the reasons fires were kept small.[5]

Another supposition can be made that lodges made of rushes and brush were very flammable and fires had to be kept small to avoid sparks setting off a quick conflagration. Women had to understand the properties of fire very well before starting to cook their meals.

Having brought fire from the chief's lodge to cook, women were aware of how capricious fire could be. It was considered beneficial to have fire from the chief's lodge, and probably kept less-skilled people from starting the house on fire by striking flint on flint. It would make a European used to a stone hearth pause before striking tinder there.[6]

Fueling Change

One of few eyewitnesses, Henry Schoolcraft, observed:

The white hunter, on encamping in his journeys, cuts down green-trees, and builds a large fire of long logs, sitting at some distance from it. The Indian hunts up a few dry limbs, cracks them into little pieces a foot in length, builds a small fire, and sits close by it. He gets as much warmth as the white hunter, without half the labour, and does not burn more than a fiftieth part of the wood. The Indian considers the forest his own and is careful in using and preserving every thing which it affords.[7]

By all descriptions, the pioneers made profligate use of fire for heat, hastening the day of fuel-wood scarcity.

Clearing wood for planting of crops, of course, was a cornerstone of the Euro-American settlers' uses of the land, hence the clearing of whole trees versus the twigs that the Indians might use. The Native American value was to leave the cover of the forest somewhat intact for both themselves and the creatures they hunted. Unlike the Osage women who used pliable saplings to build lodges, the settlers looked for large logs a team of men would cut down. An American log cabin used about 80 logs plus smaller timbers for gables and shakes and the fireplaces could hold a log, two to three feet thick. A family might burn a half to a full cord of wood per day in the winter in a drafty log cabin.[8]

The Native American Fire

Indians around their campfire shows a small fire for which the wood has been gathered by the woman tending the cooking. This is a prototype Native American rendering. The Osage shaved their eyebrows and heads, save a Mohawk down the center of the scalp (See Ma-chet-seh photo on p. 225).

Though the woods were sacred to the Osage, they had certainly modified their environment through fire. Fire was their plow, and in this case, men wielded it.[9] With it they cleared fields, cleansed them of weeds and controlled the re-growth. With it they selected ways and means to grow certain crops in certain places. With fire they kept the undergrowth in the forests checked so they could see game to hunt, form pathways for game to pass through to the hunter's advantage, and glimpse approaching war parties.

An Osage fire started by embers from this chief's fire was considered holy and could give the power of life and health to those who used it.[10] Since the Osage built large lodges of saplings and woven rushes sometimes twenty feet by 10-feet-high by 50- to even 100-feet-long and used by several families, the women stored firewood within the shelter and left open holes in the roof to let out the smoke. They sometimes even stabled their fastest horses within the confines of the shelter.[11]

The Osage had their own practices and fire myths. Men lit their ceremonial fires by using the friction method. One of two well-dried sticks had holes drilled through the center and slits that allowed air to enter the hole cut from one edge. A second stick was set into the hole and twirled rapidly between the palms. A little tinder, a little blowing and a lot of spinning created a flame that was transferred to the laid firewood. Ordinary fires were lit using the bow drill, but more commonly, borrowed from one of the "two houses in the middle" of the village, those of the chief.

Fire was both beneficial and destructive. As a tribe prepared for war, the warriors lit a big fire and danced around it. Before leaving, they pulled burning tree limbs from the fire and put pieces of charcoal into small bags each carried. When the warriors approached an enemy, they used the charcoal to blacken their faces to show the merciless quality of fire. This warning meant they would show no mercy to enemies.[12]

Meanwhile, in a typical white settlement, the blacksmith's hammer ringing steadily beside a glowing charcoal pit showed a different use of fire. The romance of flames, the reverence, had been replaced with practical labor to make things. For the Euro-Americans of the period to create fire, they carried tinderboxes with flint and steel to strike to create sparks on a bed of cotton or hemp. These smoldering embers were then transferred to kindling. Fire to them, although vital, had become utilitarian.

Because the settlers had tools such as axes and saws, they could fell large trees handily while for the Indians with their stone implements this was arduous work. The Euro-American men split the logs for building or for fire use. This required the upper body strength of men. Without the technology of the ax, wedge, saw and ox and wagon, the whites, too, would have gathered twigs and driftwood and guarded them carefully.

"If the Indians initiated America's Wooden Age, the early settlers of New England, more than any other group of European immigrants, brought this age to fruition."[13] By the 1800s pioneers from the East carried the pattern to the Missouri River. Though the state was settled by Southerners, the peoples along the eastern seaboard all lived with access to the same level of technology.

Fueling Change

The word "frontier" implies a place of greater development left behind to be replicated at the new site. Such was the case with the Euro-Americans who carried the blueprints of their mature culture from the East in hearts and minds and wagons as they approached the western edge of the new state of Missouri.

A different kind of frontier awaited the 18th century Osage when they acquired horses from the Spanish. A new energy intensity awaited them as they learned to use this magical beast to propel them off the ground and change their pedestrian ways.

The Euro-American Settlers' Fire

Settlers have an iron pot and an axe, two pieces of technology that give them great advantage in cooking and collecting wood, which is being cut by a man with the axe. The horses and wagon in the background show the high-energy system they enjoy even as pioneers on the frontier.

Chapter 3

First Inhabitants—The Osage: Foot to Horseback

*The first energy transition in this region was the introduction
of the horse into the Osage Indian population.*

Perhaps the greatest difference between Osage and Euro-American settlers was the amount and kind of animal power available and their experience and attitude toward animal use. Once the Osage adopted horses, they were inseparable from them. Whatever little else they had in the way of possessions the stature of seeing the world from a horse's back gave them pride and prowess beyond their wildest imaginations:

> As the Osage drew near, I was struck by his appearance. He was about nineteen or twenty years of age, but well grown, with the fine Roman countenance common to his tribe, and as he rode with his blanket wrapped around his loins, his naked bust would have furnished a model for a statuary. He was mounted on a beautiful piebald horse, a mottled white and brown, of the wild breed of the prairies, decorated with a broad collar, from which hung in front a tuft of horse-hair dyed a bright scarlet.
>
> Washington Irving, *A Tour on the Prairies*, 1835

This romantic image of the American Indian nobly astride his steed epitomizes the Euro-American impression of the culture. Yet the horse galloped into the lives of the Native Americans in the 16th century to inject a degree of energy never before experienced. While the Old World had had the horse for some estimated five thousand years and had built their lives around it, the New World experienced both the power and tradeoffs of a new energy source for just two hundred years before steam power again changed their energy picture. For that brief period, the horse gave them "that hauteur and sense of superiority and arrogance which horses have given all men through the ages."[1]

For Euro-Americans, life routinely included animals as beasts of burden. Animal and human muscle increased the motive power of the Wood Age dramatically. Draft horses, having been broken to the shoulder collar in Europe in the Middle Ages, worked in teams of two to eight to pull wagons and coaches and to plow the fields. The heavy draft horses eventually used in agriculture were a byproduct of the age of armor when a man fully dressed in a suit required a horse strong enough to carry him. Oxen had traditionally been used for the heavy work of plowing, but horses gradually replaced them for farm work.[2]

Contrary to popular impressions of oxen versus horses, a pair of horses could outdo four oxen in a day of fieldwork by 25-30%. Well-fed horses and oxen could also outwork men on a day long basis and do the work of thirteen to fifteen men, but oxen could get by on grass while horses required oats. Since overland travel required wagon space to be used for oats to feed the horse, few were used. Mules were more sure footed, had greater stamina than horses, were often cheaper and could get by on grass.[3]

Fur trappers' trade with Native Americans included horses for pelts.

Josiah Gregg, one of the first to record experiences on the Santa Fe Trail, noted in 1844, "At an early period the horse was more frequently in use, as mules were not found in great abundance; but as soon as the means for procuring these animals increased, the horse was gradually and finally discarded, except occasionally for riding and the chase."[4] Each animal had its niche, its devotees and its detractors, and must have been as much a subject of discussion, pride and wager as muscle cars were to their 1950s admirers.

The Osage, like their fellow Native Americans on the continent, were a pedestrian nation until the Spanish arrived with horses from Europe. They may have acquired horses from the Spanish directly or by way of more southerly tribes that traded in horses, the Ute, the Kiowa and the Comanche.[5] The Spanish arrived in the 16th century coming up from Mexico, establishing ranches in Texas and New Mexico territories.

In Missouri territory French explorer Etienne de Veniard, Sieur de Bourgmont in 1713 gave up his coat and pistol to a Padouca Indian chief, a tribe near the Osage, and was given a horse in return. A "large number" of their warriors made trips to "the Spanish country" to trade buffalo robes for horses. They traded one horse for three buffalo robes. The chief offered to Bourgmont two thousand warriors if he ever needed them. If all the Padouca warriors were mounted, that would be quite a herd of horses and an even greater bounty of six thousand buffalo skins required to pay for them.[6]

An historical marker about Bourgmont at Clarks' Point overlooking the Missouri River Valley in downtown Kansas City, Missouri. One side of the marker is in French, the other in English.

When they contacted and began to trade goods with the European settlers, they were introduced to an entirely new energy system, which created their economic system. The Osage left their self-contained lifestyle and entered the world of durable material goods, and, once begun, they could not reverse their path. The acquisition of beads, clothing, woven blankets and steel implements sent ripples through the Osage social organization because the manufacture and replacement of such goods was beyond the power of the Native Americans to replicate, and they wanted more of them. Their only currency was furs, which they began to trap at a pace that soon outstripped the supply.

A new energy level introduced by these two items imposes new demands. The change in the Osage energy level also changed their relationship with other tribes as they all acquired horses that gave them greater range, pressured the limits of their territories and with which they raided other tribes for more ponies. Suddenly, a tribe, even an individual, could acquire the currency of horses that could make one warrior more powerful than another. Horses changed the dynamics of their seasonal movement as well. More horses meant more pasture. Horses needed pasture, sometimes at the cost of field crops that sustained and amplified their diets. Sometimes, providing enough pasture for a growing number of horses meant moving out of the woodlands to the prairie.[61]

The concept of a 1,000-pound animal that one could sit astride and force to do one's bidding had to have been astonishing to them. The Indians, upon their first sight of horses, referred to them as "big dogs" or "mystery dogs" and "fled weeping" in terror from what they had seen. Later, mainly because of its size, the name for a horse was changed to "Elk Dog."[62] Still, a dog of any size could be brought to serve, and with the white man's example, the Native Americans soon domesticated themselves to the horse and vice versa.

The point of view of a people who had never domesticated a large animal, says Osage author Louis F. Burns in *A History of the Osage People* (2004) is quite different from those who had acquired them in time beyond memory. "Everyday use of animal power generates a mindset toward power sources beyond the power of human muscle. This, in turn, directs the mind to other power sources and applications." Without animals, the only power available was human, which circumscribed a much smaller area of influence, Burns argued.

Aside from power issues, the lack of domesticated animals means that meat protein in their diet must always be provided by hunting wild animals.[63] However frightened they were initially, the Plains Indians quickly passed from terror to understanding of the advantages of dominating such a beast. In some tribes they soon foreswore any notion they had ever been without the horse.[64]

Power is the result of access to energy in various forms. The horses provided power to those who had them. Those who acquired them wanted more horses and more energy at their command. Raiding soon overtook trading in many cases as the horse changed the dynamics of inter-tribal relations.

As individual warriors acquired more horses, a new idea of status was born that required accumulation of horses. One was not enough even though the horse's usefulness was limited. Without the horse collar and without a wagon or plow or freight to haul, other elements of a horse's worth were lost to the Indians. But with horses the Osage could hunt buffalo with greater efficiency and speed while covering longer distances at the same time, not to mention the utter thrill of the chase the warriors must have experienced. Where once hunting a buffalo on foot required stealth and patience, a horsed hunt transformed the hunter to a noble warrior upon his steed thundering across the plains among the heaving buffalo, an enormously daring and exciting transformation![7]

Prior to the horse the practice of raiding other villages had been confined to vegetables and occasional captives.[8] The horse brought on a much greater level of action so that they could carry off more horses plus goods. Horses began to be used as currency, a new bargaining chip beyond furs to which the Indians had access as in the Bourgmont exchange, as previously described, when the French explorer gave his coat and pistol for a horse.

The chief had plenty of horses but had never seen such a coat. A horse was an easy unit of exchange and a mark of the value he set on the coat and pistol. The horse also changed the dynamics of the tribe itself as some men began to acquire more horses than others, the less endowed were sometimes forced to borrow a horse and pay back the owner in loot acquired. This differentiation in possessions introduced caste into the previous equality within the tribe when *everyone* walked.[9]

Using horses to hunt bison increased the number killed and gave warriors the ability to travel farther. Wives of warriors had to process more hides as a result.

Fueling Change

Women were affected by their warrior's ownership of the horse since an increase in buffalo hides from better hunting methods dictated that women spend more and more of their time processing hides. Previously, they produced enough to replace worn or lost hides and a few to trade. Once hunting with a horse increased the yield and Euro-American traders demanded more hides, the women's status moved from producing for family to producing for markets.

A warrior who had acquired many horses, perhaps as many as a hundred, was rich in status and burdened with the need to reciprocate gifts with other rich men. He roamed farther from camp to hunt for commerce rather than subsistence and brought back more hides for women to process.

Meanwhile, Native American women's roles changed. They managed larger camps while their men were gone. They also married white men, forged alliances among groups of Euro-Americans, and sometimes moved their camps to new locations.[10] Slowly but surely the Native Americans were seduced by the white man's need for commerce rather than subsistence, for accumulation of material possessions, and for metal pots and pans, and steel knives. They chose to work with tools embedded with greater energy than bows and arrows, flint knives, and moccasined feet for walking.

At the same time the horse was introduced from northern Mexico by the Spanish, guns began to filter in from Canada through the English and French.[11]

While the horse and the gun both increased the Indian's power and range of travel, it injected them into a world of trade over which they had little control. As soon as manufactured goods such as brass kettles, cloth, steel knives, and hatchets infiltrated their energy system, the Osage left behind self-sufficiency and entered the web of trading their natural resources—furs and hides—for accumulation of goods they could not make for themselves.

Then they needed to produce more skins than could be sustained by natural numbers of fur-bearing animals, and still defend against further intrusion of their energy system in an effort to minimize loss of self-sustainability.

In this brief period, the Osage lived suspended between low- and high-energy systems, still in their own villages and with their own culture, enjoying the overlap of manufactured goods and horses.

Little did they realize what lay ahead for them, as more and more energy-related changes flowed in their direction.

Chapter 4

What's for Dinner? A Missouri Feast

What was the range of food available to a group in a low-energy system, and what did they have to do to get it?

The Osage diet nourished large warriors. Whether by genetic predisposition or by a diet rich in protein, Osage warriors often loomed over their American counterparts. John Bradbury in *Travels in the Interior of America, 1809-11,* was awed by the party of warriors he first observed. "The Osages are so tall and robust as almost to warrant the application of the term gigantic: few of them appear to be under six feet, and many are above it. Their shoulders and visages are broad, which tend to strengthen the idea of their being giants."[1]

A varied diet provided protein: Bear, deer, beaver, turkey, prairie chickens, water fowl, skunk, fish, birds eggs, sausage made from buffalo intestines filled with dried buffalo meat, berries, nuts, marrow and suet offered a wide choice of protein sources. Corn, squash, pumpkins, beans planted in gardens near the river, and wild plants like the wild potato or *do,* water lily roots and occasional sweets such as a kind of "fruit leather," made from wild persimmon made a varied diet. Without milk and butter from cows they substituted bear or buffalo fat.[2] Such a high protein diet gave them strength and stature. "They lived," describes John Mathews, "in a region that had long periods of lush tranquility."[3]

41

Even though they roasted and dried meat in their villages, on the plains after a buffalo kill, the entire family drank the warm blood, and ate raw the organs, tongue, eyeballs, and other parts of the buffalo before packaging the carcass for transportation. In the field, cooking gave way to packing and moving the meat before other tribes encroached. They saved the brain for tanning the hides, the hoofs for glue. Rib bones were ready to be roasted and cracked for their marrow. They fashioned spoons from horns and saved the sinews along the backbone for cord and thread. These also served as bowstrings when several were twirled together. In their villages, women made pottery and wooden bowls for cooking and serving.[4] They stirred with paddles and ate with fingers, and, like all cultures, had manners, generosity and ways of sharing. John Bradbury described a visit in his diary in an Osage village. The Osage hosts passed around a wooden bowl containing squares of cake that tasted something like gingerbread made from the pulp of persimmon and mixed with pounded corn. They called the bread *staninca*.[5]

Early Euro-American settlers had to adopt some of the same practices of living off wild game though many almost certainly had hogs and cows for butter, milk, and bacon fat and yeast for bread. Of course, they came from a culture that could create great delicacies with these ingredients and could be served on tables with white cloths and silver goblets to some fortunate few. But on the frontier, the white pioneers lived on what they could find and knew how to prepare just like their Native American counterparts.

Unfamiliarity to the countryside and the hard work of pioneering meant the settlers may have had a poorer diet than the Osage. The settlers had wood aplenty, but some had little else in those early years. Henry Rowe Schoolcraft's *Ozark Journal*, December 7th, 1818, tells this story of homesteading:

They rose at dawn and built a "cabin fire with eight-foot logs." Then, they pounded corn in a wooden mortar with a pestle attached to a spring pole, a common frontier mechanism when mills were not available to process grain. Then had breakfast and repaired moccasins, sharpened tools and so on getting ready for the day's work. The men spent their day clearing brush and felling trees until around five o'clock when they quit for dinner. They had no lunch. For dinner they ate hominy, corn boiled until it was soft, accompanied by bear's bacon. No vegetables were available because no gardens had been planted. This meal they had twice a day without variation until the pioneers could expand their diet with more complicated and varied processes.[6]

This reminiscence reveals a great deal of difference in values rising from different levels of energy use. The Osage women could not carry and would not use an eight-foot-long log to burn for heat. They had no way of cutting such a piece, means of transporting, nor a fireplace in which to burn it. They would have ground corn between two pieces of stone rather than rigging a wooden mortar and spring pestle. The Osage cleared land carefully for defensive and visual purposes but not with an ax to clear land for planting. Their agility in living in this environment meant they often ate better with greater variety of foodstuffs than their Euro-American counterparts in the early stages of settlement.

Chapter 5

When the Osage Lived Highest

Here, a high-energy system expressed its advantage to a low-energy system.

Author Louis Burns, an Osage himself, sets the zenith of the Osage domination of their territory between 1750 and 1800 when they enjoyed a "maximum margin of survival."[1] Aided by horses and interaction with both French and Spanish fur traders, they had increased their territory and expanded their dietary choices thereby increasing their health and welfare. Another tribe never conquered them; they never gave up their territory once claimed and never made war with the United States. By the early 19th century, however, the United States government had arrived at the door to their lodges and demanded more than the furs with which the French and Spanish had been content.

The Americans wanted land, and land free of native peoples. This demand started the slow unraveling of the Osage peoples. Providing furs and absorbing some articles of household use, or "cultural hardware," as Burns calls it, was one thing, but being removed from their territory was quite another. With the former, they could hold their energy system and their culture intact; with the latter, however, their energy system crumbled and their culture suffered.[2] Energy systems affected different cultures in different ways.

The Power of Temptation

Was the high-energy system thrust into their midst like a sword into the heart, or did the Osage participate in their own undoing? John Joseph Mathews, in *The Osages: Children of the Middle Waters* (1961) suggests, "the disintegration of the tribe was in a seed within the tribal organization itself and the self-esteem of each individual." Because of the Osage belief in bravery and honor they became an easy dupe for the white settlers. Every chief had "the urge to attain glory as a warrior and to be noticed and honored, the intense urge to be wise and pontifical and make statements of wisdom . . . all the elements of his makeup which had contributed toward becoming noticed as a warrior or as an orator or a generous giver made of him a half-forged tool for the trader, the United States commissioners, the military leaders, the politicians. For a few brief hours of buzzy, personal glory the chieftain might sell his whole tribe into bondage."[3] Whether their dispositions made them vulnerable, or their desires for metal knives and woven blankets to replace the grueling work of preparing buffalo hides, the Osage were deeply vulnerable to the ways and the power of the white man.

They saw the white man as foreign objects and tried to describe them within their natural context: "Their eyes and their mouths were almost hidden by hair. Their mouths were like the den of an old, male, bank beaver overhung by rootlets."[4] The Osage related as best they could to the Euro-Americans.

Every population has a rising curve, a pinnacle and a declining curve in terms of cultural expression supported by fuel and available energy. The Osage slipped from their brief pinnacle around 1800. The Osage lifestyle, in the judgment of Euro-Americans, filled an economic niche while they were needed as fur trappers. Once the fur supply began to give out and the land to fill with white farmers and land speculators, once the Louisiana Territory was divided into states, the incursions began.

The Osage energy system was legislated out of existence, beginning with the actions of President Thomas Jefferson in 1808.[5] The very lands on which the Osage then resided Jefferson had promised to the Cherokees, the Choctaws, and the Chickasaws when they were removed from Georgia and the Carolinas.[6] Clearly, the Euro-American attachment to the land did not have the same meaning as the Native American attachment. Because the Indians lived so embedded in their natural surroundings, every move they made, every aspect of their belief system keyed into the uniqueness of their natural environment. To remove any tribe from their native territory was to erode their identity and destroy their independence.

The first of seven treaties with the Osage and the United States came soon after the Louisiana Purchase. Each one trimmed away the energy system built upon their Wood Age life, erased their territory, allowed a steady stream of "intruders" into their remaining lands, and offered them the tools of an alien energy system.

The first treaty in 1808 acted as a harbinger for the new century. In exchange for all the land south of the Missouri River and east of Fort Osage—most of what is today the state of Missouri south to the Arkansas River—it offered dependence on the Americans for a startup in the new energy system, that of property to be farmed, implements with which to do it and a way to grind their grain harvest. Instead of continuing to live at the height of their own energy curve, they were asked to abandon without a fight their inherited and beautifully designed way of life and instead plow virgin prairie with alien tools and trade the harvest in an alien culture.

Gifts That Did Not Give

They would be given the greatest machine available of the stronger energy system, the mill, accompanied by a blacksmith shop, plows and cabins for the chiefs. The mill would grind the grain that the Indians ground for themselves, while the blacksmith would make and repair metal implements using charcoal and smithing tools, something in which no one had experience. The tribe members would have to learn the ways of the white culture quickly to survive and prosper in the new way of life.[7] Some former warrior must learn to be a blacksmith, another to run a mill, in fact were offered lessons in these skills. But the Osage disdained all of these gifts. They would never put their hand to a plow; they ground their own corn; they still preferred bow and arrow over the rifle; they were proud of having been given the log cabins but did not occupy them.

This 1836 map of "Indian Territory" shows the Osage nation(and others) after having been removed from Missouri. The Osage were confined to a strip south of the Shawnee and north of Cherokee territory (denoted by the arrow).

The gun could only be used for show compared to the efficiencies of the bow and arrow. The gun metal reflected the sun, and a row of warriors on a ridge shining their gun barrels in the eyes of their enemies increased their stature as warriors. The Osage had no cotton for wadding; they had to carry wood shavings, bullets and powder for the gun, so could only fire one shot. On horseback this was problematic with wind blowing the powder away and the horse moving under them. They always carried their bows and arrows with them "and used them much more than they used their guns."[8]

Fort Osage, Sibley, Missouri

Fort Osage sat high on the bluffs above the Missouri River 20 miles east of the Kansas City site and served as a trading post for the Osage Indians from 1808 to 1822.

The treaty also provided for trading at Fort Osage, twenty miles downriver from the future site of Kansas City. Fort Osage would host hundreds of Indians trading their furs for goods. A thousand at a time would camp outside the gates, particularly after they had been forced to move to the western edge of Missouri. Meanwhile, the first of the many eastern Indian tribes began to arrive with whom they would share their new territory.[9] By the treaty of 1816, the Osage reluctantly ceded three million acres of their remaining territory to the arriving Cherokees to the east.

46

The two tribes had already reacted in a hostile manner to each other in the same way the Osage had treated white intruders in Missouri and neighboring tribes edging their territory. This agreement was ratified between the United States government and the Osage. Pierre Chouteau, uncle of Francois who traded furs with the Osage at the future Kansas City site, brokered many of the treaties with the Indians, while William Clark of the famed Lewis and Clark expedition, acted as governor of the territory.[10]

Coinage That Did Not Work

The Treaty of 1822 closed Fort Osage (Sibley, Missouri) and paid the tribe about $2,500 for merchandise in exchange for furs. The Council Grove Treaty of 1825 sought protection from the Osage for travelers on the Santa Fe Trail to New Mexico. The treaty moved the Osage out of Missouri and Arkansas into Kansas. The United States agreed to pay the Osage $7,000 each year for twenty years along with 600 head of cattle, 600 hogs, a thousand chickens, ten yoke of oxen, six carts, one blacksmith and a house built for each of the four chiefs.[11]

The capitulation to the intruding energy system was summed up by Osage emissary Big Soldier who had been to Washington twice and said to George Sibley, the factor at Fort Osage:

I see and admire your manner of living, your good warm houses; your extensive fields of corn, your gardens, your cows, oxen, work houses (sic.) wagons, and a thousand machines, that I know not the use of. I see that you are able to clothe yourselves even from weeds and grass. In short you can do almost anything you choose. You are surrounded by slaves. Everything about you is in chains, and you are slaves yourselves. I fear if I should exchange my pursuits for yours, I too should become a slave. Talk to my sons, perhaps they may be persuaded to adopt your fashions, or at least to recommend them to their sons; but for myself I was born free, was raised free, and wish to die free. I am personally content with my condition. The forest and rivers supply all the calls of nature in plenty and there is no lack of white people to purchase the surplus products of our industry.[12]

He was, of course, putting too much faith in that interim period between his original way of life and the point at which "no lack of white people" would overrun it. It was a period that could not last however much he may have hoped. The Osage had been caught in the torrent of energy they themselves pulled from their land in the form of furs. Horses and guns became the least of their problems.

Once caught in the capitalistic trade of resources for money, they became indebted to their European traders and unwitting partners in their own demise. They became instruments for draining the fur-bearing animals from the natural eco-systems they called home. In one year alone in 1829 Francois Chouteau traded 150 packs of deerskins (about 10-in-a-pack), 20 bundles of good raccoons, three bundles of beaver skins and 350 otters from the Osage.

The Shawnee, who had also been transplanted from the East, brought another 100 beaver and 150 otter, along with 50 packs of deerskins. In the second hunt, Chouteau took in 236 bundles of deerskins that weighed in total about 25,000 pounds. Raccoons yielded 50 packs of skins, 10-to-a-pack. Another 500 beaver skins, 800 otter, 500 and two bundles of bearskins completed the season.[13] For this and other yearly bountiful catches that made the Chouteaus wealthy and drew in more fur traders and Indian suppliers, the Indians would receive brightly woven blankets of red and blue wool, cotton shirts, metal knives and cooking pots. They received yearly annuities from the United States government as well.

The Osage participation in the fur trade made them more dependent on the Euro-American traders and, by extension, to the American government. The increased efficiency and productivity of their hunting hastened the arrival of fur traders such as the Chouteaus and on their heels more settlers intruding into their territory. Once they had participated in fur trading, the Indians could not reverse the outflow of valuable furs and the influx of a superior energy system.

Once dominant over a large part of Missouri and southwestern territories, the Osage were soon relegated to a small strip on the west side of the state by 1825. They had been replaced by farmers whose relationship to the land collided totally with the food/water/cover ecology they had enjoyed with a natural landscape. The Osage then endured the arrival of other eastern tribes, from the Kickapoos to the Delawares to the Shawnee, Cherokee, Sac and Fox. Finally, all Indian tribes were removed from Missouri entirely and relocated to Kansas and Oklahoma in 1825.[14] The same event had occurred on the east coast fifty years earlier.[15]

The Osage had no way to defend against such superior levels of energy directed against them. At first vital links to European wealth in fur trapping, the Indians over the course of two centuries became "superfluous," as author Richard White, describes them, to American wealth.[16] The Osage became ghosts of a way of life overcome by materiality.

Axes, plows, the wheel, horses, cows, machines, literacy and capital were not the only elements of a high-energy system the white settlers brought with them. They also brought slaves. In the Wood Age, as far back as history records, some peoples dominated others and used the less fortunate to do the onerous duties seen as beneath the effort of the conquerors. Energy by way of human muscle power, intelligent, amenable, or at least directable, created many a monument to the dominant culture. The settlement of western Missouri was no exception.

Chapter 6

Kansas City and Slavery

The peculiar institution of slavery arrived with white settlers tying the community to the ancient past in terms of economics and a specific set of values.

One of the energy sources available to white settlers in the Wood Age in Missouri was the institution of slavery. The area that would become Kansas City began with slavery:

> Long ago, in 1824 and 1825, two counties sundered by the Missouri River, and flanked by the Western border line, sought at the same time their incorporation by the Legislature. On the North, the inhabitants, mostly emigrants from Kentucky, and advocating that gentleman's elevation to the presidency, calling their county Clay, and its seat of Justice, Liberty. On the South, as if in rivalry, emigrants from Virginia, Carolina and Tennessee, selected the name of Jackson for their county, and Independence for their City.[1]
>
> —William Gilpin, *Western Journal and Civilian,* 1854

Settled by Kentuckians who followed the illustrious family of Daniel Boone and his sons to the area, or from Virginia and the Carolinas where the soil was already depleted from tobacco growing, Missouri was destined to attract slaveholders.[2] It had been, of course, the slavery side of the great Missouri Compromise that created it in 1820. Missouri would become a "slave state," where slavery would be allowed, and Maine would enter as a "free state," where slavery would be prohibited. All the lands north and west of Missouri would be free states.

The Missouri Compromise reflected the wishes of its early inhabitants who had sparsely settled on the eastern side of Missouri. They represented the larger South—Kentucky, the Carolinas, Virginia—whose system of slave labor had become an elaborate and remunerative economy for those living in grand plantation houses and working larger and larger land holdings. The Missouri Compromise itself represented a clash between not only the idea of slave versus free but the design of different economies on the eastern seaboard. "[A] substantial majority of the residents had come from slaveholding states, and many of them viewed slavery as an institution essential to white supremacy. No significant antislavery sentiment existed in the territory."[3]

A population estimated at "a little short of a hundred thousand" wanted the power to govern themselves and to vote in national elections. They also wanted slavery as part of their state's rights.[4] After a good deal of wrangling in the United States Congress, the Missouri Compromise allowed Missouri to enter the union as a slave state but barred slavery within the Louisiana Purchase north of Missouri's southern border except for the state itself. Missouri was not designed, as neighboring Kansas would be, as a free state, with settlers often funded by abolitionists in Boston whose anti-slavery doctrine made settlers into soldiers for the abolition of slavery.

The General Inconvenience of Living Without Them

Missouri would be settled instead by people from a context of slavery who could not imagine life without it and pressed for its continuation. Even Patrick Henry, a Virginian, and a passionate voice for freedom as America became a nation, admitted, "I am drawn along by the general inconvenience of living without them (slaves)."[5] Among the population of the state of Missouri in 1820 of 70,168 lived a population of 11, 234 slaves, about 16% of the population. It was that imbedded convenience as well as economic value that held slavery in Missouri.[6]

Slave Bill of Sale

**Received of Thomas Johnson eight hundred
dollars in full payment for a negro girl
named Martha of a black complexion
aged about 15 years. The above described
negro girl I warrant sound in body &
mind & a slave for life and free from all
claims. --West Port Mo. May 24th 1856   David Burge**

Slavery served as the laborsaving device available in the Wood Age for those who did not have to do the labor themselves. Either human or animal labor performed most work. If someone did not wish to perform the human labor and could afford slaves, he could have a slave do it for him. Each slave was a laborsaving unit to his or her master. As such, slavery was part of the ante-bellum energy story. Until each slave was replaced by a machine driven by electricity or fueled by coal or oil, people did the work themselves, hired it done, forced slaves to do it or left it undone. Seven counties just east of Jackson were known as "Little Dixie" for their hemp and tobacco farms where slaves were used to plant and harvest. Jackson County itself showed a small but sturdy population of slaves.[7]

Slave-owning families arrived in a trickle in the 1820s. James Shepherd came to Jackson County from Virginia in 1824 with a family of slaves, and "like the rest, the men had been taught the use of the broadax." Two of James Shepherd's slaves, Pete and Sam, were "known as about the strongest men in the country, either white or black." Shepherd contracted out the two slaves to build the first courthouse in Independence, and they hewed the logs that formed the infrastructure for the building.[8] At other times Sam and Pete were hired out to cut wood for salt making in Saline County, a process that required a generous supply of wood to evaporate the brine.[9] The two men could reputedly cut and stack four cords of wood each per day and call that just "a fair day's work." Whether that is a Western tall tale or genuine output, such productivity is four times better than national statistics suggest.

H. E. Hayward and his slave nurse Louisa, ca. 1856

A 1942 government report estimated this productivity: "A skilled axman could cut, split, and stack perhaps 1 cord of hardwood in a day. An unskilled man would require two or three times as long for the same results."[10]

By the 1830s, with a Jackson County population of 2,823, the settlers owned 193 slaves held by 62 slave owners, about 6% of the population. This suggests that most settlers had no access to this source of energy and did their work themselves. One man owned 25 slaves, but most owned one to three. Male and female slaves under 10-years-of-age each numbered 41. This number would multiply in the next census.[11]

In 1832, a family set out from Nashville to the frontier—then known as Missouri, in the quintessential overland trek. James Porter, son Jesse, his wife and the 25 slaves she had been given as her wedding present arrived with cattle, horses, and hogs and purchased at $1/quarter-acre, 365-acres at what is now 23rd Street on the north and 31st Street on the south and bounded by Vine Street on the east and Holmes on the west. The demographics of the little family were typical of what made up the population of Jackson County.

> The little bunch of household goods was taken from the wagons. Axes were dug from boxes and the broad black hands of the slaves began felling trees. A clearing was made. The logs were stripped of their branches and hewed into regular lengths. The sound of axes echoed back and forth in the stillness of the forest. The growth of weeds and grass was trampled underfoot by the slaves of the settler. Plenty of rock was roundabout for the cabin's foundation. Plenty of oaken logs for the walls, plenty of walnut for the floors and window casings. James Porter and his slaves worked for weeks building the five-room . . . story-and-a-half structure with a kitchen set-off a few feet away. . . . After this house was completed, cabins were built for the Negroes. Each head of a family was supplied with one, and they were built in a sort of a semi-circle about the home in easy call of the master.[12]

> N. M. Harris, "An Old-fashioned Wedding in the Oldest
> House in Kansas City," *Kansas City Star*, 1907

Fields were cleared and planted, the harvest bounteous and life was good for the Porters, one of the founding families of the city. Twenty years later when Jesse was old enough to marry, the Porter home hosted his wedding reception at which legions of "colored servants" made and served food. No dancing was to be enjoyed because Porter was a Methodist, but the party celebrated with plenty of frivolous games and songs. In the slave quarters, however, no such restrictions prevailed. "Nothing could control the negroes' feet when the fiddles sawed out old 'Leather Breeches' or other stirring, tempting jigs," remembered one observer. "When Sam played the fiddle and Bill picked the banjo and Rafe rattled the bones I had to hike out of hearing myself to maintain the dignity of caste."[13]

In the 1840 Census, the 82 slave children under 10 had grown in number to 274 males and 244 females, suggesting an influx of slave families. The age bracket of those aged 10-24 years numbered 246 for young male slaves and 261 for young female slaves, which meant this population of childbearing age would soon increase their numbers.

The white population fell largely into agriculture at 1,703 versus commerce at 63. Those involved in commerce would have been outfitters, storekeepers, bricklayers, cigar makers, ferrymen, carpenters, tavern keepers, barbers, confectioners, Daguerreians (photographers), gardeners and such. Manufacturers and traders comprised a group of 147 who actually made articles on site such as blacksmiths, wagon makers, saddle makers, brick makers, cabinetmakers, and others who engaged in outfitting supplies for travelers and outfitting homes for residents. Learned professions and engineers, mainly lawyers, numbered 20 with nine people engaged in "navigation of canals, lakes and rivers."[14]

By 1850, beginning a golden decade of pre-war growth, the population of the county had grown to 14,000 with 2,629 slaves, 21% of the population. The under-10 group of male slaves had grown to 483 and females to 495, indicating that young men and women slaves of child bearing age were producing children, and also suggesting an influx of new young slaves. The 10 to 29-year-age group (the census had changed the age ranges) was 739 for young men and 709 for young women.

By 1860, the white population had grown to 18,882 with 3,940 slaves, about 20%. Also, by this date the census takers counted 17 Indians in Jackson County. This number was not included in any previous census.

Of the 3,944 slaves in the county, the town of Kanzas (or Kansas, later Kansas City) held 24 males and 92 females, not a large number. These slaves were owned largely in households of one or two slaves, used primarily as cooks, housekeepers and general chores. But the sheriff in Blue Springs, a village near Independence, owned 10, and a lawyer in Independence, seven. Residents in the town of Westport held 134 slaves, John Calvin McCoy, one of the founding fathers of the town, owning six.[15]

Just Step Over the Line

Pressure from "Free Staters" and local abolitionists caused a good deal of trouble in the 1850s. Missourians dreaded a free state forming on their Western flank where their slaves could be free merely by stepping over a state line drawn in the dust of wagon tracks. Missourians tried to stuff the ballot boxes of Kansas elections toward slavery, menaced the free-staters, squatted on Kansas lands, or showed false papers of ownership.

By 1859, when tensions were heating up along the Missouri and Kansas border, many slave owners had been persuaded by the agitating events to ship their slaves to the South to save their investment. Slave prices were high in the "golden age of slave values."

In 1853, a young male slave in Missouri sold for $1,000 while his equivalent in Virginia sold for $100 less.[16] In 1859, local resident Thompson McDaniels, a slave dealer, herded a group of about 100 male slaves in chains and handcuffs aboard a steamboat from the Westport Landing pier. They had been bought in Jackson County and were to be sold in the Deep South where they were considered safe, though they would probably be sold at lesser prices.[17]

Because white Southerners had much more in the way of possessions and tools, they both needed and could afford large numbers of slaves. More possessions indicated more wealth; more wealth requires more labor to care for and produce it.

In contrast to the Osage Indians, the Euro-American settlers had as part of their high-energy suite many helping hands. As a matter of comparison, the Osage took slaves but kept only children and traded the rest. Before European occupation they took slaves as revenge against other tribes.

Once the Europeans arrived, the Osage often traded and re-traded slaves with the British and French for supplies. The French tolerated the practice, but the Spanish discouraged it.[18] To the southwest of the Osage lived the Caddo tribe who sometimes fell victim to the Osage. The Osage would use "bluff war" to scare and taunt the Caddo, making threats with obscene gestures across a river. Their faces painted in red and yellow and with their stature over six feet, the Osage warriors menaced the tribe merely by showing up. The Caddo lived in fear of being captured and sold. As a result, the Caddo finally had to move away from the Osage.[19]

The land of western Missouri offered plenty of resources to both Osage and white settlers. The energy capacity of the latter was helped by their slave population that intensified the use of the wheel, the metal edge and the domesticated animal. In the Wood Age animal and human muscle were, of course, the most valuable sources of energy because they were both mobile and amenable to direction. Domesticated animals and human slaves boosted civilization to new levels of sophistication and created a class system. Slaves were the highest coinage of the realm—each obedient, thoughtful, versatile and mobile units of biddable energy.

Chapter 7

The Energy of The Missouri River

Water power used for transportation was also employed for milling. Each component played a large part in the Euro-American settlers' success, and each supported the operation of a high-energy suite introduced by them.

Part of the energy suite of the Euro-American settlers was the ability to move goods on water. Rivers were not just something to cross or the river banks just a repository for firewood. They were arteries of commerce developing in the huge Midwestern section of America. In the new age of science in which everything was measurable and namable, Lewis and Clark measured the current of the Missouri River at St. Louis at 5.5- to 7 miles per hour, a current that would make a keelboat man bend to the deck to move his craft up river. At the future Kansas City site, the expedition measured the Kaw River 400 miles later at 230-yards-wide and "wider at the mouth," while the "Missouries" measured 500 yards wide. Lewis wrote, "The waters of the Kansas is very disagreeably tasted to me." [1]

The Missouri River is about 750 feet in elevation, with Kansas City elevation about 1,000 feet. The river had been 'discovered' by the French Missionary Father Jacques Marquette and guide Louis Jolliet in 1673 and fully described and mapped by 1716 by Guillaume Delisle, a French cartographer in Paris based on the notes and observations made by Etienne de Veniard, Sieur de Bourgmont. This French explorer came down the Mississippi River from Quebec and forged congenial relationships with the Missouri, Osage, Otoe, Padouca and other nations, even taking some of them to Paris for a visit to the court of Louis XV and returning them to the wilds of Missouri in 1725-6. [2]

The Osage Indians lived along the banks of and traveled the waterways of rivers small and large from the Mississippi to the Missouri, Osage and Arkansas Rivers. They had fashioned canoes of hollowed out cottonwood, walnut or cedar logs fifteen to twenty feet long and three to four feet in diameter. Those could carry three men. These were not the birch bark canoes of the Northeast where birch was plentiful and waters more placid, but the sturdier wood canoes made for stronger Western rivers.

When white settlers began to use dugout canoes, they outfitted them with a watertight compartment in the center in which to pour bear oil or honey for transport down river since both were highly prized and no casks were available. [3] The pirogue, one of the many varieties of early boats, consisted of two canoes with a platform built between them for cargo, usually furs on their way to market. They could also, depending on size and sturdiness, carry up to 20 passengers.[4]

Another approach worth noting is the floating craft the Mandan on the upper Missouri used. Fur trappers in that area borrowed the technology. With few trees, they used the next most plentiful resource, buffalo skins. The Mandans built small round boats for river crossings using a single buffalo hide stretched across a willow frame. If wood was scarce, a buffalo shoulder blade could serve as a paddle for the smaller versions; "The bull boat," a larger version made by whites and so named because the hide of a *bull* buffalo was larger and believed to leak less than that of a female, was also round, made in the same manner and gave room enough for one man and up to a third of a ton of cargo.

John Bradbury notes in *Travels in the Interior of America in 1809, 1810, and 1811* that he rode in one across the river furnished and paddled by a woman of the Gros Ventre tribe near the Mandans on the Knife River.[5] They were met by six women, "each of whom had a skin canoe on her back and a paddle in her hand . . . . The squaws placed our saddles in the canoes, where we also disposed ourselves, leaving the Indians to drive our horses over the river. . . ." They paddled across the river (the paddle probably a shoulder blade from an elk or buffalo), which was "about eighty yards wide at this place."[6] An even larger version about thirty feet long by twelve wide could carry up to 6,000 pounds of furs; the larger ones were propelled by two men with poles. Small or large, the bullboat had to be unloaded and re-pitched every day with a mix of tallow and ashes and dried out every night to keep it afloat.

These canoes or small bullboats gave the Native Americans the transportation they needed to cross a river or paddle to a hunting ground on the opposite side, though the Indians were less often on water than on land.[7] Without sail and without means to build a boat large enough to require a crew, they loaded furs and meat from hunting grounds in smaller packages than the Euro-American settlers did on their keelboats. The lack of technology dictated the scale of their water travel.[8]

Out of the Womb of the Ark was Born the Nation

Such technology on the part of the Native Americans served them well within the context of their culture. Their bull boats and canoes made for two passengers give scale to their economy. Their use of the land as their main transportation course, their pedestrian culture that dictated light loads, burdens wrapped in buffalo robes and sinews shouldered for the walk back to the village repeat that small family scale of production without wheels, beasts of burden, or a great use of waterways for travel.

For the white settlers their command of wood as building material made larger boats available. Having already sailed across the Atlantic in 100-foot boats fashioned with large timbers, cut with saw, carved with blade, carpentered with fancy molding and decoration under full sail, Euro-Americans expected to be able to travel by water, commanded to travel by water, but in the Middle West sails were poorly used. Upstream traffic required men walking along the banks, and overhanging trees made sails problematic to use. A more practical water craft was needed.

"Out of the womb of the ark was born the nation," observed one author on attempts to conquer the western rivers.[9] It may not be too much of an overstatement to say that flatboats, often called "the ark," and keelboats, the smaller, more navigable boats, created America as a growing nation. With the political and natural forces encouraging migration, the boats became the means to an end. In the critical period between the end of the French and Indian War in 1763 and the arrival of the steamboat in some numbers in the second decade of the 19th century, keelboats birthed the trade and provided the mechanism for transport from farmer or fur trader to market and return.

In *Western Rivermen-1763-1861, Ohio and Mississippi Boatmen and the Myth of the Alligator Horse* (1959), author Michael Allen divides the keelboat era into two periods, from 1763 to 1823, the pre-steamboat or pre-industrial era, and from 1823 when steamboats began to take over the rivers until the beginning of the Civil War when all river traffic stopped. The end of the French and Indian War so agreed by the Treaty of Paris in 1763 put an end to the constraints on the population to move west.

Pittsburgh became the keelboat-building capital and the beginning point for many a cargo of staples for western-moving pioneers. Flatboats outnumbered keelboats to begin with, but by design they were a one-way ticket. Smaller and lighter keelboats could go up rivers and tributaries where flatboats could not. Each boat served two different and important purposes.[10]

Without centuries of road building available to them as was true for Europe and with magnificent and plentiful rivers, Americans demanded a boat that could take the place of a wagon on a road. That was the keelboat, the truck of the American waterways until steamboats took over. It was the only boat that could make the trip both upstream and down. Built on a keel with ribs, it could be from 40 to 80 feet long and seven to 20 feet wide with a covered cabin amidships of about five foot depth, and a shallow draft of two feet.

The boat was pointed at both ends for easy turnaround. A narrow runway along each side gave purchase to keelboat men who could push the boat up river using long poles for leverage. As many as eight to twelve men on each side poled from the bow, bending over double to increase pressure on their padded poles then walked toward the stern as they pushed the boat forward. At the stern the boatman pulled out his pole and ran forward to plant his pole again as he stood on the narrow strip of what became known as the "running board."

The boatman steered with a long rudder and the crew often rowed with oars, getting as much leverage from the water through muscle as possible. Occasionally, a sail could catch the wind and help out, but overhanging branches along the banks where they were forced to sail where the current was weakest made that problematic, or "when the wind blowing So hard Down the river that She could not assend [sic.]," making camp was the only solution.[11]

A later traveler suffered a similar situation near Fort Sibley on the Missouri River. The water was very deep and muddy. The swift current required a great expenditure of muscle power to move the boat along. The river bank itself, a dense tangle of vines, offered no progress to walk along the bank pulling a towline. Poling also had its problems. The men sometimes fell into the water leaving their poles stuck in the mud. As a swimmer, the pole man had no leverage in pulling out the pole. In one particular trip Paul Wilhelm's crew gained a distance of thirty paces in a day. Those who could swim hacked away at logs and tree limbs with axes to gain a passage for their boat. In the end they made two miles that day.[12]

When water passage even with this grueling application of muscle became impossible, the keelboat men, "sometimes rowing, Poleing & Drawing up with a Strong Rope" ascended the waterway. The flat-bottomed boats with short oars could get near a bank and be pulled by a rope from the bank. The number of crewmembers was determined by the amount of cargo, with one boatman for every 3,000 pounds of freight. The capacity of the boat ranged from 15,000 to 25,000 pounds.

The Keelboat required a full press by men on each side using poles to push upstream. The man at the stern moved the rudder while the man in the chair called out a chant to coordinate the activity on the "running board."

They may have had to use a long rope fastened to a tree trunk or boulder on the bank and then the crew on the bow pulled hand over hand or used a pulley in a practice known as "warping" snug up to that mark, while part of the crew held the boat there as others ran ahead to find another anchoring point. Or the crew could act as horses did for canal boats and walk on the bank with the rope to the boat over their shoulders, dragging the boat after them, a process known as "cordelling." In all, conditions were poor for keelboat men. Author Everett Dick remarked in his book *Vanguards of the Frontier* (1964), "Today's men could not be persuaded to endure the rigorous toil and hardships of the first decades of the 19th century."[13]

These hardy boatmen often ended the day covered in mud from working the bank. Camps were crude at best. Sometimes they had no meal more than "meet and water," as did George Drewyer and William Clark of the Lewis and Clark Expedition near the Kansas City site in 1804. "I got mired," Clark wrote, "and was obliged to Craul out, a disagreeable Situation & a Diverting one if any one who Could have Seen me after I got out, all Covered with mud, I went my (sic) Camp & [s]Craped off the Mud and washed my Clothes."[14]

A trip from New Orleans to St. Louis and back could only be made twice a year by a boat and crew as the round trip took between four and six months to complete. The ascent took seventy to eighty days though a crew could bring a boat by cordelling from Louisville to St. Louis in 25 days. The crookedness of the Mississippi River required a boat to cross the river any number of times to avoid caving banks or strong currents, snags, sawyers (submerged trees) and sand bars, finally adding an estimated five hundred miles to a trip already close to four hundred miles.[15]

> A voyage down and back sometimes occupied nine months. In time this commerce increased until it gave employment to hordes of rough and hardy men; rude, uneducated, brave, suffering terrific hardships with sailor-like stoicism; heavy drinkers, coarse frolickers in moral sties like the Natchez-under-the hill of that day, heavy fighters, reckless fellows, every one, elephantinely jolly, foul-witted, profane, prodigal of their money, bankrupt at the end of the trip, fond of barbaric finery, prodigious braggarts; yet, in the main, honest, trustworthy, faithful to promises and duty, and often picturesquely magnanimous.[16]
>
> Mark Twain, *Life on the Mississippi*, 1883

The flatboat was the keelboat's bulky, ugly cousin, "the ark itself," generally measuring from 50 to 75 feet in width. Square at both ends and built upstream to take goods from the hinterlands to New Orleans, they were simply too large for any amount of muscle power to pull, sail or pole them back upstream, though it was occasionally done, but most were broken down at journey's end to supply housing material, offering up a pile of one inch thick cottonwood planks, the wood found a welcome in the downstream building market.[17]

John Bradbury observed that they passed in one day more than a dozen arks bearing produce to New Orleans. Bradbury's keelboat put a good distance between his boat and theirs because they "made considerable distance with our oars."[18] In other words, they were rowing upstream on the Mississippi, something that could not be done with a keelboat.

Such muscle came only from the young and adventurous. Pittsburgh created a trade in keelboats and young men to man them. With a strong back for rowing, warping and cordelling, and knowledge of the river as a skill set, as many as ten thousand young men plied the western waters as entrepreneurs and crew to deliver and trade goods from one end of the western waterways to another.[19]

In this trade, the riverman was the fundamental factor. Only by means of his brawn and his genius for navigation could these innumerable tons of flour, tobacco, and bacon have been kept from rotting on the shores. Yet the man himself remains a legend grotesque and mysterious, one of the shadowy figures of a time when history was being made too rapidly to be written . . . .. It is therefore only dimly, as through a mist, that we can see the two lines of pole men pass from prow to stern on the narrow running board of a keel boat, lifting and setting their poles to the cry of steersman or captain.

Archer B. Hulbert, *Waterways of Westward Expansion*, 1903

When French fur trader Francois Chouteau brought his young wife, Berenice, and two infant sons to the site that would become Kansas City in 1821, they arrived from St. Louis in a keelboat full of household goods and trading materials for the Indians with a crew of keelboat men and slaves. The trip took three weeks or more of arduous work on the part of the boatmen to make their way up the 500 miles of snag-infested river. Berenice sailed down the river several times on a pirogue or keelboat with her growing family, and to deliver one of her nine pregnancies. A fearless woman, used to the ways of the frontier, she nevertheless, showed great courage to sail the tempestuous Missouri.

Chouteau first built a log cabin and a log warehouse, but his family and his standard of living required a real home, which he built in the French-style like those of the period in St. Louis.[20] Most lumber in the early day was shipped in on keelboats and later steamboats from Pittsburgh via. St. Louis. By 1855, saw mills proliferated on the West Bottoms of Kansas City, then known as the Kaw Bottoms, "being located in the midst of what was then very dense forests," according to Charles F. Quest, who arrived that year from Kentucky and worked as plasterer and mechanic.[21]

As steamboats made their way west on the river, Francois and Berenice Chouteau could at first make the trip from St. Louis in nine days, enjoying the social life and company on board the steamboat, but eventually made the trip in five days. The first steamboat to try going up the Missouri River, the steamboat *Independence*, made the trip in 1819, though it did not reach the site of Francois Chouteau's landing. The age of mechanization had begun for the future Kansas City.[22]

Mill Power: Corn Meal and Possum Hash

Water did not just serve as a surface for transportation, it also supplied energy for mills to grind and saw. Falling water provided the energy for inanimate mechanical energy for which there was no real substitute, but repetitious labor done by man or animal. Mills to grind and saw, or to manufacture textiles, made production of their outputs somewhat labor saving.[23]

Many smaller rivers run through Jackson County—Big Blue, Little Blue, Sniabar, Indian Creek, and Turkey Creek, plus many springs—and offered easy watering and mill sites to the settlers.

Blue Mills in eastern Jackson County, Missouri, along the Little Blue River, near its delta at the Missouri River

Water served mills as pre-industrial electricity, the energy to turn wheels to make things move, to do one's bidding in creating power to grind or saw. The big difference was that mills were both seasonal and stationary while the electricity that would later replace them could be routed to any building or light pole and produce a continuous source of energy.

For over half of the 19th century, water-driven mills accounted for approximately 25% of energy used in America, and for over 50% of energy along the western edge of Missouri where wind power was virtually unused.[24]

The only mechanized part of the lives of the Euro-American settlers was the mill, and a mill required either a strong stream of water, or horse or oxen to turn the wheel to grind the grain to produce flour. Two kinds of mills commonly operated first, the grist mill and the saw mill, the only services available in rural areas and often found side by side.

In New England the bulky, noisy, cranky "water machines" of the Wood Age could also manufacture such delicate items as nails and pins. A patent was issued in 1795 for a nail-making process that soon produced 200,000 nails per day and reduced the price over the next century to "the penny nail."[25]

Other specialized mills in the East produced paper, powder, and textiles, while still others supported iron forges, blast furnaces, foundries, salt works and sugar refineries.[26] But that was in the East. In the pioneering effort of western Missouri, the difficulty of procuring mill stones and the scarce population meant just the most elementary corn- and wheat-grinding mills stationed along a medium-sized stream. In 1840, the population of the western states combined, Missouri being the outer perimeter of that geography, had a population of over four million, with a little over 5,000 grist mills and almost 7,000 saw mills. This made one mill

61

each available to every 800 people. Population was thin, and milling hard to come by, thus the hand-held grinder and the occasional long wagon trips to the mill.[27]

Of all the energy sources available to early settlers in the Wood Age, the grist mill provided a nucleus around which to build a community. This "central expression and identification of the Wooden Age" was often the only three-story building around, imposing authority on the landscape while it squealed and roared, sloshed and growled, providing the drama of moving parts that nothing else did. The mill acted as the harbinger of the Industrial Age. It also served as a magnet for commerce. The miller often combined with a blacksmith to offer services and a store for retail business. The average capital outlay to start a mill in Missouri in 1850 was about $500. Such a mill could produce 30- to 50-barrels of flour and cornmeal a day in season with spring and summer waters.[28]

In 1840, the Missouri census showed 690 such mills; the same census for the United States showed some fifty-thousand water mills operating.[29] As in all things in the Wood Age, milling depended on the seasons. Spring floods turned the wheel swiftly; autumn's sluggish energy moved it accordingly. The winter months when the stream froze made milling impossible before the steam engine.

The miller could pay cash for the flour he ground and/or keep part, a much needed exchange not available any other way for farmers to trade in the market place. The miller often kept a portion of the flour he ground in payment for grinding. This flour the miller made available to customers who did not grow their own wheat and needed flour.[30] If a farmer were to grow beyond sustaining his family at a subsistence level, he had to break into the market with a salable crop and get cash back to reinvest, pay off debts and buy ready-made goods at the store by the mill.

Without cash, the farm family had to make everything themselves and had difficulty rising above a cash poor existence. Higher production of corn and wheat, a surplus of each sold for cash at the mill marked the beginnings of the market economy on the western edge of that area known as the "Western States," and the beginning of prosperity for families working the land.[31]

On their way up river to their new fur trading site, Francois and Berenice Chouteau would have passed the town of Franklin about halfway there. As early as 1819 farmers bringing in corn to be ground could use one of the town's two ox-powered mills to provide meal for their families in some bulk. They could get their tree trunks cut up for lumber at the second. Twelve yokes of oxen powered the larger of the two mills.[32]

In 1826, an early settler near Chouteau's Landing, James Welch, built the first mill on record at the new site. He constructed an overshot wheel with a long upright pestle of hard hickory, which rose and fell into a mortar burned into the end of a solid oak block. Welch put into the mortar a peck of corn at night and set the machinery to produce "the coveted morning's allowance of hoecake." But possums being numerous would climb into the mortar while the pestle was up only to be pounded by it "before they could take a second mouthful of the coveted prize." In the morning Welch would discover to his disgust another mixture of corn meal and "possum hash." Thus, began the pioneer effort at machinery in the "Kaw's mouth country," later to be known as Chouteau's Landing, Westport Landing, the Levee, the town of Kansas, and finally Kansas City.[33]

While scant, very early milling operations south of the river developed (with Blue Mills as an exception), a horse-driven mill in Clay County directly across the river, run by the grandfather of the eventually notorious Younger brothers, could be reached by pirogue or flatboat where settlers in Jackson County could grind their grain, "crossing and recrossing on this ferry" until 1836. By then settlement south of the river developed sufficiently to support mills.[34]

Getting grain to the mill to produce a barely edible loaf of bread represented arduous work and long suffering. James Williams recollected his trips to the horse mill in 1848 in nearby Cameron, Missouri. "Every old settler knows it was a job to get wheat ready for the mill, but it was a bigger job to get it made into flour fit for bread . . . . My, how sore our hands would get binding bearded wheat. We'd then stack in a circle, so we could put it on the ground in a circle and put horses on it and ride them around in a circle on it. We called this operation tramping out wheat." [35]

Though the mill is not extant, mill stones from the Blue Mill survive for the public to view. One is embedded in the rear courtyard of the 1859 Jail, Marshal's Home and Museum, and another is beside the main entrance to the National Frontier Trails Museum, both in Independence, Missouri.

Fueling Change

At first entirely entrepreneurial, the establishment of a mill and the subsequent rise of the "mill community" created such value that they began to be seen as a public utility. By the 1840s the Missouri General Assembly received petitions to dam streams and rivers to construct mills. The petitions were solicited with the overtones of being for the public good and stimulating community growth and stability. The Emigrant Aid Company of Kansas motivated immigration in 1854 and 1855 by establishing mills in nine fledgling communities.[36]

For farmers in remote areas and for travelers as well, a unique invention known as the hand mill could suffice to produce a small amount of meal for a family dinner. Captain Meriwether Lewis carried a hand mill with him on the Lewis and Clark transcontinental exploration. It was mentioned on June 11, 1805, as part of his inventory.[37]

Typical of the mills in Jackson County, Watts Mill was erected in 1832. Razed in 1949, the site remains part of Little Blue Trace park along Indian Creek in south Kansas City.

Henry Rowe Schoolcraft mentioned in his 1818-1819 *Ozark Journal* wandering 800 miles above the junction of the White River with the Mississippi and finding a remote cabin and fields of Farmer M'Gary who offered his hand mill for grinding corn and his smokehouse filled with bear and other meats.[38] Pounding the corn was done "with a wooden mortar, with a pestle attached to a spring pole" that repeatedly pounded the corn. G. W. Featherstonehaugh also mentioned this contrivance in the 1840s.[39]

The little village had its own mill infrastructure that over a century grew to be one of the forefronts of Kansas City industry. Early pioneer, Joseph S. Chick, arrived in 1836 and described the mill scene: "Corn and wheat were generally ground at the local mills. The principal mill was a treadmill run by Wm. Parish and located about Cleveland and 33rd Streets. Mr. Jenning (sic.) had a water mill on Brush Creek at the crossing of the Westport and Wornall Road, another was located at the crossing of Indian Creek near the state line, and James H. McGee had a corn cracker on McGee, or what is now O. K. Creek and about where Penn Street crosses. The demand that these local mills could not supply was met by a large water mill on the Little Blue owned by John and Robert Aull. It seems to me there was more water in the streams then than at present as this mill run nearly the year around."[40]

Fifteen mills in all dotted the countryside around the growing village between the early days and the Civil War. Some of them became steam-powered mills as such engines became available in the 1830s and onward. McGee's mill sold an "old engine" to Kansas-bound settlers in 1854 as they crossed over into free-state territory to set up a community at Lawrence.[41] One of the longest enduring mills was Watts Mill, the site of which is now at 103rd Street and State Line Road in Kansas City, Missouri. Built as Fitzhugh's Mill in 1832 on the north bank of Indian Creek, it serviced wagon trains ready to take off for the Santa Fe Trail. These parties would camp nearby using woods for firewood and to hunt wild game for food. The mill operated until 1939, and was torn down in 1949.[42]

From small seeds mighty industries can grow. A 1925 *Kansas City Journal* newspaper article boasted that the industry had grown to be third in the output of flour. "The combined output of Kansas City mills in 1924 was 5,412,957 barrels. Eleven flourmills, with a total capacity output of 25,250 barrels daily, are operated here. Figured at an average price of $7 a barrel, the combined value would be $367,780 daily."[43]

Mills specializing in production of wool were also important. And, the Kansas City area boasts one of the best preserved examples in the country. The 1860 Watkins Woolen Mill (which was also a grist and saw mill) became a Missouri State Park in 1964 and was declared a National Landmark in 1966.

The 20th century wheat harvest resulted from 19th century transformation of the prairie. The untilled landscape the Osage dominated with their buffalo hunting horse culture yielded to the plow. Buffalo disappeared from overhunting and mass killing. Far from woodland valleys and plains teaming with game, Indians were corralled into rectangular reservations to make the prairie available to large scale wheat production. One culture's low- energy system yielded to another's high-energy conquest.

As greater materialism changed life on the Missouri frontier, the entire United States was itself advancing into unknown territory, that of using a fossil fuel for the first time. Though

Fueling Change

English cousins in Great Britain had already adapted to coal use because of a scarcity of firewood, the young country as a whole had plenty of wood and saw little need to move in that direction. Both political events and growing scarcity of municipal sources of firewood on the eastern seaboard would force a change, however, and in the process introduce coal to wide use that would launch it as the next dominant fuel.

Chapter 8

Coal on the Way

Like an alien species introduced into an ecosystem, coal changed the fuel chain, the speed of reproduction and the offensive and defensive measures of the marketplace. Perhaps for the first time, merchants realized the advantages of a fuel in creating greater profit in the marketplace. Having taken wood fuel for granted as the only fuel, they found themselves upstaged, out priced and better manufactured by coal users.

The Coal Age dawned in America while the country still had immense forests, many as yet even unmapped, but where wood had become scarce, a new fuel was needed. By the 18th century such eastern cities of Philadelphia and Boston had already created plans to extend their grasp for wood supplies beyond the fringes of their cities or to try a new fuel. Established in 1620, Boston had run short of fuel by the end of its first hundred years. In search of new woodlands, the Massachusetts government acquired access to both New Hampshire and Maine forests as sources of wood supply for fuel, building and trade.[1]

Massachusetts competed with the British Crown over wood since the English had a fleet of ships to build and mast. The British Navy also appropriated the forests of Maine and New Hampshire for their trees were considered "the largest in the world" for masts.[2] The Maine-grown white pine and hemlock were perfect for masting, from 29-37 inches in diameter, and as long as a hundred feet. Such a tree required 36 yokes of oxen to move it through the forest to the wharf and a small army of men to load it. Indifferent to the Euro-American settlements' need for wood or the Native Americans' warring reaction to having their forests plundered, the British as well as the Dutch and the French sent mast cutters into the New England forests and loaded their ships with masts throughout the early 1700s. By 1746, all British ships were outfitted with masts from New England and losing such a supply was deemed to be "fatal to his [Majesty's] service."[3]

Britain's own forests and those of the Baltic states of Sweden, Norway, Denmark and Poland, formerly the masting forests for Europe, had already been thinned for the European flotillas.[4] Those countries looked upon New England as a prime area of national interest and defense, but the Native Americans who lived there disputed such a high-handed claim. Their strategy to stop deforestation was to slay all the oxen the mast cutters employed to move the large heavy pieces as well as to kill the wood cutters themselves who had to be protected under heavy guard to assure their survival and production of masts.[5]

Coal Mines Shall Flourish Only Where There Be Manufacturing

Lack of "Fewell" in Boston throughout Massachusetts became a problem. By the late 1700s and early 1800s, Boston citizens increasingly used coal. Complained one Captain Lieutenant Artillery (sic.) in 1783 at nearby Springfield, Massachusetts, "We have several hundred Bushells of Coal on hand . . . if I May exchange som of it for Wood . . . for at present We have no wood—nor money to by aney."[6]

Coal in the American colonies was first seen in Virginia near Richmond in 1701: "We went up to ye Cole, w'ch is not above a mile and a half from their settlement on the great upper Creeke, w'ch, riseing very high in great Raines hath washed away the Banks that the Coal lyes bare, otherwise it's very deep in the Earth . . . ."[7] It is not known when coal began to be commercially sold, probably in the middle of the 18th century, but it eventually found its way to the wharves of Hampton, Virginia, and into the boats that took it north to growing cities.[8]

Wood was presumed to be the preferred fuel for home and hearth if available and coal only for "Forges and great Towns, if ever they happen to have any; for, in their Country Plantations, the Wood grows at every Man's Door so fast, that after it has been cut down, it will in seven Years time, grow up again from a seed to substantial Fire Wood."[9] This, written in 1720, shows an optimism of an abundance of fuel in both coal and wood to be had for the taking in the years ahead. Indeed, that proved to be true for a century and more.

Bituminous coal was mined first in both Virginia and Pennsylvania.[10] Once anthracite fields were found in Pennsylvania in 1768, that, too, was mined and used.[11] Unlike the soft, smoky bituminous coal, anthracite was hard and brittle, virtually odorless and smokeless, difficult to light and also hard on the grates made for wood, but consumers adapted to it. Until 1845, when people talked about coal in Pennsylvania, at least, they meant anthracite.[12] This "hard coal" was in demand in Philadelphia by 1790.

Artisans and blacksmiths "accepted hard coal as superior fuel for doing business. The hotter temperature and time saved" made anthracite the preferred fuel for those using it in small industry, having learned it was "a more efficient type of fuel."[13] Citizens increasingly needed it for their own hearths, and came to rely on shipments of coal from the mountains in northeastern Pennsylvania as well as from Ireland at around a thousand tons a year.[14] White settlers had manufacturing in mind for coal use, had mentioned in letters and maps the outcroppings of coal and other minerals all over the eastern portion of the United States from the 1600s onward. Europeans knew metals meant value and coal meant greater efficiency.

The only reference to Native American industry in coal in the entire country surfaces in the written record of "Lieutenant Beckwith in 1853 near Westport, Missouri, on the Santa Fe road near the Kansas River. He was probably in Kansas, past Fort Leavenworth. His record of June 26 states: "On a branch of the Wahkarrussi, where the Oregon trail strikes it, a seam of bituminous coal crops out. This is worked by the Indians, one of whom we met driving an ox cart loaded with coal, to Westport." This is the only mention that the Indians had any interest in commercial mining."[15] Which tribe was represented there would be a guess at best.

But they drove a wagon! They hauled coal! They adopted the white man's economic model to take stuffs to market.

The Osage, as was true of their fellow Native Americans, did very little, if any, underground work. They defined their lives as living between the impenetrable earth and the endless sky.[16] They met their needs there, valued the fellow occupants of their lands, both human and animal, and honored the vault of night and day above them. They worked gardens, hunted for food and furs, and traveled distances with the seasons, all done on a horizontal plane.

The Euro-American's ancestors, whose descendants were now represented on the Missouri frontier, had once done the same, but over millennia had discovered the "three Ms" of high-energy civilizations, minerals, mining and metallurgy, so that the verticality of life of populations moving into high-energy systems may have set in about the same time as mining.[17] Metallurgy accompanied mining and helped to enhance wealth versus enduring relative or extreme poverty. In other words, the deeper the mines, the greater the mining work force, the greater the wealth pulled from the depths, the greater was the wealth of a few compared to the many who labored for it.

The horizontal and bi-pedal pedestrian approach to life to which the Osage limited themselves—with or without horses—offered everyone a fair share of resources.

The Osage and fellow Native Americans were not the only peoples to overlook mineral wealth. The Australian aborigines did as well. Metals were not necessary for a rich cultural existence. "In taking his first steps from the Stone Age into the Age of Metals, man crossed a great divide. But considering his long and skillful use of the other materials around him, that advance took place quite late in human history. In fact, in some parts of the world it never took place at all."[18] Certainly it did not among the Osage.

But in the minds of the Euro-American settlers, though working against a western backdrop of enormous forests, those resources had become out of reach for cities on the Atlantic coast. Transportation of cut timber had been a problem for all of human history. If it could not be readily cut at a river's edge and sent down stream, timber was very difficult to transport.[19] For this reason the young American cities looked to the next available fuel at hand: coal had a future with them. They had experienced firsthand the superiority of the industrializing strength of Great Britain, understood the source of that strength, and envied it for themselves.

Coal found its way into daily life in Virginia in the early 1700s, though living in a land as wooded as colonial America made it less necessary to use than it had been by their British cousins. By the turn of the 19th century, however, wood had grown scarce enough that Philadelphia, engaged in burning coal delivered by British ships. Two early steam engines using Virginia coal operated the water works in the center square during this decade. By 1810 and 1811, some 13,000 tons of coal were delivered to American ports per year, but as the War of 1812 took over the waterways, coal tonnage fell to under 3,000 tons a year. By 1814, only 691 tons were delivered.[20] Clearly, Philadelphia, if not all of East-Coast America, entered its first major fuel crisis.

The British showed their wealth, power and energy in the War of 1812. The loss of coal shipments by sea forced local merchants in Philadelphia and Wilkes-Barre to scramble for local supplies. By April 1813, the British blockage of coal had caused Virginia bituminous coal to triple in price. Artisans had to pay high prices for coal themselves and were forced to pass on the increase to local citizens.[21]

The early years of the War of 1812 saw a slow increase in coal from the Lehigh coal field of Pennsylvania destined to become one of Pennsylvania's most flourishing anthracite regions. Those who used the hard coal found it efficient. It reduced production costs, heated iron in half the time and increased production. By the time the war was over in 1815, anthracite had a firm hold on the coal market.[22] Another byproduct of early coal use was streetlights invented in England in 1812 and used in Baltimore by 1816.[23]

The War of 1812 was fought over British restraint of trade and impressments of American sailors on the high seas. It had the unexpected consequence of initiating an independent coal mining industry in the United States.[24] With that would come the coal gas industry in Baltimore to light the streets of the city and the increase in iron working that made the proliferation of the railroads possible.

In this way coal use began in America: The ripples of the scarcity of trees in England by the 16th century forced the mining of coal there. The need to clear the mines of water with a better mechanism than horse, pulley and bucket forced the invention of the steam engine. Increased coal as fuel and parallel experimentation of coal conversion to coke in place of charcoal from wood led to increased iron making in England. The increased manufacture of cannon and cannonballs led to its supremacy at sea, making it possible to found colonies on the eastern shore of what would become America.

This 17th century series of events led to the dominance of Great Britain over the colonies that led the forests of New England to be sacrificed for masts as well as for building and fuel. Fights over wood rights between colonists and British navy became grievances to match others the colonists had against the British throne. The ensuing Revolutionary War led the United States of America being founded as a separate and equal nation shortly to be challenged again by the British on the high seas that led to the War of 1812. The ensuing coal embargo and resulting scarcity, along with the realization that Britain's power came from coal and that the United States had its own coal mines, forced the young nation to start its own march into the Coal Age.

Though the tiny settlement on the western edge of Missouri would feel little of this turbulence directly, the combined strength of British industrialism and the eastern states' borrowing their technology and creating their own would send wave after wave of collective enterprise, innovation, optimism, growing populations and westward-moving urgency to the shores of the Missouri as it turned north. The steamboat that would soon arrive on the western waters of the recently purchased Louisiana Territory, of which the new state of Missouri would become a part, is a direct descendant of the steam engine in England invented because of that country's scarcity of wood. The pre-steam world of wood, that 100% saturation of wood as humankind's only fuel, was forced to open to another fuel.

Chapter 9

Steam Comes to Kansas City

The use of steam in propelling water craft was . . . the lightning of heaven
subdued and put in harness by the genius of man . . ..
—William Z. Hickman, *The History of Jackson County, Missouri* (1920)[1]

Perhaps nothing in the 1830s onward was more exciting than having a steamboat arrive at the limestone pier then known as "the levee," or Westport Landing, that would become Kansas City. Villagers, passengers, merchants, wagon masters, hawkers and gawkers ran to the waterfront to greet passengers, do business, and just generally watch the amazing scene of a mechanized river boat laden with people, animals and goods being unloaded by sweating slaves and free men amid the din of hundreds of voices raised at once. The steamboat had summarily replaced the keel boat and all that sweat, danger and toil was now a thing of the past.

This was something new in the fullest sense of the word . . . never seen before. Yet the fuel was old. The steamboat was a Wood Age invention. This combination of new and old, old and new courses throughout this part of the narrative. As soon as a new fuel was introduced into the picture long dominated by wood, new technology was invented to capitalize on its properties. Though the boat burned wood at this point, it arrived powered by mechanically generated power, not wind, human or animal energy, but by an *engine* within, "the lightning of heaven put in harness by the genius of man." Nothing like it had ever been seen before. The engine built in the Wood Age was a response in Britain to a new fuel. It would soon burn coal and become a bridge to the Coal Age.

The arrival of the steamboat increased the energy flow through manufactured replication and signaled the raw beginning of the next fuel age that ushered in the Industrial Revolution. *Industrial* meant machines, metal against metal, chugging, heaving, moving, making, burning, heating . . . "Lightning of heaven" was an apt description. In the mindset of the 19th century, the steamboat could only be seen as a favor bestowed by God.

The use of the word *harness* is a subtle reminder of the main motive power of the Wood Age, the horse, that had been the prime mover. An old image described a new invention.

Fueling Change

In this 50-year period between 1820-1870, coal would become the fuel of choice for railroads, steamboats and iron makers. It would change the face of labor throughout the western world as mechanical extraction replaced human hand and back, and mechanical production made inroads into the long, long history of hand-crafted work.

As if that were not enough change, the ability to extract oil from the ground was developed in 1859 in Pennsylvania, and its rise as the next new fuel was meteoric.

In just 10 years the demand for oil rushed it through the many steps of Stage 1, *Discovery and Development,* into Stage 2, *Systems Organization.* People understood, at last, what a new fuel meant in terms of wealth, transportation and manufacture though they barely had technology to handle it.

Forthcoming chapters reflect the changing fortunes of the three fuels at work at the same time within a 50-year period.

After eons of one fuel, and 100 years of two fuels, now communities would soon have the choice of three fuels *plus* mechanical power!

The introduction of the first mechanical converter to transform fuel to energy would change: 1) the way things were made; 2) the speed of travel; and, 3) the fuel and energy components of their world.

In the last decades of the Wood Age, different forms of fuel and different levels and kinds of energy clashed and flourished.

Coal brought change to the world ushering in a period of chaos as old and new components matched and re-matched in their evolution toward a new balance.

A brief comparison of these fuels shows the increased fuel power available in moving from wood to coal to oil:

A cord of wood is a 4' x 4' x 8' stack of wood including air space and bark.

One cord contains approximately 1.2 tons of dry wood or 2,400 pounds.

A barrel of oil is 42 U.S. gallons.

About 7.2 barrels of oil equal one ton of coal.

The per unit mass of coal varies greatly among different types of coal.[2]

Chapter 10

The Marvel of the Steamboat

The marvel of a fleet of steamboats on western rivers made demands on the work force to extract both wood and coal to keep them running and meeting schedules.

An energy suite has been defined as a matched set of components with a common fuel denominator, and the Wood Age described in Chapter 1 offers ample example of that suite— human labor, wood as fuel, centuries-old patterns of clearing land for farming.

The little communities that would become Kansas City lay at the far edge of the mechanical growth fueled by coal. As the easternmost settlement at the western edge of the United States, the area was caught in the ancient patterns of the Wood Age but repeated in a new place. This wood-powered suite would be exploited up to the 1870s even as steamboats became a real force and railroads began to encroach. As the end point in water travel, pioneers to points west totally depended on Wood Age systems to cross overland.

Mark Twain said about himself, "The reports of my death are greatly exaggerated." So, too, the reports of the demise of wood are greatly exaggerated. As a fuel, it was about to come into its finest hour. In its last moments, as ubiquitous fuel to humanity for hearth and blacksmith forge, wood was reborn as fuel for motive power and a bridge to the Coal Age. Flame took on a new persona altogether. For the first time in human history flame provided movement by heating water under pressure to move a boat upstream under its own power without sail or human or animal muscle. This amazing event created the means to stitch together the far-flung settlements beyond the Allegheny Mountains. Mechanized water travel became a daily miracle that owed its life to wood. As Brooke Hindle, author of *America's Wooden Age*, noted, wood was the first fuel used by both steamboats and railroads, thus the

steam engine belonged to the Wooden Age. It took decades of steam engine use to shift to coal-driven engines.[1]

Through the steam engine the old fuel provided new energy in a barely settled world. Any new systems being built to create lines of trading, transportation or farming were still supported by both a wood (fuel) and a wooden (building material) infrastructure. While the steam engine added mechanical power to their lives, the settlers still had to fall back on their old fuel for the miracle to work. Wood was now being used for both passive and active fires as well as for building.

Fortunately, the Kansas City area had an abundance of wood. Pioneers without exception commented on the thickness of forests, their grandeur and inexhaustibility, and lamented their loss while enthusiastically chopping down trees in the name of establishing home and business. At an "old settlers meeting" of Jackson County in 1871, founder of Westport, Missouri, John Calvin McCoy, reminisced about his life in the area still wild even in 1840:

> Around on all sides was a dense forest, the ground covered with impenetrable brush, vines, fallen timber and deep impassable gorges. A narrow, crooked roadway winding from Twelfth and Walnut streets, along down on the west side of the deep ravine toward the river, across the Public Square to the river at the foot of Grande avenue. A narrow, difficult path, barely wide enough for a single horseman, running up and down the river under the bluff, widening its way around fallen timber and deep ravines.[2]

Even as late as 1859 "the way from the limestone pier to the village of Westport (a distance of about four miles) "led through almost unbroken forest," "a dreadful state of mud, mostly uphill and through a considerable piece of oak and walnut timber."[3]

Gushing promoter of the Kansas City mystique C. C. Spalding noted in 1858, "A good portion of these grounds is, indeed, prairie, and the balance is covered with heavy growths of timber, which will forever furnish us with a bountiful supply of framing lumber. Opposite our city there is one dense body of timber of over 2000 acres, while to the east and south of us every one of our rich and fertile farms is supplied with large quantities of the first quality of timber."[4]

During the years of the early settlement, the West Bottoms along the Kaw Riverfront as it merges with the Missouri River was known as the French Bottoms in which lived a small settlement of French trappers. William Mulkey, "sold saw logs for years off the land where now lies the residence portion of the western section of the city. The squirrels and deer were so bad that they were pests, rather than game. It was nothing in those times for a party to start out and come home with 700 or 800 squirrels. The deer were also extremely plentiful and could be shot so easily that it was not sport to kill them. When I first came here (in 1828) there was nothing on the site of the city but dense forests."[5]

Another citizen, Charles F. Quest, observed this in 1855: "At this time all that part of what is now Kansas City except the river front, where the business was carried on, was heavily timbered and broken only at rare intervals by little farms. The West Bottoms, then known as the Kaw Bottoms, (the name had changed in the intervening years) were given up to the saw mill business, the mills being located in the midst of what was then very dense forests."[6]

But it was not just the forests but the stretches of meadows and streams that challenged and excited the pioneers in their travels. This part of the story emphasizes the geography of the spot, the rivers, the plains, the "unprecedented proportions" of distance and natural ecosystems. It was a time to be stunned by the plenitude and beauty of undeveloped places while eagerly planning ways to break them down into smaller pieces, usable commodities, economic building blocks. Wonder and a zest for conquest rode side by side. Fortunately, the plentiful wood supply would stoke the engines of steamboats and progress.

The Lightning of Heaven

For lack of population in the first two decades of steam boating not much traffic made its way up the Missouri River, though Cadet Chouteau, half-brother of Francois, financed the *Yellowstone* in 1830-31 for a total cost of $8,950 (the steam engine being half the cost), to go to the upper Missouri River to bring back loads of furs. He surprised Francois and Berenice by his arrival on April 30, 1831, after only two weeks on the river from St. Louis. The rest of the trip upstream, however, was fraught with difficulty and disappointment. The *Yellowstone*'s draft was too deep, and the boat became stuck for 12 days. The crew found, to their dismay, even in spring only four- to four-and-a-half feet of water, "when the river is very low, and one's steamboat is 'drawing all the water' there is in the channel," as Mark Twain describes this kind of condition in *Life on the Mississippi*. The *Yellowstone* arrived at Fort Tecumseh, 1,300 miles upriver from St. Louis, on June 19 and shoved off on June 30 to return carrying among its buffalo robes and furs, 10,000 pounds of salted buffalo tongues. The *Yellowstone* made the return voyage to St. Louis on a higher river in two weeks.[7]

Most of the early steamboat traffic confined itself to fur trading for which reason the comparative speed was profitable. Whoever could get to market faster with the furs gained the most; but, soon other passengers requested transportation. Missionaries to the Indians, trading supplies for the Indians, Indians themselves as delegations to St. Louis and even Washington and back, children on the frontier from families like the Chouteaus who could afford to send their children to school farther downriver—such was the nature of steamboat passengers and traffic in the 1820s and 1830s.[8]

Town of Kanzas (later, Kansas City) Waterfront, 1853

The ferry in the foreground takes cattle across while a Conestoga wagon waits. The single line of buildings against the bluffs behind and the rocky pier in the middle foreground accurately depict the geography and population of the Town of Kanzas. The steamboat and the ferry overlap energy components from two different energy suites, the ferry in the Wood Age and the mechanized steamboat moving toward the coming Coal Age.

The town of Franklin, opposite today's Boonville some 250-miles down the Missouri River between St. Louis and Chouteau's Landing, had welcomed its first steamboat visit in 1819 by the *Independence*. It had no regular service until the 1830s.

In 1819, the *Independence* took 13 days to make the trip to Franklin from St. Louis.

By 1831, the *Yellowstone,* with improvements, reached the Kansas City site in five days. The *Western Engineer* chugged its way farther up river to Chouteau's Landing in that year as well.

But, not until 1834 did the *John Hancock* make "the first landing of record" at Chouteau's site, and regular service may have said to begin at that date.[9]

The very idea of steam boating drew on a complex series of materials and techniques. From old materials and old ways came the new invention. The first steam engines were often anemic and offered little in the way of energy for the amount of fuel they used.

Racing Steamboats on the Mississippi

This scene is similar to the race described on the Missouri between the *James H. Lucas* and the *Polar Star*. The sailboat and small passenger boat suggest an overlap of energy suites.

On the western edge of the Missouri River, the settlement joined the nation in the unavoidable clearing of wood for fuel for their Wood Age life style. The river, once exclusively used for canoes, bullboats, keelboats and flatboats, now welcomed the mechanically driven newcomer. The steam engine burned wood and needed a constant supply. No sooner had steamboats proven their ability to move than captains began to race them as well. A little of the romance from the early 1850s shows up in a boat race between two powerful steamers.

The fastest boat to hold the speed record was the *James H. Lucas* from St Louis up the Missouri River to St. Joseph. A challenger, the *Polar Star*, demanded a race; the prize was a rack of elk horns legendary in their size. The *Lucas*'s captain used pine, barrels of rosin, "a few tons of fat pork" while his bow "turned the water like a plowshare." The race was bow to bow until the *Lucas* pulled ahead between Kansas City and St. Joseph and won by three hours and twenty minutes. The elk horns with silver plaque were duly awarded the *Lucas* that kept the record without further challenge.

Not only does this vignette on a small stretch of the middle Missouri River display some of the excitement of the new technology, it also suggests that the captain of the *Lucas* picked his winning fuel to be pine, rosin and pork fat, evidently fuels either plentiful and power-packed, or just those available in an emergency.[10] It also shows that the American fascination with speed now had a new expression in mechanized travel. What a thrill it must have been to move faster than a horse could run, to move *up*river *quickly*, and to race another mechanized behemoth on the surface of the previously unyielding current.[11] Fifty years later an author would remark that the transportation world had matured: "Their sporting, drinking, gambling, fighting, have given place to business, temperance, prudence, and refinement, while wealth rolls up in the cities as a result of the speedy and cheapened transportation which the steamers have effected."[12]

Wooding Up

Originally, boat crews had to stop and cut their own wood but did not have to worry as would the crews on ocean-going steamships of taking up most of the deck or hold space for a supply of wood or coal to make the distant shore.[13] As traffic increased, the obvious commercial exchange presented itself and "wood hawking" became a new way to earn a living, albeit a seasonal one.

Early steamboats, of course, found no ready-cut cords of wood waiting along the banks of the rivers. Supplying wood to a steam engine caught the enterprising frontiersmen unaware of such an opportunity. Farmers fortunate enough to own riverfront property discovered an unexpected cash crop, sometimes their best one, particularly if they possessed good wood. Well-seasoned cordwood, the captain's best hope for speed, varied from one wood yard to the next and from one riverbank to the next. Hardwoods like oak, ash or chestnut were favored for long-lasting fuel, cottonwoods least favored for burning quickly or green wood with its high-water content.[14]

Competition for wood at good prices depended on individual wood hawks lowering their prices to beat another farther upstream or on the amount and kind of wood available. Competition for passengers and freight also became fierce, according to travel stories of the time. Captains ranged from duplicitous to undependable to quixotic. Boats were loaded to the gunwales with deck passengers plus those who paid for cabins. The boats lined up at the piers, literally miles of steamboats, "some two to three miles long, of tall, ascending columns of coal-black smoke," diagonally parked at major ports to take on their loads, but none of it moved without fuel, usually wood.[15] A Kansas City observer wrote this about a steamboat that stopped to take on over a hundred cords of wood. "The captain ran the outside wheel to keep the boat close to the bank and burned up the entire hundred cords of wood in doing so."[16]

Wood Hawking

This scene of passengers who signed on for wood hauling in exchange for passage plus crewmen loading the steamboat was common until wood hawking grew more organized. Also see the map of a river's wood lots on page 81.

A hundred cords took the work of over a hundred men and perhaps as many as a hundred acres of woods to yield the wood for this particular event. Across the state at this time, St. Louis in 1852 received some 3,000 steamboats yearly and the total rated capacity of these was about 50,000 tons, making St. Louis the third largest port in the country in the amount of steam tonnage exceeded only by New York and New Orleans.[17]

The multiples of cordwood per steamboat per year become staggering in a short amount of time. Woodcutting, wood hawking and wood procuring became a major industry almost overnight as steamboats moved as far as wood could take them. In hardwood forests an acre would yield a cord and more of good wood. Marginal lands would yield about a third of a cord per acre.[18]

Coal was simply not to be found on the western rivers until the 1840s, and not in any abundance until the 1860s. Though coal fired the first steamboat's maiden trip, the *New Orleans,* in 1811-12, which departed from Pittsburgh, the soon-to-be epicenter of the coal country, coal scarcity could only be cured with time. Coalmine operators by the late 1830s began to advertise in such eastern newspapers as the Cincinnati *Gazette* and the Pittsburgh *Daily Gazette and Advertiser* the availability of coal over wood. Soon coal mine owners set up coal stops along the river banks and coal boats with bags of coal for ease of handling followed along to transfer their bags to waiting steamboats.[19]

Modifications needed to be made to the fire box for coal but could not be made if coal was not consistently available, all of which slowed the progress of coal. Sometimes a combination of wood and coal kept the engines humming in spite of the inadequacies of the firebox.[20]

Steamboat captains and engineers created a number of small systems for themselves in procuring fuel, particularly if they were in competition with each other to arrive first. For a race, the wily captain contracted in advance along the route with dependable wood hawkers for coal flats and wood.[21] If he is in the lead in the race, he might buy all the seasoned wood and leave only the green wood for his competitor. The racing boats from New Orleans did not slow down before St. Louis (the route on which keelboat men had previously labored so mightily against the upstream current) except to allow a wood hawker to intercept them.

During the race, wood hawkers would meet the racing steamer by a pre-arranged signal, a series of whistles or bells, with a wood boat bearing as much as thirty cords of wood. With a double crew for quick loading, work went fast: "You should be on board when they take a couple of those wood boats in tow and turn a swarm of men into each; by the time you had wiped your glasses and put them on, you will be wondering what has become of that wood," Twain commented.[22]

The best boats in a race made fourteen miles an hour compared to keel boating up river at sometimes as little as three miles in a day. Other times on the Upper Missouri where wood became scarce, the engineer or captain might contract with wood hawks on the way up for fuel to be used on the way back. Ever resourceful, he might send a yoke of oxen to shore, his crew throwing a chain around a few logs and taking them on deck where his men could saw the wood while on board. Other times, crew members rousted out "deck passengers" paying the least fare or none at all who traded passage for labor in "wooding up," to cut and carry wood

Wood Lots along Ohio River

This map of river ports along the Ohio River indicate the MANY stops at woodlots along the river bank. Quite literally, each steamboat would need to dock and reload their wood coffers, as it would be consumed quickly…especially while running up river.

After the Civil War the focus turned to the railroad. Steamboats began to burn coal and wood hawking died out.

It is presumable that a similar map of the Missouri River woodlots, or any western river in the prime of steamboating days, may exist in some little-known archive.

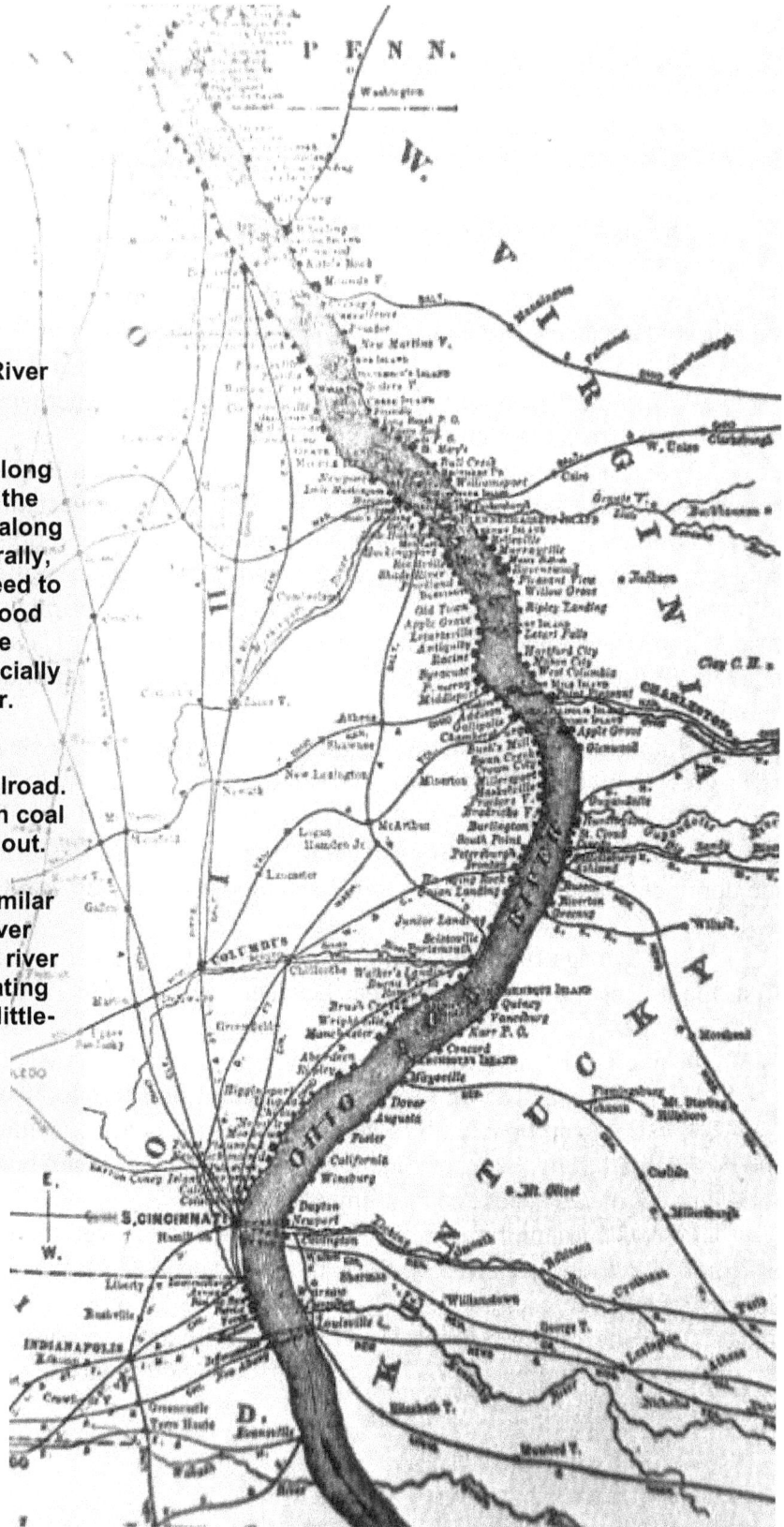

back on board. In some cases a farmer could leave wood at riverside with a mark on a stump as to price, and the captain would leave money or a chit in exchange for the wood, but, in the early years, at least, a good deal of wood was simply stolen along the way either by steamboat crews who needed wood and found no one to pay along the "almost untenanted shores," as described by Twain, or because many of the wood hawkers lining the river bank were squatters with no title to the timber or the land.[23]

The supply line that could be loosely called a system was made up of many, small, wood and some coal sellers vying for attention along the riverbanks. Their sheer numbers made the system work though they were for the most part individually owned and operated. Their supplies were uneven, and their practices often questionable, but over the course of the 1830s, 1840s and 1850s, the opportunity to sell wood and coal to over a thousand steamboats plying the western waters gave employment to countless men—perhaps the very ones who had formerly been keelboat men.

Wood delivery as a system remained "catch as catch can" even as other parts of the new transportation mode evolved. The Pilots Benevolent Association grew out of necessity to relay information on the challenging and changing river conditions. Pilots quickly sensed a power position and flourished in its secrecy and stringency, controlling traffic on the river until pilots took on an imperious role and a steamboat could not move without a pilot from the association. The number of pilots increased through the kind of "hands-on-the-wheel training" that Twain himself experienced, cuffed about the ears by one pilot, respected and taught by another. [24]

Both pilots and steamboats proliferated. The number of steamboats on the rivers after 1811 grew to 69 by 1820; to 151 by 1830; to 494 in 1840; and, to 638 in 1850.

By 1860, the numbers in the "stately procession," as Twain fondly described them, had grown to 817, and by 1866 to over 1,000···the year of greatest traffic for steamboats before the continental railroad began to erode steamboat traffic. By 1868, the number had fallen to 874.[25]

The average running time, or season, for steam boating increased over the years. At first, the average round trips per year between the two ports of Louisville and New Orleans was three. By the Civil War period the trips had increased to 12. Also, in the early years before 1820, the average running time or season for a steamboat was 90 days.

The season in 1850-60 for boats between Louisville to New Orleans had increased to 141 days per year, probably 30 to 40 days fewer for boats in colder climates.[26] During 1857, the river remained open and profitable for nine months of steam boating in Kansas City with a total number of 725 steamboats calling at the levee.[27]

Wood consumption became more voluminous over time as engines became more efficient in creating steam, and, thus, more powerful: Average daily consumption rate was approximately one cord for each 20 tons before 1820; one cord for each 12 tons during the 1820-29 decade; one cord for each 10 tons 1830-39; and one cord for each eight tons 1840-60. Price per cord before was at $2.25. From 1830 to 1860 it was $2.50.[28]

The greater number of steamboats increased the demand on the countryside for fuel. In 1818, a 400-ton steamboat took 20 days to travel from New Orleans to Louisville, and it consumed about 360 cords of wood in the process. In this case, the consumption rate was about one cord of wood for each 22 tons every 24 hours, one cord for each 12 tons of the boat's measurement. The average fuel consumption rate of New Orleans boats (about 275 tons each) around 1840 was about 35 cords of wood per day, or one cord for each eight tons every 24 hours.[29] On the round trip the steamboat could burn upwards of 500 cords of wood at a cost of approximately $1,250.[30]

The 1850 census reports for the vessels operating in the Louisville/New Orleans trade again provided a basis of comparison. Based on those returns the annual fuel costs of a 310-ton steamboat would be approximately $11,600. Those for a 360-ton steamboat would be approximately $12,250 round trip from New Orleans to Louisville.[31] None of these abstract statistics, however, tell of the furious activity among wood hawkers to supply this amount of fuel from the receding forests. These unsung heroes of early industry personally uprooted, chopped, sawed, cut and delivered to the banks of the middle western rivers the mountains of wood to be used for early motive power.

Wood Hawks

Wood hawking, though piecemeal, awkward, unreliable, amateur and sometimes illegal, supplied the nation's hunger for speed and transportation in the form of cut wood, lard, coal in bags . . .. whatever a crewman could throw into the boiler to keep the ship moving. This was Stage 2, evolving *Systems Organization* at its earliest: rudimentary technology, scarce labor, spotty supply and continual scavenging to create the "lightning of heaven subdued and put in harness by the genius of man." The one constant in this fledgling system was the demands of the growing steamboat fleet. That only increased. Speed, convenience, eager pioneers, advancing trade and highly profitable routes pressed more and more boats into service.

The first reliable statistics for wood use in America show a per capita consumption in 1850 of all wood use of 4.39 cords of wood compared to 0.36 tons of coal, which meant Americans burned an estimated 100 million cords per year for all purposes, almost entirely for heat and cooking. So that even though these prodigious amounts of wood were wrenched from the nation's ecosystems for steam boating on the western waters, they were small compared to the nation's need as a whole for its citizens to heat their homes and cook their food. By 1860, wood use had dropped to four cords per capita and an almost 10% decrease in wood as fuel. By 1900, it had fallen from an all-time high of over 90% to 21%, an amazing decline, and mute testimony to the changing fuel procurement and labor patterns.[32]

The wood hawks themselves represented some of the working poor of the western movement while assisting to move masses of people on their way west. If they lived along the river itself, they commonly suffered "ague," or malaria, living in clouds of mosquitoes and fighting nettles, chiggers and snakes. Paul Wilhelm, Duke of Wurttemberg, noted a similar experience during the same period: "Barely penetrating a hundred paces into the thicket, we were swarmed upon and covered by mosquitoes to such an extent that we could scarcely see and recognize each other at a distance of twenty paces."[33]

Sometimes wood hawks harvested wood stocks without permission or ownership for a little ready cash or built their humble shacks on stilts over the muddy bank. One traveler visited a tidy whitewashed cabin with furniture and stove while waiting for wood to be loaded, while another remarked at the clay-colored men who toiled in the mud at the river bank to load wood.

Living a meager, hard existence by even the standards of the day, these men used their muscle to power the beginnings of steam-powered industrialization.[34] Unless they had a spring nearby from which to drink clear water, the wood hawker may also have had to use the river water "so charged with mud and sand that it is perfectly opaque, and in a few minutes deposits a sediment an inch thick in the bottom of a tumbler," according to Francis Parkman, chronicler of *The Oregon Trail* in 1847 remarked on the grittiness of Missouri River water.[35]

Wood hawking was rough work and they often tried to earn a little extra by disguising a stack of poor wood with an outer cover up of good wood. One steamboat captain recited his experience in dealing with these wood hawks in his early days: "As a second clerk, I was early taught to hold my own with the pirates who conducted the woodyards scattered along the river." Twenty cord stacks piled eight feet high and 10 lengths of the measuring stick (eight feet long) was the unit of measurement most often used if that much wood was available. (This is *Discovery and Development* at its source, always raw.)

The wood hawks often hid green or wet wood in the interior or rotten or crooked stock or "sticks," and the clerk had to inspect not only the length but take out the ends of the cords and peer within to check the quality of the wood. If he detected cheating, he discounted the price appropriately. Then the woodmen and the crew "exchanged a blue-streaked volley of vituperation," which often passed for entertainment among the passengers until the clerk and the wood hawk agreed on the deal or broke contact.[36]

The Gilliss House

This was a famous hotel on Westport Landing, "beautifully furnished" and "the best hotel in the western country," according to the *Daily Western Journal of Commerce*, August 26, 1860. The hotel was torn down in 1890.[37]

**Kansas Governor Andrew Reeder (left)
The governor escaped Southern
sympathizers by hiding at the Gillis House.
Dressed as a wood hawk—note sack of
kindling on his back—he fled to the East to
tell his harrowing tale of life in the wild West.
Above, 'The Woodman' a fine stipple
engraving by Francesco Bartolozzi after the
painting by Thomas Barker of Bath.**

The wood hawks along the river who supplied the bulk of the fuel were so common as to be unscrutinized, made invisible by their numbers and appearance, embracing and emitting the necessary grit and grunt of their station in the economic life of the frontier. A former governor of territorial Kansas dressed himself as a wood hawk or woodchopper to flee from border ruffians in the Town of Kansas in 1854. It turned out to be the perfect disguise. The pier upon which was unloaded vast piles of cut wood ready for city burning stands by this hotel. Wood piles were common sights.

The slavery question heated the border town to a boiling point as the former Indian lands across the river were proposed to come into the Union as free states Kansas and Nebraska. The governor of the Territory of Kansas, Andrew H. Reeder, a staunch abolitionist, had a price on his head and hoped to escape with his life. To do so, he had to cross the Kaw River and catch a steamboat going east. A few leading citizens of the town of Kansas City, including Colonel Kersey Coates and Dr. Johnston Lykins plotted to help the governor escape. In the dead of night, he was secretly rowed across the river and hidden in the waterfront Gilliss House hotel until the Southern militia came to search for him. Colonel Kersey Coates of the still-standing Coates House, then guided the governor up the steep limestone cliffs behind the levee town to a one-room cabin occupied by an elderly couple who agreed to take him in and use their attic as a hideout.

Reeder hid there for several days until, disguised as an Irish woodman, and carrying a sack of kindling, an ax over his shoulder and a long clay pipe in his mouth, he climbed down the hill and sat on a wood pile in the wood yard adjacent to the pier. In his disguise he only had to wait for the next steam boat. He escaped to Illinois and eventually to Washington D.C. to tell the tale of life on the Kansas border and his anonymity as a woodchopper. A photograph capturing him in that guise survives. A painting was later made from the photograph.[38]

Reeder's persecution was based on his refusal to certify fraudulent voting results to make Kansas a slave state, an act that riled pro-slavery factions on both sides of the river. He was made to resign by President Franklin Pierce for "private, speculative interests" because Reeder moved the capital of Kansas to Pawnee where Reeder had property.[39]

Wood or Coal?

Coal became more available for steamboats even on the shores of the rivers and both supplemented the wood hawks' wares and competed with them. The records from the steamboat *Columbian* show the use of wood and coal over a period from 1849 to 1851.[40] The receipt book, predated with an "184_" [blank] accommodates the two fuels with column one for amounts of coal received and column two for amounts of wood received. This shows the reality of two fuels in use with coal in the first column and wood in the second, indicating the rising availability of coal.

The records show that when farther east and nearer the source of coal, the steamboat used coal with occasional injections of wood. Farther west, the boat used more wood. On the Pittsburgh to St. Louis run the *Columbian* used more coal than it did on the Pittsburgh to Cincinnati run, bearing out the impression that wood was used farther west because coal was not that available. Assuming that it took a day on average for a skilled man with a broadax or saw to chop a cord of wood, each of the loads of multiple cords of wood sold required a good deal of concerted labor. Of course, digging coal did as well, and it may be that this coal came from outcroppings along the riverbanks or slope mines hauled to the riverbank in wagons.

A few named wood yards are listed as sources. Coal ports on the list competed with the wood yards. Unlike the wood hawks, coal dealers began to advertise in local newspapers to notify the public of their existence as an alternative fuel to wood. Sometimes the boat took on several loads of fuel in one day, suggesting supplies may have been undependable or meager. Mark Twain noted both coal and wood barges plied the river during his years as pilot in the

1830s.[41] Since the *Columbian* shared these waters with many other ships per day using the same fueling stops, the output of wood and coal among these stops was tremendous.

An army of woodcutters and coal diggers with little more than broadaxes, picks and shovels had to work to supply this insatiable demand for fuel. The number of small purchases in this record suggests that the boat rarely had enough fuel to go far. On two dates, one in July and one in September of 1851, the boat picked up 2000 bushels of coal. No explanation for this is currently available; but, given the loads of goods and passengers these boats carried, room for such a load of fuel would have been at a premium.

Taking on such a load of fuel meant that the boat may have been empty of cargo. Also note that the measurement of a "bushel" (35 liters of dry goods) originates in an agricultural context, not an industrial one.[42] Twain noted that "in the heyday of the steam boating prosperity the river from end to end was flanked with coal fleets and timber rafts, all managed by hand," suggesting supply was adequate and the shores teemed with producers of fuel.[43]

The map on page 81 of fuel stops on the Ohio River bears this out. Twain later lamented in the 1880s that "when there used to be four thousand steamboats and ten thousand acres of coal barges and rafts and trading scows, there wasn't a lantern from St. Paul to New Orleans, and the snags were thicker than bristles on a hog's back; and now when there's three dozen

MAKING UP RAFTS ON THE SUSQUEHANNA RIVER. A SCENE ON THE LINE OF THE ERIE RAILROAD.

steamboats and nary barge or raft, the government has snatched out all the snags, and lit up the shores like Broadway, and a boat's as safe on the river as she'd be in heaven."[44]

Master of the Levee

In the 1850s in Kansas City "all business was conducted at the levee." In this "Golden Era" of pre-fossil fuel driven machinery, with sixty regular boats running between St. Louis and Kansas City on a constant basis plus a fleet of coal and wood barges—wood hawkers flourished here, too—and transient boats or tramps, the levee dominated water commerce as the wagon trains dominated land. "It was not unusual at this period to see five or six large steamboats at the Kansas City levee at the same time. In the 1857 season, 729 steamboats arrived at Kansas City. So great was the volume of business that the steamboats ran day and night."[45] As early as 1840, it was not uncommon for 200-300 men to assemble at the river landing to buy and trade when the boats arrived.[46]

In 1856, the steamboat Arabia hit an underwater snag in the Missouri River and sank with 200 tons of cargo near the Kansas City landing. Built in 1853 its short life nevertheless proved profitable in 14 repeated trips up the Missouri River. One night in August 1856, the Arabia hit a snag in the river and capsized 130 passengers before sinking into a muddy time capsule of history. The Arabia was rediscovered 45 feet underground in a farmer's corn field in 1987 some distance from the river's current flow, and its precious cargo is now exhibited in one of Kansas City's best museums, Treasures of the Steamboat Arabia.

A boat might arrive with two hundred or more passengers, her hold almost bursting with freight besides being crowded with horses, mules, oxen and wagons on the main deck, and with furniture, boxes, even a piano or two piled on the hurricane deck as high as it would stick. In 1857, in the seven months of seasonal navigation, the village at the limestone pier still known as Westport Landing, Kanzas, or increasingly more often as Kansas City, played host to crowds night and day. The hotels on the landing hired boys to approach a passenger and ask if he or she were looking for a hotel. If the answer was yes, the boy would snatch the passenger's satchel and run for the hotel that paid him a tip while the startled passenger, adding screeching and shouts to the noise level, scampered after the boy to retrieve the disappearing luggage.[47]

The middle decades of the 19th century witnessed an elaborate and extensive series of systems created to manage the westward thrust of population and trade. The wagon master, the steamboat pilot/captain duo, the local merchant and the wharf master formed a nucleus of focused energy as they each directed traffic in their spheres of influence. Nothing could happen without the work of all in concert. Everyone else worked to support these positions one way or another: the investors and owners above them; the supporting legions of men below them; the townspeople who ran small retail and industries because of this traffic, and their customers using the flow of goods from one end of the trade to the other.[48]

89

The cattle, freighting and delivery belonged to the firm-handed wagon master. The steamboat traffic's success belonged to the skilled pilot to navigate among the many snags in the river and the captain to manage the fuel, the guests and the cargo. The buying and selling belonged to the shrewd-eyed merchant. The success of unloading and loading goods and passengers successfully at the levee belonged to the wharf master.

Perhaps never before or since have so few professions carried so much weight in a community. During the raucous and fluid scenes at the levee, these professionals supported each other's ventures and together hammered out systems on a daily basis to meet the needs of the town and its hordes of visitors. In this way the Wood Age was given its greatest expression. Not only was wood used as fuel for the engines of the steamboat, but to power the engines of commerce, along with its necessary concert of animals serving as carriers, water as the highway, timber as the raw material. (See Appendix C for the complete description of the Master of the Levee. It is hard to believe, and rivals any modern-day occupation, but without computer).

The sheer volume of activity forced systems to evolve. Stage 2, *Systems Organization,* required a greater and greater draw of wood from the surrounding forests estimated at 13,000 acres to supply fleets of steamboats as well as armies of eager emigrants their fuel and shelter while camping out and readying for the great trek west.[49]

For the towns, a steady supply of wood was needed for blacksmithing and wagon making, as well as hearth and home. Both lumber and finished wagons were, in the early years at least, according to Josiah Gregg, steadily manufactured and shipped in from Pittsburgh.[50]

The energy system required an intricate network of communication on paper by agents, merchants and bankers with orders for finished products sent out near and far. Resources from around the world were turned into everything from calicoes to windowpanes. Then they were packed and shipped from as far away as India, China, England and the East Coast of the United States.

Closer still, the great depots of Pittsburgh, St. Louis and New Orleans shipped them on to arrive at the levee in Kansas City to be split out by sweating laborers to thousands of hands and households in the great seasonal surge from April to November.

As soon as the ice went out and until it formed again, goods changed hands in little towns fully engaged in outfitting these hordes in everything from western attire to hotel service before the hullabaloo died back down for the winter and its original, if growing populations breathed a sigh of relief. There is something to be said for seasonality and its enforced downtime.

CHAPTER 11

Traveling Overland

Overland pioneer travel west from the Missouri River's elbow at Kansas City meant exploiting the Wood Age energy components to their fullest extent. Scale, time, and distance found new meaning on the overland trails when fully-loaded wagons were pulled by invaluable livestock.

Though using the water highway remained the preferred transport, overland travel to the West of necessity began at the western edge of Missouri. Upon arrival, settlers found they still had water to cross . . . either the smaller Kaw River or the nearby Blue River. To cross to either bank of the Missouri River remained a challenge, and a brisk business in ferries began to flourish. In one way or another the pioneers had to cross the river by ferry or "take the bank" with cattle power. In 1827, the first ferry went into business three miles south of the site at a place called Uneaw's Ferry and competition for local water transport began.

After the Chouteaus settled in and others began to gather in the 1820s, the clerk of the Circuit Court issued a license for one year against a security tax of $2.00 which allowed said ferryman to charge $1.50 for a loaded wagon and five horses, $1.00 for an empty wagon and five horses and $.75 for a light wagon or Dearborn, 12 ½ cents for every head of "meat cattle," each head of hog, sheep or goat, five cents, each footman 12 ½ cents.[1] Ferries proliferated up and down the Missouri River and across the Kaw River from both banks as travel to the area increased and teams and wagons crossed the frontier's last waterway on flatboats to begin the great American pioneer adventure of the 19th century.

91

Dugout canoes gave way to rafts that gave way to primitive ferry boats of logs lashed together. These gave way to sawn timber and were guided by poles then oars then drawn by ropes. Eventually, horses were employed to turn the stiles until steam engines replaced them in the early 1850s.[2] This quick evolution of simple technologies to cross the local rivers showed the speed at which old ways were replaced by the new. Until the railroad bridge was built at Kansas City across the Missouri River in 1869, the local population used one of these forms of energy to cross the Mighty Missouri.

Taking the Bank

As the trickle of settlers increased to a flow, the Independence, Missouri, landing six miles down river lost popularity. Though the town served as the county seat and remained an outfitting center for wagon trains, the wagons from Independence starting the long trek west had to cross the Blue River, often a treacherous event, while the limestone pier on the Missouri River farther west was just that—farther west on water, and the temptation to go even five more miles on water caused Independence to lose some of its luster. In 1824, one party in crossing the Blue had to "dig down the banks and lower the wagons and dearborns on ropes." The Blue was uncrossable at high water, which sometimes delayed a train for as long as two weeks.[3]

Wagons at 2nd and Delaware in Kansas City waiting to cross the Missouri River. The bluffs behind, with buildings on the edge, were later excavated.

For those who started from Independence, the Blue River was their first obstacle. Crossing a river with a wagon train often began with a man on horseback testing the depth and current. If the stream was found to be deep enough, all the cracks in the wagon needed a coat of pitch from the bucket hanging on the side to keep the wagons from leaking. A river as large as the Missouri could only be crossed on rafts or ferries, but a smaller, shallower river like the Blue could be breached by wagons.

After the initial foray by a lead rider and a route chosen, nearby underbrush had to be cut to line the slippery banks to give traction to the horses or oxen to pull the wagon down into and out of the river. Then a "great deal of yelling and swearing" helped drive the whole venture across and up the opposite bank.

If travelers were lucky and the ground was not too soft or the brush all gone, a crossing could be accomplished with minimal risk and struggle. A great deal of energy was expended by man and animal with no help from fuel as we have come to know it though certainly participants were fueled by food.[4]

Doctor and merchant Josiah Gregg, of the Mexican trade, observed:

When caravans are able to cross in the evening, they seldom stop on the near side of a stream—first, because if it happened to rain during the night, it may become flooded, and cause both detention and trouble; again, though the stream be not impassable after rain, the banks become slippery and difficult to ascend. A third and still more important reason is, that even supposing the contingency of rain does not occur, teams will rarely pull as well in 'cold collars' as wagoners term it—that is when fresh geared—as in the progress of a day's travel. When a heavy pull is just at hand in the morning, wagoners sometimes resort to the expedient of driving a circuit upon the prairie, before venturing to 'take the bank.'[5]

Pioneers clung to the river for these reasons, and C. C. Spalding in his 1858 book, *Annals of Kansas* pridefully proclaimed:

. . . Kansas City stands upon the outpost of our internal navigation, the last and extreme western locality, with a geography giving command and connection with our vast river marine . . . . Directly here, in the Great Bend of the Missouri, the westward wake of the steamboat ends. There is no more west to pay respect and tribute to the genius of Fulton.[6]

And so, from there the "overlanders" as they were called, began the long walk eight hundred miles to Santa Fe, Mexico, double that to the coast of California or Oregon. They set off with good cheer and more than a little naiveté about what the trek would require of them. The frontier town of Kanzas became the "jumping off" point to abandon the last water transportation available, to literally jump off the deck of a steamboat and start walking. Thousands did.[7]

Fueling Change

By 1833, John Calvin McCoy built a cabin along the trail a full 12 miles west of the Independence landing. This soon became a store that attracted other businesses to spring up. McCoy laid out streets and named the growing community Westport, as it became the entrance to the West. Indian country lay less than a mile beyond, where the end of the state of Missouri and the beginning of the Indian Territory began, populated by relocated Indian tribes.

Westport was indeed "the last town in the West under the Stars and Stripes."[8] McCoy and his community influenced steamboat captains to drop their cargo farther west at the new landing, the limestone pier, at what is now the foot of Grand Avenue, three miles west of Chouteau's Landing, and six miles west of Independence. Since the goods deposited there were largely ordered by Westport businessmen, the limestone pier became known as Westport Landing. The town of Westport on the overland trail four miles southwest of the levee soon began to compete with Independence for trade with the growing traffic of pioneers along the three trails that converged here, the Santa Fe Trail going southwest to New Mexico to trade with the Spanish, and the California and Oregon Trails going west and northwest.[9]

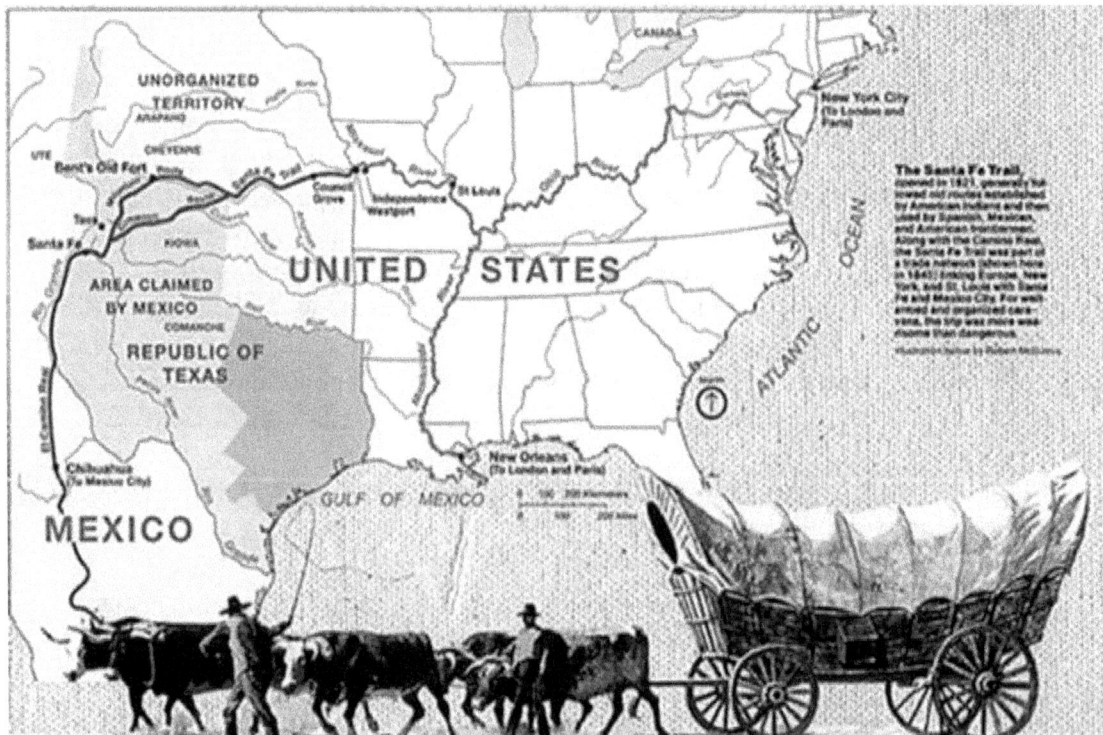

"The Santa Fe Trail from Missouri to New Mexico"
From the first, Westport's buildings clustered around the stream running through the area and a mill began business at the intersection of Mill Street and Westport Avenue. Large bodies of people from the eastern United States as well as foreign immigrants flocked to Westport, stepping from the decks of steamers at Westport Landing and making their way through the timber and mud to the village to outfit and organize their wagon trains. They needed cattle, mules, horses, most of which were supplied by the counties east of Kansas City in an area called "Little Dixie."[10]

94

Wagons, harness, cookware, earthenware, foodstuffs were all for sale in Westport with all the outfitting trade done in cash. Since the pioneers arrived in droves, money was as plentiful as they were. The tents of the migrants blossomed on the fields "like the camp of a great army. These parties made themselves up into trains, as they were termed; some employed mules for transportation purposes, some oxen, other horses, and not a few strong-spirited men loaded a few supplies into a cart drawn by a single mule and walked beside it."[11]

The Mexican American War slowed the traffic to Santa Fe in the 1840s, but the discovery of gold in California in 1849 brought a torrent of opportunity seekers who flooded the Missouri border. Each of the small towns from St. Joe to Westport was surrounded by campers. Three thousand Mormons camped on the spacious fields, a plus for that location, between Westport and Westport Landing waiting to begin the trek to Salt Lake City.

"They were in a fine forest. Some were sleeping in their wagons, but the most had tents and the woods and fields in all directions were covered with these white and fragile dwellings. Oxen are used for teams. Men, women and children were scattered about on all sides. Blacksmiths' hammers were heard, and the hum of preparation came up from all parts of the camp. It was a singular sight . . ."[12]

To the Spanish Country

After outfitting themselves from eager merchants, the travelers usually spent their last night camped out around Westport, Independence and the levee by the thousands waiting for all manner of small events to occur so they could begin their trek. Eyewitness Josiah Gregg rejoiced at the moment of departure: "At last all are fairly launched upon the broad prairie—the miseries of preparation are over—the thousand anxieties occasioned by wearisome consultations and delays are felt no more."[13]

Nearby farmers provided mules, oxen, horses, ground corn and flour from mills; saddle and harness shops provided miles of reins and harnesses; wagon makers turned out wagons of every type for the many who came in by steamboat.[14] The many forests provided fuel. Wood was still the reigning monarch of materials here as well as the absolute fuel.

Wagons had to be made of seasoned wood or calamity was sure to strike. Wood was deceptively temperamental. It had to be "thoroughly seasoned and dried" to avoid shrinkage. Once the wood shrank from the iron bands holding the wheel together the wagon breaks down.

A loaded wagon could weigh over two tons and could be loaded with 3,000 to 6,000 pounds of freight. To raise a wagon with jacks in mud or dirt, to set props under it was an art in itself as well as a herculean task. The entire job could take a day and delay the entire wagon train.[15] Wagon masters hated the delays; they were costly and laid the wagon train open to raids and lack of water.

Independence bustled with workshops typical of the 19th century . . . small, often open-aired, with primitive tools, a few men, and fewer amenities. On sites around the square stood small manufacturing shops of wagons, harness, saddlery, blacksmith making shoes for horse, ox and mule, and at least one place making for those oxen "a great many oak yokes and bows." Up front in these busy shops a customer could find a counter perhaps and beyond that a small group of men in each shop industriously filling orders for waiting wagon trains. "A large number" of workers crafted leather works, from tanners to saddle makers. Merchants brought in or had made on the spot every kind of necessary item for the wagons to take west.[16]

What wasn't shipped in from Pittsburgh or St Louis or New Orleans was fashioned in Independence or within a few counties as soon as the local population could muster the raw materials and expertise to do so. Even something as small but vital as a whip was crafted in Independence to use on the trail to urge on oxen and mules. Local author William Z. Hickman, growing up in Independence, remembered that the same slaves, Sam and Pete, who could cut four cords of wood in a day with a broadax also braided 10 to 12-foot-long whips on a winter evening. In fact, the whip-making business belonged to the "negro men of the country" who spent any idle time in the winter braiding whips to be sold in the spring when the traffic on the Santa Fe Trail started up again. They bought up hides, cut them into strips and braided the whips for sale to merchants or bull-whackers for about $.50 to $.75 cents each.[17]

Sam and Pete's work once again became legendary. As the wagons left the levee in the 1850s to start the long trek to Santa Fe, "a team of 24 mules would have four to six Mexican drivers. They would start down the levee and around up Grand Avenue. Every driver prided himself on the loudness with which he could crack his whip, and in a train of ten or twelve wagons the whip cracking would sound like the firing of muskets, only louder."[18]

Before the hordes arrived in the 1840s and 1850s a thin thread of commerce between "the Spanish Country" and the little settlements of Independence, then Westport and finally Kansas City established itself. The destination was Santa Fe, New Mexico, where manufactured goods from the American East could be traded for Mexican silver.

William Becknell of Franklin, Missouri, organized the first trip overland to Santa Fe in 1821, making the trip successfully with 17 men and returning in six months using pack horses only. Until 1830 the expeditions left from Franklin then moved to Independence. Overland travel required large numbers of animals and patient endurance on the part of both traders and travelers. Becknell had taken a long shot in organizing the trip; Mexico had just separated from Spain and the politics of changing markets attracted this man from Franklin, Missouri. For some reason Becknell, a rural businessman and deeply in debt, felt it was his destiny to gather men to make the overland trip.

Profit lay out there close to 800 miles and over 65 days away, the kind of profit not available at Boone's Lick on the Missouri River. He was right. Along with other goods he sold he made a small profit and was able to forestall his debtors.

On his second trip he sold his $150 wagon for $700. Becknell had discovered a silver mine! Once started, overland trade leaped forward with as much organization and as many intrepid men, hardy cattle and goods available. Overland trains soon grew to over 300 oxen,

36 wagons, and 30 men to load, guide and carry 60 to 75 tons of goods from Independence to Santa Fe or farther north to Fort Laramie and Salt Lake City.[19]

Whatever commercial venture left from Kanzas, however, had to contend with the Indian populations who had been relocated on land foreign to them, had been systematically disenfranchised from their way of life, and may have been provoked to defend themselves against hostile trespassers through their newly acquired land.

"The Crazy Osage"[20]

In the summer of 1823, a new expedition started out from Franklin, Missouri, to Santa Fe in Mexico.

Three hundred miles out, two men from the expedition in search of stray horses were captured by the Osage and were "stripped, barbarously whipped, and robbed of their horses, guns and clothes."[21] The Osage, already removed from the ancestral lands and on the government dole, did not like the intrusion of more whites moving through their newly acquired territory.

"Various circumstances combine to fix this outrage on the Osages, who receive regular annuities from Government," Becknell wrote, "and have a school among them through its beneficences and the charity of individuals. They have before been guilty of similar offenses and have long been distinguished for their predatory habits and are daily becoming bolder; and unless checked by prompt measures we fear they will cause a great disruption to western intercourse."

The Treaty of 1825 between the Osage and the United States government signed at Council Grove was created to stop the Osage from raiding the new trade to the Southwest.[22]

Wagon masters protected their wagon trains from marauding Indians by driving the wagons in four parallel lines. In that way they could circle quickly and avoided the vulnerability of a long, single line of wagons.

> Thus far also we had marched in two lines only; but, after crossing the Pawnee Fork, each of the four divisions drove on in a separate file, which became henceforth the order of march till we reached the border of the mountains. By moving in long lines as we did before, the march is continually interrupted; for every accident which delays a wagon ahead stops all those behind. By marching four abreast this difficulty is partially obviated, and the wagons can also be thrown more readily into a condition of defence (sic) in case of attack.[23]

March of the Caravans
As part of organizing systems in the Wood Age the wagon masters learned that a "four abreast" series of wagons proved to be a stronger and more efficient way to cross the open prairie. Note the outriders along both sides who served as scouts and messengers.

As a result of such attacks, another treaty was drawn up in 1837 to protect travelers to and from the New Mexico territory. This treaty included the Kiowas and Muscogee tribes as well as the Osage. Their names bespoke their mindset just as the European settlers' names bespoke theirs. The Indian names ranged from the Learned Dog, to the War Eagle, to the One Who Gives Horses, to the Crazy Osage, a completely separate and exotic mindset from the other culture indicative of forests and wildlife, open vistas and identity with living things with which they were familiar. They signed the "talking leaves" of the white man and relinquished their territory once again. (See Appendix A)

Dispossessed from their original lands, the Osage showed by signing their names to this latest contract that their origins were from another time and place. The need for such an agreement shows they felt violated by further intrusions in their new territory. Their lives were not the same, and to fight the wagon trains or to let them pass were their two unhappy choices. The treaty asked that citizens of the United States be "freely permitted to pass and repass through their settlements or hunting ground without molestation or injury, on their way to any of the provinces of the Republics of Mexico or Texas or returning therefrom."[24] Whatever injury they gave in the way of property damage they would have to repay from the annuities from the government or from their crops or buffalo robe trade. Caught between two energy levels, the new one foreign, their own repudiated, they lived marooned on the plains neither conquerors nor conquered.

Trains of Unprecedented Proportions

Overland trains to Santa Fe continued. Mexican silver dollars and a hungry and isolated market lay in the shimmering distance. By 1839, the first prairie schooner was introduced to the Santa Fe Trail. Before then caravans of pack animals and a few wagons had been used. Yokes of six oxen (12 oxen) or, four to six spans of mules (eight to 12 mules) drew these wagons with sufficient muscle power to pull a load of about three to seven tons. In that same year, the first large shipment of goods was sent from Westport using 63 wagons each carrying about 6,000 pounds and drawn by six yoke of oxen.

With extra oxen for replacement, a herd of some 800 would have had to be provided for going and coming back. The level of organization became a matter of larger and larger scale for a trip of this magnitude, the trip being about 775 miles, according to Josiah Gregg's chart measuring from Independence to Santa Fe. Agents Boone & Bernard in Westport now organized and directed shipments to agents Meservey and Webb in Santa Fe. Formal business dealings instead of entrepreneurial expeditions had extended across the wilderness from one high-energy location to another.[25]

Between 1822 and 1843, when the Santa Fe trade was interrupted by the increasing hostilities over the Mexican-American border, freight increased from a total of 15,000 pounds carried by pack animals and 70 men to 450,000 pounds, 230 wagons and 360 men. Such animal labor would include a herd of around 3,000 animals.

This increase created a large industry, the demands of which the towns of Independence, Westport and Kanzas rushed to fill.[26] By 1861, in spite of the Civil War, wagon trains headed out with 400 wagons, 4,000 to 5,000 head of oxen, 70 mules and around 400 men to Denver, making two trips per season.[27] This output was before what author William Lass calls "the freighting boom of 1864-65," during which overland hauling reached "unprecedented proportions."[28]

Lass suggested the irony of increased Indian attacks on oncoming wagon trains: "The energetic thrust of organized freighting exposed the Indians to an even greater struggle of abrasive civilizations." Still connected both emotionally and physically to buffalo and local habitat, the tribes had two choices, to either accommodate the white man or to try to resurrect and protect their vanishing way of life. One meant giving up and embracing the new energy system while the other meant war. The Native Americans who disrupted the trade and emigrant routes inadvertently stimulated the traffic through their lands. The trade required military protection and the military, once there, required supplies, stimulating even more wagon trains.[29] More wagon trains meant more money.

Border Money

Material goods and property meant a kind of infrastructure the Osage along their rivers and trails of central Missouri could never have imagined, nor could their Indian compatriots on the Great Plains. Meanwhile, Indians along the Indian Territory border, so-called until it was renamed the Kansas-Nebraska Territory in 1854, had annuities to spend. The government paid them for their lands in 20-year annuities of several thousand each year plus mills, blacksmith shops and cabins for their chiefs. The annuity money was profitable trade and brought even more people to the frontier to take advantage of it.

The three scrappy frontier towns of Independence, Westport, and Kanzas formed a tiny triangle four to twelve miles apart on the face of the vast continent (see Jackson County map on the following pages). But they were electric with potential. Their citizens were eager and able to serve the political and economic waves of the rising West. Each settlement had the luck of either political or natural geography. Independence, still deemed the "very frontier of civilization," capitalized on the Santa Fe Trail trade with the first steamboat landing.[30]

Westport, on the other hand, about 12 miles west had situated itself right up against Indian Territory from which streamed Indians with annuity money to spend at local trading posts. They engaged in the "truck and dicker" trade with the Indians and "the sale of last minute knickknacks to emigrants."[31]

This was no small trade and Westport became the hotspot to go to for the local tribes. By 1858, Westport factories turned out 240 new wagons, 2,000 ox yokes, 3,000 tarpaulins and 25,000 dollars' worth of harness. Between 1855 and 1858, Westport reached the zenith of its prosperity with a population estimated at 5,000.[32]

The third point on the triangle, the levee itself, four miles north of Westport and six miles from Independence, had the advantage of the limestone pier on the river. The steamboats first brought trading goods for the Indians at Westport, then goods for the emigrant trains and outfitting business, and, finally, served the residents of the growing town itself. The pier had been known from the days of the fur trade and continued to grow unaffected by the change of hands of the territory from European powers to the United States. Once John C. McCoy, founder of Westport, had a road of sorts cut through the limestone banks to the river to accommodate the wagonloads of goods from the steamboat deck, Westport's future was assured. The future of Westport Landing depended on the town's trade, and Westport's trade depended on agents at the levee to do their work for them.

Westport served the Native American trade. Delawares, Munsas, Stockbridges, Shawnees, Kansas (or Kaws) Kickapoos, Osages, Pottawattomies, Weas and Peorias all now lived beyond the border and had government money to spend at the crude stores where they traded in blankets, pots and pans and trinkets. The Sacs, Foxes, Otoes, Missouris, Wyandots and Cherokees would also settle in across the Kaw River. [33] Ninety thousand Indians lived across the state line, each tribe with a 20-year annuity of some $1,000 to $3,500 that was proportioned to tribe members.[34] That alone offered a worthy market to stimulate business.

Between 1820 to1830, Alexander Majors of the famous freighting company, Russell, Majors and Waddell, noticed that "there were a great many peaceable tribes of Indians, located by the government all along the western border of Missouri in what was then called the Indian Territory and has since become the States of Kansas, Nebraska, and Oklahoma Territory . . .. They were paid in silver, either in whole or half dollars, and the head of every family received every cent of his quota."[35]

Westport did a great business selling blankets, pots and pans, trinkets and foodstuffs. Francis Parkman in the spring of 1846 described the scene that had matured over two decades: "Westport was full of Indians, whose little shaggy ponies were tied by dozens along the houses and fences. Sacs and Foxes, with shaved heads and painted faces, Shawnees and Delaware's, fluttering in calico frocks and turbans, Wyandots dressed like white men, and a few wretched Kanzas wrapped in old blankets, were strolling about the streets, or lounging in and out of the shops and houses."[36]

Parkman does not mention the Osage standing a head taller than some of their compatriots, but they, too, traded at the stores though they had been relocated farther south and may not have shown up as often. In the space of a generation the wilderness the Indians knew, the way of life that had integrated them into natural ecosystems had been overtaken by the bustle and commerce of capitalism. Hunting and gathering in the wilds of Missouri had been replaced with shopping in Westport!

Blessed with a confluence of geographic circumstances that boosted it above other just established, hardscrabble towns across the West, the area played host to thousands each season preparing to make the march west as soon as the grass on the prairies could support livestock. Every May the retreating woods hosted more legions of travelers making arrangements. This income gave the three little communities hard cash during a time when many towns their size existed on agricultural crops exclusively and bartered their goods while scrambling for hard currency.[37]

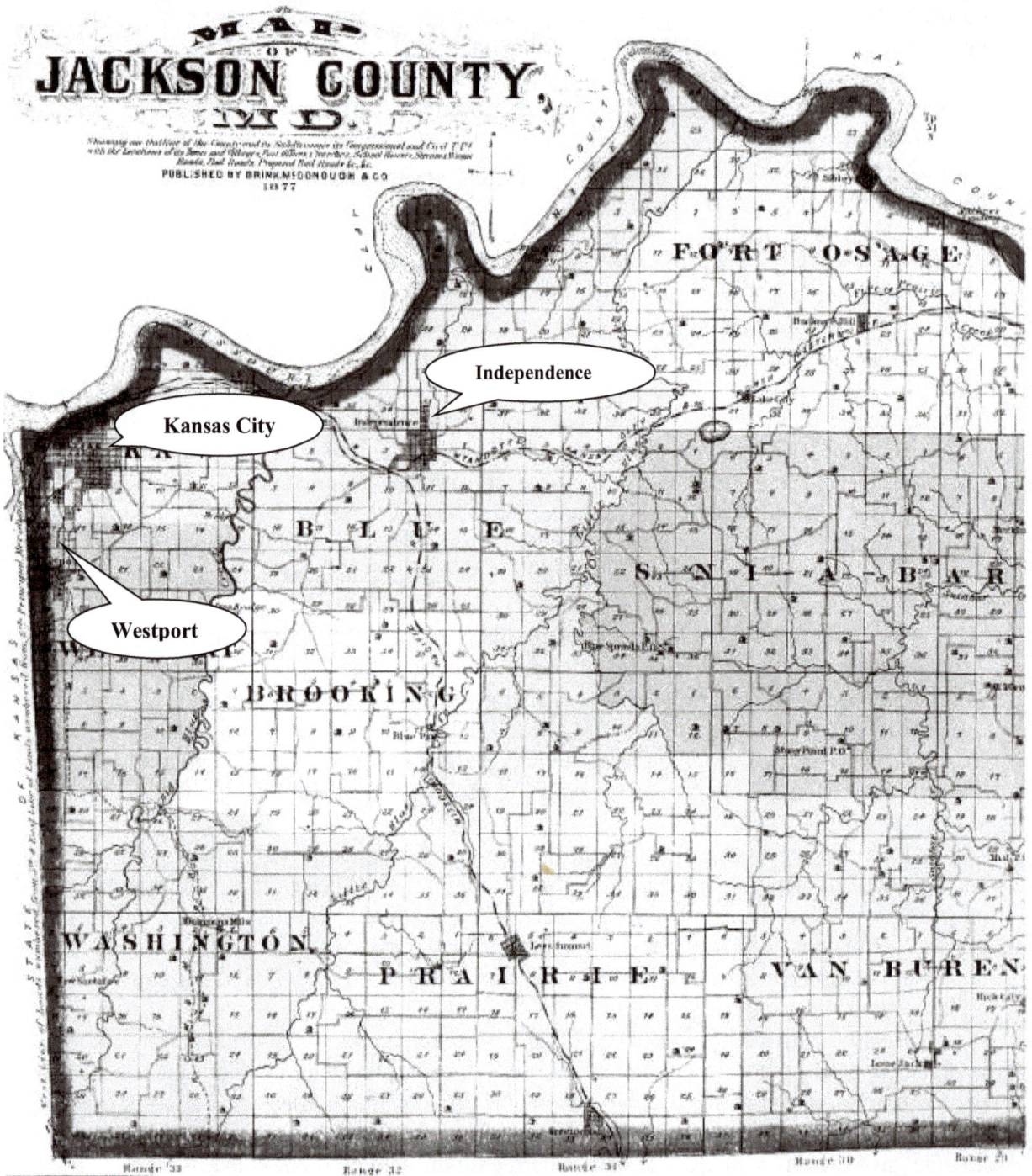

Jackson County, Missouri, 1877. The map shows the three small towns of Westport, Kansas City, and Independence near the western border across which lay Indian Territory.

The market economy of Kansas City was not dependent on agriculture alone. Spalding admits that not all that trade yielded hard currency···that a fair amount of bartering went on. "The trade of the city for the last year, which has been done exclusively with currency and exchange, amount as near as it can be estimated by our best business men to $1,200,000." Such income including the trade from those white settlers moving into the Kansas Territory after 1854 estimated at about $700,000 for the year of 1857, led the St. Louis *Leader* to exaggerate just a little. "[T]he business of Kansas City is now more extensive than the business of any other place in the world, in proportion to its population."[38]

By 1857, one of the golden years of steam boating for Kansas City, Spalding wrote this: "It is the river, and our commerce thereon, that gives us position and command. . .. Without the Missouri river we should occupy no more commanding position than any inland

town or hamlet." [39]

Town of Kansas (later City of Kansas), 1855
This view across the river shows the two opposing energy systems at mid-century.
The Indian tribes of the Delaware, Kickapoo, and Shawnee view the rising Euro-American city
on the banks at the convergence of the Missouri and Kansas Rivers
as it took over the former hunting grounds of the Osage Indians.

But they did occupy that spot; the river was no ordinary secondary tributary but the mighty Missouri, the shores of which received thousands of emigrants in a season. The overland migration to Oregon, California and Utah between 1849-1860 grew from an estimated 45,700 in 1849 to 250,000 in 1856, and, to nearly 300,000 in 1860. A good number of those pilgrims arrived at the limestone pier by steamboat; the remainder came overland by wagon train. To a town of 700 people, this flood of humanity meant an incredible flow of cash, and residents jumped at the chance to partake of it. The armies of people arriving and departing overworked both facilities and townsfolk to attend to their needs.[40] One hotel on the levee boasted of having served 29,000 people in one season![41]

Though all these figures are estimates, many emigrants kept records of passing wagon trains along their own route. One traveler reported that their wagon train passed 250 wagons one morning in 1850, then were passed by a hundred others before noon and passed by at least 500 more on another day. The highway was crowded with travelers. Another emigrant wrote that he had observed a thousand wagons passing Fort Kearny one day in May in 1850.[42] Of course there was no cross traffic and very few wagons heading east!

Fort Laramie staff attempted to keep an accurate record of emigrants, or "overlanders," and offered their own figures for that route in 1850. On May 14, 1850, a recorded 1,950 men (no women or children mentioned) passed through on 215 wagons. By June 2, 9,972 men and 2,797 wagons passed by. On the last date of August 14, they recorded 39,506 men and 9,927 wagons passing through. They did not mention the enormous numbers of livestock that had to have accompanied such a flow of humanity. Such numbers must have kept an army of observers attentive to the stream of traffic. This record is from one vantage point on one route, so it suggests enormous numbers who traveled west on the various routes.[43]

Such Acres of Wagons! Such Herds of Oxen!

Perhaps the Wood Age offered its greatest expression of vitality, strength and range in the combination of men and animals that performed amazing feats of directed energy to cover long distances. One example is the wagon trains from Kansas City to Santa Fe and their return. Another is the Pony Express from St. Joseph, 50 miles upriver from Kansas City to Sacramento and its return. Each combined men, animals, scale and distance to stretch the capacity the Wood Age to its greatest potential. Their journeys were no one time Greek marathon to be extolled as a single event throughout history. The trips these men and animals took made their colossal expression of energy, bravado and endurance commonplace in their repetition. To pull off this kind of energy expenditure over and over again required more and more refined systems of efficiency.

First came the trek to Santa Fe, New Mexico, a distance of 800 miles, which began with pack mules in 1822, and then wagons only from 1826 onward. They carried from 150,000 pounds in 1828 to 450,000 pounds in 1843, according to the records of Josiah Gregg, one of the first diarists of the trail. The 1843 trip included 230 wagons, 350 men and at least 3,000 head of oxen at six yoke (twelve oxen) to a wagon and spares, plus mules for the men to ride and a few horses. They brought back 300,000 pounds of goods.[44]

Such an outlay to fit and fill a wagon train required tremendous stores of supplies to begin a journey. Horace Greeley, the editor of the *New York Times*, remarked in 1859 as he witnessed a similar event at Leavenworth, Kansas, that had to be repeated at every departure point: "Such acres of wagons! such pyramids of extra axletrees! such herds of oxen! such regiments of drivers and other employees!"[45] He goes on to explain: Each wagon carried a couple of extra axles lashed under its body, to be used "in case an old one gives way under a heavy jerk." [46]

The men drove their teams of oxen by walking beside them between twelve to fifteen miles per day since that was the only way to keep the oxen steady on their route. Alexander Majors ran a highly disciplined crew whom he trained with a watch before letting them start their wagon train, thus instituting systems of efficiency on the trail along with organizing and loading supplies before the trip started. Majors trained his drivers to each find six pairs of oxen at once out of the herd in the corral, to yoke them together and to hitch all twelve to their wagons in 16 minutes! Majors showed "how quickly the men who are thoroughly disciplined could be ready to 'pop the whip' and move out, when unskilled men were often more than an hour doing the same work."[47]

The men were divided into "messes," six to eight men in a group with each an assigned duty to carry water, fuel and stand guard, plus the best cook of the lot to serve up the grub. They guarded the cattle day and night, watched for overgrazing by avoiding two trains camping together, and killed swarms of rattlesnakes as well. "The rattlesnakes on that road (to Santa Fe) in the beginning of travel were a great annoyance, often biting the mules and oxen when they were grazing. At first, mules were used altogether for traveling, but they would either die or become useless from the bite of a rattlesnake, and the men would sometimes be sent ahead of the caravan with whips to frighten the snakes out of the pathway, but later on, the ox teamsters, with their large whips, destroyed them so fast that they ceased to trouble them to any great extent."[48]

In the spring of 1859, the last of the golden years of steamboat traffic, the Kansas City paper, the *Journal of Commerce*, described Commercial Street at the levee to be "jammed with Santa Fe wagons."[49] By virtue of the herculean work by teams of oxen and "messes" of men millions of dollars changed hands every season from April to November. These figures available from 1854 could only grow larger by 1859: Some $8,266,463 dollars exchanged hands among the merchants, the wholesalers with their warehouses, the wagon masters, the steamboat captains, the banks and the small manufacturing shops.

A fourth of that money, $2,138,200 included livestock and draft animals, to a large degree supplied by "Little Dixie" up and down both sides of the Missouri River, merchandise at $3,815,502, warehousing at $545,000 and exports at $1,767,761. The exports were comprised of the goods brought in from New Mexico and the western mountains. The hard discipline of the wagon masters and their hardy men paid off. Though the teamsters earned $1 a day for themselves, they earned the growing city a thriving economy.[50]

The Pony Express: Full of Pluck and Daring

The epitome of Wood Age exploitation of available means came in the form of man and beast attempting to compete against the growing excitement of speed generated by the new machines. While steamboats churned and whistled upriver representing the new energy suite, man and beast, the perennial combination of the Wood Age, attempted to take speed to new levels in a time-honored combination. A last-ditch effort to prove that the old ways were still strong, still good enough to compete may have motivated these efforts. The following is a story of an innovative use of energy in the last moments of the Wood Age using what had been available for eons but whose stretching of ability and endurance had not been considered until faced with such lucrative trade and competition.

The progenitor and inspiration for the Pony Express, it is said, arose from the example of a single man whose ride, witnessed by no less than Alexander Majors, made the impossible seem available for those with "pluck and daring."[51] The amazing feat of traveling the 800 miles from Santa Fe to Independence was done by F. X. Aubry in five days and thirteen hours beginning September 12, 1853. Aubry, a guide and trader, had already made the same trip the year before in eight days on a bet of a $1,000 that he could make the ride in ten days.[52]

Aubry did not stop except to change horses and resaddle, though he had to deliver messages to several trains on the trail. He walked 20 miles, broke six horses during the ride and slept in the saddle by roping himself to it. A 24-hour rain made the trail muddy and streams high. Aubry arrived in Independence, by some accounts stuck to the saddle with his own blood and was carried into the hotel where he first ate ham and eggs before retiring on the evening of September 17th. His "foaming horse half ran, half staggered" the final few steps.[53] Aubry carried only a canteen of water and "a bundle of sun-dried buffalo meat." He rode each horse 100 to 125 to 200 miles before changing, picking up a horse at a pre-arranged spot or buying a new horse "at any price" if needed and letting the spent one go. His own yellow horse, Dolly, Majors said "was one of the finest pieces of horse flesh I ever saw."[54]

Aubry understood the business of speed. When he started running wagon trains to Santa Fe it was customary for only one trip to be made in a season. Aubry soon doubled that to two and then increased the run to three and increased profits proportionately. Not satisfied with that, he rode ahead of his wagon trains to Santa Fe, launching them as early in April as newly grown grasses would support his livestock. Upon arriving he placed an ad in the paper of the arrival of his goods and sold all from the wagons when they arrived, bypassing warehouses and retail as the first wagons of the season while his competitors were still in Missouri. The Santa Fe *Republican* called him "the Telegraph," or "Skimmer of the Plains," and said he traveled with "a rapidity that was almost supernatural." Aubry's exploits were reported nationally in the *New York Weekly Tribune* and later retold in *Harper's Weekly*.[55] His rides have remained an unbroken distance/speed record.

Inspired by Aubry's audacity, reckless speed and using his example of having mounts stationed along the route, Alexander Majors and his partners Russell and Waddell organized the Pony Express in 1859, at the behest of the governor of California who urged sending mail across the expansive West from St. Joseph to Sacramento.[56] Without the telegraph, news had to go by way of a southern stagecoach route that took months. The telegraph had been tested by Samuel Morse with the completed line in 1843 from Washington to Baltimore with the message "What hath God wrought?" Telegraph companies sprang up and began relaying train schedules on the East Coast by 1851. It was still new when Aubry made his most famous ride to Independence in 1853, had rested there overnight and made his way to St. Louis by steamboat and carriage, arriving a scant 10 days after leaving Santa Fe. He handed a letter to the editor of the St. Louis *Daily Reveille* from the editor of the Santa Fe *Republican* dated September 12th that began "Allow me to introduce you to the man to whom the telegraph is a fool."[57]

The telegraph, that harbinger of industrial energy, had already competed and won against horses in the East, but not in the West. The telegraph ran from San Francisco to Sacramento on the West Coast; from the East Coast it ended in Kansas City, which had acquired it in 1858, and to St Joseph on the east side of the Missouri River.[58] That left another 1,500 miles or so to cover for communication with the growing might of the new state of California. Two of its major cities, San Francisco and Sacramento, were connected by telegraph.[59]

Fueling Change

St. Joseph was chosen as eastern terminus since it was the furthest point west reached by the railroad and the telegraph from the east. The Pony Express route began there. The first task of the rider was to take a ferry across the Missouri River, and then to ride ten to fifteen miles to a station to change horses for which the driver was allowed two minutes to change his *mochila*, or saddle bags with mail—papers as "airy and thin as gold leaf," according to Mark Twain's account—and get his log verified by the station master. The riders themselves changed out every 80 to 100 miles and kept the mail running both day and night during all seasons. The company guaranteed delivery in ten days for most of the year though allowed twelve to thirteen days in winter. The horses averaged about ten miles per hour in good weather.[60]

Twain's famous eyewitness account captures the drama and the impossibility of the endeavor after the stagecoach driver shouts, "Here he comes!"

> Every neck is stretched further, and every eye strained wider. Away across the endless dead level of the prairie a black speck appears against the sky, and it is plain that it moves. Well, I should think so! In a second or two it becomes a horse and rider, rising and falling, rising and falling—sweeping toward us nearer and nearer—growing more and more distinct, more and more sharply defined—nearer and still nearer, and the flutter of the hoofs comes faintly to the ear—another instant a whoop and a hurrah from our upper deck, a wave of the rider's hand, but no reply, and man and horse burst past our excited faces, and go winging away like a belated fragment of a storm!
>
> Mark Twain, *Roughing It* (1872)

The ad to recruit riders in the St. Joseph *Daily Gazette* read, "Wanted: Young, Skinny, Wiry Fellows not over 18. Must be expert riders willing to risk death daily. Orphans preferred. Wages—$25 per week."[61] The average age turned out to be about 20—the youngest 11 and the oldest 40—and the average weight about 120 pounds. Eventually 183 men rode the Pony Express for the eighteen months of its existence.

The trail led through Kansas, Nebraska, northeast Colorado, Wyoming, Utah, Nevada and California, across the Continental Divide and over both the Rockies and the Sierras. It was not the easiest route geographically and was populated as well by Indians and white gangs eager for confrontation. The rider carried no pistol which would add to the weight. His only defense was to outride any aggressors. A series of 165 stations serviced the trade and provided for about eighty pony riders on route "day or night, stretching in a long, scattered procession from Missouri to California, forty flying eastward, and forty toward the west, and among them making four hundred gallant horses earn a stirring livelihood" over the nearly 2,000 mile distance.[62] As soon as the telegraph reached Sacramento, the Pony Express disbanded and became a legend of speed and distance in the Old West.

"Think of that for perishable horse and human flesh and blood to do!"[63] The combination of man and animal overcame distance, hardship and expense to achieve the dreams of the entrepreneurs who put together the logistics. No combination of these sources of energy seemed too great to conquer the remaining portion of the Wild West. The Pony Express combined a single man and rider on a route laid out like a delicate string of beads, a series of stations at which first horse then rider changed while the mail continued on in a highly organized mechanism. The wagon trains contrasted in bulk, speed and weight, but held to the same kind of organizational structure. Each was designed to wrest from the animals the maximum the Wood Age could offer in the way of speed and efficiency. Men's minds could grasp the coming speed of industry even as they forced animals to do their best to carry out the scale and distance. Human energy provided the daring while the animals provided the muscle.

Chapter 12

Wood, Coal and The Civil War

The clash between North and South played out in western Missouri and a civil war was fought by the two polarizing edges of the Wood Age... hand labor in the form of slavery in the old paradigm, and mechanical labor in the form of technology in the new. As the Wood Age faced its demise there were those who were willing to fight to the death to detain its passing. The most compelling energy component on land was the railroad.

Can it be that the great American Civil War was actually fought over fuel and energy systems? Ultimately, yes. Old and new systems clashed to answer what system shall replace another. At the time the South seceded from the Union, layer upon layer of insult and injury, righteous indignation and resentment, protectivism and exploitation may have obscured the fact, but, quite simply, a waning Wood Age and a growing Coal Age came to blows, and the Coal Age won.

Between Two Fires

Fire burning wood was undoubtedly the South upholding its manual labor system powered by slavery. A growing industrial base powered the opposing fire burning coal in the North. In retrospect, they may be seen as the open flame of the Wood Age and the enclosed furnace of the Coal Age.

If human energy is part of the Wood Age scene, then it is irresistible to look through the energy lens at the institution of slavery and its sudden and final termination as an energy system. It is also important to look at the Civil War as a means to that transition. This four-year event was a political war with energy consequences. When it was over, industry replaced human labor as the prevailing mode of doing work for the nation, though the South would lag for another 100 years.

The first set of fires was the political division between the North and South. The other was industry versus slavery, or active versus passive fuel. As long as wood was a passive fuel—no machinery obeying its flames—hands and horses picked up the slack. Once wood became active in a fuel box and turned wheels by creating steam, machines began to replace living flesh.

As the Kansas Territory opened in 1854, both Abolitionists and Pro-slavery factions rushed to settle. Naturally, the Pro-slavery families brought slaves, or had them shipped in, or so the St. Louis *News* announced on March 21, 1856. Once the Kansas or Kaw River opened to steamboats in 1856, emigration of slaves to Kansas began. At least 500 slaves arrived from the Ohio River, down that river to the Mississippi at Cairo, up that river to the Missouri at St. Louis and up that river to the town of Kanzas to go on up river into the interior of that state to work on farms. The slaves were "in almost every case taken in the cabin, while poor white families going to the same place take passage on deck."[1] Thus was the South continuing to expand its way of life in a formally declared free state.

Across the Kaw River by 1860, 15% of the population of Kansas City, Westport, Independence, and Jackson County as a whole were slaves. The seven counties hugging the Missouri River on both north and south banks directly east of Jackson County known as Little Dixie engaged in agriculture at a commercial level. With emigrants demanding large numbers of mules, oxen, miles of rope from hemp, plus bacon, tobacco, and other agricultural produce, the legion of slaves in Little Dixie rose as high as 25-30%.[2] Even if the farmers had started out as immigrant farmers from Kentucky, Virginia and Tennessee working at a subsistence level, the demand for large supplies of goods and fertile loess soil drove farmers to expand and use forced labor to increase production.[3]

Each slave was seen as a mechanical unit of energy to do work. ". . . [T]he negro slave was absolutely subject to sale at such times, to such persons, and on such terms as pleased his master. The ownership was as absolute as that of a horse or a watch . . . and able-bodied slaves who began to lose their vigor and vitality were sometimes sold because no longer (sic) profitable as work hands."[4] A slave could be bought or sold but not paid. He or she could be worked but not educated. The conditions of destitution and illiteracy forged as strong a series of chain links as did the leg irons themselves. Instead, their power lay in their backs, their arms, their legs and feet. The blueprint for freedom hid in their muscles.

Individual and collective human labor to do work at the bidding and direction of others made up slavery as a system. These slaves labored for fear of punishment—being "sold down the river," or whipped or otherwise punished for failing to do the work they were compelled to do. Their labor, however freely given, was dictated by another, not chosen by them. As an energy system, slaves served the needs of the owners of large plantations in the South to till, plant and harvest crops of cotton, tobacco, rice, indigo and hemp.[5]

In a pre-industrial world, men took the place of mechanized labor that allowed acreages to be planted far beyond the powers of a single farmer and his family. Slaves also chopped wood, built houses, cared for livestock, and supplied the domestic labor of childcare and household duties from cleaning to cooking to serving food. The acquisition of slaves increased the energy supply on a plantation. As the Osage acquired horses their energy flow increased. As the plantation owners increased their slave holdings, their energy flow increased. Each group was able to do the kind of work needed to support their lifestyles. The Osage needed to hunt farther and faster for which the horse was ideal. The plantation owners needed to produce more crops over larger acreages, for which a good number of slaves was necessary.

Slavery produced more agricultural products than could be had by any other form of labor or mechanization at the time. Owning slaves increased wealth because slaves were property and favored the accumulation of capital. "That other countries and other states were prosperous without slavery, and had greater accumulations was neither understood nor recognized by the south."[6]

SLAVE POPULATION OF THE UNITED STATES FROM 1790 TO 1860.

WITH THE RATIO OF SLAVES TO THE WHOLE POPULATION IN THE PRESENT SLAVE STATES, BY EACH DECENNIAL CENSUS BY THE FEDERAL GOVERNMENT SINCE ITS FORMATION.

	1790	Ratio to pop.	1800	Ratio to pop.	1810	Ratio to pop.	1820	Ratio to pop.	1830	Ratio to pop.	1840	Ratio to pop.	1850	Ratio to pop.	1860	Ratio to pop.
Maine.............	..	..	..	..	..	..	..	..	2	..	..	..	..	..	..	..
New Hampshire....	158	..	8	..	..	..	..	..	3	..	1	..	..	..	..	..
Vermont............	17	..	..	..	..	..	..	..	..	..	..	..	..	..	..	..
Massachusetts......	..	..	..	..	..	..	..	..	..	..	..	..	..	..	..	..
Rhode Island.......	952	..	381	..	108	..	48	..	17	..	5	..	..	..	..	..
Connecticut........	2,759	..	951	..	310	..	97	..	25	..	17	..	..	..	..	..
New York..........	21,324	..	20,343	..	15,017	..	10,088	..	75	..	4	..	..	..	..	..
New Jersey.........	11,423	..	12,422	..	10,851	..	7,557	..	2,254	..	674	..	119	..	..	..
Pennsylvania.......	3,737	..	1,706	..	795	..	211	..	403	..	64	..	..	..	..	..
	40,370	15.0	35,811	9.5	27,081	5.7	18,001	6.2	2,779	4.3	765	3.3	119	2.5	..	..
Delaware..........	8,887	15.0	6,153	9.5	4,177	5.7	4,509	6.2	3,292	4.3	2,605	3.3	2,289	2.5	1,805	1.6
Maryland..........	103,036	32.2	105,635	30.9	111,502	29.3	107,398	26.3	102,994	23.0	89,737	19.0	89,800	15.5	85,382	12.7
District of Columbia.	..	..	3,244	..	5,395	..	6,377	..	6,119	..	4,694	..	3,687	..	3,234	..
Virginia............	293,427	39.2	345,796	39.2	392,518	40.2	425,153	39.9	469,757	38.7	448,987	36.2	473,026	33.2	495,826	30.8
North Carolina......	100,572	25.5	133,296	27.8	168,824	30.3	205,017	32.0	245,601	33.2	245,817	32.6	288,412	33.2	328,377	33.9
South Carolina......	107,014	43.0	146,151	42.2	196,365	47.3	258,475	51.4	315,401	54.2	327,038	55.0	384,925	57.6	407,185	57.2
Georgia............	29,264	35.4	59,504	36.6	105,218	41.6	149,656	43.8	217,531	42.0	280,944	40.6	362,996	42.1	467,461	43.7
Florida.............	..	..	..	..	..	..	..	..	15,011	44.6	25,717	47.2	39,341	44.9	63,809	44.0
Alabama...........	..	..	..	..	..	..	47,439	32.7	117,549	37.9	253,532	42.9	342,894	42.4	435,473	45.1
Mississippi.........	..	..	3,489	39.4	17,088	42.3	32,814	43.4	65,659	48.0	195,211	51.9	309,419	51.0	479,607	55.1
Louisiana..........	..	..	..	..	34,660	45.2	69,064	45.0	109,588	50.8	168,452	47.8	236,807	47.3	312,186	46.9
Texas..............	..	..	..	..	..	..	..	..	..	..	..	..	58,346	27.3	184,956	30.0
Arkansas...........	..	..	..	..	..	..	1,617	11.3	4,576	15.0	19,935	20.4	46,983	22.4	109,065	25.5
Tennessee..........	3,417	9.5	13,584	12.8	44,535	17.0	80,107	18.9	141,603	20.7	183,059	22.0	249,510	23.8	287,112	24.8
Kentucky...........	11,830	16.1	40,343	18.2	80,561	19.8	126,732	22.4	165,213	24.0	182,258	23.3	221,768	21.4	225,902	19.5
Missouri...........	..	..	..	..	3,011	14.4	10,222	15.3	25,091	17.8	58,240	15.1	89,289	12.8	115,619	9.8
Indiana............	..	..	135	..	237	..	190	..	3	..	3	..	..	..	..	..
Ohio..............	..	..	..	..	..	..	..	..	6	..	3	..	..	..	..	..
Illinois.............	..	..	..	..	168	..	917	..	747	..	331	..	..	..	..	..
Wisconsin..........	..	..	..	..	..	..	..	..	..	..	11	..	..	..	..	..
Iowa..............	..	..	..	..	..	..	..	..	..	..	16	..	..	..	..	..
Michigan..........	.	..	..	..	24	..	..	..	32	..	..	..	..	..	..	..
Total..........	658,527		857,230		1,164,283		1,525,667		2,096,264		2,486,590		3,179,470			
General total..	697,897		893,041		1,191,364		1,543,068		2,009,043		2,487,355		3,179,589		4,002,996	

United States Slave Population, 1860

This report from the 1860 U.S. Census indicates the slave population in Missouri before the Civil War. Though Kansas City's slave population was small, about 500 in Jackson County and far fewer in the town itself, this work force provided vital services in planting crops, supplying fresh vegetables, providing manual labor, tending cattle, doing household work among other duties that kept the community running.

The war was fought because those within the slave-based energy system could not give up their mental construct of what "should be." Like the Osage before them who organized their world around fitting into their natural surroundings, slaveholders organized their world around slavery as an institution. They built their economic life, the home life and their morality on their position as slaveholders with the right to command labor to do their bidding. To consider another way of life by freeing the slaves whose freedom they suppressed and feared was an idea they could not entertain at all. Standing on the verandahs of their plantation mansions they could not, for the life of them, think of another economic system that would supply them with the life to which they had become accustomed. And since they held the capital, the influence and the sale of crops with which to keep the South running, the only way to change things was to wrest from their hands the entire fuel chain—slave to master to market to bank to community at large.

The plantation owners were also overwhelmed by the superiority and intensity of energy systems powered by machinery. While the Osage were overpowered by Wood Age energy, plantation owners were overwhelmed by Coal Age energy. Their defeat in the Civil War was a capitulation to the growing industrial might of the Northern states and that was increasingly powered by coal. It became clear that the Northerners "were marching with modern civilization, while the defenders of slavery were standing for the obsolete, the abnormal and the impossible."[7] The two opposite forces of energy—coal-fired factories in the North and slave-dependent plantations in the South—could not be reconciled. Once the war started, it could not be stopped until the case for industrial strength had been made on the battlefield, in the factories and across the fields. Barbara Freese, in her book, *Coal: A Human History,* summarizes the industrial advantage of the North:

"Northern trains brought in thousands of troops and a constant stream of munitions to the battlefields, enabling larger and bloodier battles. And industrialization ultimately ensured a Union victory. The North had a decisive industrial advantage of the South with 10 times more factory production, 15 times more iron, 32 times more firearms production, most dramatically, a 38 to 1 advantage in coal."[8]

Though the northeastern portion of the United States had moved to a combination of wood for home use and coal for industrial use, Kansas City on the frontier fought the Civil War in the Wood Age. No railroad yet ushered in the Coal Age. Coal may have been available by the wagonload pulled by horse or oxen from nearby outcroppings, but wood could still be had in ready quantities and aside from the steamboat traffic and more mills running on steam engines, the city could boast of few industrial works and fought the war with the last vestiges of the old order.[9]

Because of the "border troubles" of the 1850s when the Kansas and Nebraska Territory opened as a free or anti-slavery territory in 1854, "the city was virtually right between two fires during the entire period of the war."[10] Missourians had voted to stay in the Union but as a Confederate state. Kansas City was "a pro-Union island in the midst of a confederate sea" which meant that many business relationships with surrounding commercial establishments were severed.[11] The wagon trains continued to the Southwest now under military guard as far as Fort Larned, Kansas, about 150 miles out, and the town continued to trade with the military at Leavenworth in Kansas about 50 miles northwest and upriver.[12] Many commercial establishments suffered a total decline, however, and quickly went out of business.

With little energy coming into the town in the form of trade and with large numbers leaving to escape the tension of war, the town "fell into disrepair" and no further building or upkeep continued until the war ended.[13] Such was the sudden loss of business, steamboat traffic and tax base that at the close of 1861, the city treasury reported cash on hand of $87.73.[14]

The last issue of the Kansas City *Daily Journal of Commerce* came out on June 16, 1861. (It would resume in April of 1862). The newspaper had been reduced to one page and called for 50,000 men to fight invading federal forces. Bushwackers, Red Legs and Jayhawks already terrorized the countryside on behalf of real or imagined insults against their beliefs. It was not safe to go beyond the city limits without escort, even to travel the four miles to Westport. Inside the town itself in and around the levee "strains of martial music, flying flags, and the rumble of artillery had taken the place of the busy hum of commerce, painfully reminding the citizens of how the times had changed."[15]

Union Army soldiers from Kansas entered Jackson County and often set any slaves free they met along the way and provided escort across the state line. "It was but a step across the line to a land of freedom, and nearly all took advantage of the opportunity. Wherever the Kansas soldiers found a family of Negroes on a farm, they would order them to load up their master's wagons with what they wanted and follow after them. Owing to this removal of the Negroes, there was no one left to harvest the crops and cultivate the fields around Kansas City."[16]

**Freed slaves make their way under protection
of Union soldiers as the Civil War drew to a close.**

115

The valuable property of individual slaves as much as $1000 apiece disappeared before the eyes of their owners. Young adult males, especially, brought at least $1,000 before the war, though by 1863 none could be sold for even as much as $500.[17] The area was soon without slaves, but the point became moot with the *Emancipation Proclamation* signed by President Abraham Lincoln on September 22, 1862, early in the war. As the Union Army penetrated the Confederate states, they freed thousands of slaves each day they marched into new territory. An estimated four million were set free by July 1865, and the United States Congress ratified the *Emancipation Proclamation* as the Thirteenth Amendment to the Constitution on December 18, 1865.[18]

Realizing the inevitability of the political situation, the Missouri government had voted to end slavery within the state on January 11, 1865.[19] The end of slavery is the only energy transition that took place in so short a time, in one day, so to speak, with the issuance of the Proclamation, though it took another three years to dismantle the structure of slavery. It is unlikely that another energy transition will occur so completely and so suddenly. The only comparison of that kind of swift energy transition today would be the permanent loss of electricity, a force that has created the many labor-saving devices we now depend on, including remotely fueled heating and light. If we can imagine that occurring now, we may understand some of the harshness of the loss of slaves as energy to slave owners on the one hand, and the sudden freedom and loss of accountability of the slaves on the other.

Many slaveholders gave up their slaves to Union forces to join the army in hopes of getting reimbursed for their generosity in supplying troops. The *Proclamation* made it possible for former slaves to join the armed forces. The Union Army's Provost Marshal in nearby Lexington in Lafayette County took in 70 blacks in one day. "Every negro received saves a white man," he said, "and we must confess that our sympathies are decidedly for the white man. We advise all the owners of slaves to put them at once into the service taking a receipt therefore."[20] Whether the former owners received anything in return is not clear. By the end of the war an estimated 400,000 former slaves had served as liberators of their own people.[21]

War itself by virtue of its definition comprises a high intensity of energy as well as fuel. Massive troop buildups with firepower and armaments supported by an infrastructure of supply and fuel creates an energy force of dreadful power. The losing side nearly always has to reconstruct itself from disconnected pieces of former systems often found obsolete and in need of replacement with newer, more energy-intensive systems. While the winning side has amassed its energy flows to some pinnacle and proceeds to grow from there, the losing side has lost its intensity through destruction of infrastructure and decimation of skilled personnel to organize, repair, build and lead the new energy structures. Such was the case with the South.

The former slaves who became free, having served as property, now had no leadership for their new paradigm. "Emancipation signaled change, but it provided no blueprints for growth."[22] No longer supported by their former masters, some wandered the countryside looking for subsistence, for employment, for someone to make decisions for them as they had been taught. Some turned down jobs from their former masters and stood idly on street corners without an alternative.[23] Not unlike the Osage before them, they had been freed of the structure that dictated their way of life and could not immediately create a new one. [24]

116

Emancipation Ordinance of Missouri

The U.S. Census of 1870 showed more than two-thirds of the freedmen worked as farm laborers in Missouri. Women took in washing and ironing, worked as domestics, as cooks and seamstresses, depending on their skill level. One black woman entrepreneur, Alpha Smith Minor, opened a dress shop in Kansas City, "Lady's Ready to Wear."[25] The freed blacks had no political power, and though the men had the right to vote, most could not do so for lack of literacy or courage to go to the polls. Looking for places to congregate, the freedmen and women formed all-black churches that became their places of strength and in which emerging leaders would be trained.[26]

The whites also suffered from uncertainty and loss of stature. "The slaveholders' institutional structure of social control had vanished." Those who had been slave masters now had neither "the racial supremacy nor the security which slavery provided. . . . Although slavery as a system of forced labor had ended abruptly, the racial accommodation persisted tenaciously."[27]

The economic loss was a bitter pill to swallow. The social loss may have been even greater. "One of the great evils of slavery," noted Berenice Morrison-Fuller who had been born and raised on a Missouri plantation, "was the arrogance it created in the master. Absolute power over the lives and destiny of others is a terrible responsibility and few are capable of sustaining such an ordeal. . .. It was a terrible problem for a man of tender conscience, quite impossible for the fanatical abolitionists to understand. Ideally and theoretically, their ideas were right, but practically, they were fraught with a great injustice and cruelty."[28]

The Southern plantation owners now had to hire farm workers, which many of them did from the ranks of their own former slaves who became tenant farmers, or work the farm themselves, or sell their land. "We may be mistaken," wrote one newspaper editor, "but we think all intelligent gentlemen will hear us out that the farmers of the county will begin a crop in the spring of '63 with a thousand field hands less than they did in '61."[29]

Arthur Jackson (1856-1931)

At his home in the Westport district of Kansas City, Missouri, where he lived from 1913 until his death in 1931. Members of his former slaveholding family lived blocks away.

Many freed slaves continued to work as sharecroppers for their former owners. Others remained loyal servants until their deaths decades later.

One Franklin County, Missouri, slave, Arthur Jackson, great great grandfather of co-author David W. Jackson, continued to live with, or very near his former master's family— Richard Ludlow and Lucinda Edwards (DeAtley) Jackson—for 66 years after his 1865 emancipation. Arthur, who was born a slave in 1856 when the Jacksons lived in Charleston, Kanawha County, Virginia (today, West Virginia) claimed the Jackson surname. The family moved to Franklin County in 1859, when Arthur was three years old. As an adult, Arthur married a Caucasian woman, Ida Anderson. They named three of their children after members of Arthur's "white family." These Kansas City families were intertwined in ways that descendants on both sides are rediscovering five generations later.[30]

More former slaves, however, turned to nearby towns and cities, sometimes crowding 40 into a tenement to provide a roof for themselves. A mass migration of freedmen headed west as participants of the Exoduster Movement.

Dislocated poor whites also fled to cities and lived a day-to-day existence.[31]

PART 1
Conclusion

The scenes depicted in this part may be called the world of "Peak Wood." Life in the Wood Age is described here at its finest, reenacting the age-old pattern of the frontier, with all its expenditure of animal and human muscle, harnessed and unharnessed water power, pace, and level of material possessions.

Peak Wood was a seasonal as well as local world. When the weather changed, activity changed. When the water froze, it froze mill power and boat use. Peak Wood belonged to the seasons, and because of the weight and awkwardness of logs, to neighborhoods.

There was no insulation from the seasons. Each one demanded its activity and if that was missed that year, there was no way to replace a missing part of the cycle by artificial means. Peak Wood lasted from at least 350,000 to perhaps a million years of human control of fire.[32] That wood-oriented way of life was practiced with gusto and precision by both low- and high-energy cultures alike. As coal began to be used on America's East Coast, what happened there would soon enough be exported to the western edges of the country.

The little hamlet that clung to the Missouri River's edge in 1821, a mere scattering of cabins, did not hint at the metropolis to rise. Little overt evidence of the fuel revolution that began in England in the 1600s reached this far into the wilderness; but, as the fuel revolution gained momentum in Europe, it would crash the shores of the new United States and break on the shores of the Missouri River like a tidal wave of energy. That energy was embodied in coal mining, in the steam boat, in the influx of population, the pent-up desire for wealth that propelled the westward trek of thousands of people and wagons assembled to cross the Missouri River and be on their way. That surge of energy changed the economy from agrarian subsistence to market economy. The transformation of the land from intricately woven pastoral ecosystems to separated natural resources swept across the area. It divided, subdivided, commoditized, priced for sale and harvested for immediate use what had been inviolate in its natural state. That revolution from ecosystem to natural resource would signify a transformation in the way people lived and enriched their culture with material goods.

The tradeoff was clear. Every acquisition and transformation of the ecosystems the settler took over meant a loss of context and storehouse from which the Osage drew their life. The Osage carried out their culture rich in beliefs and ceremony without a high level of energy available to them. Both populations would be impacted by the change to coal, first in Great Britain in the 17th century, then on the American side of the Atlantic in the 18th century, and finally at the mouth of the Kaw in the 19th century. Once the transition to coal had begun, its superiority in metallurgy and its relative cheapness because of its abundance would promote its use. As author Martin Melosi says, "[T]ransitions are not necessarily due to energy scarcities. Price, technology, transportation accessibility to sources, consumer preferences, environmental impact, and several other economic and non-economic factors can influence a transition."[33]

Fueling Change

The first energy transition was the arrival of the horse for the Osage into a Wood Age, low-energy, pedestrian system. The second energy transition would be for the American settlers, a mechanization of transportation, the steam engine. The engine would outstrip the ability of wood to supply its fuel needs and add to the demand for coal.

Wood's dominance as fuel for unknown millennia had been penetrated. It would take less than a century for coal to replace it as the preferred fuel, but never at the level at which wood functioned for all those eons. Wood was humanity's cradle in every sense of the word. Coal came along and launched humanity into an energy-driven adolescence.

This part of the story is split between Wood Age *energy* and Wood, Coal and Oil Age *fuels* at work. Animal and vegetable elements began to phase out; fossil fuels eased in, and with them a growing use of fuel and an eventual decrease in human and animal energy. In 1850, fuel use was probably 10% fuel to 90% energy. It also consisted of 90% wood and 10% coal. By 1870, increased flow-through of fuel with use of coal as well as increased use of wood changed the fuel picture to 25% coal and 75% wood. Too many undefined variables stand in the way of an easy conclusion, but over the course of the next 50 years, hand labor turned into machine labor and animal energy fell accordingly though neither was in any way quickly eclipsed though animal labor was less than 6% of the energy scene by 1920.[34]

Early diaries describe the beauty of wilderness, while also narrating the struggles with undeveloped land, distance and privation, all of which took prodigious energy to engage in with only a little help from fuel-driven mechanisms. First-person accounts extol the virtues and the dangers with a breathlessness of appreciation for the scene they know will soon vanish even in the days in which the diaries were written. They sensed then, as they stepped from throbbing steamboat decks, that the arrival of machines would change the world they had come to savor. Europeans had invaded America and brought their level of energy and its exploiting power with them. The pioneers carried that west as soon as circumstances permitted, willingly sacrificing the level of energy being enjoyed by the Native Americans and replacing it with their own. The previous generations of Europeans had carried disease that destroyed native populations. Now the 19th century arrivals carried with them the machinery to destroy the roots of the energy level on which the population based their culture. Observers could not help knowing they had arrived at a vanishing point of some kind.

Wood use in the post-steam world increased from a possible one cord per person for the Osages in 1800 to 4.5 cords per capita estimated for the then United States in 1850.[35] Wood use was still primarily used to heat homes. In spite of the numbers of steamboats plying the western waters and rapacious cutting of timber to feed them, only about one tenth of the amount was used for steamboats. However, that amount would change after the Civil War as railroads began to compete for wood sources. Both steam-driven machines would use wood when they could; both would have to change to coal to expand their development to the fullest extent. Both owed their beginnings to wood as fuel for motive power. That fuel had to be delivered by some system to continuously feed the mighty machine.

Fuel Wood and Coal Consumption Per Capita[36]

Date	Fuel Wood (cords)	Coal (net tons)
1850	4.39	0.36
1860	4.00	0.60
1870	3.46	0.69
1880	2.71	1.58
1890	1.90	2.48
1900	1.31	3.45
1910	0.98	5.28
1920	0.78	5.59

Systems as we know them in the 21st century, far removed from the fuel that powers our world, may be more complex than we can grasp. Human desires get translated into actions that get organized into sequences that include all the parts of actors and objects at some point in time and space. All is powered by fuel burning at remote locations. In the beginning of fuel use, however, systems were simple enough. The early fuel systems may seem comical now, but that rough scramble up and down the banks of the western waterways to fuel steamboats signaled the country's best effort to work with wood on a quick turnaround.

To be transportable wood had to be close to the riverbank when it was cut. The roadless forests from which the wood was commonly cut did not lend themselves to hauling wood long distances by wagon though some of that was surely done. Wood's bulk and weight worked best on water. Wood's finest moment of supremacy could not support so much effort in terms of harvesting and supplying the needs of industrializing demands.

Humans still sawed and cut wood under poor working conditions, while animals still conveyed it distances, or flotillas of wood made their way downstream, not up. The upstream direction was the wonder of steamboats. To go upstream without cordelling! That was a miracle that wood brought to the steam engine before coal had much significance in supplying that effort.

Activity was organized around the physical characteristics of the fuel itself. People did whatever it took to turn trees into a readily available fuel. Starting at the bases of the uncut tree, men organized tasks as efficiently as they could with the technology at hand. That first organizational layer became more complex and sophisticated the farther from the fuel site.

Layer upon layer of organization of tasks less directly identified with fuel and its delivery became evident and was carried out. (See Coal Grid, *Systems and Organization*, page 123.) Ultimately, the energy from the fuel itself via available technology and the fuel's energy components dictated transportation systems. The systems created by the steamboat pilots' association and those developed by the wharf master are examples of those systems built around wood as fuel in the new Wood Age.

Fueling Change

The wood hawks provided the fuel that went into the steam engine that drove the steamboat that gave the pilot and wharf master reason for being. The merchant took advantage of the greater energy to buy and sell goods and organized his tasks accordingly in long paper chains of producers, distributors and customers. The wagon masters could afford to field wagon trains with thousands of head of cattle and thousands of dollars of goods to sell that came in quantity by steam engines powering the riverboats relying on wood for fuel.

The population along the Missouri River's edge in the scrappy town of Kansas City found their lives improving dramatically by the amount of goods delivered to them, the industry springing up around them and the increased communications with others, whether taking the boat upriver to Leavenworth to shop for the day or to send and receive goods and messages from great distances.

Systems are comprised of parts that work together in both time and space to achieve a particular end. In this particular time and place, the heyday of the Wood Age and its exuberant expression on the Missouri frontier showed that Herculean tasks could be accomplished with the components of the Wood Age energy suite available. The activity around coal was similarly dictated by that fuel: shovels not saws, buckets not axes, flatboats to float coal downstream and so on.

Unlike timber that could be seen and whose types and quantity could be instantly estimated, the mystery of how much coal was available remained a question from the beginning up to the present-day estimates. Wood was still abundant across the country as coal came into use, but the increase in industrialization that British industry had already demonstrated for a century began to be put to use in America.

The activity around oil was uniquely dictated by the characteristics of that fuel. Liquid fuel confounded people at first, but efficiencies immediately emerged as soon as participants in the scene could invent both technologies and systems to fit the needs of the oil on one side of the equation and their own needs on the other. Humans have manipulated the combination of fuel, energy and technology to suit their desires for millennia. Fuel requires only one thing from its users, understanding of its demands and limitations.

COAL

Essential Requisites for Fuel Use	Stage I: Discovery and Development	Stage II: Systems Organization	Stage III: Expansion and Defense	Stage IV: Niche and Decline
Dates:	1701-1758	1758-1885	1855-1955	1955
1. Good Quality of Fuel for Use	VA residents used coal locally for years before exporting	PA mines opened during War of 1812. Anthracite a new kind of coal	Coal fields developed throughout East and Midwest	Coal is a niche fuel but not in decline: Electricity and manufacturing
2. Sufficient Quantity of Fuel	Exploitation for commercial purposes in 1758	Anthracite mines expanded to supply coastal cities	RRs become controlling factor. Miners strike for better pay, conditions	The U.S. one of largest repositories with 22% of world total
3. Cheapness and Regularity of Production	Often sold in coal bags for easy handling from flatboats to ship	Many inventions to increase production-- electrification of mines	RR monopolies and miner strikes make coal undependable	Now organized by mega companies with money, markets
4. Cheapness of Transportation	Sold by boat load to go up the coast to northern cities. Required multiple handling	1. Extract coal. 2. Load wagons. 3. Load on to flatbed boats in bags to waterfront or shovel on	U. S. Navy used coal until 1911. Transfer from collier ship on high seas problematic at best	Will continue to provide electricity, manufacturing, 5 times more truck than rail delivery now
5. Sufficiency of Transportation	Uncertain supply but miners and boat captains kept coal flowing	4. Wagon from flatboat to cruiser up the coast 5. Wagon from ship to yard 6. Yard to customer	RRs made to carry coal; coal mined for RR fuel. Diesel oil took over in 1950s	More local and regional transportation forecast as cost is too high for inter-national trade
6. Good Market (i.e., End-Users)	Many users from England knew coal	Anthracite difficult to learn to use. Consumer education required	Widespread coal use into the 1950s but air pollution decreased use. Replaced by natural gas	Consumers in a golden age of electronics use powered by coal, natural gas, nuclear, & some solar

Fueling Change

PART 2

Good-Bye, Wood:
Hello, Coal Age, 1890-1970

*. . .Innovation was in the air—because the mid-19th century, especially
in the United States, resembled a great laboratory both for the debut
of intellectual invention and for the nurture of the alchemy needed to
translate it into revolutionary applications to the physical world . . .*

--Francis Schruben, *WEA Creek to El Dorado: Oil in Kansas*, 1860-1920 (1972)

Alchemy, indeed! The chief stimulus for the nation's inventions was its two new fuels, coal and oil. With more fuel available than ever before in history and new processes for making iron, intellectual invention had a rich road ahead. Using the new fuels as prodigiously as they could be extracted, manufacturers, railroads and households made sizable inroads into wood's territory.

In this brief period of 30 years, coal rose in 1885 and soon surpassed and replaced wood as the dominant fuel for the first time in human history. Goodbye to the hearth!

Meanwhile, oil (initially in the lighting and lubrication fields), natural gas and hydropower show little of their future status as critical fuels of the 20th century.

If hands, horse, water and wind were the pillars of the Wood Age, how did coal replace those? Hands still handled fire but now increasingly it was from coal. Horses still pulled their weight in city transportation but increasingly were replaced by streetcars powered by electricity. Wind as motive power was often replaced by steam engines by this time, and in this period, water would become turbo power to generate electricity.

Such a wholesale overhaul of the fuel-energy network would bring about enormous changes in the workforce, in manufacturing, and in social classes. It was a fuel revolution that brought about an industrial revolution that began with coal being used to make steam engines in place of wood. Once a mechanical user of fuels, i.e., an engine, could be replicated ad infinitum, coal production flourished and began to replace the costlier wood.

Coal then occupied a two-pronged effort, first as fuel to manufacture the steam engines and then as fuel to be burned in the end product. As making coke was mastered, a century-long struggle between charcoal and coke finished with coke the clear winner. The finite amount of wood available compared to the seemingly infinite amount of coal was not a match. Coal won.[1]

The chapters ahead show the human side of coal production, the beginning of electric lights on a scale so small as to seem quaint, the transformation of transportation from live animal to mechanically powered conveyance, and the beginning of steel production. Even as small as oil production was in this period compared to coal, its qualities were so exciting and its promises so great that people could easily see oil was going to be a necessity in the fuel picture.

No one could have imagined that the very quick displacement of wood for coal as the dominant fuel would happen within a thirty-year period. Once coke began to replace charcoal, and once steel-making in quantity took hold, coal grew over a thirty-year period in the exact dimension that wood declined. Meanwhile, oil continued on its organizational path to solidify the gains in the illumination business. As far as fuel was concerned, these were busy decades. The East pushed forth its multiplicity of goods, the West gladly received them and grew apace on the frontier. Fortunately for Kansas City coal deposits lay nearby.

Chapter 13

Kansas City's Railroad Beginning

*The expansion of the railroad saw the arrival of the "iron horse" in the west,
as oil arrived in the east. Railroads increasingly run on coal had hardly made inroads
to Kansas City when oil was discovered in Pennsylvania. Nevertheless,
the ripples of change would keep "chugging" forward.*

When the railroad arrived at the juncture of the Missouri and Kaw Rivers, the Wood Age settlement was overtaken by an undeniable statement of mechanical power from the Coal Age flourishing farther east. Until then inroads had been small. Like the first knives given to the Osage Indians, steamboats laboring up the river had constituted a small invasion of an old energy system. Then steam engines began to replace mills, though by no means all of them, some of which endured well into the 20th century. The telegraph had coursed its way to the river and then on to California, but land traffic remained Wood Age and the river the time-honored route of travel. Now all that would change.

An Abundance of the Raw Material

Coke from coal, the mineral equivalent of charcoal from wood, began to be developed in England from 1709 onward by Abraham Darby to work with metallurgy. In his area of the Midlands, wood had become prohibitive in price. Darby began to experiment casting iron with coal and had no success until he learned the process of "purging the coal of sulfur and other unwanted elements before using it for fuel." This trial and error period on some small scale lasted decades. Abraham Darby II took over his father's work in the 1740s. While his father had sold cast iron cookware at reasonable prices, Abraham II thought to sell the furnaces themselves. Eventually, he was able to demonstrate that coked coal could produce "more iron with coal than had any conventional charcoal furnace in the history of the trade."[1]

Coke's density created a much higher heat than wood charcoal. Coke made large quantities of cast iron possible and the material ranged in use from the first cast-iron bridge in Shropshire, England, in 1780 that still stands, to ornamental gates for estates of the rich to the humble cooking pot that became ubiquitous at every hearth.[2] Coke replaced charcoal as the heat element of choice in that country by the 1750s, but not until more than a century later in the United States because of the relatively ample supply of wood available in this country.[3]

On the Missouri frontier they could boast of knowing coal, of advertising coal-and-wood-burning stoves, of having cannel coal available to steamboats at the limestone pier. In fact, they seemed to have plenty of coal, and, as always, wood, according to early Kansas City promoter Henry Spalding, who in 1858 said, "We have an abundance of the raw material for the furnace, and all kinds of machinery, either for the construction of the labor-saving implements of the country, or the manufacture of useful or ornamental fabrics."[4]

Not surprisingly, the above quote linked fuel with the city's destiny.

Fifteen years before Kansas City embraced coal as a fuel, Henry Spalding, the voice of the business community of the still nascent Kansas City, knew what fuel could do and where it belonged--in the furnace, as well as the fireplace. The town was ready for manufacture. Furnaces meant machinery; machinery meant manufacturing "labor-saving implements," and ultimately progress and prosperity.

Wood could readily be identified with hearth and home, but even here moved to the forge and furnace, while from the beginning, coal served as much of an industrial fuel as for home heating. But until the 1870s, Kansas City worked with coal as an alternative to wood, not as the mainstay. By 1858, stoves of both wood and coal were being advertised for sale in the city directory. Both fuels were available. In what quantities is unknown.[5]

The experimentation with coal happened on the East Coast. Coal burned hotter than wood and required an enclosed structure to focus the heat for metallurgy, hence the arrival of the furnace and the grate to hold the fuel. Wood in general burns from 9 to 17 million BTUs while coal burns from 16 to 26 million BTUs.[6] The difference in heat intensity challenged inventors when all metallurgy was created with wood charcoal. A grate that would withstand the heat of a coal fire was a constant challenge. This problem was solved in 1808 when Jesse Fell first designed a grate to burn anthracite coal. By 1818, coal stoves made by Texler in Bethlehem, Pennsylvania, were sold locally, but weight, cost and transportation kept them from being widely distributed.

By 1821, metal workers experimented, using anthracite in blast-furnace smelting instead of charcoal. This marked the difference between low and high productivity in iron in America as it had a century before in England. Abraham Darby's breakthrough distillation process of "'cooking' off the volatile gaseous matters, including tars, oils, and gases, at a temperature between 900 and 1150 degrees Celsius, so that the fixed carbon and ash are fused together" may have been the industrial shot heard round the world. Repeated in America in the 1830s, the process of the hot blast furnace using pre-heated air to fire the coal in 1837, took less fuel and less time to reduce the coal to coke. [7]

The first anthracite-fueled hot blast furnace was fired up in Allentown, Pennsylvania, on July 4, 1840.[8] Experiments with both anthracite for metallurgy and the hot blast furnace technique had gone on for at least eighty if not more years. Scores of men had contributed to the process, some coming from England to sell their knowledge to American iron forgers. Eventually, the process would be called successful and America could and would produce greater quantities of iron than Great Britain by the end of 1890s and any other nation by the beginning of the 20th century.[9]

By 1825, anthracite was used to fire boilers of a steam engine in a nail factory in Pennsylvania. By 1831, coal-burning stoves with serviceable grates came into general use on the eastern seaboard. In 1838, the Reading Railroad began to convert to coal-burning engines using anthracite, and by 1840, anthracite smelting of iron ore had become doable thus increasing the output of pig iron and lowering the price at the same time.[10] By 1840, over a million tons had been mined; its use quadrupled by 1850. Within 20 years coal would dominate fuel use greater than any other fuel other than wood at 72%. Bituminous coal, the next-densest grade, comprises 42% of the coal available.

By the 1830s, bituminous was used in manufacturing for steam engines for both railroads and steamboats and in-home heating. Its black smoke pouring from chimneys was once seen as more of a blessing than a curse. Smoke meant employment but at the same time it meant air pollution that would grow as a problem and have to be dealt with in later years. The remaining coal reserves of the United States are made up of 88% sub-bituminous and 29% lignite. Only anthracite and bituminous contain enough density to work with metals.[11] Bituminous soon began to be mined and used for manufacturing along the East Coast and in some cases home heating.[12]

The introduction of coal increased fuel usage. For the first time in history, humanity had two fuels to use, one for home, the other for industry. By 1850, the first time-verifiable statistics are available, Americans burned an average of 4.39 cords of wood per person, and .36 of a ton of coal.[13]

Two fuels! A choice of fuel! This was new in human history.

The Iron Horse Drinks at the Mouth of the Kaw

The railroad boom began in Kansas City in the 1850s along with other towns in Missouri to gain access to eastern markets. "It was one thing, however, to plan roads in every direction, and quite another to construct them. The Kansas Citians never had enough money to invest heavily in railroads, so they concentrated on persuading outside interests to build them."[14] Throughout the pre-war years, the leadership of Kansas City kept up continual pressure on both citizens and members of railroad companies to bring the "iron horse to drink at the mouth of the Kaw" by this busy little town on the levee.[15] They gave barbecues, speeches, rallies and parades to keep the spirit high. In the summer of 1855 the Missouri Pacific was completed as far as Jefferson City from St. Louis.

In the autumn all the produce and crops north of that terminus were handled by steamboats with deliveries made inland by horses and wagons. Interior cities like Sedalia, Marshall, Warrensburg, Holden and other towns transported their goods from Westport Landing by freight wagons drawn by several pair of oxen or horses.[16] Meanwhile, the Union Pacific approached from the West toward the town of Wyandotte across the Kaw River. A bridge had to cross the Missouri River at some point and Leavenworth, whose population had grown to 18,000 by 1865 because of the Army post there, and St. Joseph at 10,000 and Kansas City at 4,000 all vied for the bridge to come to their town. Without it, they would sink into relative idleness while the victor would grow into an urban empire.[17]

In spite of the war, construction continued on several lengths of track. In 1864, the railroad proceeded in Kansas toward Wyandotte across the Kaw River from Kansas City. The first locomotive for the Kansas Pacific arrived on a steamboat from St. Joseph, Missouri, and was brought to the Kansas City levee. (Imagine the amount of fuel, probably wood, that took. An entire forest would burn to bring the next technology to town!) Though "the weather was exceedingly severe" on February 11th, attempts were made to unload the locomotive when it slipped into the Missouri River "from whence it was subsequently fished out with great difficulty and put on the track."[18] This brief summary can only give a glimpse of what a miserable event that must have been. Of course, the locomotive had to be pulled out by teams of oxen and mules, the old form of energy that could tug and heave the new form of energy into place!

As the townspeople fought to reinvigorate the town, the "Bushwackers" still threatened them and the town needed to be protected. The guerillas cut the telephone lines daily between Kansas City and points south, and all messages received were routed through Omaha and Leavenworth. The Battle of Westport had yet to be fought on October 22 and 23, 1864, and the townspeople and Union soldiers put up fortifications while men drilled their maneuvers for three days. The *Journal of Commerce* exhorted its citizens: "There should be no disposition to yield the town save in the last extremity."[19]

Union Major General Samuel R. Curtis with Kansas and Colorado troops 22,000 in number defeated the Confederate Major General Sterling Price with 8,500 troops in a "severe battle" at the Big Blue River, Brush Creek, and what is now Swope Park and Forest Hill Cemetery where Price retreated leaving a field of dead and wounded of about 1,500 from each army. Survivors were "humanely attended" by the women of the town, including some at the Wornall House across from what is now Jacob L. Loose Park, named in 1927—in more peaceful times—for the founder of Sunshine Biscuits. (Now that is an energy transition!) "By the low cost of the wounded patriot is the peculiar province of woman," wrote Thomas S. Case, one of the city leaders of the time. "It is her light footstep that brings comfort, her gentle hand that smooths the rough pillow, and her soft voice that cheers the sinking spirit and recalls visions of happiness and home."[20]

Map of NORTHERN MISSOURI Showing the HANNIBAL & S.T JOSEPH RAILROAD LANDS. THE SHADED PART SHOWS THE EXTENT OF THE R.R. LANDS.

The traffic of 30,000 troops at war left the area a wreck. "Kansas City suffered in the loss of everything that goes to make up a town. Her trade was crippled, her population divided in sentiment, and all energy and enterprise dead."[21] But even before the war was over, the leadership of Kansas City had revived and continued its efforts to bring the railroad to

Kansas City. The Missouri Pacific had not come through, so the city fathers approached the Hannibal and St. Joseph railroad instead.

Having since set their sights on a link with Chicago rather than St. Louis, the Kansas City leaders believed the latter railroad to be the better choice. That railroad was farther north, and the Hannibal and St. Joseph proposed to build the bridge across the Missouri. Numerous meetings with railroad leaders in the East and lavish promises of their readiness to service a railroad somehow swayed the decision makers to turn south at Cameron, about fifty miles northeast of Kansas City and directly east of St. Joseph. The Kansas City promoters had promised the railroad executives that the track from Cameron to Kansas City had already been surveyed and graded when, in fact, the surveyor had only walked what would become the route.[22] Kansas City leaders won the argument with relentless pursuit of the prize. This insatiable spirit to improve their city would eventually become known as "the Kansas City Spirit."

In true 19th century prose, the 1870 city directory rejoiced: "At length the war cloud broke away and the sun shone out once more upon the hills," and continued to describe the fast recovery of the city:

> May 1865 found Kansas City with a population of about 6,000 and its real prosperity set in. Emigration poured in from all directions, business sprung up, trade became active again, laborers were in demand, houses could not be built fast enough to accommodate the new arrival; again the work of grading the streets was begun, the high banks along Main and Delaware streets gave way to large business houses, and were rented before built, and filled with goods immediately thereafter. And so the work has continued and still continues.[23]

Building the Hannibal Bridge
Construction began in 1868 (this image was taken May 16). It opened July 3, 1869.
This scene overlaps the steamboat of the Wood Age
with the bridge for the railroad that would usher in the Coal Age.

131

Fueling Change

In January 1867, the population had increased to 15,064, and the real and personal property of the city was valued at a little over $4,000,000. The railroads began to converge on Kansas City though the bridge across the Missouri, the key to Kansas City's future, was still to come.[24]

The bridge became a major challenge for two reasons. The first was that many believed the Missouri could not be bridged. The river was too turbulent and unstable to support a bridge strong enough to bear the weight of locomotives and cars. The second was that Kansas City had no facilities for manufacturing the parts. "Kansas City at that time was almost on the frontier; there was but one small foundry and machine shop in the town, while not a barge suitable to carry stone could be found on the river."

"Special tools had also to be designed and erected . . .a steamboat was also found necessary to tow the barges . . . ." Everything had to be imported or built from the ground up.[25] The masonry and quarrying of stone was contracted for locally, but the superstructure, not surprisingly would come from the Keystone Bridge Company of Pittsburgh. With appropriate festivities the corner stone was laid on August 21, 1867. The bridge was finished in May 1869 and opened with the first engine crossing on Saturday July 3, 1869. The promise of the finished bridge drew people like a magnet.

During the time the bridge was being built, the population of Kansas City more than doubled from 13,000 to 30,000, and "from being little more than a way-station on the Missouri Pacific Railroad, it had become an important railway center, from which no less than seven lines of railroad were in full operation, while several more were projected."[26]

Kansas City had come of age, had been connected to the intercontinental railway system, could compete with Chicago and St. Louis in various markets, could and would brag about itself endlessly in the years to come.

Though still a Wood Age city, the abilities of coal in eastern factories had brought it to the door of the Coal Age. "These trains were not yet burning coal, but they ran on rails formed with coal, were pulled by engines made with coal and were financed by empires built on coal."[27] Coal and everything it could do in factories in the east beckoned to the growing city.

Bird's Eye View of Kansas City

Hannibal Bridge is on right. The West Bottoms are beyond in upper right. Railroad engines and steamboats chug through this picture, another scene overlapping wood and coal. From this time forward the emphasis was on the railroad and not on the steamboats.

132

Chapter 14

Oil: An Excitement Unparalleled

The beginnings of a third fuel was introduced for the first time in human history: oil production. Extraction was more exacting than either wood or coal, delaying the start of oil drilling. Once the technology met the fuel in the right combination, wells sprouted like mushrooms—first in a small, remote location in Pennsylvania, then eventually across the country, and around the world. Wood had been the cradle, coal the sturdy child, but oil was an adolescent going into young adulthood. It would bring the country of age with all the advantages its citizens could possibly imagine…and then some.

Before atomic power grew in a science laboratory among documenting attendants, no other fuel source has had its beginning marked by such a well-remembered, single-recorded day in history. Not that oil had not been used since time immemorial, but without a means of lifting it from the ground in quantity, little of it could be used at once. Only seepage from "oil springs" gave enough to sell in small bottles as a curative for most anything, if patiently gathered in some quantity by wringing out a blanket thrown over the water to absorb the oil.

Beginning of the Oil Age

Saturday, August 27, 1859, could be called the beginning of the Oil Age. This is the day officially entered into history as the moment when oil would soon be abandoned as a medicine and would became a commodity as fuel. Edwin L. Drake's tedious efforts near Titusville, Pennsylvania using salt-mining equipment to *purposefully* raise oil instead of salt water with oil in it finally paid off. His innovation was to drive a three-to-four-inch pipe 60 feet into the ground using a five-horse steam engine for help to get to that level without cave-ins or water seepage. Salt-digging methods had always been to dig to bedrock before starting to drill.[1]

On Sunday, August 28, 1859, Drake's helper, "Uncle Billy" Smith, having actually spied the oil at the wellhead of the 69 ½ foot pipe, took that as proof of the first oil strike. Drake, a former railroad conductor, had, by a circuitous route been hired by four partners in the underfinanced but optimistic Pennsylvania Rock Oil Company. Drake knew nothing about oil drilling, but then no one did, but he was willing to put forth the effort to drill for oil the

partners agreed was there, and to prove that enough of the liquid lay underground that it could be marketed in quantity. When Drake arrived at the wellhead summoned by Uncle Billy's urgency, he rigged a pump to stop the flow that Billy and his helpers had tried to catch in washtubs, jugs and bottles, a total of about eight to ten gallons.[2]

The news traveled quickly, and prospectors of black gold went berserk. One of the original investors of Drake's well, attorney George Bissell in a partnership with three others who had backed Drake's prospecting, visited the area in November of that year. He wrote home: "We find here an excitement unparalleled. The whole population are crazy almost. Farms that could have been bought for a trifle 4-months-ago, now readily command $200 & $300 an acre, and that too when not a drop of oil has ever been discovered on them. So much for the bare hope of there being by any possibility a substratum of oil."[3]

An oil strike,
or gusher

134

In testimony to oil's strong reputation as a curative, Bissell came down with a heavy cold while visiting the well but saturated a strip of red flannel "with Rock Oil, about my neck and took repeated doses of the oil. I really think it would have resulted badly for me without this remedy. It is positively a specific for throat ailments of such a nature."[4] The powers of "snake oil," as it had always been called, would hang on for many decades after oil's "discovery," but its power as fuel was undeniable.[5] Before it left behind the healing arts, "snake oil's" medicinal qualities were extolled in a poem for Seneca Oil, bottled as medicine and named for the Indian tribe that occupied the lands where it was first found:

> The Healthful balm, from Nature's secret spring,
> The bloom of health, and life, to man will bring;
> As from her depths the magic liquid flows,
> To calm our sufferings and assuage our woes.[6]

Little did the writer realize the last two lines would become a metaphor for wealth and not health.

The partners suspected that the oil could be used for much more than medicine if found in enough quantity. They envisioned its being used for illuminants and for lubrication, but when quantity arrived via "Drake's well," as it was always called, no forethought had been given to managing the flow. The first problems oilmen faced were containment and transportation. Today we might expect such an anticipated fuel discovery to be approached with forethought, but at the time the idea of liquid fuel in large amounts simply could not be grasped. No tank cars, no barrels, no pipelines, no prepared roads or rail siding awaited the birth of the oil industry.

The nearest railroad lay twenty-five miles away in one direction and forty in another. Standard width of rails had not yet been decided, so oil in whatever container available shipped on one rail would have to be unloaded and reloaded on another to further its journey. Teamsters with horses and wagons provided the first transportation from well to rail and from rail to rail and charged a fee per barrel. At the end of that rail journey, the barrels would have to be loaded on wagons and drayed by horses or mules across the uneven streets of the town to the waterfront and loaded on board vessels for coastal delivery, then unloaded from the ship, reloaded on wagons and so forth.

It was an inauspicious beginning. For over two years the new oil drillers scrambled for containers and transport and wasted enormous amounts of the new fuel and time to get it to a market. As one observer noted, it was "a unique type of mining industry, with distinctive features of its own."[7]

Drake had a six-horse-power steam engine at his disposal, but that kind of help was occasional for the hordes of wildcatters who came in search of oil.[8] Many of them drilled without mechanical help using two men to "jig" back and forth on a board at right angles to the drill that sent it down and back on a spring pole. They could complete a jig twice a minute and eventually make some progress in deepening the well at three to six inches a day. Horses

135

were also used: they walked around the center of a shaft that supplied motion to the drilling bit. Oil was usually found at around 200 feet below the ground.[9]

Getting a well drilled was one effort; getting it capped was another. At first drillers did not know that natural gas could lift the oil from the depths of the earth and send it flying skyward. By 1861 the first spouting wells spewed oil 60 feet in the air at three thousand barrels a day. The outcome of such events was enormous waste. Said one observer: "When the first [flowing] wells were opened . . . there was little or no tankage ready to receiving it, and the oil ran into the creek and flooded the land around the wells until it lay in small ponds. Pits were dug in the ground to receive it, and dams constructed to secure it, yet withal the loss was very great."[10]

An earlier effort at the illuminant market had already resulted in an underfinanced but optimistic company, the North American Gas Light Company in New York, that would crack the illuminant market with a liquid fuel from coal called kerosene. A Canadian physician and geologist Abraham Gesner had come to New York after being poorly received in his home country to capitalize on experiments he had done in Canada, and to produce the liquid from coal he himself had named kerosene or light from the sun, "which could be manufactured at a lower cost than the various burning fluids now most in use."[11]

Coal gas had been used for illuminants since the 1820s. The best light came from whale oil candles, also the most expensive. Those were made from spermaceti, the liquid found in the skull of sperm whales. Other illuminants included camphene derived from turpentine from wood that burned in newly developed glass lamps, and the usual animal fats burned in a shallow dish with a bit of cotton for a wick. That practice went back to earliest times, beyond the ancient Romans, beyond the Greeks even. Not much had changed.

The time was ripe for better illuminants. Growing numbers of factories required greater light on short winter days than could be achieved with present light sources. This convergence of needs and experimental fluids forced the bottleneck to open for illuminants just before the Civil War.

The decades of refining both whale oil and coal gas had given the country a certain knowledge of chemistry that led to a great deal of experimentation. Such refining had created an infrastructure to experiment with other liquids as whale oil supplies dwindled from overhunting during the very decade in which this fever to create a new light source gained momentum. Kerosene from coal oil arrived in the mid-1850s and awaited only 1) a steady supply of burnable liquid that did not smell of smoke, and 2) a lamp in which to burn it, preferably one that would control these two problems. Furthermore, both liquid and lamp needed to be available at a price affordable in quantity.[12]

Coal oil was already being produced in some quantity in Kentucky, Ohio, Maine and Pennsylvania. Soon coal *oil* competed as a light source against the earlier success of coal *gas* in cities using the gas as street and home illuminant, forcing the gas companies to lower their rates. What the Pennsylvania Rock Oil Company needed was a steady stream of rock oil that could piggyback on the infrastructure of coal oil as a competitive and, hopefully, cheaper alternative illuminant. It had to be cheaper than the two-step process of mining coal and taking it through the process of distilling.[13]

With all the light sources looking for a place in the market, whether good and expensive or inferior and smoky and/or smelly, the miracle that Drake had created galvanized people to champion this new and better illuminant. Once the technique had proven fruitful, the frenzy broke out on the remote Pennsylvania landscape.[14] By 1860, landowners and stock companies purchasing leases peddled them for an acre or less of ground. During the 1860s, the Oil Creek valley was "cut up much like a sheet cake, but then swapped and sold with each piece swapped and sold many times before anyone took a bite."[15]

Between 1860 and 1870, the oil industry worked to find its legs and get its new product to market. Wildcatting was at a fevered peak, but an unmistakable sign of underground wealth had not yet appeared until April 17, 1861, when the first gusher came in at Titusville, blowing 60 feet in the air powered by a pocket of natural gas and pumping oil at three-thousand barrels a day. Another appeared in May. Others followed soon after. Now the mad scramble moved to transporting the liquid to refinery facilities to keep up with the increased flow. Investors, now convinced of the riches available in the oil industry, stepped forward to underwrite exploration and drilling, transport and refining while the original coal oil quietly began to fade away.[16]

The decade from 1860-1870 showed eager discovery and urgent development of the Oil Creek field, or the Oil Region, as it became known, or even shorter, simply the Region, the area surrounding the original well in Titusville, Pennsylvania.[17] It was, after all, the only one at the time.

The discovery came just before the Civil War broke out, but the fact that development proceeded apace against the backdrop of the Civil War is interesting to imagine. Unlike coal that could be taken from the ground and thrown into a furnace, oil's use was predicated on a number of containment and distilling steps before it could be put to work.[18] The decade from 1860-1870 not only saw the destruction of war but the construction of the basic elements of oil's rudimentary infrastructure upon which the whole industry would later be built. Beginning with the simple task of containing a liquid fuel, then transporting it, then distilling it, then finding a market for its various properties, then organizing these pieces into greater efficiencies, and finally finding ways to use it in the marketplace—in a world unused to its advantages, oil's early life was very busy.

Barrels, Barrels, Are the Great Want Now!

The many iterations of technology that followed the prodigious flow of oil virtually overwhelmed the early participants in Pennsylvania while distance overwhelmed commercial efforts for frontiersmen. Missouri's frontier and the Civil War combine with the early oil to suggest three theaters of energy at work at once.

The first was the last act of the Wood Age on the Missouri frontier, case in point being the beginning of the Pony Express a year before oil was discovered.

The second was the introduction of the Oil Age in 1859 in Pennsylvania.

And, the third was the Civil War itself, a prodigious user of energy, mostly men and horses, railroads still burning wood—a nationwide mix of fuels and energy urgently focused on different ends.

Stage 1 of oil *Discovery and Development* (see Oil Grid on page 246) was telescoped into a decade because it happened so quickly. Unlike coal's slow, scattered, grimy and underground beginning that provided no pyrotechnics or flumes of spouting oil, what happened to oil happened quickly. The coal industry had done a good deal of the hard work by the time oil came along. Distilling from coal oil was a ready-made industry, railroads, though still primitive and far flung, nevertheless could be built to the site as soon as an oil yield developed. As one author noted, "The coal industry developed; the oil industry was created."[19]

Chapter 15

Coal in Kansas City

The coming of fossil fuel to the local scene shows the many resources available in the area to service the new arrival.

The state of Missouri had ample supplies of coal, and as the railroad came to town coal mines within the city limits flourished. Coal mines erupted in people's back yards, along the creeks and near the industrial area as if by magic. Though the deposits had rested their undisturbed, their time had now come, and eager hands dug out the resources of the Paleozoic laid down some 290 million years ago.

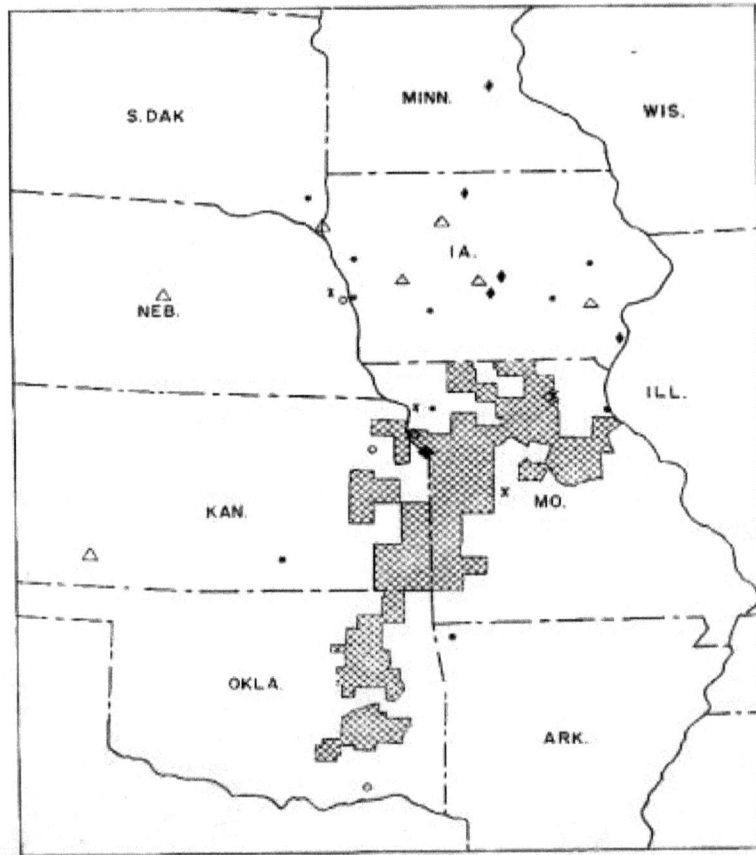

DISTRIBUTION OF COAL MINED IN THE 15th PRODUCTION
DISTRICT*

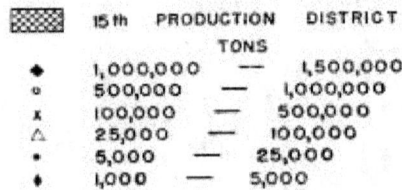

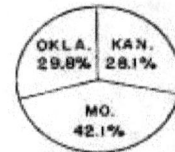

15th PRODUCTION DISTRICT

TONS

◆	1,000,000	—	1,500,000
○	500,000	—	1,000,000
x	100,000	—	500,000
△	25,000	—	100,000
•	5,000	—	25,000
◆	1,000	—	5,000

OKLA. 29.8%   KAN. 28.1%

MO. 42.1%

PER CENT MINED IN
EACH STATE IN 1946

*SHIPMENTS OF LESS THAN 5,000 TONS REACHED WESTERN NORTH AND
SOUTH DAKOTA, WESTERN MINNESOTA, NORTHWEST TEXAS AND NEW ORLEANS

DISTRIBUTION DATA FROM U.S. BUR. MINES, MINERAL MARKET REPT.,
M.M.S. NO. 1559 AND M.M.R. NO. 1558

COUNTIES   WHICH   HAVE   PRODUCED   MORE   THAN
100,000   TONS   OF   COAL   IN   ONE   YEAR
1889-1947 INCLUSIVE

NUMBER   OF   YEARS   IN   WHICH   100,000   TONS   OR
MORE   WERE   MINED   SHOWN   BY   NUMBERS

25,000 Square Miles of Coal

Missouri offered its early residents an abundance of coal for its greater fuel demands in the late 1870s and early 1880s. The estimate of coal deposits for the state in 1900 was 25,000 square miles in area, of which 10,400 were upper and exposed middle measures of coal. The remainder, 14,600 square miles were exposed lower measures.

The upper measures contain about four feet of coal; the middle measures about seven feet, and the lower measures about five workable seams, varying in thickness from 18-inches to four-and-a-half feet, and thin seams varying from six-to-11 inches . . . in all, about 13-and-half feet of coal.[1] Ninety years later, the coal report estimated 25,000 square miles of coal, giving strong credibility to the earlier estimate. The coal is bituminous with a medium to high sulfur content.

The difference between the two dates is in the point of view of the population involved in mining. In 1900, coal was seen as the "most abundant mineral in Missouri, and there are more persons employed in mining it than in mining any other." But in 1992 the federal Energy Information Administration found that "coal mining is a relatively small industry in Missouri, but coal is the principal mineral fuel produced, and the value of coal production accounted for an estimated 6% of the total value of all mineral commodities produced in the state, including oil and natural gas." The first year that coal production was documented was in 1840 with 9,972 short tons (two-thousand pounds). The peak year for coal production in the state of Missouri was 1964 with 6,733,000 short tons.[2] Coal fueled 81% of Missouri's electricity generation in 2017.[3]

The Pattern of Modern Enterprise

Immediately after the Civil War the town that would become Kansas City began to reconstruct itself. By 1869, it had brought back the booming business of outfitting emigrants with supplies, had engaged in a building boom and, most importantly, had built and opened the Hannibal Bridge, the first bridge to cross the Missouri, and welcomed the first railroad train service from across the river. Kansas City already a hub in the nation's network of transportation, had become part of the Coal Age, though use of coal had been in its infancy due to lack of railroads.

The Kansas City *City Directory of 1867-8* showed an ad for coal, a harbinger of things to come: "Always keep on hand at Kansas City the best of Lexington Coal. Office and Coal House, Corner of Delaware Street and Levee." This coal came from Lexington County, the next one east of Jackson County, and a large producer. This advertisement showed with a silhouette of a train and coal car that the coal yard was at the levee by the river, and its coal would do for both steamboat and railroad engine.[4]

Kansas City had its own local supply of coal to exploit. Jackson County, though having some coal deposits, would not become one of the major coal fields of the state but would need a strong, reliable supply of fuel to meet the needs of the flood of emigrants growing daily at its doorstep. The city residents numbered just 3,500 in 1865.

By 1870, however, they had increased to 32,263, a tenfold increase in growth that kept the town busy.[5] (In 50 years it would increase tenfold again). Besides accommodating such an increase in residents, the *City Directory* of 1870 estimated that in the past year 260,000 people had passed through the area, of which 150,000 arrived by wagon or private conveyance, 70,000 by railroad, and 10,000 by river. Clearly, an amazing land rush in progress passed through the gates of Kansas City to the West.

The Santa Fe Railroad connecting Kansas City and Santa Fe would soon be reached by mechanized rather than wagon train. The train changed the way people crossed the plains and introduced them to the luxuries of traveling without travail.

Though wagons still brought the majority by twice the margin, the new railroad promised transportation across the Hannibal Bridge to the Far West in a degree of comfort previous emigrants could hardly have imagined. The newly built train station in the West Bottoms handled the traffic way beyond the power of the levee to do so. "The trickle of westward pioneers who had braved the wagon trails turned into a flood of settlers riding the rails. Now the door was open to ranching and farming, because the surplus could be shipped by rail to the urban markets of the East."[6] These figures give some reality to the expression "western migration." Accommodations and outfitting of these emigrants became an all-consuming business for Kansas City, and more and more fuel was needed to support personal and industrial demands.

Kansas City's use of coal slowly began to rise as one prospector after another sank shafts even within the city limits itself. One coal mine operated at 43rd and Kensington near the current Country Club Plaza and employed over a hundred men. Brush Creek Coal and Mining had a coal yard at 2nd and Wyandotte and offices in the Gibraltar building downtown.[7]

143

Other mine shafts cropped up around Kansas City, one in Rosedale, a suburb of to the southwest where "working beds of good coal eight feet in thickness within two miles of Kansas City" were found in the Rosedale coal vein. A shaft was sunk to a depth of 345 feet to find the eight-foot vein. Gas was also found at this site.[8] Still another coal mine flourished for a time on Indiana Avenue known as the Cedar Springs coal mine. This was active from the 1880s onward.[9]

The Bolen Coal Company was one of the largest houses in the coal line in Kansas City, "one of the integral parts of a chain of corporations controlled by the Gould family."[10] Jay Gould, who headed first the Union Pacific and then the Missouri Pacific Railroads, was "a builder and organizer of systems and as a promoter of local resources along the lines he controlled." Gould realized that a railroad alone could not prosper without local business, and "pushed the development of resources and new industry along the line." Gould inspected his properties and sent agents to buy property, as he did for Rich Hill, Missouri, which would become a coal supplier for Kansas City. Gould built a series of railroad branches from Fort Scott, Kansas, to serve the mining operation at Rich Hill, across the state line.[11]

The main office of the Bolen Coal Company at the corner of 9th and Wyandotte streets (above the bluffs from the river), handled direct from the mines different well-known varieties of coal. They were each named for the mine of origin, would supply most of the local trade and could be shipped in large quantities all over the West. The list sounds parochial and romantic in terms of mine of origin, a reminder of how local the world of Kansas City once was that coal could be identified and requested in this manner.

Word of mouth must have played a part in one's choice of coal: Eureka, Ouita, Russelville, Denning, Coal Hill, Jenny Lind, McAlister, McAlister coke, Cherokee, Wier City, Pittsburg, Fleming, Yain, Inola, Oolagah, Lexington, Pasdus Lehigh, Labeled Farmers, Rich Hill, Panama, Foster, Worland, Richmond, Illinois, Iowa, Rock Spring, Wye, Colorado, Piedmont, Blossburg, Connellsville coke, Pennsylvania, Lehigh Valley Anthracite, Lackawana, and Connell. Coal varied in size, weight and sulfur content and could be sorted by that criteria and/or by originating mine. A coal yard nearby would have coal piles of those varieties and sell them directly to the customer.[12]

The list of coal varieties above testifies to the many different railroads going to the many different coal mines to bring back an array of coal for the growing industry of Kansas City. Some coal in that list, specifically, Connellsville coke, Pennsylvania, and Lehigh Valley Anthracite were imported from Pennsylvania. Both the coke and the anthracite would supplement the bituminous production of coal in Missouri, which produced small amounts of coke and no anthracite, a coal local to Pennsylvania.

Size mattered in coal. Each had a different market and user. Three main sizes were usually separated at the mine and loaded into different cars and were available for domestic purposes: block coal meant a chunk larger than six inches (it would pass over a screen with a six-inch opening), lump, between three- and six-inches, and nut coal between two- and three-inches. Slack coal or screenings, one-half-inch or smaller in size, eventually found a market feeding steam-raising plants.[13]

Chapter 16

The Production of Coal on a Human Scale

The underground world of the coal miner in these early days of mining is revealed.

Even though trains charged in and out of Kansas City on a daily basis and passengers scrambled on and off in the new West Bottoms Union depot, the scramble for fuel took place underground hidden from view to arrive in wagons and eventually in rail cars. Discovering, mining, producing and transporting coal created a patchwork industry that was both local and national.

Miners and Their Trade: So Degraded and Abject a Condition

First keelboat men, then wood hawks and now coal miners as well as oil men toiled at creating motive power in overlapping efforts in the 19th century. Unlike keelboat men whose every muscular effort moved their boats upstream, or wood hawks who saw the steamboats burn the wood they chopped and sold, coal miners did not see the end result of their work.

They belonged to another world underground taking part in an intricate concert of cooperative digging and hauling large chunks of coal out of the dark reaches of tunnels. These chunks saw daylight before the miners did, were sorted and loaded on wagons or railway cars and disappeared toward the growing cities of the young republic.

As early as the 1860s coal miners knew their lot was a hard one and wished for some way to improve their work. One of them wrote the *Industrial Advocate,* a pro-miner Missouri publication, early in 1867: "Politicians may grow eloquent, armies may be raised to fight, and philanthropists may wail over the poor 'Africans,' but let me tell you, and through you the whole world, that never were the negroes in slavery in so degraded and abject a condition as the miners here are, and for a long time have been."[1]

A miner's day began by being lowered in a cage with up to ten other miners into a deep shaft or by walking the distance of perhaps a mile into a slope mine to get to his room, an underground cavern leading off a more central hallway and mined by an individual miner.[2] As an independent contractor or "tonnage man" the miner was assigned a room perhaps 30 feet by 150 feet from which to extract coal. His room was linked with many others below ground in a rabbit warren of organized mining activity threaded together by rails to move the coal to the surface.

The miner's first task was to pick up the chunks of coal left from the blasting done the night before. Every afternoon before he left his room, the miner had bored holes in the coal face with his own auger, packed it with explosives he himself had bought and mixed, then set the charge and fixed the fuse with dirt to deflect the force of the blow backward toward the coal wall. The miner did not fire the shots himself. He had the fuses inspected by the "shot firer" who lit the fuses set by all the miners at noon and after they had left for the day.

Before cleaning up the coal, rock and dirt from the previous day's blast, the miner stopped to test the roof of his room with his pick head to hear if the ceiling sounded solid. If it did, he stopped to take a look at the timbers supporting the walls and entryway to see if they had been weakened or dislodged by the latest blast. In the dim light available only from his own oil lamp fastened to his helmet, and sometimes with a hand-held lantern for added light, he made the inspection of his room on which his life depended. If all stood firmly, if no water had accumulated that needed to be bailed out, he set to work; if not, he had repair work to do, timbering, supporting, building a "pack wall" with stone and dirt both for support and for disposal of debris.[3]

If the miner had an apprentice with him, a son, a nephew or neighbor boy, he set him to work cleaning up, building the pack wall or bailing water while he lifted the large chunks into the cart. The miner determined the size of the chunks by the depth, width and angle of the undercut and by the number of explosives used to chisel them out.[4] Loading the cart well, he had learned, meant the difference in better pay at the end of the day. The art of loading he himself had learned at his father's or uncle's side, for he received no instruction booklet on coal mining before he entered.

Large chunks he loaded up front and on the corners of the cart to stabilize it, filling in with smaller pieces in the middle. He may have already measured the height his load could take by riding the empty car back to his room with has elbow resting on the edge of the cart and hand raised upward. When his fingers brushed the roof of the tunnel he knew exactly how high he could load his cart and still get it through the passageway.[5]

It would not do for coal to fall off the cart. That meant loss of hard-dug profit, a tangle of carts in the passageway, a pileup, delay of other miners' work. The cart ran on narrow-gauge rails laid down from the mine entry or elevator cage down the main tunnel. From there the rails spread out to each of the rooms where miners labored in sometimes elaborate layouts of many rooms and haulage ways covering several acres underground. The miner and his young apprentice pushed the cart, weighing as much as two tons to the entrance of their room where, if the passageway were tall enough, a mule driver attached the cart to the train and pulled it along with others to the shaft entrance. There the cart was hauled up by winches pulled by horses above ground, by steam engine or eventually by electric motor.[6]

The miner and his apprentice, having cleaned up after the last blast and having loaded and sent out the first cart of the day, set to work to make an undercut on the coal face for the next blast. The miner began to chip away at the bottom of the seam next to the floor. He used his pick, the primary coal-mining tool, to dislodge gravel and dirt from the edge of the coal face while the apprentice swept up.

The miner picked away on his knees or by squatting until the undercut got deep enough that he had to lie on his side to continue to deepen the cut, approximately three to four feet into the face of the coal seam. The deeper the cut, the bigger the chunks of coal would fall with the next blasting. Some men developed an ambidextrous approach to the undercut work and could pick with their right hand to the end of the wall and then turn over and pick with their left hand all the way back.[7] Of course, the miner faced the danger of his coal face collapsing on him as he dug deeper into the undercut.

This primitive form of mining required muscle, vigilance and concentration. The miner and his apprentice usually stayed below for lunch and resumed their labor, picking, loading, picking and loading. With each load the miner placed a metal disk on a hook on the cart's side with his number on it so that on the surface, in the light of day, the "weigh boss" would credit his account. The miner was paid by his production, which varied by the quality and kind of coal, the absence of slate or dirt, the amount of coal available in the seam, the speed at which the miner was given an empty cart and other variables.

Each day the miner set a couple of charges to loosen the face of the wall. Each time the shot examiner or in some cases the shot firer inspected the shot before lighting it while everyone stepped out of the room, then, if all went well, returned to clean up the latest chunks. Later, as electricity infiltrated the mines, the shot firer used it to ignite the charge.[8]

Company men or "day men" supported the miners in their work. They spent their days timbering the roofs, checking for gas, greasing the wheels of the carts, driving the mules, laying track on the mine floors, directing traffic underground, minding the ventilation shafts and returning empty carts to be refilled. All these simple skills the daymen learned by the "helper system" of apprenticeship where many older boys got their training before taking over a coal room of their own. Since this miner had an apprentice to help him on a daily basis, he got an extra "turn" or cart per day to fill though, depending on the age of the youngster, the miner may have had to work twice as hard to fill the cart until the child became old enough and strong enough to relieve the miner from some of the heavy work of loading chunks of coal to best advantage in the cart.

Though the miner worked as an independent contractor, he was at the mercy of the mine operator in many ways. In an intricate balance between tonnage and fairness, the miner and mine operator worked for each other. The operator provided the miner with carts and other services, but not at such a pace that the miner could wrap up his two- or three-ton day by two o'clock and leave. The operator, as a company man himself, needed to oversee the other company men for their full day's work, so the operator sometimes slowed the return of empty carts to keep the miner there all day every day the mine was open.

As cutting machines were introduced at the turn of the 20th century, production increased. The machine operator and assistant moved from room to room undercutting with two large jacks for which they were responsible to keep in good working order. This was a new and expensive piece of equipment that changed the rhythm and skill set of the miners. The machine cutter was expected to be available and operate the machine every day to increase production. He had less knowledge of the coal face than the tonnage miner and concentrated more on operating his machinery. [9]

Lighting was always a problem. Before electric lights were installed, dim light offered the miners their only chance to make out the coal seam and assess its direction, to check on the timbers, and to avoid tripping over obstacles. Before electricity men wore a variety of oil lamps attached to their helmets. The typical oil lamp looked something like a coffee pot with a spout from which protruded a wick that the miner lit. The miner filled and lit it each morning and worked until it became too feeble to give any more light. This lamp dripped a little with the miner's movement, and by the end of the day, his skin glistened with a mix of coal dust and oil that required real devotion to remove.[10]

It would be wrong to assume that the haulage ways were level and men could stand upright in them. When they were, a mule could haul the carts out; otherwise, the miners and daymen pushed the carts out themselves. Nor did coal seams lie in accessible and continuous outlines. "The beds roll and pitch to such a degree that the average haulage ways in the mines resemble in plan and profile a roller coaster speedway," observed one engineer.[11]

One of the problems with coal from a consumer's standpoint was dependable supply. Mines dried up; accidents closed them down; weather became uncooperative; markets changed. At best mining did not keep everyone busy fifty-two weeks a year.[12] While the coal and the conditions to mine it lasted, miners worked hard. The average mine lasted perhaps ten years, occasionally twenty, often much less, hence the necessity of "coal camps" that were built to service a particular seam while it lasted, perhaps as little as two to three years before the whole community picked up and moved to the next seam. On the other end of the production process, miners were frustrated by lack of railroad cars that came only two or three days a week to carry away the fruits of their labor. This slowed the work and decreased the wages.[13]

Another problem was the ever-present danger of injury, collapse, even asphyxiation. Even going down and coming up the shaft presented dangers. At the beginning and end of the day, a conscientious mine operator would not carry two family members in the same elevator in case it capsized or the cable broke.

Danger, darkness, toil, uneven wages, primitive living conditions, but men would sooner mine coal than to start into manufacturing as an unskilled laborer or be a farmhand at half the wages. One miner turned poet wrote about the ways in which he had seen boys and men die in coal mines "All for Coal." They were overcome by deadly gas, blown up by a delayed fuse, dragged between the coal car and the rock wall, crushed by a rock fall, drowned in a cave in, killed by fire.

CHAPTER 17

Give Us Light!

An all new electric light industry is illuminated.

Is there a happier marriage between fuel and its offspring than between these two forces of fuel and energy? The great goal of illumination by some means other than oil or gas had been reached. Electric light did nothing less than achieve new heights for civilization, as some thought at the time, an idea that would become abundantly true in the years to come.

Electricity had not only been put to work for transportation, but also for lighting the night. The centuries-long process of understanding, refining and learning to control this magic medium had finally paid off. Factories could be lit at night and so could the streets. One enthusiastic mayor extolled the arrival of electricity as a panacea for everyone:

"Give us the opportunity of attaining the highest civilization we can enjoy, give us sound and healthy bodies, give us no more darkness, but give us light! More light! Give us the electric light! It is the poor as well as the rich man's light! It will light the suburbs, as well as the central portions of your city. It is in fact the light for all."[1]

In 1885, electric light was still a marvel, a bit of wizardry hanging from a pole and brightening the night. The eloquence of this speech suggests both the hyperbole of the 19th century and the esteem in which electricity was held as a solution to the dark, to ill health, even to class differences. The speech was titled "The Superiority of Electricity over other Illuminants for Public Lighting," and was made at the newly formed National Electric Light Association at the first annual convention in Baltimore in 1885. The association was small, perhaps thirty to fifty men assembled from cities along the East Coast and as far west as Kansas City, plus representatives of a few businesses providing their own lighting systems, but the conversation was enthusiastic, urgent and probing to understand the phenomenon these men were now responsible for delivering.[2]

Electric lighting was new; the arc light had made its debut in 1879; but, by 1885 every city of any size had arc lights blazing against the sky at night.[3] City and industrial representatives in charge of establishing or growing electric lighting systems formed the association to exhort their fellows and to solve the challenges of electric lighting powered by coal. The membership gathered "electricians," a new term with somewhat undefined connotations to discuss and educate each other on efficiencies and profitability.

Electricity had been made possible by the use of coal as fuel. The one thing that coal could do that wood simply did not do was to generate electric light. It may be that wood was occasionally thrown into a furnace in a stop-gap move to keep the boilers going, but coal gave light. The process with coal as fuel sounds like a child's nursery tale: Coal heated metal that could be shaped into steam engines that burned coal that heated water that turned to steam that turned a dynamo that gave off electric current that caused the sparks to arc between two carbon rods that lit up the sky more than 150 times greater than the gas lamp then in use.[4] This combination of electro-mechanical processes was not attainable with wood. Where once gaslight had lit homes, coal, through this process, now gave brilliant light at night.[5]

Coal and electricity lit the cities of the world in a way that no amount of wood burning had ever done. Coal gave speed to ships, trains and steamboats; it gave power to standing steam engines to mass produce goods; it would power streetcars, but perhaps the most exquisite service coal would perform in this era would be to create electric light.[6] To compare a lump of coal to a burning electric light was to be confounded by the miraculous process of turning fuel into remote light. Nothing like it in the world had ever been seen. To eyes already accustomed to gaslight, electric light made by arc lights was thrilling, blinding, freeing to some, threatening to others. Mayor Hodges of Baltimore in a speech to the association noted: "Electric light is a nocturnal joy to an honest man, but a scarecrow to a thief."[7] Intense enough to be seen from a distance, night time skylines lit by electric arc lamps filled viewers' hearts with wonder:

A Port Huron, Michigan, paper of December 31, 1884, said of Detroit:

This city by night has been for some months the amazement of travelers approaching by boat or cars. The steward of a lake steamer said to me the other day, 'Whatever hour of the night, whenever we approach Detroit, I always call up the passengers to look at the electric lights, and they all considered the view a glorious one. Approaching on the railroad, the view is equally enchanting. It seems like a glimpse within the walls of Paradise to see the multitude of dazzling lights, flashing in the distance.[8]

The Arc Lamp

This light source briefly dominated outdoor night lighting before the incandescent bulb was perfected. It shone brilliantly at five-hundred watts but needed its carbons replaced on a daily basis.

Arc lights seemed like magic because they offered light a step removed from the burning fuel that created them. This step would become the first of many steps away from the fire that creates our heat and light. It is a wonder of modern systems delivery that we live nowhere near the fire that provides these miracles.

Instead of a torch or a gas flame for light, electricity allowed the coal furnace to hide in the background, heating the steam, making the belts whirl and generating light in the street. Coal would do the same for the electric trolley. Without flame present at the point of transportation, coal-driven engines via cable or overhead lines would soon pull the trolley along the street.

Arc lights glorified the night by 1879. They were a combination of the dynamo, acting as the generator, established by 1867, and the hard graphite carbon tips necessary to create the arc of electricity in the lamp itself.[9] This technology emerged as two systems, one known as arc lighting and the other as incandescent lighting. The dynamo generated electricity and was often set up in a separate building dedicated to the dynamo and the coal that fed it. Wiring carried the current to the arc lamp. To create the light electric current ran between the two carbons when turned on at the dynamo, then, as soon as the current heated them, the points slightly separated. The air between the heated tips became a conductor and the electricity leaped in the form of an arc or curve between the tips creating the bright light.

Arc lights came in 500 to 3000 candlepower creating light too bright for interior use.[10] If the current were diminished in any way, the mechanism that controlled the distance between the carbon tips, either a clockwork or a gravity-driven mechanism, adjusted the distance and the light burned steadily. The drawback to arc lights was that the carbon had to be changed daily. The carbon tips burned well for a few short hours and then died. The incandescent bulb that would replace it burned entirely without oxygen and would last several days.[11]

Lighting with gaslight was well established before electric light appeared. By 1870, some three-hundred-ninety establishments produced manufactured gas from coal in the entire United States, employed over 8,700 workers with a total value of products at $32,048,850. Over $70 million dollars in capital supported the trade. Between 1850 and 1870 the industry had grown from 30 establishments in 1850 to 390 twenty years later. Gas lighting was at its height when electric lighting shouldered its way in during the 1880s.[12]

Like most cities, Kansas City still functioned largely in the Wood Age in the 1870s. Fewer than 2,000 customers used gas lighting in a city of 55,000 and the "patient mule furnished the sole motive power for the few street railways connecting downtown districts."[13] At the end of that decade, power was confined to milling and packing houses that used steam engines. People still found mechanical power itself a wonderful thing. Electricity would be another of God's gifts to His people. "Electricity is one of God's motive powers that are given to us to handle for the good of God's creatures," said the mayor of Chicago in 1885.[14]

By 1879, Thomas Edison had worked through the filament problem to create what we now call the electric light bulb and had developed a system to power it. The dynamo he invented was called a "Jumbo" because it dwarfed both size and stability of the previous models. Its efficiency was also superior. It could produce a kilowatt hour of electricity with as little as ten pounds of coal. Arc light dynamos of that era burned as much as 30 pounds of coal for the same production.[15] Members at the second semi-annual meeting in Detroit, August 31st and September 1st of the National Electric Light Association in 1886 would be reminded that in that year of 1879 "there was not in existence in the whole world a central station for electric lighting."[16] Progress by the mid-1880s produced arc lighting in most cities and incandescent in a very few.

151

Fueling Change

An amusing anecdote shows Edison, the creator, very much involved with his craft at a time when electricity was still a very local event. While attending the opening of the play "Iolanthe" in the Bijou Theater in Boston one evening in 1882, Edison was dismayed along with others in the audience to see the lights dim and flicker. But *he* could do something about it. Dressed in top hat and tails, Edison left the theater to help shovel coal "back at the powerhouse." Whether in the back shed or a block away, the amount of coal burning in the furnace had a direct effect on the quality of light, and Edison did what he had to do. The show had to go on![17]

Gas lighting, now a customary form of indoor light by the 1880s, held danger for its users in a number of ways, asphyxiation, explosion, structural fires, and personal injury, but the century had been filled with experimental lighting and the public gave gaslight a respectful acceptance. City officials across the country had given gas lighting companies licenses to operate to provide indoor as well as street lighting for their citizens. Small improvements in burner design, gas pressure and composition of gas and lower prices encouraged loyalty by its city users, but gas lighting really stood little chance of survival as electric lighting became available on the market.[18] Still, progress with electric lighting was slow.

By 1879, only three electric light and power systems showed up in the 1880 United States Census.[19] One year later, gas companies had invested a $150 million in municipal lighting with more than 500 companies participating in furnishing both street and indoor lighting. Arc lamps had taken about 10% of the outdoor lighting market by then; the incandescent light market threatened to take over the rest.[20]

Tireless experimentation in electricity over the course of the 19th century had finally produced workable products. While gas lighting companies experimented with burner improvements, electric light enthusiasts experimented with the electromagnetic field and dynamos. Gas companies worked with end-use improvements typical of a mature commercially dominant industry while the other light source worked to refine the delivery of the electricity itself. The early commercial activity typical of emerging technology. Early manufactured-gas experimentation had taken place from 1816 onward when the first system was installed in Baltimore. Wooden pipes were replaced with cast iron by the 1820s. Better burners, fixtures and the development of meters improved delivery in the early decades of the utility. Decisions had already been made in terms of fuel, distillation processes, technology and distribution.[21]

Looking back from a century and a quarter later it is difficult for us to imagine the meager beginnings of the electrical industries and the painstaking incremental improvements that made the entire industry blossom in the 1880s. In 1879 the telegraph held first place in this country as the premier electrical wonder, according to the 1880 census. Seventy-seven "establishments" or companies of telegraph works produced that wonder in the United States that year, employing almost 15,000 workers and bringing in $93,602,922 in revenue.[22]

Telephone systems were more numerous with 148 different companies employing 3,338 workers and capitalized at $15,772,135. Even more numerous were 221 electroplating shops doing contract work, employing 1,441 workers and with capital of $865,890.

The production of telephone and telegraph apparatus kept 40 shops busy and employed 893 with capital of $38,458. Production of other electrical apparatus and supplies kept 36 shops busy and employed 378 workers with capital of $873,300. Electrotyping and stereotyping outside of printing establishments kept 45 shops busy with capital of $536,000 and employed 642. These were encouraging signs of new industries birthing at the end of the 19th century.

At the very bottom of the list in 1879, three companies offered electric light and power systems--nationally, employed 229 workers and had capital of $425,000. The combined value of all the electrical products and services in 1879 amounted to $25,608,529.[23] As robust as this effort sounds, these were national figures sprinkled across a nation struggling to embrace the power of the new fuel-driven technologies.

Electric light came of age in the 1880s. Other electric technology had already made their debut. Telegraphy had been well established since the late 1840s; electro-plating had been around since early chemical batteries in the 1830s.[24] A series of improvements in arc lights and dynamos would create a viable industry by the early 1880s, hence the establishment of the National Electric Light Association by 1885. Enough cities then had electric light systems—between fifteen and twenty--to warrant an established professional discussion. Other electrical entrepreneurs were drawn to the prospect of working with the new medium. Since dynamos stood alone to generate electricity in the early years before Edison created his system with electric lights, a factory, for instance, could have its own lights managed on site. "Mill men," as opposed to municipal lighting representatives, among other entrepreneurs, attended the conferences. Early in the life of the association, members held a long discussion about associate members. A man could join and become an associate member who might be generating light for a few hundred lights.[25]

In other words, anyone with a little capital, a dynamo, a coal supply and a willing customer could produce electric light.[26] Before Edison's system infiltrated city streets, store, hotel and mill owners installed their own systems for arc lighting on their own properties.[27] The incentives to develop a new and better light source were enormous. Both entrepreneur and capitalist stood ready to reap the possible rewards of fame and financial remuneration.[28]

In Kansas City in the 1880s, electric lights started within stores and other buildings before going outside, while gas companies monopolized the street lighting business.[29] Nationally, the gas industry saw itself as the illumination system and defiantly hung on to that service while facing increasing threat from kerosene lighting and the incandescent electric light. Gas companies would eventually be forced to change their methods, market, technology and production, but not without a fight.

Arthur Bright, Jr., in his classic book, *The Electric Lamp Industry: Technological Change and Economic Development from 1800 to 1947* (1949) summarizes the tactics the gaslight companies used that have remained common. The gaslight companies belittled the advantages of electric lighting. They played up the dangers of electricity and attempted to dissuade city councils against adopting it. The two franchises battled it out in newspapers and brochures while trying to influence standards in their favor established by the insurance companies.[30]

153

In spite of such defensive measures nationwide, electric light came to Kansas City, March 23, 1881, with a three-hour display between 6th and 8th on Main. The event was highly anticipated, and crowds arrived to see it. The newspaper quoted one awe-struck bystander's words: "You just pull a lever and there's your light."[31] None of the business of making light by other means was required.

G. Y. Smith, operator of a hardware store at 712-16 Main Street, had financed this electrical demonstration with Edison's arc lights, each of which had two-thousand candlepower. Two exterior lights hung over Main Street itself illuminating the crowd and the muddy ruts of the street.

On April 6, *The Star* announced Smith's "Grand opening …with the 'Electric Illumination' upstairs and down," so that throngs of shoppers could shop…and buy…by electric light. The arc lights had been designed by Edison with magneto and carbon tip. They produced about eight hours of constant light powered by a Brush dynamo located in a large building 22 x 32 feet one block to the west. *The Kansas City Star* the following day harshly described gas light by comparison: ". . . such gas lights as were to be seen, looked yellow, ghastly and ashamed of themselves."[32] The truth about arc lights was that they were white light, bright to the point of blinding and caste black shadows by the contrast of lighted to unlighted areas.

Still, other Kansas City merchants followed suit. Louis Hammerslough, "the great clothier" announced in *The Star* on April 27, "A Combination of Wonders," bringing together their prideful inventory "brilliantly illuminated" every evening "with the wonderful electric light."

Shortly after this event, financiers contracted to begin electric lighting for the city. Kansas City became one of the first cities in the country to develop electric lighting with the organization of the Kawsmouth Electric Light Company in February of 1882. The company was licensed by the American Electric Light Company of Connecticut that held the patents of Elihu Thomson and Edwin Houston whose system it would use.[33] The first powerhouse for the dynamos was built at Eighth and Santa Fe Streets in the West Bottoms. It soon supplied the Quality Hill residents, the old Union Station and the Union Avenue district with arc lights used indoors mostly for business houses.[34] Edwin R. Weeks was made superintendent in 1882 and remained so, representing his company and city with dignity and expertise at national electric lighting conferences until his retirement in 1900.[35]

Going to Strangle Gas

In the minds of electricians, gaslight belonged to the same era as oil and candles and needed to be replaced as soon as practicable.[36] From the 1870s onward different fuels, their dedicated technologies, their devoted supporters and eager publics vied for position. "Now incandescent lighting has reached that point of development where in many places, it has been able to compete with gas and with arc lighting," said one representative at the semi-annual National Electric Light Association at the Union Square Hotel in New York in August of 1885. We have an infant seven years old, that, I think, is going to strangle gas with one hand and petroleum with the other. That infant is a robust one. He is today competing with a very well-developed man. He is competing with arc lighting. He is also competing with gaslight and is he to stop his growth in his seventh year?"[37] This rhetorical question could only hint at the growth to come. Meanwhile, kerosene had already become a popular illuminant in the 1870s and a fall-back fuel for the vagaries of gas or electrical lighting. The lighting of Kansas City had become a many-splendored thing.

In Kansas City, competition sometimes took on almost comical appearances. The means for transmission for telegraph, telephone, gaslight, arc lighting, incandescent lighting and trolley lines all collided in the streets of the growing city. Several electric companies (there were five altogether) and two gas companies further muddied the scene. The positioning of poles along the city streets posed a problem. The Kansas City Electric Company had received from the city permission to "enter upon any street, avenue, lane or alley of the city, erect poles or lay down pipes."

Ultimate Light Pole

This photo shows the **complexity of lines carried by the average light pole** in the early years of electrical production. Notice the one line swooping down in the left foreground as a result of an ice storm.

155

Were telegraph poles also to be added? What about the other companies? If every company were to install poles, what then? One Saturday night in 1891 the American Electric Light Company (AELC) put up a line of sixty-foot poles in the West Bottoms on one side of Santa Fe between 12th Street and the Union Pacific tracks working under cover of darkness to avoid a confrontation. This act compromised the lines of the Kansas City Electric Company (KCEL) creating dangerous interference. The problem was solved when KCEL employees cut down the poles of the AELC on Monday morning!

Four Kansas City Electric Companies

Their different offerings indicate various levels of development.

In 1896, a similar competitive moment between the United Electric Light Company and the Consolidated Electric Light and Power Company in Kansas clashed in the West Bottoms and each company cut down and removed the other's poles during the night.[38] Imagine the numbers of men required to cut down sixty-foot poles and remove them, probably by kerosene lamps, without electrocuting anyone. The poles were loaded on horse-drawn wagons and pulled down rutted, muddy streets and unloaded somewhere else--nefarious deeds stealthily carried out for market share. These hijinks were committed more than once in Kansas City before the squabbling was settled between gas and electricity.

Rate wars and crossover marketing between gas and electricity worked well for customers but could be ruinous to the companies themselves. The two gas companies participated in a rate war in 1897 that dropped their price of artificial gas to fifty cents per

KANSAS CITY ELECTRIC LIGHT CO. . .

Licensee Thomson-Houston Electric Co.

★ ★ ★ ★

NATIONAL BANK OF KANSAS CITY BUILDING.
KANSAS CITY, MO.

★ ★ ★ ★

Electric Light and Power Service in Kansas City, Mo., and Kansas City, Kas.

EDISON ELECTRIC LIGHT & POWER CO.

Licensee Edison Electric Light Co.

★ ★ ★ ★

NATIONAL BANK OF KANSAS CITY BUILDING.
KANSAS CITY, MO.

★ ★ ★ ★

Incandescent Light and Power Service.

SPERRY ASSOCIATE ELECTRIC CO. . .

Licensee Westinghouse Electric Co.

★ ★ ★ ★

NATIONAL BANK OF KANSAS CITY BUILDING.
KANSAS CITY, MO.

★ ★ ★ ★

Incandescent Light and Power Service.

AMERICAN ELECTRIC LIGHT CO. of Kansas City.

Licensee Ft. Wayne Electric Co.

★ ★ ★ ★

GIBRALTAR BUILDING.
KANSAS CITY, MO.

★ ★ ★ ★

Arc and Incandescent Lighting.

156

thousand feet from an original $2.50. The electric companies reduced the rate on arc lights to one dollar per month per lamp. The gas companies also began to offer electric service as a means of joining the competition.

Then, even some electric companies began to offer gas service before things were ultimately sorted out in the 1900s![39]

This **early electric substation** shows the primitive technology then available.
Wood sufficed as infrastructure until more sophisticated materials could evolve. Notice the horses in the lower right as an indicator of scale. Most remarkable in this picture is the absence of flame. The coal furnace turning dynamos to create electricity to send to the substation appears to be housed in the shed in the background.

The gas companies also used the media to form negative impressions of the new electrical technology. A few small gas companies formed a syndicate and hired someone to represent them against the competition. "Whenever they see any little paragraph which is detrimental to the electric light, they have it printed and published in all of their local papers and paid for by the gas syndicate as an advertisement." The speaker—again at the National Electric Light Association--went on to suggest that the electric industry ought to publish the many tragedies of explosions and asphyxiations caused by gas. "Why, we could make a Bibleful of these things; they are everyday occurrences."[40]

Kansas City Gas, Light and Coke Company Gas Holder, 1895

The national companies also fought for position. Mergers and acquisitions were a way to beat the competition. *The Electro-Mechanic* editor in the Kansas City-based publication complained in 1889 about the state of industrial mergers: "At this rate, between the two great cannibals Westinghouse and Thomson-Houston, not to speak of the more fastidious but still capacious-mawed Edison, there won't be many independent manufacturing electric light companies left by next Christmas."[41]

By 1885, in spite of early growing pains, the original Kawsmouth Electric Company in Kansas City increased its customer base to serve businesses and residences along Union Avenue, Main, Walnut and Grand Streets from Third to Fifteenth Street.[42] Even at the time of the cable car's origin (1885) Kansas Citian John C. Henry started his experiments with an overhead electric trolley that would in the next few years become the dominant form of local transportation. It also required its own dynamo station.[43]

The Kawsmouth Electric Light Company incorporated in Kansas in 1881 and by 1882, the company had been reorganized as the Kansas City Electric Light Company with capital of $20,000. The plant had four small dynamos with a capacity of ten lamps each and an improvement that allowed lights to be turned on and off on the circuit without hand adjustment at the plant each time, a considerable improvement. By 1883 the capitalization had increased to $100,000 and Edwin Weeks oversaw every improvement. Larger dynamos and Corliss engines increased the station capacity to three hundred arc lamps, all used for business houses and stores.[44]

Kansas City Gas, Light and Coke Company Gas Holder, 1895

Note two people in foreground indicate the scale of the installation as manufactured gas arrived In quantity to Kansas City

We Must Watch Our Coal Pile

The ratio of coal to candlepower began to be explored as electricity expanded its reach. Greater quantities required greater savings. Edwin Weeks, Kansas City's pioneer electrician, was a fastidious manager and particularly adept at watching the ratio of coal to output. "In regard to the cost of coal, and the steam part of the plant, I think that is a matter of great importance. It comes right home to every one of us. That is where the solution must be made in regard to the commercial success of electric lighting. We must watch our coal pile." Weeks went on to detail the intricacies of setting boilers, keeping records, lighting lamps and keeping them going. This was an industry in its infancy.[45]

At another point at the same meeting Weeks urged the members not to work their engineers and firemen on "too long a watch." They needed to be vigilant in their attention to the coal fire: "Basing our calculations upon a good mixture of slack and nut coal for a 200-arc plant, at an average distance from the fuel supply, the cost of the power department should not be far from 32% of the whole operating expense."[46] Over time, best practices would become standard in the trade, but in the early years, individual watchfulness provided the data.

In New York in August of 1885, at the meeting of the Electric Light Association, Weeks again approached the coal question educating his cohorts on the distance between grate and fire and the amount of coal to be burned on the grate surface "depends on the amount of grate and draft." He noted that companies "in no less enlightened a portion of the country than New England" operated by "very intelligent men" were burning six pounds of coal every hour. That he found to be "simply ridiculous." Boilers and pipes also had to be considered. The Westinghouse engine "takes more steam than any other engine in Christendom," Weeks announced and the boilers in question were set 20 inches from the bars. "I think if he (the questioner) will raise his boilers about a foot and a half or very near that," he offered, "that he will find that he will make a great saving in coal."[47]

Another observation of Weeks was the pipefittings. "In regard to size of pipe, many put in too small steam pipes and insufficient heaters to create heat. Proper size steam pipes, setting of the boiler, settings of the grate, the draft, size, kind, and price of coal, and many other details had to be worked out during this period." [48]

One of the disadvantages of gaslight for street lighting was the manual turning on and off of each light every night and morning. Men were hired to do that city block by city block twice a day. The refrain from the song "The Old Lamp Lighter" gives the picture:

> Now if you look up in the sky,
> You'll understand the reason why
> The little stars at night are all aglow,
> He turns them on when night is here,
> He turns them off when dawn is near,
> The little man we loved so long ago.

One of the electric-light practitioners at the association conference in Baltimore in 1885 compared that practice to electricity: "Today a hundred men are required to light and extinguish the gas burners in the city of Chicago, at a great expense. The entire city of Elgin is illuminated in an instant, by simply turning a switch at no expense or loss of time, and Chicago, with its 600,000 citizens might be lighted in the same manner."[49]

Gas companies and electric companies rankled each other with petty arguments until December 1885, when the gas works exploded in Kansas City and inhabitants were plunged into darkness except for those portions lighted by electricity.[50] Mr. Weeks was quick to suggest the benefits of electricity while the gas company built a new fire-proof building for itself. The Kansas City Electric Light Company, of which Weeks was manager, installed a 25-lamp circuit for outdoor use, the first-time electric light was used for public lighting in the city.[51] The city population at the time was around 125,000, having grown from 55,000 five years before.[52]

By 1886, two incandescent light plants were put into service. They had 150-light capacity of sixteen-candle-power lights and required no hand regulation at the plant when individual lights were turned on and off. The company soon realized, however, that without meters they were losing about a third of their output. The company adopted the Edison meter the following year increasing revenue by 25%. Company officials soon realized that the Edison system was superior and formed still another company, the Edison Electric Light and Power Company in 1886 with capital of $100,000 with Edwin R. Weeks again as general manager. This plant had continuous current of 220 volts (110 on each side) using the Edison three-wire system. It served a district about a half-mile square with an initial load of about 2,600 incandescent lamps, all at sixteen candlepower.[53]

The gas interests realized by 1890 that electricity was a serious threat to the gas lighting business. They built a new electric powerhouse with the Brush system of arc lighting using Corliss engines and "all improvements known to science." The company was soon bought up and consolidated with other small electric companies into the Kansas City Electric Light Company. Inducements to light with gas and cook with gas were offered customers including fixtures and gas stoves. Despite the financial panic of 1893, the twin industries grew. They extended their lines five miles into the suburbs, introduced alternating current, powered a scattering of elevators and introduced incandescent lighting to several residential districts.[54]

Nationally, the brilliant, mesmerizing arc light hit its highest peak of use between 1880 and 1893.[55] Ten companies produced arc-lighting fixtures across the country. Edison's first company to produce fixtures, the Edison Lamp Company, established production in 1880, followed by such companies as the United States Electric Lighting Company, the Consolidated Electric Light Company and the Swan Lamp Manufacturing Company, all established between 1881 and 1883.[56] They produced arc lamps, switches, wiring and dynamo systems. They sold the ability to make light. Once installed in cities, the owners of these systems contracted through franchise with the city for street lights to be turned on at sunset and turned off at eleven or twelve p.m. or at sunrise. "Calendar lighting" allowed them to avoid moonlit nights and to supply lighting on cloudy and overcast nights.[57]

The Coates House

American and European Plan

Interstate Hotel Co., Props.

Edison's followers formed an association in 1880 as the incandescent light begin to flourish and met for their ninth convention in Kansas City. The event was held at the Coates House on February 15, 1889. John Peak, a city official, welcomed the visitors, "Gentlemen, we may not welcome you to a city filled with beautiful parks and handsome thoroughfares, but we point to our network of electric wires, our great cable system, to the marvelous growth of the city as an example of western energy." In 19th century style he continued, "Edison is not unknown here, and if he lives for fifty years more and keeps on inventing, we may expect to see aerial ships sailing through the air to Mars and other planets, and the moon used, like the Samoan Islands, as a coaling station, upon the heavenly voyage."[58] His was evidently a coal-fired vision.

161

A further treat for the convention attendees was to visit Edwin Weeks' residence to inspect the model electric light plant with which he lit his home. The *Electro-Mechanic* magazine reported that he used a "2016 c. p. light, Thomson dynamo run by Baxter motor by current taken from the arc circuit (from the street, a now illegal practice). All present expressed themselves as much pleased with their visit." The magazine also reported on one final touch of modernity during the event: The Missouri and Kansas Telephone Company put up a phone at the door of the convention room in the Coates House for the use of the members.[59]

The fears of the gas industry in the end were unfounded. So great was the demand for both light and power that the gas market grew from fewer than 2,000 customers in Kansas City to over 20,000 users. "It is a fact growing into general recognition," wrote one author, "that, while gas is losing its position as the leading illuminant, it will be the fuel of the future."[60] The future of electricity certainly seemed assured; the Kansas City Electric Light Company paid its shareholders dividends amounting to more than 200%.

By January 1, 1900, Kansas City generated enough current in isolated plants to operate no less than 1,000 incandescent lamps, 3,000 arc lamps, and 4300 horse power in motors, exclusive of street railways which were rapidly converting to all-electric systems. General manager Edwin Weeks had presided over that growth. He retired from it in 1900 when the company was purchased by Armour & Company of Chicago.[61] "One of these days," he said, "the best electric light is going to be formed by taking the best in all the systems and putting them together as one system. That time is coming."[62]

By 1901, the wages for electric light employees in Kansas City looked good: for a lineman they were $2.25 per day; trimmers of the lamps, which had to be done daily in the case of arc lamps, received $56.50 per month; dynamo men the same per month, assistant foremen $60 per month, the foreman $65 per month, and the line superintendent $75-per-month. Mr. Weeks earned $175 per month by 1896. The men worked 10-hours-a-day six-days-a-week. They also received double time for Sundays and holidays and time and a half for overtime. A union had been organized in 1891 and helped to create standard wages and hours.[63] Kansas City by then had a national reputation, due largely to Mr. Weeks' participation in various organizations that gave him one-on-one communication with representatives from other cities. The city was considered to have "the best electrical facilities of any city of its size in the country" in the late 1890s, according to the *Kansas City Star* in 1898.[64]

Kansas City enjoyed 100,000 incandescent lights, all at sixteen candle power, 3,000 arc lamps for outdoor and factory lighting, and 4,300 horsepower motors beyond those that operated the street railway by 1900. The city was on its way.[65]

Chapter 18

The Horse Leaves the Carriage

One of the primary catalysts of the Wood Age, the horse, is let out to pasture.

It was inevitable that the horse would leave the carriage and only a matter of time now that mechanization had entered the lives of city folk. The horse in the city became a foreign object, a shard of a retreating energy suite, one of the first to be realized but one of the last to go.

A Substitute for Human or Brute Labor

As with every other task in the 19th century, mechanization arrived to assist the miner in his trade. By the turn of the century a certain transformation had taken place below ground: "There is hardly a country in the world and hardly any department of mining in which electrical appliances are not employed, and in many instances the installation and equipment are of a most extensive character," wrote Thomas Commerford Martin, in "Electricity in Mining" in the special report, *Mining and Quarries* for the 1902 Census.[1]

The work would always be arduous and dangerous, but the new power of electricity, itself fed by coal, supported reaping its own fuel. The symbiotic relationship between coal and electricity found its way to the very mouth of the mine. In 1900, electricity still alternated between direct and alternating current. Water generated electricity for the first time and wires from waterfalls could span a distance of 25 miles to light a mine. "A great many mines and mining camps in regions where fuel was either very costly or difficult to obtain have been brought within the range of profitable working through the use of some distant waterpower."[2]

In the early stages of electricity, lighting was applied to mine work. Who needed light more than those who worked under ground and mined the coal that lit the homes of the nation? They, too, should benefit from their own labors. The lights that lit the corridors of the mines at 24 watts each were feeble by today's standards, but they were steady. Because of the intricacies of the mining landscape underground the cost of wiring all the hallways and rooms for electric light was prohibitive. Instead only the main corridors were wired for electric light leaving the rest of the minescape in the gloom of oil lamps or eventually lights operated by portable batteries. The average coal mine at the turn of the century worked with 227 horsepower for lights, motors and other uses.[3]

163

Beyond lights the next improvement allowed electric motors to replace horses, mules and humans as traction in the mines. Rails had been laid in the mines in America during the 19th century; at the beginning of the 20th century electric motors would do the work formerly done by "brute force." The haulage in the mines was originally by rope driving and by mules, a system nearly two miles long. With electricity a system of 5,600 volts of alternating current at the mine mouth generated current to a substation in the mine itself near the actual mining operation and about nine thousand feet from the power house.

Static transformers and a rotary converter generated 275 volts of direct current to the haulage circuits. The two-mile system with mules grew to a five-mile system with electricity.[4] The electric mine locomotive weighed about five tons with thirty-two-horsepower electric motors. The motor turned the driving wheels by a chain and cog or sprocket connection and hauled up to fifteen cars, each of which weighed one ton when empty and carried 2.35 tons of coal. The current was supplied by a trolley arm and the track rails were used as the return circuit. This motor was operated by a man seated on the machine. The cost of haulage by mule power was estimated at six-and-a-half cents per ton while the cost of electric haulage was at two-and-a-half cents, a savings that was eagerly accepted.[5]

Electricity provided another great improvement to mining--the cutting of the coal face itself. Instead of a pick, miners now used electric cutting machines, one of the largest classes of mining machinery employing electric current. A recent development, the number of coal mining machines in use in the United States in 1898 was 2,622, but by 1902, it had increased to 5,418. All of these were employed in bituminous mines.

Early Electric machines gave miners ability to extract coal faster than with hand methods. Note electric cord lower left.

In 1891, mining machines produced slightly less than 7% of the total production of bituminous coal. In 1902, they produced somewhat over 20%. The first machines were powered by compressed air operating like a jack hammer, but improvements created a chain form driven by electricity like a chain saw. In 1902, almost 60% of machines ran on compressed air while the other 42% were electric or chain machines.[6]

A machine could cut 50 tons of coal in an eight-hour shift. Since most of these machines were operated by two shifts of workers, the output of a machine working in a "thin vein" of perhaps 28-30 inches could cut up to 100 tons per day! The machines were about 100 horse power, which allowed for simultaneous operation of power for lights, pumping, ventilation, drilling and shot firing.

The cost of pick mining in rooms was ninety cents per ton, while the cost of machine mining in rooms was eleven cents with a cost of $.52 ½ for loading the coal after the machines left the room. This is a savings of $.26 ½ per ton of machine over pick miner, an appealing increase. Of course, operation and depreciation would leave a net savings of $.13 per ton, but four machines could produce at least 75,000 tons per year.[7] The cost of operating such a machine ranged from $1/10^{th}$ of 1% up to $.02 per ton depending on the hardness or softness of the coal and the skill of the operators.[8]

Other benefits of the machines included the very small amount of slack coal falling out of the cutting process, decreasing the loading and cleanup time. The speed at which the chain machine could cut the coal decreased from hours to minutes: Once the machine had been placed in position, it could make an undercut 44-inches wide, four-and-a-half-to-five inches high and six feet deep in five minutes. The cutting machine weighed about 3,000 pounds, was about 18- inches high and was operated by two men.

This turn-of-the-century electric coal cutter, though very primitive, markedly increased energy to increase production.

To set up the machine and make a cut that size took less than 10 minutes. One machine team cut 1,700 square feet in nine and a half hours, a record beyond a pick miner's wildest dreams. Many, many mines, of course, never used such undercutting machines and pick mining was the norm for decades to come, but the machines came into use soon after electricity became a force in the workplace. Most of the original machine mining took place in Pennsylvania and West Virginia at the turn of the century and worked their way west to Illinois and beyond.[9]

The power-generating plant was located at the mouth of the mine and coal from the mine kept the electricity going. At some mines, all of the machinery from tipple to mine opening was driven by electric motors, a trolley line with electric locomotives bringing the pit cars from the main entry to the tipple. Electric augers and shot firing completed the ensemble of coal mining supported by electricity. At this early stage with the mixed use of direct current and alternating current and distances from the power source making it remote, electricity was a miracle worker that needed to be handled with great respect.[10]

Competence in handling electricity in mine settings became just one more of many skill sets needed to operate a coal mine. Miners doing everything by pick and oil lamp could only be astonished by the arrival of the machinery and its electrical motive power. The miner's skills changed as he worked in concert with machines to greatly increase the coal production of the nation.

Demise of the Equine

Perhaps no transition shows the shift from wood to coal better than the phasing out of the horse from city streets. Through the many iterations of change from horse-drawn to motorized vehicles, city populations struggled to adapt, invent, expand and replace transportation systems to serve their fast-growing populations. By the 1870s the "urban horse" was differentiated in the census from the other horses in the country.[11] Their numbers increased with the need for city transportation. As city populations became dense, as factories gathered in the midst of population centers and increased the need for a way to handle numbers of people and piles of goods, something in the way of mass transportation became necessary.

Both transportation by steam engine and transportation by horse grew at the same time. Though steam propelled both steamboat and railroad engine, the technology had not yet been applied to vehicles that could move beyond river or rail. All other engines stood stationary in support of industrial processes. Until the point at which the changeover was complete, and the horse had been replaced by engine-driven transport, the horse would supply muscle as a vital link from Wood Age to Coal Age. It would then give way to the horseless cable car that would shortly be replaced by the electric car, two products of the Coal Age.[12]

As an agrarian animal, horses and their required services had always been built into the fabric of the farmer's life. He watered and fed the horse from materials close at hand; the manure he shoveled into a pile to be plowed into cropland. The city dweller of means kept a stable and hired stablemen to look after the horses. The poorer classes walked or hired "hacks." In the city, as horses began to be used in areas of concentrated population, their needs became somewhat problematic.

Horses were a product of natural ecosystems long since adapted to human use as a Wood Age energy force. In their final years as bearers of burdens and pullers of wagons, horses inhabited an increasingly mechanized, man-made environment that had less and less tolerance for their needs. Horses had to eat and drink as much as five times a day to keep up their strength. They each required from 16 to 47 pounds of hay and oats daily. Like the wagon-train drivers to Santa Fe before them, city drivers had to provide oats along the way for their horses.

The 1870s city offered numerous places at which a driver could stop to purchase a meal or two for his horses, though to stop meant the driver expended both time and money. Horses worked best with an ample supply of oats, their best fuel. Their droppings and urine were the resulting pollution. Horses defecated freely, roughly 16 pounds of manure to a thousand pounds of horse. [13] Add several gallons of urine to each horse's waste, and a city already operating on rudimentary services for its human population has a sanitation problem of sizable proportions. On the Santa Fe Trail horse waste posed no problem, but in the city, those who used horses as labor force were responsible for cleaning up after an urban horse population.

Manure was known as a profit center in some cities as farmers in the surrounding countryside adjacent to cities hauled in hay and grains for daily use and hauled out manure. This exchange set up a long series of efficiencies in hay growing, standardization of crops of hay, oats and other feed, baling, pricing and transportation to accommodate the growing urban horse population. The farmers frequently bred horses for the urban horse trade as well. They often contracted for the manure from stables and streets for their fields to grow more hay. Water for horses presented a need for water troughs or fountains though some teamsters carried water with them.

As a facility for horses, water troughs did not last long. First instigated after the Civil War, they were removed for public health reasons by 1910, leaving the remaining horses to be watered by carrying their own water or by the driver arranging for private service. A horse could feed from an oat bag or on hay thrown on the street, but the driver did not always address the task of manure removal. He had promises to keep and moved on, hence the cycle in which the farmer grew hay and oats to feed the horse and then picked up the subsequent byproduct to plow into the fields to produce more. [14]

In the first decades after the Civil War the 1860s and '70s mixed coal and wood, animal and machine in whatever form and quantities could be found. Business went on; the Coal Age encroached from the East while the Wood Age stretched out from the riverfront community all the way West. Kansas City was a city in both a fuel and an energy transition.

The wave of mechanization rising from the East reached St. Louis and then subsided by the time it reached Kansas City. The Santa Fe Trail trade, for instance, continued as it had before. In 1867, two years before the Hannibal Bridge opened to railroad traffic, W. H. Chick & Company, one of the original "town company" owners and a substantial businessman of long standing in the community, loaded 1,420 wagons for Mexico, the value of which was $2,200,000.

Two other firms put together smaller but profitable ventures at $300,000 to $500,000 each with fleets of horses, oxen and mules to provide the energy along the way. [15] The trail to Mexico still invigorated trade in the city and demanded servicing by large amounts of animal energy. Kansas City businessmen continued to lace together the markets they serviced with the goods their customers could depend on from what arrived at the steamboat landing.

167

Good-Bye to a One-Horse Town

As early as 1860, the first commercial horse car transportation was organized as the Kansas City Railroad Company. Poorly financed, it faded in a short time. No further efforts were made until after the war.[16] As the emigrants flowed back into the city after the war, however, entrepreneurial opportunities once again abounded. In 1868, a freight company, marking the revival of business in town at the levee, began business with one horse and one wagon and two men to haul goods around the city.

By 1870, as the population had increased tenfold to 32,260 from post-war figures, twelve horses, six wagons and twelve men actively engaged in delivery for this one company.[17] "Some idea of the increase in the express business may be formed," boasted the city directory author, "when it is remembered that in 1866 one horse did all the drawing, and now fourteen horses are kept continually busy."[18] Kansas City had moved from a "one-horse town," literally, to a metropolis in three years.

Commercial transport of pedestrians began when one enterprising citizen, Nehemiah Holmes, started the first street railway in 1869 between Kansas City and Westport, a distance of about four miles. The Kansas City and Westport Horse Railroad Company completed the four-mile run by 1871. Holmes "was the leading spirit of the enterprise, and but for him it would doubtless have failed." The company's office and stables were at 16th and Grand Ave, about equidistance between the two towns.[19]

Coal furnaces in Pittsburgh or St. Louis had produced the first inter-urban rails for the two separate populations of Kansas City and Westport whose citizens rejoiced that they were now "linked together by indissoluble iron bands." Like the railroad itself that had just arrived to link the city across the state and the nation, Kansas City had suddenly entered the age of iron rails.

By 1873, the Kansas City population had grown to 40,740, a jump of 8,000 in three years. Clearly, public transportation needed to grow along with the city. Holmes's railroad did not pay, however, and upon his untimely death in 1874, the company was sold and reorganized as the Westport and Kansas City Railroad Company. It would not become profitable until 1880. Meanwhile, the Jackson County Horse Railroad Company was organized to run from the corner of Fourth and Main at the levee along Fourth to Wyandotte, on to Fifth Street to Bluff street and Union Avenue to Mulberry Street, on to Ninth and on to the State Line to connect to a new company organized in Wyandotte.[20] The "horse" in the name of the railroad would indicate it as the hybrid of its day. Part horse, part mechanical, it bridged the old and the new.

The city grew and changed along with its transportation and reflected the changes in both regional and national events. Competition for the Kansas City and Westport Railroad started up in the form of the Jackson County Horse Railroad Company, which established offices and stables at 4th and Walnut on the levee.

As far out as 20th and Cherry, a hospital was listed for the second time in a city directory, clearly not yet served by public transportation. "Barar, C & Son, Car-builders—street" had a factory between 19th and 20th at Grand Ave, becoming part of the growing industrial section of the city. Brick works were now "steam-pressed," and "hoisting machines" steam and hand-powered were available by local agents.[21] The levee along Delaware Street, "the great wholesale mart of the valley of the Missouri is teeming with an activity never before witnessed, and we are positively assured that its trade alone will reach 40% in excess of any preceding year in its history."[22]

The city was taking on the characteristics it would retain to the present time—wholesale district at the levee where the great storehouses of furs were once held by the Chouteaus, then the real downtown of banking and retail, and then to the industrial section beginning around 16th street and running to the outskirts of Westport at 37th streets.

The Future of This System is Filled with Possibilities

Not surprisingly, New York and Boston started their horse railroads around 1838, thirty years earlier than the frontier of Kansas City, though until 1850, only one road carried small horse-drawn cars in New York City. By 1870, twenty lines of passenger railroads prospered in New York City, employing nearly eight thousand horses. Their gross earnings equaled about $1,000 per horse or $8 million for the company per annum. Brooklyn, Boston, Philadelphia, Cincinnati and Chicago had nearly as large fleets; all other cities of 20,000 inhabitants or more had lines of similar but smaller dimensions.

Collectively, the roads in American cities extended almost 2,000 miles and carried more than 300 million passengers per year.[23] Horses still supplied the energy, not with wooden wagons, but with metal streetcars instead. Coal as coke had created the ability to produce metal in large pieces to create such a thing as a street car, though in the beginning the urban horsecar was also built with wood and covered with a metal covering.

Innovation began in Europe first and then crossed the Atlantic. In 1881, the first electric railway was built in Germany but struggled with technology. The Germans had already moved beyond steam for railway purposes and had invested in electricity in the form of battery-powered street cars. "The machinery for converting coal into the power, or rather extracting power from coal, is not portable, but stationary and can be placed in the most convenient spot." The mechanism they used was a central rail though it sometimes became encrusted with dirt and could not "communicate" with the battery itself.

This problem also crossed the Atlantic and became a matter of concern at the next electricity conference. The Second Annual Proceedings of the Electric Light Association, electric pioneers, discussed the significance of this in Baltimore, Maryland, February 10, 1886 with prescient forecast. At the same time this discussion gives a snapshot of the cautious understanding and progress being made in electricity. One delegate explored the subject:

From all I can gain on this subject, it is my opinion that the most practical way will be to use wires and poles. The poles can also be made available for stringing electric wires for both incandescent and arc lighting. The future of this system is filled with possibilities. It will eventually become the motive power of all the present horse railways.[24]

Members of the Association of Electric Light agreed that the "present system of making steam in locomotive-boilers is expensive as well as wasteful." The ratio of evaporation of pounds of water to each pound of coal consumed to make steam in locomotive boilers was the *key to profit*. The then-current ratio of making steam in locomotive boilers of three-and-a-half pounds of water to a pound of coal using the best grades of bituminous coal was too costly. At the same time the stationary boilers, set to burn coal screenings (a lesser grade of coal) for fuel evaporated nine pounds of water to one pound of fuel, reducing the cost of fuel from one third to one half.[25]

The discussion continued on to forecast the next step in augmenting electricity and phasing out the horse:

It is only a question of time when all the different electric lighting stations in this country will use their engines in the daytime to make power to be sold for manufacturing purposes, the same as they sell power in the form of electric lights now. They can also furnish power to run electrical railways, elevated or surface. The economy of this system over the cost of running horses, as used now, will be over 50%.[26]

Daytime use of electricity was an idea then in formation. Lighting was seen first as the real reason for pursuing electricity, its use beginning in the evening. But with the advent of electric railways and electric coal cutters and other mechanical uses of electricity, the daytime hours began to be productive as well.

In April of 1882, as part of the mix of horse and machine in Kansas City, the city council approved a franchise for another horsecar railway to operate along part of Eighth Street to part of Main Street, to part of Ninth Street to part of Jefferson Street, a small line but one that serviced a business district growing in density and importance.[27] Then along came a new combination of energy and technology, the cable car.

Along with the horsecar endeavor, Kansas City could boast of being one of the first in the cable car business. According to local historian and eye-witness Colonel Theodore Case, Kansas City was third in cities just behind Chicago and San Francisco in that order. In 1880, the nation had only 16-miles of cables in operation.

**Laying Cable
on Kansas City's
Main Street in 1886.
These men worked on what would
become a sophisticated system of
cable-car transportation
in Kansas City rivaled only
by San Francisco and Chicago.**

By 1884, the total number of miles of cable had increased to 34. By 1888, the list of cities using cable cars included New York, Philadelphia, Cincinnati, St. Louis, St. Paul, Omaha, Oakland and Los Angeles. Beyond American shores London, Melbourne, Sydney and Auckland, New Zealand, each had started their own lines.[28]

The systems were often powered by two 500-horse-powered Corliss steam engines turning a wheel with cables running under the surface of the street. The original power house in Kansas City was located at Ninth and Washington but expanded to a new powerhouse at Eighth and Woodland in 1887 with two Corliss engines of 750 horsepower each and became, at the time, the largest institution of its kind in the world with 130 cars, 210 employees and car designs "of the latest and best patterns."[29]

The effect of the cable car on the city was intoxicating. The stock of the KC Cable Company appreciated more than a 100% to $255 a share. Real estate prices along the routes shot up as people envisioned the cars penetrating to the farthest reaches of the suburbs. While the horse railway was viewed as a great improvement over carriages, the cable car appeared to be an invention unique in its ability to elevate the expectation of the city toward modernity. Theodore Case noted the following about the growing interest in all things mechanical:

"Real estate men saw their opportunity, and with the sagacity peculiar to their class, seized upon it. They saw that ultimately cable lines, annihilating distance and removing time, would penetrate to the exteriors of the city and additions were laid out as fast as they could be surveyed, and the plats filed. The problem of rapid transit through the city, across the ravines and over the elevations was solved."[30]

Carried the People as They Had Never Been Carried Before

The city transportation discussion continued worldwide on the merits of horse versus cable versus electric as the energy transition took place in small increments. The horse was clearly on its way out with two new systems to choose from, though each had its problems. The cable car system worked "where the traffic is exceptionally large, but its cost prevents its adoption except in places where the transportation is extraordinarily large." The storage battery system was "destined to failure."[31]

The conversation ranged from storage batteries to trolleys electrified by rail or pole. A visit to Richmond, Virginia, reported in the pages of the *Electro-Magnetic Journal* published in Kansas City showed the very latest in electric trolleys:

"We started for Richmond. What we found there was perfectly surprising and amazing to all of us. There in the city of Richmond, a city of 90,000 inhabitants, was a road twelve miles long over grades and around curves. It is operated by a system of overhead wires, which is positively unobjectionable; the cars ascend grades of 9% at the rate of six miles per hour and are under the most perfect control."[32]

The Ninth Street Incline ran from Union Depot in the West Bottoms up to the growing downtown Kansas City atop the bluffs.

Perfect control, however, did not mean perfect success. The theme of "communication" between car and surface again came under discussion. The track itself was in "exceedingly bad order." It was laid without any paving at the sides, "laid in Virginia mud; the cars would get off the track continually, and one thing and another would happen." But the inspection team left satisfied that they had seen the future and that it included an "electric road." The Richmond road was "carrying the people of Richmond as they have never been carried before, and with entire satisfaction to everybody." It would soon have from 75-100 cars running on the streets of their town.[33]

The Kansas City cable car line, meanwhile, in spite of its success would soon be overtaken by the electric streetcar. The Corrigan system, named for its owner Thomas Corrigan, powered by batteries was also changed to cable, followed by the construction of the

10th Street cable road, which paralleled the lines of the Kansas City Cable Railway Company, a competitor line. This was followed by the construction of the 10th Street cable line, paralleling the lines of the Kansas City Cable Railway Company, proving "immediately on its completion and operation that cable roads in Kansas City had been overdone."[34]

While the cable dominated the scene, however, it offered a certain cache to the city and adventure to its riders. After numerous delays and tribulations, a start was effected, and only one trip made over the road. Such an experience has rarely if ever been equaled. The rollers in the grip jaws made a noise like a threshing machine, and when they did succeed in gripping the cable, the car shot forward with a jerk sufficient to throw one off his feet. In fact, the entire trip was a series of jerks and jumps, the rollers slipping from one end of the jaws to the other. On the completion of that trial trip every creditor made a rush for his money. Liens were filled, and suits instituted to such an extent that for years that road stood as a monument to the folly of the enterprise.[35]

This scene, amusing now, had a hair-raising quality to it, that made new-found technology less friend than frightener. The Ninth-Street Incline was an ebullient testimony to cable car riding that both terrorized and inspired riders as it moved between railway station in the West Bottoms and the growing town on the cliffs above.

The Decision as to Electricity versus Horses

The comparative cost, not to mention the pollution of horses, became a decades-long part of the conversation. Each was calibrated to equate with the other. The article in the *Electro-Mechanic Journal* published in Kansas City in January 15, 1889, observed, "The life of a good battery should be about the same as that of an ordinary tramway horse; if both are used with care they should last for about four years."

This remark was followed by a discussion of battery-powered tramcars as part of the mix among horse, cable and electric rails. "For one car, two sets of batteries would be necessary, and supposing that each set weighed one-and-a-half tons, there is a total weight per car of three tons. One set is sufficient to carry an ordinary tramcar for about thirty to forty miles on average roads, that is half a day's journey. Two sets therefore will be enough for each car per day; and the batteries will only need changing once."[36]

Across the Atlantic, the Germans had been hard at work on the same problem. German observer, Herr Zacharias, gave a comparison between horse and electricity in stables in Berlin to settle "the decision as to electricity vs horses"

He estimated that less than half the annual expenses were needed to work with batteries rather than horses. Herr Zacharias stated that the figures given were derived from actual working on the Berlin tramway lines and may therefore be given credibility. The *Journal* editor commented that the cost of working the horse cars may have been overestimated; 10-15% depreciation were sufficient for "properly worked and well supervised batteries."[37]

By February 1889, the question the Kansas City-published *Electro-Mechanic* posed was about the weather. Could the electric car handle snow and ice? What would be the effect of low temperatures on the batteries? The news from Davenport, Iowa, proved heartening:

> Though the tracks were covered with ice and snow and snowplows and scrapers had left hard ice on the track, the electric cars brushed away such obstacles with steel brushes. "The electric cars moved along without a break with almost the usual speed, and with much less difficulty than motive power on horse car lines encountered." Two horse cars did their best with the weather. They had two mules on one and two horses on another but each electric car had 15 horsepower. The electric car even did better than the Chicago, Rock Island & Pacific freight train that "did not move for half an hour."

The electric car moved "a very heavy load" up the hill on the icy track in less than six minutes. "Two teams of horses could not have done the same under similar circumstances in less than fifteen or twenty minutes." The satisfying results of this scene emboldened the writer to announce that the "electric system will be adopted in both Sioux City and Aberdeen" in the near future.[38] In this manner each city found its way to the new technology and chose what worked best for its population, but all agreed to leave the horse behind.

Twelve Miles for a Nickel

By August 1, of 1889, the *Electro-Magnetic Journal* proudly announced that electric tramways had arrived in Kansas City:

> The city now has the finest system of street railways in the world, and the new line will compel all rivals to admit the fact. A person will be able to board an electric car in the extreme northeastern part of the city and travel to the extreme southwest and over into Kansas City, Kansas, over the electric and cable roads at a speed of not less than eight miles an hour. Or he can travel in the same manner from the southeast to the northwest. On the Metropolitan Company's lines alone he can travel from the western limits of Kansas City to the eastern and southeastern limits of Kansas City, Missouri, a distance of from ten to twelve miles, for a nickel. No other city in the world can show such a system of interior transportation.[39]

By January 1, 1896, the *Journal* newspaper reported that their Metropolitan Street Railway Company ranked among the greatest of the street transportation companies of the country. It owned 135 miles of cable, electric and horse railway, penetrating the two Kansas City's in every direction like a network and extending to Independence, Westport, Rosedale, Sheffield and other suburban towns within a radius of ten or twelve miles. The capital stock of the company was $5,600,000. The company owned 147 grip cars, 249 cable trailers, 109 cable cars, 54 electric motors, 15 electric trailers and 47 horsecars. The company furnished the power to this impressive system with an engine and boiler capacity of over 6,000 horsepower, distributed through eight power houses around the city.[40]

By 1900, the exchange between horse and machine had largely been completed. The above mix of batteries and horses, cables and power houses typified the necessary exchange of one technology for another along the line of the transition itself. The next exchange would be from the remaining individual horse carriages, necessarily remaining, to the automobile that would encroach on the streets of Kansas City in the early years of the 20th century.

A broader view of the exchange of horse for electricity was voiced by author James P. Boyd in his 1899 *Triumphs and Wonders of the 19th Century*. In speaking of the passing of the horse-car and its substitution by the trolley, a distinguished writer indulged in the extravagant expression of the period to capture the awe and enthusiasm that electricity brought to the public. Nothing like it had ever been seen in the life of man, and the ability to actually use it as a matter of choice and convenience excited everyone.

To use it to replace the plodding, obedient, and often misused and abused horse came as a relief to many. The Society for the Prevention of Cruelty to Animals was created in 1866 to protect the horse from its grueling life.[41] People sensitive to the abuse of the horse must have been pleased to find an alternative land transportation they could embrace, not only for its amazing powers of self-propulsion, but for not having to sit behind the haunches of a horse straining in its traces.

> Humanity in an electric car differs widely from that in the horse-car, propelled at the expense of animal life. It is more cheerful, more confident, more awake to the energy at command, more imbued with the subtlety and majesty of the propelling force.... There is no dragging down and subjugation of a physical force. There is only a going out, or up, of genius to meet and to grasp it. Its universal application means the raising of mankind to its plane. If electricity be the principle of life, as some suppose, what wonder that we all feel better in an electric car than any other. The motor becomes a sublime motive. God himself is tugging at the wheels, and we are riding with the Infinite.[42]

Transportation used electricity soon after lighting found its magic. Small appliances would come in the 20th century, but the problem of getting around, the challenge, the smell of horses and their deposits would soon be at an end. Yes, animals would still work, problematic and expensive as they were, while electricity seemed like "God himself tugging at the wheels."

Chapter 19

From the Missouri River
To the Missouri Pacific Railroad

Geography shifted within the cityscape as a new energy component was introduced.

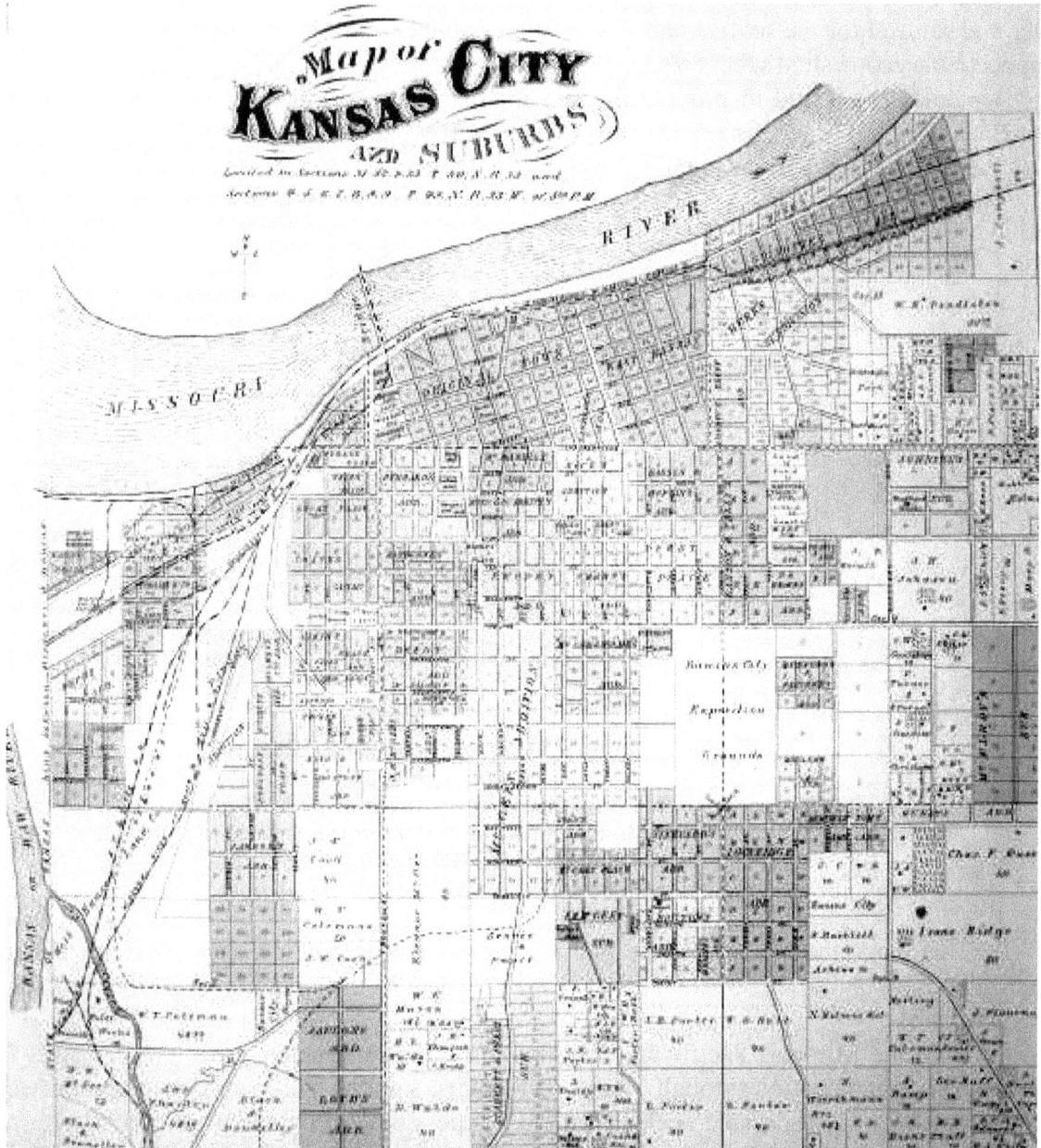

Fueling Change

A less obvious energy transition but a signal of the influence of coal was the change of focus from the riverfront to the railroad yard. Even though the railroad would eventually take over the burdens of the river traffic, steamers still discharged 28 million pounds of freight as late as 1888.[1]

The Hannibal Bridge of 1869 made the Kansas City area not only the crossroads of railroading to the West, but the nexus of more and more railroad connections to all points of the compass. With the railroads arriving from the West and from the East, the obvious place to put the connecting points was in the West Bottoms on the state line between Kansas and Missouri. That spot that had been a dense forest for the French, a hunting ground thick with deer and squirrel for the settlers, the firewood and lumber yard for the growing city, the once impenetrable eco-system spent on supporting Euro-American life blueprints--had by the 1880s been completely cleared to provide the site for the Union Depot and numbers of railroad switches. It may be that remaining woods were swiftly cleared out and used for fuel for the first trains arriving since coal supplies would be tenuous.

Opening the Hannibal Bridge, Kansas City, Missouri

**This is a never-before published image of the engine "Marlboro,"
identified on the original photograph as the, "new engine, first to cross bridge."
The bridge across the Missouri River connected eastern
and the newly developing markets of the southwest.**

This made the West Bottoms the most important area of the city. The city council appropriated $60,000 for street improvements that led to the opening of Third, Fifth and Twelfth streets.

Both the Missouri Pacific and the Union Pacific terminated there and demands for passenger accommodation through hotels, restaurants, saloons and local transportation were soon supplied. "It now became evident that the business base of the city would be transferred

178

from the levee where it had always been . . . and that Kansas City was destined to become a railroad center, rather than a steamboat town."[2]

The river could not, in fact, handle the traffic that deluged the town and of which Kansas City was justifiably proud. In 1893 the Commercial Club of Kansas City, a group of professional businessmen who also promoted the city issued this report: "During 1892 Union Depot handled 970,000 pieces of luggage, an increase of 50,000 pieces in one year. The baggage department handled 33,823,750 pieces of United States mail and 3,408,000 letters and packages for railroad departments."

At least 134 trains arrived and departed on a daily basis, including specials and extras that themselves made a total of 120 per day! The riverfront landing was simply unable to handle that kind of traffic. The embodied energy of passengers, freight, and letters going to multiple destinations beyond the river itself impacted the Kansas City area to eclipse river traffic for its earlier purposes. The simple days of linear river boating and delivery were over.

By 1893, Kansas City had nine passenger depots and 36 railroad warehouses and freight depots mostly in the West Bottoms. "Unequaled switch facilities" provided access to 450 commercial houses, which loaded and unloaded goods there. The railway facilities were "unsurpassed by any city in the world." Kansas City had as many railroad lines as Chicago (26), which was more than St. Louis (19), more than New York City (17), more than Cincinnati (15), Buffalo, St. Paul, Omaha (11 each), Philadelphia (9), Indianapolis (8), New Orleans (8), Pittsburgh (8), Boston (6), Denver (6) or San Francisco (5)![3]

Even though 1892 had been a year of economic depression, the city had handled over a $100,000,000 worth of merchandise that did not include their mammoth market for livestock and grain. The yards had shipped 38 million bushels of grain, had processed in the local slaughter houses 1,358,588 cattle, 2,654,700 hogs and 484,000 sheep.

To carry the stock and grain required 158,000 railroad cars. With a population of 134,000 in the city proper, and another 90,000 in Kansas City, Kansas, across the Kaw River, "which is, in fact, nothing but Commercial Kansas City," the metro had 225,000 thousand "bona fide" population.[4] The little village beside the limestone pier had vanished into a railroad destination of world-class proportions.

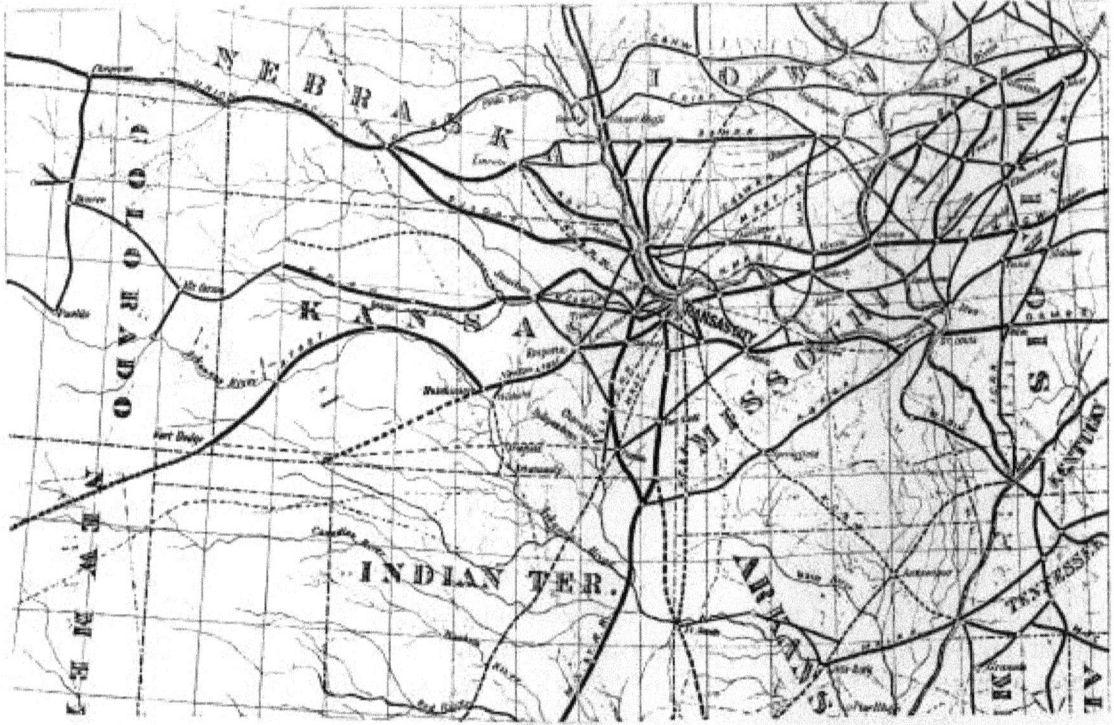

Regional Railroad Map, 1873

**Railroads serving Kansas City in 1873 overlays the landscape
that once knew only the curves of Native American Indian territories.**

Chapter 20

Wood as Building Material Instead of Fuel

During this period wood became an industrial building material as the combination of coal, railroad, and market turned this natural resource into a commodity that could be moved far beyond its local and regional setting for the first time in history. This story is important because post-war cities were built with this technology and fuel combination, and woodlands once thinned for local fuel were never habitually clear-cut and never replanted or encouraged to recover.

Mammoth Interests of Both Lumber and Coal

In the 1870s, wood reached its height as both passive fuel for home heating and active heat for steamboats and locomotives.[1] Consumption of fuel wood burned in 1870 was 138 million cords, the zenith in quantity of fuel wood use at 73% of the fuel picture. By that same year coal had increased in use to over 40 million tons and had become over 26% of the fuel picture.

Because of the weight and the difficulty of hauling wood by team and wagon, it had always been a local fuel and building material until steamboats made it possible to bring both fuel and lumber great distances.[2] Now railroads would burn fuel and carry lumber as well. Though wood had been used as both fuel and building material from the beginning of time, the supplies needed for burgeoning cities like Kansas City required a railroad for transportation to keep up with demand.

Wood was still a very relevant material in the last quarter of the 19th century. Wood from species no longer known to the average consumer today were in demand for building. This quote suggests the irony of importing wood from forests far away from the standing timber in the state, such exchanges made possible by the railroad's ability to crisscross the states with raw materials formerly carried as short a distance as possible by horse and wagon:

> There are many excellent varieties of timber for fencing, agriculture and mechanical implements, for cabinet work and for carriages. These varieties comprise twelve species of Oak, four of Hickory, two of Walnut, two of Maple, two of Elm, two of Linn, three of Ash, two of Locust, two of Cottonwood, two of Hackberry, besides Box Elder, Cedar, Cherry, Coffee Bean, Mulberry,

181

Sycamore, Birch and Willow. The introduction of machinery will give us more of these fine hard woods in our houses, and thus save the expense of poor imitations in paint. Were it not so common, it would be a matter of surprise, that we finish our houses and churches in pine from Wisconsin, that we may cover it with paint in imitation of the oak, walnut and cherry, which grow so abundant in our forests. Boone County burns up much of her best lumber and pays Ohio and Illinois many thousands for the same kinds manufactured into implements, vehicles and furniture.[3]

Since coal also required railroad transportation from mine to market, the two resources often intertwined in the same business. Railroad spurs were specifically built to reach remote coal mines and timber lands making them accessible in large quantities delivered in an efficient style. One such local company controlled "mammoth interests of both lumber and coal."

Beginning with a capital sum of forty-four dollars, Richard H. Keith, a repatriated Confederate soldier, established a small coal yard on Bluff Street in 1871 (two years after the bridge opening) "when Kansas City had very little industrial or commercial importance and handled not more than thirty or forty carloads of coal per day." (A carload measured ten to twelve tons at that time.)[4] The city proved a profitable marketplace and by 1893 Keith had reorganized the Keith and Perry Coal Company into the Central Coal and Coke Company.

He opened one mine after another in Missouri, Kansas and Arkansas. Starting with two or three men at the original coal yard on Bluff Street, the company grew to employ about 10,000 men with an output of 120,000 cars (probably of greater capacity than twelve tons since they grew by the turn of the century to hold from 30 to 90 tons) from mines in Kansas, Missouri, Indian Territory, Arkansas and Wyoming.

The company established 25 stores and coal yards and offices in Wichita, Kansas, St. Joseph, Missouri, Omaha, Nebraska, and Salt Lake City, Utah, and became the leading coal company in the Southwest.[5] One of Kansas City's downtown office buildings was called the Keith and Perry Building at 9th and Walnut:

**Keith and Perry Building
Kansas City, Missouri**

182

The steep slopes of Ninth Street looking west from McGee are pictured on an early hand-colored post card, published by Fred Harvey. A streetcar crosses the intersection on Grand Avenue.

Flags fly from the tops of the U.S. Post Office and the Scarritt building at the right side of the card, as well as from the Grand Avenue Temple building (and church), at the left side.

In the background, the much older six-story red brick building with the pointed turret is the Keith & Perry Building. It was erected in 1887 by Richard H. Keith and John Perry, who made their fortune in coal. It was the design of architects Holt-Price & Barnes. The offices of the coal company were on the sixth floor.

Keith, a former Lexington, Mo., confederate soldier, became a resident of Kansas City in 1871 and invested his entire capital of $40 in the establishment of a little coal yard on Bluff Street. As Carrie Whitney wrote in her history: Kansas City then had but little industrial or commercial importance and handled not more than 30 or 40 carloads of coal a day. Mr. Keith lived to witness the growth of the city and its business development until between 350 or 400 carloads of coal were handled daily.

He eventually became one of the most prominent and successful retail coal dealers of the

Richard H. Keith

country as the president of the Central Coal & Coke Co. Constantly watchful for opportunities to expand, he opened his first mine at Godfrey, Bourbon County, Kentucky, in 1873, and later opened other mines at Rich Hill and in the Bonanza district of Arkansas. By 1909 his businesses were producing 4 million tons annually. When Colonel Keith opened his little coal yard on Bluff Street he employed but two or three men and ere his death the employees of the Central Coal & Coke Co. numbered about 10,000, mining coal in Kansas, Missouri, Indian Territory, Arkansas and Wyoming.

Charles S. Keith, a son, became a member of the firm in 1891, first serving as a bookkeeper, and by 1907 president and general manager of what was then the largest coal and lumber enterprise of the southwest.

John Perry came to Kansas City from England in 1869 to seek his fortune. He went into the coal business with Keith and shared in the thriving business. His wife and four children, returning to England on a trip in 1898, were drowned when the French liner Bourgoyne went down at sea. After the tragedy, Perry returned to England to live, but visited here from time to time.

The Keith & Perry Building (as pictured) was occupied by doctors, lawyers, coal and lumber dealers as well as the Central Coal & Coke Co. One occupant was Dr. Arthur Hyde, defendant in the long, drawn-out trials in the Thomas Swope murder case.

[In 1979,], the site…was occupied by the Columbia Union National Bank and Trust Company Building.[6]

With the help of the railroad the lumber enterprise grew rapidly. Keith purchased a small lumber company in Texarkana, Texas, along with twenty-five acres of forest within the city limit. He modernized the small plant and within eight years had cut into lumber the entire marketable timber from the Texarkana property, and then moved the operation to Carson, Louisiana to start anew, "owing to the exhaustion of the timber supply of the company at the former place."

The Carson mill cut about five million feet of lumber per month and shipped them via the Missouri & Louisiana Railroad, virtually owned by the Central Coal and Coke Company. Then Keith formed a new corporation, the Louisiana and Texas Lumber Company, for the purpose of harvesting 165,000 acres of pinelands in Houston County, Texas. The lumber was handled by the Central Coal and Coke Company and shipped to outlets around the Southwest.

Another leading lumber and coal business, the Dierks Lumber & Coal Company ranked as one of the foremost local yards at 16th and McGee streets in Kansas City covering fully half a city block, including a large, two-story office and store house. The company started up around 1875, and by 1900 had a daily capacity of about 200,000 feet of lumber, "principally, yellow pine lumber as well as fine fuel coal, the local house supplying most of our builders, manufacturers and also doing a large family trade."[7]

Another businessman, Alfred Toll moved to Kansas City from Hannibal, on the other side of the state, after having successfully run a lumber business there in 1866. By 1873, he had enlarged this organization as the Badger State Lumber Company with mills in Wisconsin and in 1886 moved to Kansas City to make his headquarters there. This business having prospered, he also organized the Fort Smith Lumber Company of Fort Smith, Arkansas, where four mills operated. He owned 94,000 acres of timber land in that area and used much of that lumber to build the Central Railroad of Arkansas. By 1900, he was president of the Badger Lumber Company, the Fort Smith Lumber Company, the Central Railroad of Arkansas and the Choctaw Investment Company, a series of businesses that complemented and supported each other in the marketplace.[8]

Well-known lumberman and pioneer conservationist John Barber White (1847-1923) also combined lumber and mining. He helped to organize the Missouri Lumber and Mining Company in 1879. As a conservationist he came to the notice of the White House, and President

Theodore Roosevelt appointed him to the National Commission on the Conservation of Natural Resources in 1908.

During his administration the President put under government protection two-hundred-and-thirty million acres, including five national parks, eighteen national monuments and twenty-four reclamation projects. He was in touch with naturalist John Burroughs on the East Coast and John Muir, founder of the Sierra Club, on the West Coast.[9] Roosevelt also pioneered the idea of selective cutting in which mature trees are carefully removed to avoid damaging new growth.

As the nation's forests yielded to massive cutting and the outcry for conservation could be heard throughout the nation, it was coal mining and the fruits of those who labored in the dark that took over the national economy. Both lumber and coal thrived on organization and mass production. Systems of organization augmented by steam engines and rail multiplied the processing of the nation's resources.

As business history author Alfred Chandler noted, "Coal mining brought the pattern of modern enterprise with it—a need for organization, managers, coordination of transportation and output."[10] Jay Gould saw this need and systematized transportation and coal production on a large scale. The Kansas City coal and lumber companies did the same on regional scales, far beyond the confines of the city or county, into states in the South and Southwest. These coal and lumber companies exemplified the changing nature of the raw resources industry. No longer a farmer's supplementary effort with either wood or coal or a small-time coal mine or woodyard with a half-dozen hands, coal mining had gained a whole new level of exploitation and organization.

The role of wood began to grow in all directions after the Civil War. In the1870s Missouri ranked eighth among states in quantities of timber cut at twenty-nine million board feet, compared to Michigan as number one at 2,251,000,000 board feet. Kansas did not qualify with a ranking its numbers were so low: 750,000 board feet. These were reports of sawmills cutting lumber, not wood chopped for home heating and cooking.[11]

The Kansas City *City Directory of 1870* proudly lists the lumber yards in the growing town: Corner of Fifth and Delaware and Santa Fe Street, Latshaw, Quade & Co., sold during the year ending 31st August 1869, 5,480,699 feet of lumber; shingles, 3,881,000; and lathes 1,808,840, amounting to $240,000. Other lumber yards lined the streets: 1) corner Walnut and Twelfth, 2) Walnut Street from 11th to 12th, 3) corner Main and Eleventh, 4) west side Main between Court and Eighth Street, 5) between 18th and 19th streets, and 6) Grand Avenue, McGee's addition, corner Grand Avenue and 18th. Clearly the building boom marched forward with ample supply.[12]

The age-old product of wood had expanded to furnish a superstructure that included in its arc the use of wood as fuel, the supply for steamboats and then for railroads and then clear-cutting of forests to build dwellings and shops in cities. While the nation's forests filled the building needs of an influx of population in the final decades of the 19th century, coal picked up the fuel needs. The commercial dominance of wood as fuel in 1870 was three-quarters wood to one-third coal. By 1900 the reverse was true.[13]

Energy Content (heating value) of Fuels

Wood 20% moisture	6,400 Btu/lb.
Lignite/sub-bituminous coal	6,500-8,200 Btu/lb.
Dry wood	7,600-9,609 Btu/lb.
Bituminous/anthracite coal	11,500-13,000 Btu/lb.
Charcoal	12,800 Btu/lb.
Gasoline	115,000 Btu/gallon
Petro-diesel	130,500 Btu/gallon
Barrel of oil	138,095 Btu/gallon

The "abundance of the raw material" of coal required more than horses and wagons for transportation. It required furnaces, grates, processing into coke and railroads to carry it. The qualities of coal itself at BTUs higher than wood along with the process of turning coal into coke for metal smelting made greater production of iron possible than the charcoal plants tied to nearby forests. The final cost of charcoal as fuel remained steady at $20 a ton as far back as 1845 versus coal as fuel at $3.25. [14]

Coal and railroads formed a symbiotic relationship, the one being the fuel for the carrier, the other the carrier for the fuel, while iron to make the carrier was made accessible with anthracite coal--all to serve the rising field of enterprise. Coal, iron and transportation in the form of the "iron horse" created an unbeatable combination. Other business partnerships and evolving systems from merchants to bankers had formed on the Kansas City waterfront in the antebellum years to serve the emigrants, but only the arrival of coal as fuel unlocked the potential of capitalism on so grand a scale.

Chapter 21

The Structural Expression of Coal: Steel

A new building material would replace, or offset wood and stone,
as the process of using coke from coal made steel plentiful.

Wood and stone for building material would now be replaced with steel in quantity made possible by the Bessemer process of making steel. While steel had been available historically, each piece had been beaten out by a blacksmith on a forge in small quantities, an inefficient method that kept steel expensive. Now all that would change as a new process would make cheap steel available in large quantities.

Bessemer: Eight-Hundred Pounds of Metal in Thirty Minutes!

One of the great bottlenecks in 19th century industrial development was the inability to make quantities of steel at a rapid rate and a reasonable price. Although the hot blast furnace developed in the 1830s and 1840s and the growing exchange of coke from coal as fuel was replacing charcoal from wood, steel was "still a luxury product."[1] To make it commonplace was the goal of English inventor Henry Bessemer (1813-1898) who patented a process rather than a formula. In one of the early recycling efforts of the Coal Age, he used the waste heat from the blast furnaces to heat the blast air. With this simple closed circuit, Bessemer reduced his fuel consumption by 40%. His process, like that of his fellow Englishman Abraham Darby a century earlier and his exchange of charcoal for coke, was slow to be adopted.

In 1856, Bessemer presented his paper called "The Manufacture of Iron Without Fuel" in England. He claimed to be able to "do" 800 pounds of metal in 30 minutes against the puddling furnace's output of 500 pounds in two hours."[2] Early licenses to use the process, however, left other iron makers unenthusiastic, and Bessemer was forced to experiment on his own without benefit of income from licenses until he proved the worth of his process by providing steel at $20 less a ton than his competitors. By 1859 he was making steel with his "pneumatic" or forced-air process. American iron makers first adopted it in 1865, while experimentation went on in this country on various ways of decarbonizing steel, dealing with chemical combinations of pig iron, fuel and blast, conflicting patents by other early experimenters and financial constraints. Steel on a mass scale evolved in a complicated fashion.[3]

One of the first uses of steel was to replace iron rails for the railroads. Steelmakers were not able to guarantee quality, however, which kept the iron-rail makers in business for another twenty years.[4] To assure greater control over the rail-making process, the Reading Railroad built its own steel mill in 1868. Steelmakers also began building integrated works where they could combine iron smelting as an "adjunct to steelmaking." This combination of processes to support the creation of a final product from start to finish would become more common. While doing so would increase speed and quantity through mechanization and greater scientific understanding of what made good steel, at the same time the combined factory processes reduced individual workmanship from artisan to employee.

"The knowledge of materials and how they could be expected to behave was inexact, and the tools for measuring the chemical content of materials were imperfect. People tested their materials in somewhat impressionistic ways, both for physical and for chemical properties, and tried to build their findings into a unified description of the phenomena observed."[5] The Bessemer process produced at least 50 % of the steel in this country until the beginning of the 20th century when a much-evolved puddling process took over.[6]

What once had been an art of reading the molten iron, the rising vapors with careful, individual attention to small batches of metal became an assembly of interacting parts on a grand scale. "Union and business leaders, in their quest for political and economic power, lost interest in the intellectual content of work and were willing to connive artisans' creativity with rigid work rules and bureaucratic control of the shop floor. As they did these things, they put in place the forces that would later bring about the demise of the great American steelworks."[7]

Bethlehem Steel Works in Pennsylvania, 1881

Chapter 22

Old King Coal

Coal flexed its muscles as the dominant fuel in amounts excavated by the underground army of miners who did their best to meet national demands.

Coal mining had come a long way since women and children dragged out baskets of coal on their hands and knees while husband and father hewed the coal face with an ax in a small space lit only by a candle. By 1900, coal had exchanged with wood the supremacy of fuel dominance. Peak Coal was in full throttle from 1900 to 1920 at 72% of fuel consumption. What that meant to the industry, to its competitors, and to the consumer is a complex tale of chaos and growing maturity. Peak Coal included the use of animals and timber from the Wood Age that would slowly be eased out of the picture by mechanical equipment and steel beams. It included greater management efficiency, in fact, "the science of management" was promoted in the *Coal Age* weekly, a publication started in 1911 that became the organ for the coal industry.

This period for coal is Stage 3, *Expansion and Defense,* for this fuel. The two terms could not be better chosen to describe these years. As it assumed commercial dominance, the coal industry stretched to meet the demands of the position. Local and regional shortages became national shortages during these two decades, when one bottleneck after another choked production, transportation, delivery and markets. The rewards for the coal industry for being dominant were great, but the pain was also enormous. The reputation of being part of "King Coal" had certain psychic satisfaction to those involved, but to others it was a power to be dethroned as quickly as possible.

The *Coal Age* weekly magazine was started to give the industry a professional face to its readers and to the public. It added power of voice and solidarity of practice, promoted efficiency and educated miners to both mining production techniques and to the morals of leadership, patriotism and alcohol-free mining. Its pages are a treasure trove of insights into the mining industry. The following threads show the state of the coal mining industry during this time. The first is the use of animals in large-scale production.

Goodbye, Old Mule!

Animals still played a part in coal mining as the Wood Age and its animal complement hung on in the Coal Age itself as well as in the pages of *Coal Age*. Evidently a consciousness of cruelty to animals as a negative practice had lodged itself in the coal industry since the industry organ consistently printed material instructing handlers how to treat their mules. On the 4th of July 1913, as reported on the "Sociological Department" page, the United States Coal and Coke Company "used the occasion . . .. to promote a kindly interest of drivers for their mules and to enliven the dull routine of a line of mining camps which are shut in closely in narrow valleys between forbidding hills."[1]

Twenty-eight mules ridden by their drivers "dressed in comic costumes representing the nationality of each, the marshal of the cavalcade being the stable boss. The mules were caparisoned in muslin with 'First aid' in gold letters." Following that came the sawmill department with a large, log, float, twelve-feet-long and four-feet-thick, drawn by eight large mules, decorated with bunting. Woodsmen marched in the rear. (These would have been the men charged with finding and cutting mine timbers.)

Another float was led by a horseless carriage pushed by a mule draped in all the colors of the rainbow and marked as generating 100,000 mule power. This entry took first prize as being the cleverest by far of entries from a parade that lasted over an hour.[2] A model miner's house, the "sanitation machine," and a float with Sunday-school children and 12 mules in working harness followed. All the workers from mines no. 4 and 5 of the United Supply Company, a nearby plant, walked with their wives and 22 mules gaily draped. First aid figured large in these gatherings and a float of members of the first-aid corps followed with a patient in bed "swathed in bandages, and thirty-five decorated mules and their drivers making a striking cavalcade."

190

The entrant who expected to carry away the prize "as always before" showed off "thirty lively mules tricked up in bunting and mounted by as many drivers," admittedly a striking and expensive entry; but as a sign of things to come, it had been trumped by one mule-pulled horseless carriage! This entry was followed by a Hungarian band of 16 pieces, another float of Sunday-school children and twenty-five "fine mine mules without a scratch on any of them, and all dressed in comic costumes." Another float filled with miners carrying flags followed thirty-nine mine mules "gaily decorated," and so on flowed the parade as an example of what we might now call "community relations." Whatever the purpose, mules figured largely in numbers, in examples of good health and in more than pulling wagons. They starred in the show above ground as they provided important services below and were a vital part of the mining community.[3]

The magazine featured other articles and ads reminding readers in subtle ways that the Wood Age hung on in their workaday world. One editorial observed that "the use of animals for haulage purposes underground is generally unprofitable if the distance to be covered exceeds two-thousand feet.[4] Wire-grid eye guards for "horses underground," looking something like a hockey-player's mask only smaller, were advertised in a 1912 edition of *Coal Age* with the copy that this would save their eyes from being scratched by passing walls or to keep falling coal away from their eyes.[5] A 1913 ad for a Whitcomb Engine advertised that a motor using only fifteen gallons of gasoline "discarded 22 mules for gasoline engine" power. Interesting is the word "discarded" rather than "replaced," a choice of words that has a subtle lack of feeling to it, as if many mules had already been discarded before for failing to qualify as adequate mule power.[6]

In search of a means of testing the air for toxic gases, canaries and mice had both been used, but miners complained that these animals were too small and sensitive, and their alarms sounded too early. The men could have worked longer after these small animals keeled over. What they wanted was an animal that was just slightly more sensitive than humans so that the miners could work longer before leaving a dangerous situation. To that end, miners in India tried using chickens. Two miners took a chicken to the pit bottom where a fire had raged and was being put out. Both men "fell to the ground in a collapsed state," but the chicken was fine. Another group of miners tried a chicken in a similar circumstance in another mine. The men "were knocked over" but the chickens "were quite unaffected." A bit of trivia for the reputation of chickens, perhaps, but not a reliable means for detecting toxic fumes. [7]

By 1917, the carbide lamp test for air quality had given some solution to the problem of depleted oxygen in mines. A miner's life is not endangered until the oxygen content falls below 10%. The carbide lamp now preferred required 12 1/2% oxygen at its lowest point. The color changed in the flame when the oxygen content reaches 17 1/2% and allowed a miner some ways from an exit to return before the oxygen level dropped to a lethal level. The acetylene lamp "certainly presents more positive warning than anything else of a practical nature that has yet been devised (including chicken, mice and canaries). Irrespective of whatever else may be said of a carbide lamp, this point alone is a strong recommendation for its use."[8]

Years went by and still mule care was a concern in the pages of *Coal Age*. A series of instructions was offered in 1917 as a definitive look at mule treatment. "Humane Treatment for the Mule" leaves no harness unexamined. (See Appendix E). These mules were animate units of energy employed to do the work that men could or would prefer not to do with greater efficiency. It is difficult to think of mules in an industrial setting, but the roots of the Coal Age grew from the Wood Age and carried forward with it certain components of that era until ultimately replaced by inanimate labor.

A mule lasted from five to ten years in a mine, "some mines use them up faster than this because of specially hard and adverse working conditions." The mule, better than the horse, was well suited to this work and displayed "an almost human sagacity in getting about the mine and avoiding the many dangers incident to his precarious life, such as being run down by trips of loaded cars, etc." They responded well to kind treatment, as the article above suggests, but could sulk and become vicious when abused.[9]

Mules worked in dark passageways, did dangerous work, breathed air filled with all manner of dust and odors and got minimal sympathy and only fair care. Whatever problems machines challenged workers, the difference between animate and inanimate power was enormous. Just as electric cutters saved the miner's back, carts powered by electricity saved the mules. The coal industry embraced mechanical devices to compete in the marketplace increasingly powered by them.

In 1920, an article on "Mine Electric Lighting," recommended 25-watt lights spaced at 300-foot intervals for safety purposes, a very dim lighting system by today's standards, and instructed readers on lighting the mule stables. "Underground rooms, mule stables, and the like may be illuminated with 40-watt lamps equipped with angle reflectors mounted on the wall as high as possible. One unit can be used for each two stalls." Frequent whitewashing of the walls of the stables would increase materially the illumination of this part of the mine.[10] Mules spent years in the mines sometimes being hoisted out for pasturage during the low-producing summer months.

At what point mules were finally replaced forever by mechanized equipment is hard to say. Animal power increased until about 1910, but by 1920 the work output of animals had dropped to about 6%. In 1910, animals provided 18% compared to machines offering 142%. Animal power dropped slightly in 1920 to 15% while inanimate or mechanical power increased to 268%. By 1920, then, animals still held a portion of the work force while machines quadrupled their output. As for mules and horses in mining, they were still used in some mines as late as the 1940s, when, at last, it was "goodbye, old mule![11]

All this is to say that while coal held its place as provider of 72% of fuel consumption for the nation, it did so with uncounted animal power still laboring in an industrial setting. This overlap between the Wood Age and the Coal Age shows a remarkably long and well-used bridge between the two as industry-built replacement units of machines powered by coal, natural gas and electricity to take the place of animal power.

The 1910 census indicates a huge output of coal using such combination of methods (it does not count mines producing less than a thousand tons a day nor does it mention mules. These two may be in combination with each other. Mines operated without mechanical power fall into this category. Missouri had 78 mines without power out of a total of 220, and Kansas had 48 out of a total of 202 mines.)[12] Of the more than 6,000 mines operating in the United States, a third of them operated without power, and these produced more than a thousand tons per day.

Mechanical power was still small. Steam engines and electric power together made up 1,227,400 horsepower with an increase of 148.9% over the decade. The average increase of steam engines was 80.2% in number and 145.5% in total horsepower. The average horsepower per engine increased from 75 to 102 horsepower or 36%. Electric motors run by current generated by the mine increased 635% in number and 400% in total horsepower. The total output of coal increased 45% and the total horsepower increased 150%.[13]

Not surprisingly the greatest percentages of increase in mechanical horsepower appeared in the states producing the largest amount of coal: Kentucky, West Virginia, Texas, Tennessee, Pennsylvania and Alabama with an average increase of 221%. (The states are listed here in order of increase with Kentucky at 267.1% and Alabama 194.7%.) Their coal production increases averaged 63%. Those states with the lowest increase in horsepower included Missouri and Kansas with an increase in mechanical horsepower of about 50%. Missouri showed 238 steam engines with a total of 11,619 horsepower and 78 electric motors with horsepower of 2,042 which amounted to over 1,000% increase in electricity use and a 25% increase in steam power.[14]

Production of coal for the state of Missouri was 293,000 in 1909. Kansas sold locally 679,500 tons and shipped out almost seven million tons. Missouri shipped out three-and-a-half-million tons.[15] In 1909 the United States produced 460,049,000 tons of coal (17.6% anthracite and 82.4% bituminous) valued at $552,895,000. The coal industry controlled 8,182,749 acres of land throughout the producing states.[16]

Growing Scarcity of Mine Timber

Another thread in the *Coal Age* pages is the need for ready supplies of timber to shore up the roofs of the rooms where miners work. A series of articles addressing this problem appeared over the two decades from 1900 to 1920. Some quite profitable mines left wood behind and went for metal posts that were proposed as early as 1913.

Timbers supporting coal mine ceilings were replaced by concrete in years to come; an overlap of energy suites shown here.

These particular ones were imported from Belgium. Each post had a metal sleeve of 4.8 inches in diameter that is closed at the bottom with a wooden plug. The sleeve is split lengthwise and fastened by three collars making it a telescopic kind of tube. It is then filled with coal dust, broken stone, cinder or other filling to give it strength. This becomes the pillar part of a three-piece set that forms an arch for holding up the roof of a chamber.[17]

Costs and difficulty in handling argued against its use. Timber supports cost $1.78 versus $12.75 for the metal post. The metal post weighed over a hundred pounds and was difficult to handle. The cross rail weighed about 158 pounds. Plus, filling the tube with some kind of filling required time, material and skill. Still the article thought the metal mine posts were worth the cost. Other articles suggested concrete supports with similar arguments.[18]

The reverse in cost proved true for a steel derrick and drilling rig advertised in the *Gas and Oil Journal*, a rival publication, in 1911. Offered by the Carnegie Steel Company, it extolled the virtues of steel against the growing scarcity and rising cost of wood:

"While wood is still plentiful in many districts our steel derricks are fast crowding out the wooden rigs. The first cost may be slightly higher but consider the ultimate saving when you can use the same rig over ten wells; the immunity against fire, lightning and decay; the lower steam pressure required for operation, as the rigidity of the steel does away with lost motion. You can erect the derrick, take it down, move it to a new location and set it up again at less expense than when using wood."[19]

This is another overlap between the Wood Age and the Oil Age with coal as the fuel that bridges the gap between the two. Soon enough, coal producers would move to steel derricks for the reasons above and another component of the Wood Age would fall by the wayside.

Other mines stayed with timber and crews of saw men. A timber would last four or five years, the length of most mines' service, if they were treated with creosote. Like the green mule, a green timber should never be taken into the mine and used as a prop. It would be unreliable, prone to dry rot and disease and would soon have to be replaced.[20]

Another aspect of mine timbering was the source of the wood. Timber preserves were proposed in this article, citing the use of unvalued timber. The attitude was toward cultivating timber tracts beyond the government's role in this. Mine timber needs about 10 to 20 years to grow to the appropriate size and can be grown on hilly regions nearby the coal fields, which "would seem a practical solution of the problem of the impending scarcity of timber." [21]

Timber scarcity is often associated with agriculture since tillable fields were the motivating force for forest clearing when agriculture began. It is less known that both coal and oil production destroyed whole countrysides that needed to be replanted. That replanting has often been a slow and begrudging process, but the roots of restoration around coal mines started early in the 20th century.[22]

Chapter 23

Is Petroleum a Necessity?

The rise of oil supplanted coal. America's infrastructure swiftly adapted
to the changing fuel source.

Though it took coal more than 80 years from first recorded shipment (1758) to reach a production milestone of a million tons, oil reached the equivalent of that in ten years. Fledgling wells pumped 500,000 barrels in 1860 and a strongly organized industry increased that to nearly 5,000,000 in 1870.[1] In 1873, the Titusville, Pennsylvania, *Morning Herald* asked the editorial question, "Is petroleum a necessity?" and went on to suggest that it had already been proven to be of "such commercial and social importance to the world that if it were suddenly to cease no other known substance could supply its place, and such an event could not be looked upon in any other light than of a widespread calamity."[2] This praise was based on illumination and lubrication, not on internal combustion, an idea whose time had not yet come. Coal, however, had received no such prophetic welcoming. It did not bring to mind that kind of proclamation though it had and would provide the stepping stones for oil's success as wood had done for coal.

Using the distilling infrastructure of coal oil (that had borrowed whale-oil distilling practices, a light-source coal oil was replacing in the 1850s), producers and distillers quickly adapted the process to refining oil, separating products and marketing them. The first decade had also seen the bumbling attempts to contain a liquid fuel get organized to solve those problems with barrels and tankage.

The transportation industry had taken on the task of moving liquid in quantity and evolved in short order from horse team and riverboat to railroad transportation and pipeline. The lightning progress not only could be attributed to the infrastructure already available that coal built, but "partly it was because innovation was in the air—because the mid-19th century, especially in the United States, resembled a great laboratory both for the debut of intellectual invention and for the nurture of the alchemy needed to translate it into revolutionary applications to the physical world . . . The oil and gas industry was one of the earliest of a bevy of American businesses that would combine 'future shock' changes in science and in economic theory and management methods."[3]

Perhaps no greater example exists than the new and ever-expanding oil industry. The remaining thirty years of the 19th century would witness the rise of the Standard Oil Company, incorporated in 1870, as an organizing and threatening force in the marketplace, the expansion of prospecting from "the Region" in one state to many regions both in and beyond Pennsylvania and the world, the building of large refineries, the "vertical" organization of the activities of the oil business into fewer and stronger companies and the competition with foreign markets. The new fuel was irresistible as a light source, and as soon as practical problems were overcome at the production end, it was universally accepted by consumers.

Who could not welcome a cheap and brilliant light that once poured into the new glass lamps lit the room better than any previous fuel ever used? By the early 1870s, 89% of foreign kerosene shipments went to Europe, almost 3% to China, and about 2% each to North and South America. Over the course of the next 10 years, Europe would import less and Asia more as each market responded to the new fuel either by increasing tariffs to encourage exploitation of their own oil deposits as in the case of France and Spain, or in replacing glass lamps with tin, and bean oil with petroleum as in the case of China.

Cost and availability of the glass lamp at about $3 each prohibited many from using it in the beginning, but over time costs of both fuel and containers came down. For the first time the modest homes of the low and middle-income workers around the world could be lit against the night. The "trading class" in China found a kerosene lamp on desk or passageway a boon to extending hours in retail and wholesale business.[4]

These barrels of kerosene (sold by container or barrel) from the Standard Oil Company lie in retreating 1903 flood waters in the West Bottoms. Kerosene was sold by the barrel or by the size container the buyer brought to the corner drug store or other outlet for fuel.

The business in oil products consisted primarily of axle grease, kerosene or other lantern fuel, naphtha, benzine and gasoline used as cleaning fluids, and paraffin for a wide variety of uses including sealing jars of canned goods. Though nine other countries by then produced oil, borrowing technology and process from Drake's approach, still Pennsylvania produced over 90% of the world market.[5]

The Standard Oil Company approach was first to buy up small refineries and reorganize them under the Standard banner to increase their yield. The next step was to take over transportation, first railroads and then pipelines. A third step and coinciding with the first two was to go beyond the boundaries of the state of Ohio where the company had been incorporated to other states via the legal mechanism of the trust held by officers of the original company, the trustees.

The trustee idea eventually became a holding company of businesses bought in other states whose shares and profits were passed on to Standard Oil shareholders.[6] In 1877 Standard Oil of California was formed by local businessmen in Ventura to spur oil drilling there and bought by Standard. In Maryland that same year the United Oil Company, formed of many smaller firms, joined Standard. In 1878, Waters-Pierce Oil Company of Cincinnati joined the Trust.

In 1879, Standard Oil of Ohio marketed to Ohio, Indiana, Illinois, Wisconsin, Michigan, the Rocky Mountain States, and California. They also acquired Standard Oil of California by way of their Pacific Coast Oil Company. In 1880, the company founded Imperial Oil of Canada. They added the Vacuum Oil Company that year from the Rochester, New York, a company that manufactured lubricating oils by vacuum steam distillation, and the Chesebrough Company that made the already famous "Vaseline" petroleum jelly in 1881.

That same year the company moved into pipeline installation and operation by way of their National Transit Company. New Jersey laws allowed corporations to own stock in other corporations, so the Standard Oil Company of New Jersey was formed to provide administrative coordination to the Trust in 1882. Standard Oil Company of New York also formed that year and oversaw most of the foreign territories.

Another company, the West India Oil Company formed to handle refining plants in Cuba and the Caribbean. Needing transportation for the West, Continental Oil was acquired to distribute Standard products to Colorado, Montana, Utah, Wyoming, and New Mexico. Regional company Gilbert and Barker were acquired by the Trust. In the Midwest in 1885, the Standard Oil Company of Iowa was given responsibility for marketing along the Pacific Coast. The Buckeye Pipe Line, still listed on the New York Stock Exchange in 2018, was formed in 1885, along with the Solar Refining Company while Standard's Vacuum Oil Company sailed across the Atlantic and opened offices in Liverpool, England.

By 1886, the Trust had taken up residence in Kentucky, establishing the Standard Oil Company of Kentucky and absorbing companies there. The same was true in the North Central states where Standard Oil Company of Minnesota absorbed another regional company in Wisconsin, Minnesota, North and South Dakota. In 1889, skipping over some lesser acquisitions in other states, Standard Oil of Indiana built a refinery in Whiting, Indiana, the "production end of the business" being its only task. That same year South Penn Oil Company was formed to further explore Pennsylvania and West Virginia to produce more oil. Standard Oil Company of Illinois was then forming in 1890 and absorbed the assets of P. C. Hanford Company.[7]

In other words, though many independent producers, pipeline companies, refineries and transportation companies still existed, they all felt the pressure and threat of the mighty Standard Oil. In 1892, due to court action in Ohio where the original company still operated, the Standard Oil Trust officially dissolved and gave the responsibility to the New Jersey standard Oil Company to become the controlling organization for the Standard brand.

Over the next decade this pattern of acquisition continued throughout the United States and throughout the world. Offices were opened in China, Japan and Germany. At home, Standard of Kentucky sold to Indiana Standard to Iowa, Nebraska, Kansas and Missouri. Two new companies, bowing to anti-Standard sentiment, formed Standard Oil of Kansas and Standard Oil of Missouri. Kansas was particularly upset; Standard operated only one large refinery in Neodesha in that state.[8]

Standard Oil arrived in Kansas City in 1880. In spite of the hue and cry against Standard, the law suits and the vituperation, the following quote written from a distance of twenty years later describes in very positive terms the influence of the company on the local scene:

> The great Standard Oil Company practically controls the coal oil trade of the world. And yet it has been through the very operations of that company's vast aggregation of capital, resources and facilities which enabled them to produce more oil, to handle more oil and handle it at far less expense than a widely scattered and large number of small operators working under primitive methods and with deficient equipment. The local yards of the company cover not less than four acres of ground upon which are located 30 extensive tanks and other necessary belongings of the oil business, including a handsome new office building covering 5,000 square feet. This business was established here in 1880 and has been under the management of Mr. George W. Mayer for many years.[9]

Clearly, Standard Oil epitomized the corporation of the late 19th century. First, it had capital. Without that, all the other companies were destined to local and regional strength at best. Because of that, and the way oil required various steps of organization from prospecting to drilling to production to storage to transport to refining to more transport and marketing, Standard was able to integrate those many parts of the process that may have remained separate industries without their leadership.

"John D. Rockefeller's Standard Oil worked to squelch competition in the Kansas oil market by manipulating it to secure better prices on freighting and refusing to operate its pipeline as a common carrier. Producers suffered from a rapid and drastic drop in the price of crude resulting from large stock piles and a lack of competitive buying, dividends on stock declined, and consumers continued to pay for refined products at elevated prices. With Standard in control of the Kansas oil market and everyone else suffering the effects, investors, retailers, and consumers raised their voices in angry protest, as politicians in a campaign year sought out solutions to curb Standard's activities and restore competition. One suggestion, endorsed by the newly elected governor E.W. Hoch in his inaugural address of January 1905, was the construction of a state owned and managed refinery."[10]

Cartoon at the left shows Kansas (the stove) fighting back as
John D. Rockefeller, dressed in women's attire, pouring Standard oil into it.
As he pours, the stove (Kansas) explodes, toppling a pot of "Profits"
and blowing Rockefeller away.

Cartoon published in the *Chicago Daily News*, February 13, 1905

Through their financial strength and managerial talent, they assumed the risks of the new industry and moved quickly west as fields in Pennsylvania began to die out. In Ohio they learned to refine high-Sulphur crude that would prepare them for the Texas crude to come. In becoming national they stood ready to move from illuminant to fuel oil.[11] But John D. Rockefeller, "who took a dim view of using crude for fuel purposes," wrote this comment to the Whiting, Indiana, plant managers when he learned that it was producing just 60 barrels a day of paraffin, one of the most profitable by-products:

> With wax at say $15 a barrel and fuel oil between $.50 and $.60, it seems we ought not let our valuable paraffine (sic) plant be idle in order to supply fuel oil . . .. My view is we should distill all the production of Lima oil, run our paraffine plant to full capacity and supply tar and benzine, if necessary, for fuel.[12]

This short quote says much about Rockefeller's approach to business. He was legendary in watching his pennies, though at the same time, he seems to be unaware of the fortune to come in fuel oil. Whether Rockefeller liked it or not, fuel oil would soon be the order of the day. The empire he had built on illuminants and lubricants was but a prelude to the 20th century.

Part 2
Conclusion

The Great Fuel Exchange, the first of its kind in human history, occurred with some kind of mathematical precision in 1885 as the abundance and higher energy content of coal crossed over wood. In a mirror reflection, the two fuels proceeded toward their destinations, coal as the new dominant fuel and wood toward its demise. Had it been a sporting event, it could be said that "coal trounced wood," or "wood's defense was weak," or that "wood was unprepared for the contest," but little of that observation was ever made.

The crossover was probably unnoticed at the time since "innovation was in the air," but the results of it were certainly noticeable, and citizens of Kansas City were kept exceedingly busy responding to wave upon wave of energy in the form of people, trains, building efforts, cable cars and the other inventions and artifacts that fairly flooded their lives. Compared to the pioneer days before the Civil War, this thirty-year period had to be a cornucopia of increased materialism.

"The pattern of modern enterprise," as historian Alfred Chandler noted, required "organization, managers, coordination of transportation and output." A clarity to effort must have emerged from the melee of events occurring in this outpost turned steamboat town turned railroad town. The sheer numbers of people and trains drove organization and coordination. The careful steps of organizing the electric light industry is such a view into a fledgling industry whose most ardent fans could not have imagined the foundations they were laying would support the structures to come.

Fuel, meanwhile, was becoming a more distant commodity. Though the city had a few coal mines, most of the coal supply would come from neighboring counties and from even farther away. Fuel gathering was no longer a local affair; still regional but by and large beyond the sight of town citizens whose coal came delivered much like the kindling man—the disguised Governor Reeder—might have done, a coal bucket at a time. Or citizens would have bought from the local coal yard, an accompaniment and replacement for the local wood yard—beginning down by the river, but increasingly moving southward.[13]

The advantage that wood had as a fuel source was that it was visible and cut in daylight. The light of day never reached to the depths of the mines. The miners worked by the thinnest of light sources, problematic and dangerous deep underground. The outcome of their efforts, however, were visible everywhere one looked around the growing city. Whether the citizens actually connected the huge city activity to the labors of men in the dark mines is unclear, but they certainly enjoyed the fruits of the miners' labors.

Nothing so wonderful from those labors appeared better than electricity for it truly changed the way mankind lives. The early beginnings seem quaint and amusing now, but electricity had the feel of magic to it and was gingerly handled even by the 1880s as seen by the speeches made by the men at the Electric Light Proceedings in cities along the East Coast. Both creators and users of the new light source lived in wonder at its feeble light. To do away with candle, gas light and kerosene was to put an amazing distance, once again, between the user and the fuel source itself.

Now that gritty transformation occurred "out back" or "down the street," not far at this point since direct current had a short tether, but the raw flame of lighting could disappear with electric light. It did not replace any of those flammable fuels by any means, and in another overlap between fuel and energy sources, appeared side by side for some years before the fuel and energy picture settled into its current profile.

Distancing from the source is a theme of this part of the fuel story. That distancing included the long farewell to the horse. It was much more complicated than uncoupling the animal from the wagon and turning it out to pasture. Legions of coal miners had to produce the coal underground to replace it. Coal had to be shipped to any number of factories for making cable cars, steel rails, steel cable and for every piece, part and connector of the new mechanical world that would replace the horse.

The horse could not be replaced by an equivalent element packaged in a single unit in a quid-pro-quo; but must be replaced by the many inventions great and small that would create a cable car system or a streetcar system or a rail *system*. A single horse could carry a rider to a destination, but a single cable car without its cable, its rails, its personnel, was useless. For this reason, the horse faded slowly over the next fifty years as whole systems evolved to replace it. Even during World War II, armies had mounted cavalry units going into battle.[14]

Like the Wood Age itself, of which the horse was a key part, the animal as energy unit declined but found its niche in pleasure riding and horse racing as wood found its use in fireplaces and bonfires. The arrival of new kinds of fuel and energy provided the much-welcomed retirement for the horse that had served mankind for some five thousand years.

Thus, the Stage 3, *Expansion and Defense,* worked its way through the energy components and slowly exchanged one element, one component for another across the decades of the 1870s, '80s,'90s and on into the 20th century. No energy component could retire until all its parts had been replaced by a new fuel and its systems. Meanwhile, competitors of new technologies slugged out market share and jostled to find their places. The expansion of any of the new fuels met with retaliation and undermining of the others.

Though this part of the story is undeniably about coal and wood, in the background oil moved along at a swift pace organizing and refining its product as much as its fuel system. The fact that it could do all its basic work in 10 years is a testament to the groundwork already laid and many lessons learned from whale oil and coal oil.

The industrialization of lumber—the transformation of local wood into a new commodity of national lumber sales made possible by coal and railroads. Kansas City had its fair share of notable lumber barons, from Robert A. Long, to Hans Dierks, S. Z. Schutte, and Robert A. Sutherland.

The Long Bell Lumber Company, owned by Kansas City's Robert A. Long, fells a tree.

The arrival of steel in quantity changed the way the building industry did its work. Steel allowed buildings to be erected beyond the four or five floors to which they had been limited, not just in structural measures but because architecture had to adjust to building tall structures.[15] Structural steel interior walls had to be designed to take the load formerly supported by outer walls. The effect of fuel as coal and oil as light source impacted daily life and changed it forever to become a society of large proportions.

Part 3

Good-Bye, Coal:
Hello, Oil Age, 1900-2020

*The rapid development of all material resources during the closing years of the
19th century and the opening years of the 20th has brought business enterprises up
from the day of small things to gigantic proportions, where millions of dollars take
the place of hundreds and where men are required to handle thousands as carefully
and as successfully as their grandfathers handled hundreds.*
—Robert Alexander Long, Kansas City Lumber Baron, 1850-1934

This part explores coal's expansion as wood fuel fell into decline and heavily used as building material. Coal worked to maintain its position in the marketplace at 72% of the fuel consumed in this country. Meanwhile, oil continued on its systems-organization path as it reshaped itself into a fuel that burned in engines rather than in lamps. At the same time due to geographic patterns of geologic deposits, oil became a national fuel available from coast to coast, something that coal was not able to do. Coal was an eastern fuel; natural gas became the western fuel for cities like Phoenix and San Francisco.[1]

Coal's period of commercial dominance from 1885-1920 contained the trauma of World War I with its fuel shortages and shortcomings as a fuel—pollution, labor strikes, huge industrial demands, and an up-and-coming rival, the aggressive oil market. Its power as a fuel destroyed individual artisanship in iron and steel making and created instead employees of endless furnaces, intense heat, declining wages, and avaricious and unfeeling overlords.[2]

Coal had a heavy footprint very distinct from wood and oil. The Coal Age was Herculean in its might, whose support of human activity provoked such descriptions as "city of the big shoulders" that poet Robert Frost saw in the city of Chicago. From 1885 to the 1920s coal abundance, shortfalls, delivery problems, pollution--its personality as a fuel--dominated people's lives from electric-powered streetcars to increasing number of small appliances to the shopping experience itself. At the consumer level the increased cultural artifacts available from Montgomery Ward's and Sear's catalogues in the last decades of the 19th century came from coal that fired the furnaces that created mass production. Cities concentrated workers in urban areas where coal supported factories en masse.

Skyscrapers came from men conquering the metallurgical process on a grand scale through coal. Railroads epitomized coal's strength as both medium and message. Coal introduced electricity that began to erode the efforts of human- and animal-muscle for mechanical output. Mining and forging iron and steel with coal provided a backdrop for labor rights to evolve. Coal would retire animals from the picture slowly but surely. It made fortunes for men like Carnegie, Frick, Gould and Vanderbilt, while laying the groundwork for the Rockefellers and the Morgans. Coal gave America, not just the city but the *nation,* big shoulders. More than any other force, it unleashed the human acquisitiveness on the American continent to harvest the resources of a deeply rich and varied land. It also bridged the chasm between the Wood Age and the Oil Age. The latter could not have achieved its meteoric rise had it not stood on those shoulders to begin its own work.

In this period, fuel use increased exponentially as technology developed to take advantage of it. In 1900, the Btu value of oil as percentage of the total consumption of mineral fuels was 3.1% with coal at 93.4%. By 1910 oil had grown to 7.1% and coal had shrunk to 89.2%. By 1920, oil had grown to 13.9% and coal had fallen to 81.6%.[3]

Oil had made a sizable gain, though undoubtedly coal still had the upper hand. Consumption rates followed similar lines. Nevertheless, coal had been the primary fuel since the 1880s (it had crossed over and changed places with wood as leading fuel in 1885), was referred to as "King Coal," and would gain its "Peak Coal" height in this period with 72% consumption.[4] In the first decade of the 20th century alone, mineral fuels and hydropower, excluding wood, increased their consumption by 95%.[5]

The coal industry scoffed at that idea of being replaced. Even though oil increased to only 12.3% by 1920, it may have been the ease of handling that the Navy discovered, or the much lower prices than coal, or the promise of less air pollution or the magic and wonder of automobiles and flying machines, or just that it was the new, untried fuel and therefore, had none of the problems of the old. Psychologically, these facets of oil's personality gave it a boost, though the quantity used did not bear out the supremacy often claimed.

Chapter 24

The Multiplication of Small Things
To Gigantic Proportions

*With several fuels being used at once, a complex society of things
and their originating birthplaces was created.*

The multiplication of fuels was bound to expand "small things to gigantic proportions" by the 20th century. John D. Rockefeller alone created that kind of mathematics. Not content with one refinery, one pipeline, one railroad siding, or even a few, he replicated like functions into a system of prodigious production. The small amount of oil used as illuminant, lubricant, cleaners, and waxes—less than 3% of the fuel picture for the country by 1900, nevertheless generated an enormous amount of human energy and enthusiasm. This energy rippled across the nation in the form of more refineries, railroads, terminals, pipelines, labor, dollars and other services, not to mention the fever of speculation, and, in turn, helped to infuse Main Streets across the country with expansive activity. One such refinery was built between Kansas City and Independence in 1904, founding a small town called Sugar Creek and helping both of the larger towns to grow.

Kansas Oil: Mining in Its Liquid Phase with a Wheat Field Lid

Prospectors discovered oil in the states of Kansas, Oklahoma and the Indian Territory before the end of the century and the state of Kansas eventually became the last of top seven producers in the country at the turn of the century with production of 75,000 barrels of oil from 103 wells.[1] The center of crude oil production had moved west from Pennsylvania to Ohio, Indiana, Illinois and on to the Midwestern Prairie. Standard Oil moved into what became known as the "Mid-continent field" before 1900 and made its presence known by leasing several hundred thousand acres of land with likely deposits of oil.

By then the technology of refinery and pipeline served four large, "integrated" companies, among the hundreds of startups: Gulf Oil, the Texas Company, Sun Oil and the Security Oil Company, a subsidiary of Standard of New Jersey.[2] These companies soon overpowered the smaller ones and dominated the market. Standard built a refinery in 1897 with a capacity of about a thousand barrels a day at Neodesha, Kansas, (pronounced NeOdeshay) about 150 miles southwest of Kansas City. The refinery produced 3-5,000 barrels a day by 1904.

Victor Murdock of the *Wichita Eagle* drove in 1936 with C. Q. Chandler of Wichita's First National Bank to view the oil and gas developments on the western Kansas prairie. Though thirty or more years had passed since the first such scene, the combinations and the contrasts were what struck him: "Here is found," he wrote, "a mixture of mining in its liquid phase with agriculture in its agronomical phase, a mixture which immediately arrests the imagination. Perhaps its most appealing manifestation in central terms is the way the derrick has jostled with the windmill on the skyline of the prairie landscape . . . . There is no statute against any victim of the oil contagion sharing the general thrill which invariably quickens the closer you get to its source . . . . [The oil and gas] under its wheat field lid is an enormous volume and it crouches there like a lion."[3]

Standard then built a second plant in 1904 between Kansas City and Independence on the bluffs overlooking the Missouri River. This latest addition to Standard's Mid-continent holdings opened with a capacity of seventy-five hundred barrels a day, mostly of kerosene production. The region was producing some thirty thousand barrels, however, and an extension pipeline to Whiting, Indiana, would have to be laid along with a tank farm for storage to handle the overflow.

Workers from the Whiting refinery had been brought in to build and operate the intricate equipment of the Sugar Creek refinery since local labor pools had little experience in this type of work. At both refineries Standard hired as much local talent as it could find and paid them the same wages as their counterparts in the East. "Indeed," one author concluded, "Standard attained the image of the hero-employer during the early years of the first decade of the 1900s."[4]

In spite of such largesse, the skirmishes between Standard Oil and the independent Kansas producers created long-term friction that provoked anger and panic on the part of Kansas citizens and aloof entrenchment on the part of Standard until somewhat more equitable terms for refineries and pipes were worked out over the objections of the state's "anti-pipers" who objected to their lack of access to pipelines.[5] The oil was destined for Kansas City through miles of pipeline to be refined at Sugar Creek, so named for the sugar maples growing along the banks of the Missouri River. The boat landing area along the Missouri River that is today part of Sugar Creek, Missouri (officially incorporated in 1920), was once known as Wayne City Landing originally Duker's Landing) by about 1845 when steamboat landing itself was new. No one there could have imagined such a thing as an oil refinery growing on the spot where early pioneers left the river and headed west on foot.[6]

A railroad line between Kansas City and Chicago had been laid through Sugar Creek in November of 1887. By the following spring passengers could travel by train between the two cities though no stop was made at Sugar Creek until the refinery opened in 1904.[7] The refinery held great hope for the nearby Kansas oil producers and their expected access to the Sugar Creek pipeline. The refinery plus its new tank farm would be connected by what would become one of the world's largest trunk-line systems, to the Whiting, Indiana, plant, which, in turn, would be connected to points east.[8] Local residents were proud of their trans-continental oil system. In 1904 the *Kansas Derrick*, a local oil-industry periodical, wrote: "Probably 80% of the refined products of crude petroleum used in home consumption find a market east of the

Mississippi. The economy of the pipeline system will thus effect a great savings of the cost of transportation, and at the same time it will permit the Kansas product to participate in the economies of manufacturing."[9]

Sugar Creek Refinery, Standard Oil Co.,
near Kansas City, Mo.

Sugar Creek Oil Refinery
The refinery was constructed along the Missouri River east of Kansas City in 1904,
first to produce kerosene and then to refine other products.

Connections from Kansas to Sugar Creek, Missouri, to Whiting, Indiana, formed part of a Standard Oil strategy to satisfy the producers and their demands to access to refineries on the one hand and to restrain competition from other companies by buying all the oil available. The strategy failed to work, however, because sufficient local markets had not yet been developed for the kerosene and byproducts produced.[10] Standard also needed to develop pipelines from Kansas to the Gulf of Mexico, but those were still on the drawing board. Abundance and scarcity on a grand but regional scale stalled Standard Oil in the Midwest. Rivals that sprang up around the Texas oil field—Gulf, Texas Company, Sun Oil, Royal Dutch Shell, Sinclair and Cities Service, soon bit into Standard's territory, and from its original 90% share of refining in 1900, it was reduced to 64% of national production by 1911. The Standard Oil Company Trust was broken up in that year by federal action that also caused it to lose market share.[11]

Standard had been on the field first and had devoted itself, not to production but to refining and transportation. It had used predatory pricing to control independent producers to buckle, to be bought out, or to be left using railroads and *their* predatory pricing rather than pipelines, a cheaper and more efficient transportation technology. Advantages of scale had given the company capital for both vertical efficiency and technological advantages. Pipeline access had been wielded like a blunt instrument against small producers but also against the railroads that lost their loads to a new technology. The prelude to the eventual breakup were a series of reports by the Bureau of Corporations confirming predatory pricing, railroad rebates and non-competitive market conduct.

The federal government followed that with passage of the Hepburn Act of 1906 to make regulation of oil pipelines a federal matter under the control of the Interstate Commerce Commission. This same commission would step in again during World War I to regulate the delivery of coal during the nation's fuel crisis.[12] "By the early 20th century, pipelines were the key element in the expansion of the industry. In 1910, 20,000 miles of trunk line and 24,000 miles of gathering line were operating; by 1920, 70,000 miles of all pipeline were in place." Not that Standard was dead by any means, only forced to reorganize for the second oil revolution—fuel.[13]

The Sunbelt oil discoveries meant the populations there jumped right over the Coal Age and into the Oil Age. Very little coal had made it to those areas, so their growth was dependent on oil and natural gas. This fuel discovery and production promoted rapid industrialization and made clear, as the new fuel was used ubiquitously, the advantages of oil over coal. The railroads in the Sunbelt were among the first to appreciate fuel oil. The Southern Pacific Railroad's use in El Paso rose from 100,000 barrels in 1900s to more than 5,000,000 in 1905. Coal use fell in proportions to oil's rise. Railroads across the Sunbelt followed suit. By the 1920s, railroads became the major market for fuel oil across the area from Texas to California.[14]

This Locomobile, a steamer, was tried on the up and down streets of Kansas City and found to be "peppy" enough to handle itself.

It may not be too much of an overstatement to say that the intersection of easily refined oil in quantity, some derivative of that fuel for internal combustion, grease for bearings, the internal combustion engine itself, railroads for transportation of fuel, metal produced in sufficient quantities by coal use to provide car bodies, paved streets, demand for goods outstripping current infrastructure, and eager users created one of the great harmonic convergences of human history. The idea of self-propulsion had arrived.

Perhaps nothing else since the domestication of the horse some 5,000 or so years ago has quite hooked the human consciousness the same way as auto-mobility.[15] While each of the aforementioned streams of material and technology evolved separately or in concert with each other throughout the latter part of the 19th century, nothing combined them better with greater long-term impact than the automobile.

To leave the horse behind, to no longer *be* behind a horse for locomotion on an individual basis was a dream beyond comparison. In fact, no one *did* dream it because they could not imagine a replacement for a horse before that replacement emerged. It would take another three to four decades to phase out the horse entirely after its very long service to humanity, but that was done as expeditiously as manufacture and technological alchemy could support the flip of the switch.[16]

Could the convergence of such materials NOT have produced the automobile? Human values dictate such choices, and those values indicated at the top of the list of wish fulfillment that transportation sans horse be possible and then imminent. To think of transportation without horses was a revolutionary idea that slowly filtered into the public psyche as technology replaced animal power. The idea was not a goal as much as a byproduct of flow of energy from new sources that shunted aside the horse in its forceful takeover of the daily scene.

New sources of energy, new ways to apply them, new mechanical processes, faster and easier and non-horse, non-animal appeared in a steady stream and the choice became inevitable. The old power of the animal—horse, mule, oxen--was replaced by the then new power of steam engine, then *that* to be replaced by an engine that burned an oil derivative, and the footprint of the Wood Age shrank in the early decades of the 20th century along with the use of its most steadfast servant.

Horseless Carriages Conquer

The horse shared the street scene in Kansas City with electric streetcars at the turn of the 20th century, but a newcomer encroached.

"The horseless carriage," the next step in the long evolution in individual and collective mobility took to the streets in Kansas City in November 1899, when the *Kansas City Star* reported, "Kansas City is so accustomed to up-to-date things that the horseless delivery wagon which appeared on the streets yesterday created no surprise and attracted little attention." Kansas City and Jackson County historian and author, David W. Jackson, writes, "Within a week the situation was markedly different. The one and only automobile in use in Kansas City, driven by A. D. Boyer, an electrician with West Bottom meatpackers Swift & Company, 'filled every requirement.'"[17]

"*Locomobile*"

DAY AUTOMOBILE CO.

Tel. 1472 Main.
1407 E. 12th St.

Kansas City, U. S. A.

Kansas City's *success* was reported in the summer 1901 article, "Horseless Carriages Conquer: Kansas City's hills after many trials have been overcome by the Locomobile," in the magazine, *The Kansas City Manufacturer*.

211

. . . At the present rate, it will only be a short time that all business and pleasure vehicles will be propelled by steam on the hills of Kansas City. The only successful carriage, so far, has been the Locomobile, as shown by past experience, and to it is due much credit for making Kansas City up-to-date with Eastern towns, and showing that the hills here are no obstacle to automobiling, if the Locomobile is used.[18]

Indicative of the mixed fuel scene of the era, different engines had been tried, a gasoline engine and two different "steam carriages." This particular news story announced a peppy little carriage that was indeed "horseless," with a small steam engine attached under the two-passenger seat.[19]

The steam engine had served Kansas City well since its introduction by steamboat in the 1820s. Now it was time for it to leave the water, leave its stationary stance in the coal shed as a provider of electricity and take to the roads of the city. The future seemed rosy for cars using a small steam engine. The little Locomobile fanned the desire of people to be self-propelled--without a horse. They had done it collectively with the streetcar, now they wanted true automobility—to go wherever and whenever they wished to go individually.

**Streets traveled by a horse and buggy, an early automobile, and a streetcar. Left: Northwest corner of 10th & Walnut.
At right: 12th St looking west.
In 1907, equal space in the city directory listed automobile companies and carriage and wagon works.
That would soon change.**

Experimentation continued. In 1905, the Sunday *Journal* advertised an electric car, the Columbus Electric, as the "only *successful* (sic) Electric Auto on the market. It will run all of the time, 75-miles on one charge. Speed 20-miles-an-hour. It will climb any hill in Kansas

City. NOISELESS! Isn't that comfort for you? And any lady can operate it too. In details it is perfect. Has graceful lines and trimmed in the latest style." The Columbus Buggy Company would sell the electric car at 922 Walnut at a price of $1,600.[20]

The auto industry in 1907 offered "the 14-horsepower wonder," the Maxwell, that had "the marvelous simplicity that eliminates the necessity of a chauffeur and makes it the ideal car for the untrained owner." (One can read between the lines here on the cautious approach to horseless carriages and their ease of handling.) The Maxwell sold for $825 and had 9,278 owners to "proclaim its superiority." Whether that number was local or national is unclear. The Auto Dealers Association of Kansas City held its first annual automobile show in 1907 in the convention center. Lighted lamp posts, lavish use of potted palms and patriotic bunting announced the serious role cars were taking in Kansas City.

At least 35 cars were on display. The President of the Buick Automobile Company wrote an article in the 1907 *Annual* saying that Kansas City was an "automobile market." The city welcomed "both American and foreign cars from the most luxurious and finest appointed gasoline, steam or electric cars to the popular priced Runabouts."[21] Along with the 60-horsepower Thomas Car, "America's Champion," evidently uniforms for drivers and chauffeurs were sold at Central Automobile and Livery Company, R. C. Greenlease, proprietor, at 1316-18-20 East 15th. There was a flux in energy choices and the energy transition from horse to car was a great example of the energy transition in motion!

Three simultaneous modes of transportation on Kansas City streets
(horse and wagon, streetcar, and the automobile)

The Studebaker, ("[T]he entire line of self-propelled vehicles from the dainty electric to five-ton truck"), the Packard ("enclosed body cars our specialty"), the Stevens-Duryea, ("this line based on seven years' of experience in the business") the Woods Electric, the Jackson, ("No Sand too Deep," "No Hill too Steep") the Buick, the Pierce Arrow, the Moline, the Maxwell and the Mitchell ("Not only the most economical car to buy but to keep") all advertised for sale in 1907. The Buick Automobile Company built an impressive three-story building at the northwest corner of Admiral Boulevard and McGee Street. Ads that did not mention either electric or steam must presume to be an internal combustion engine of some kind. By 1908, the 30-horsepower White Steamer sold in Kansas City, the "incomparable White, the car for service."[22] This advance in technology assured prospective buyers that "the steam pressure remains constant under all conditions. The persons driving one of the new models for the first time will get the same results as the most experienced operator," along with such welcomed features as "absolute silence, freedom from vibration (the absence of all delicate parts, genuine flexibility (all speeds from zero to maximum by throttle control alone), and supreme reliability." Owners were assured that the car would run "at least 150 miles on one filling of the gasoline and water tanks." Missouri Valley Automobile Company sold the White at 1112-1114 East 15th Street. Clearly, machines of power and personality took to the roads in droves in the first decade of the 20th century. No one yet knew which fuel would rise to the challenge and bring uniformity to the fleets of cars.

Keep Your Bearings Cool

A look through the pages of "The Kansas City Manufacturer" of the summer of 1901 gives a picture of the varieties of fuels, technologies and uses to which the new fuels have been put. Lubricants in an engine were still a topic of conversation as suggested by this ad: "Reduce your oil bill 75% and keep your bearings cool by using Finch Oil Cups, Crampton-Farley Brass Company, 221 Main Street, Kansas City, MO." An oil cup contains a wick of wool or cotton that drips oil onto the bearings to keep them from overheating, an important part of making a steam engine last.[23]

Another ad for "King Bee Oils" shows they are made in "Kansas City, U.S.A. Cylinder, Engine Dynamo, Roller, Harvester, Harness and Castor. Pure, and will lend life to machinery." These oils were "manufactured by Interstate Oil Company, Kansas City, Kas." What kind of oil, unfortunately, is not stated though the company was the "only refiners of lubricating oils in the two Kansas City's, and whose products deserve and receive general recognition from users of machinery."[24]

Gasoline was being used in a variety of ways such as in "gasoline stove ovens," manufactured by Gille Manufacturing Company at 1053-1059 St. Louis Avenue in Kansas City, Missouri. Since gasoline has a high volatility, the idea of using it to heat an oven seems chancy. This manufacturer also made gasoline and oil tanks in "tin plate, galvanized iron, sheet steel and tinners' supplies, granite, galvanized, stamped and Japanned ware and stove hollow ware," all of which meant benefits to the buyer who understood these advantages in 1901. Witte gasoline engines were advertised as "Kansas City's Best," with electric ignition.

214

This bustling view of Kansas City in the early 20th century,
skyscrapers risingin the background, combines all energy systems at once,
the steamboat, the barge, the railroad, and the factories.

They promised steady regulation, economical fuel consumption and were guaranteed for five years. Witte offered models in two and three horse power and recommended them for "printing offices, blacksmith and bicycle shops, small pumping outfits and all places where small and steady power" would be required. This little engine would be replaced by electricity later, but for now a small gasoline engine in the shop would take the place of handwork. Over a thousand of these engines were in operation in July of 1901 made by the Witte Iron Works Company at 51 West 5th street in Kansas City, Missouri.[25]

The editors of the *Kansas City Manufacturer* described each entry at The Homes Products Exhibition opening May 27, 1901 in glowing terms. Their comments will remind some readers today of business icons that have come and gone or lent their names to streets in the city. William Volker, manufacture of picture frames and window shades was mentioned along with Woolf Bros. Manufacturing Company that would show "the latest fancies" in the essentials of shirts and "gents' furnishing goods."

Fred Wolferman, "who has the most complete establishment of retail groceries in Kansas City will have an attractive display of the goods he carries that are made in Kansas City, U. S. A." (The use of the phrase "Kansas City, U.S.A," seemed to be an editorial decision to position the city as an internationally known entity, suggests an early attempt at what we now call "globalization.") In another part of the exhibit "a concord of sweet sounds will emanate" from the booth of J. W. Jenkins' Sons manufacturer of a line of musical instruments "which are known throughout the world," including the "famous Harwood guitars and mandolins."[26]

The news of the building of the "largest retail structure" in the city, the Jones Dry Goods Company

Witte Gasoline Engines

Kansas City's Best.

Electric Ignition, Steady Regulation, Economical Fuel Consumption. Guaranteed for five years. Catalogue L tells more.

WITTE IRON WORKS CO.
510 W. 5th St.,
KANSAS CITY, MO.

216

at Twelfth and Main Streets was announced. Small stores at the site were "being wrecked" to make room for the retail giant, eight stories high, of white enameled brick, glass and iron. "The Christmas trade," the ad said, "will be accommodated in the new house."[27] The highly lauded Day Locomobile would be represented in the hall in a "very attractive manufacturing exhibit, and as the Locomobile will be new to many visitors this exhibit will attract attention from all."[28]

The automobile had arrived in Kansas City and meant to stay. It required more paved streets, more navigable roads, garages, ultimately gasoline stations. The infrastructure of the auto would replace the infrastructure of the horse. Watering troughs would be replaced by service stations. Parking spaces for cars would replace the stables. Another feature of the Wood Age would give way to modernity powered by the Oil Age.

These early autos were a harbinger of growth to come in all sectors. The city itself boomed with activity and experienced a real estate bubble from which the developers learned hard lessons.

The Lesson Was Severe

By 1900, the city and its environs had grown to a population of 210,000, an amazing increase of growth considering its enfeebled condition and resurrection from the Civil War when in 1865 it had about 4,000 residents hanging on.

From then onward, miles of railroad tracks along with acre upon acre of building and growth marked the city as it accommodated the emigrants going west and the wheat and cattle that would fill the railroad cars going east. As with all building booms, this one required thousands of feet of lumber and every kind of attendant business to support rapid expansion. Then the boom collapsed in the 1890s, until the city once again resurrected its building plans after losing "a number of valuable business enterprises, due solely to there being no suitable building and location to accommodate them." [29]

A full-page article reported on the lumber business: "Shipments are exceeding the cutting and there is a visible depletion in the supply of stocks. Very few, if any, of the southern mills have been able to keep even with the pace set by the call for lumber and stocks are badly broken. . ... The demand has continued to steadily increase, and prices are stiff."[30] Perhaps this shortage helped to lead to the use of steel for building material.

The year 1901 was hailed as "the greatest building year and will lead all records in number and substantial buildings." Kansas City had suffered its own inflated building drama in the recent past reminiscent of the housing problems of 2008: "During the boom of unhallowed memory the city went building mad and structures of all kinds were erected in such number as to preclude even the earning of a fair interest in the investment. The lesson was severe and costly and capital has fought shy of a repetition."

The report went on to describe the building of warehousing along Southwest Boulevard, the erection of the "largest elevator and warehouse in the West," more warehouse building at Eighth and Broadway "going up so rapidly that while the men are blasting out the rock in one end of the lot the piers are up, and the superstructure is begun in the other end." The Savoy Hotel was expanding on Ninth, and the New Century building for stores and offices was rising on Grand Avenue. "The lumber is arriving for this and work is going on there every day. It will be finished this fall and will be six stories high." The aforementioned retail giant, the Jones Store, was part of this list that ended with the description of the Willis Wood opera house being built at Eleventh and Baltimore at a cost of $350,000. It would be "the finest in the West." "The steel is here" for this building, the story said, and suggests it had arrived from somewhere farther east, and that steel-built buildings would slowly take the place of wood-built infrastructures. (See Care of Coal appendix).[31]

Above: A 1907 Ad for the "Good Luck" Range, a natural gas range showing that fuel was finding its new niche in home heating and giving up the lighting sector. As advanced as it was, it took only "twenty minutes" to learn to operate, suggesting lighting a gas range was still a tricky and potentially dangerous process. It was probably called "good luck" because the range provided ease of lighting and performed better than others.

Right: For home and industrial uses, coal needed to be encased in a furnace, an idea barely entertained even a hundred years earlier. Within the confines of the furnace a coal fire could become as large and as intense as necessary to do the work of industry versus the work of hand laborers. This furnace on the left is a small version for home heating with pipes leading to individual rooms.

The home and kitchen at the Homes Exhibition received its fair share of the spotlight with the Herrick tile-lined "Refrigerator," though still an ice box, the technology had advanced to include "circulation of pure cold air, absolutely dry, never sweats, therefore is perfectly hygienic, iced from outside the house. Unequalled for economy of ice."[32]

The Kansas City Steel Range manufacturer showed a new cook stove, a definite cut above the cast-iron range, and the Kansas City Milling company had "one of the most striking exhibits in the hall" especially interesting "to lady visitors" who used Imperial Flour.

The furnace for the home had arrived in Kansas City. The Prest Heating Company, manufacturers of the Prest Furnace, of which there are "more in use in the best homes in Kansas City than any other kind, will show the superiority and general excellence . . . over those of any other kind in the market." The fuel is not stated, but the furnace could have burned either wood or coal and perhaps both.[33] The engraving here is not a Prest Furnace, but the formidable structure shows how far home heating had come from the open fireplace. Coal required an enclosed housing to make the best use of its qualities as well as to remove as much smoke as possible. The multiple pipes indicate room-by-room heating outlets and the size of the furnace itself a testimony to the breakthrough in working with metals made available through the use of coal in the last decades of the 19th century. Technology had caught up with the coal stream.

Two thousand "editors of country dailies" would attend the exposition and would carry back to their small towns the wonder of a multi-fueled, energy-rich Kansas City at the turn of the century. Among other wonders they would see was the manufacturing of wind mills their readers no doubt used on their farms. The American Wind Mill Manufacturing Company, a newcomer to Kansas City, was the only manufacturer of wind mills in the area.

Armour Packing Company had an elaborate display of canned meats and "products and by-products which are produced by a first-class packing house. Their exhibit was in the nature of a revelation." Nearby would be the American Can Company with an "artistic line of their

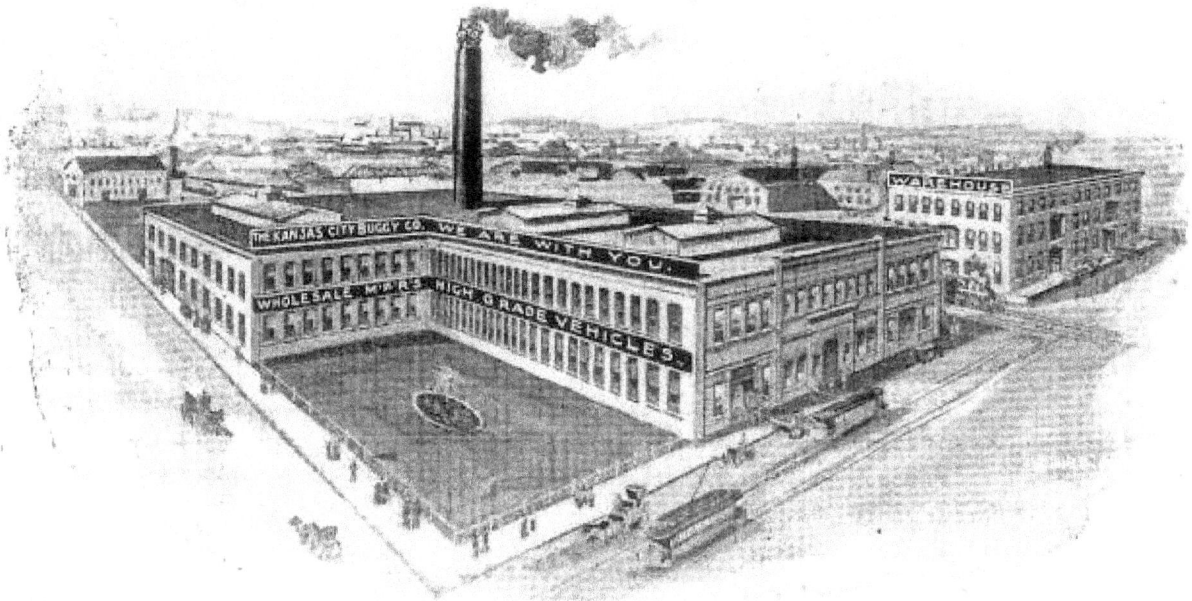

goods, which practically covers all lines of products in tin cans, from the ordinary fruit can to the highest grade of art lithograph tin packages."[34] The Novelty Manufacturing Company displayed "scores of useful and labor-saving novelties for workshops and household and many other uses," indicating the phrase was a come-on for the curious and hopeful.[35]

Though the city had achieved some control over its water quality by installing a waterworks in 1875, the Standard Filter Company, manufacturers of Standard and Climax filters for the home and factory would demonstrate "how the non-pellucid Kaw and the sometimes-turbid Missouri River water can be made as clear as crystal," a welcomed relief to those drinking the water and trying to wash clothes with it.[36]

In spite of the obvious advantages of the horseless carriage, the Kansas City Buggy Company is pictured on the front of the July issue of *The Manufacturer*, a huge factory that would burn down shortly thereafter. Little did people know in the early years of the 20th century how quickly buggies would become obsolete. The size of the buggy company factory suggests a strong market for their product, but around the corner a little Locomobile chugged up a hill toward commercial dominance.

The "California Connection" to oil drilling was sold in shares by a realty company in Kansas City, Missouri.

Sedalia and California Oil Company.

Incorporated under the Laws of Missouri.

250,000 Shares of the Par Value of $1 Each.

50,000 Shares in the Treasury.

Stock Absolutely Non-Assessable.

Company owns 40 acres of Absolutely Proven Oil Land in Sunset District, Kern Co., Cal.

We do not ask investors to buy stock on a probability of striking oil.

We now have one well completed and pumping one hundred and fifty barrels of oil per day.

Purchase of this stock is absolutely safe and a reliable investment. It will bring dividends and profits to every investor.

DIRECTORS:— Judge W. S. Shirk, Wm. H. Powell, W. F. Walker, J. D. Donnohue and W. P. Cunningham.

We invite your most rigid investigation and solicit your subscription. A limited number of shares are now for sale at eighty cents per share. For further particulars, address or call on

WHIPPLE-WOODS REALTY CO.,   110 W. 8th St., Kansas City, Mo.

220

One of the city's other firms was described as "the line of rapidly developing businesses in the production of buggy tops in Kansas City. The largest single plant devoted to this line is operated by the Gille Hardware and Iron Company. Improvements in the machinery, equipment and additions to the capacity were made "as fast as a rapidly growing demand enforced it. The result has been a factory modern in every feature and producing a complete line of goods varying from the medium rubber top to the highest grades of hand buffed leather." In addition to buggy tops, cushions, lazybacks and aprons were also made.

Standard Oil Filling Station, Kansas City, Missouri. Gasoline $.14 per gallon.

This merchandise was distributed to all parts of the West and Southwest, and "an ever increasing trade offers good evidence that the goods are right in quality style and price."[37] This product is not quite akin to the buggy whip rushing to extinction, since the buggy tops were probably used on little Locomobiles, but they certainly were of the old paradigm and no one is seemingly aware that the multi-fuel picture and horseless runabouts had already numbered their days.

One of the most interesting ads in this edition is the "Sedalia and California Oil Company" offering 250,000 shares of stock in an oil well in California brokered by a local realty company. This ad shows the level of financing for the oil fields at the time. This Missouri company, straddling half the continent between Sedalia, Missouri, and Kern County,

Fueling Change

California, had local backers and California equipment to bring in a sure investment, not the "probability of striking oil" but one already producing.[38]

The next chapter in Kansas City's oil history combines the very old occupation of the Osage Indians with the very new arrival of oil as motive power.

Chapter 25

The Osage in the Oil Age

This chapter reveals the fast-paced, unsteady and sometimes harsh path
of modernization the Osage nation took to become 20th century citizens of America.

At this point in its fuel history Kansas City has one of its most ironic twists. The original inhabitants, the Osage Indians and other neighboring tribes, were removed in 1825 and suffered a century of humiliation, disease, mistreatment and thievery in many forms during the following decades. Their revenge was to enjoy the fruits of their newly acquired lands in Indian Territory, Osage County, Oklahoma, that would become the largest county in the state when statehood was conferred in 1907.

Oil was discovered there at the turn of the 20th century and made them "the richest tribe in the world." As if that were not an ironic enough twist, natural gas and oil found on their reservation was piped back to their former homeland to Kansas City in the form of money and dividends in the early 1900s. According to the *Greater Kansas City Annual of 1904-05* "gas exists in a great many places in the Indian Territory on both sides of the line separating the Cherokees from the Osages."

In an article entitled "Heart of Oil and Gas Belt, Great Productive Territory at Kansas City's Doors Assures the Cheapest Fuel," the author writes that "for many reasons the large supply of petroleum and natural gas in Kansas and the Indian Territory has an important bearing on the future development of Kansas City." In a telling judgment of the future he writes, "The great development of this product is having an unusual influence on the material development throughout the areas producing them, and as the productive territory is tributary to Kansas City this alone would yield no small increase to her commercial and banking accounts." [1] In so many words, the author connects the oil and gas fields of the Indian Territory with the "material development" being enjoyed in Kansas City.

Once again, the Euro-American settlers of Kansas City drew on the natural wealth of the Osage, first profiting from taking their land in Missouri, then from taking the oil from under their land in Oklahoma. What the arrival of oil did for the Osage was another matter.

We began this story with the long-suffering Osage Indians after their first removal from Missouri in 1825 to becoming the "richest tribe in the world" through oil discoveries on their reservation. Their 19th century experience at the hands of the higher energy suite and its presumption of civilizing the Indian into "citizen's clothes" to at least "resemble white men" is a cautionary tale with that double ironic twist at the end.[2] First feared, then disdained, then enriched and envied, the Osage felt the full force of the influence of both energy and fuel over the span of a century from 1825 to 1925.

The Euro-American settlers matured with the incremental changes of moving from one fuel to another over time. Meanwhile, the Osage had to telescope a longer adjustment of understanding and accepting Euro-American materiality as well as changing fuels. This collapsing time frame forced them to relinquish time-honored ways with sudden loss and to acquire modern ways with forced acceptance.

Walking the Narrowing Path of Accommodation

The Osage, originally residents of lands south of the Missouri River and down into the Ozarks and Arkansas, were forced to give up those lands once Missouri became a state. They moved along with numbers of other tribes onto the plains of Kansas in 1825. Having been both plains and woodland Indians, this arrangement removed them from their woodlands cover and made them exclusively Plains Indians. Lost were the rushes to weave into walls for their dwellings. Lost to them was the forest and its abundance of sounds and whispers that told them that the bear, the deer, the turkey, the badger had gathered there for cover as had the Indians themselves. Lost to them were the stalwart trees, sentinels to the Indians' comings and goings among them.

The Osage had originally had the good fortune of being located in a geographically powerful position and became "a perfect buffer" between the competitive French and Spanish in the 17th and 18th centuries. In that position the Osage had spread their borders and increased their territory through raids, fighting, and bluff warfare with other tribes on their periphery. Fierce warriors with a tremendous pride of battle and bravery, they were feared by the other tribes as well as by the Europeans who felt they could do little with this nation of tall warriors "until the time when they could overwhelm them."[3]

Eventually that time came for the Indian removal. What the Osage gained by living on the plains was proximity to the seasonal movements of the buffalo and grasses for their horses year around. They gained antelope and prairie dogs. They also gained from the United States government farm implements, a mill, blacksmithing tools, a log cabin for the chief and other material goods typical of 19th century Euro-American farmers. And, they gained annuity payments for their lands. This seemed like an unequitable and undesired tradeoff for having given up their homeland.

The Osage lived in reasonable harmony with their neighboring tribes, given the dislocation all of them had experienced, until 1868 when treaty negotiations began again. Once more the United States government asked the Osage to give up their lands and move. When Kansas became a state in 1861, only the Civil War slowed the land rush that brought increasing pressure from white settlers for the Indian lands, and the tribes were again forced to relinquish the place they had made home.[4]

The first land confiscation after the war came from having been associated with the losing side. An unknown number of Osage men served the Confederate Army, while nearly 400 served with the Union army. At the close of the conflict the North had won, federal authorities, taking a dim view of confederate service, forced the Osage to give up nearly half of their Kansas lands in retribution.

In an 1865 treaty the federal government also allowed non-tribal members to settle on the remaining land the Osage still possessed. Post-war conflicts found the Osage beleaguered from both East and West forces. They had been unable to complete their fall buffalo hunt by the "allied" tribes of Arapahos, Cheyenne and Sioux who had united to harass the oncoming flow of emigrants and to stop the intercontinental railroad from being built. Not only had the Osage come home without their buffalo meat but they had lost over 325 horses to the allied tribes as well. Meanwhile, settlers encroached on their land, and the Missouri, Fort Scott and Santa Fe Railroad Company asked to buy a third of the remaining Osage reservation for right of way. The white man had all the power at this point. The tribe was "very destitute," reported Indian agent G. C. Snow in Kansas. "Something must be done for these people at once." They were starving.[5]

During negotiations the tribe leaders were told their game was disappearing and that they could move to the Indian Territory where "the white man would bother them no more." The Great Father, they were told, "would be sad," if they refused to sign the treaty, he would believe, then, that the Osage "could get along without him." Without supplies from the government, the Osage would have to stand alone against the Plains Indians to try to hunt buffalo while the settlers gathered on their land wanting to plow and build.[6] The Osages eventually "touched the feather," signing the new treaty.[7]

Osage Indian, Ma-chet-she, adopted modern clothing while keeping his signature hair style to show his tribal affiliation.

After 1870, the Osage relinquished all of their remaining land in Kansas for which they were paid, and that money held to buy land in Indian Territory, what would become Oklahoma.[8] They had $8,500,000 from the sale of their land earning 5% in the United States Treasury.[9] Since 1825 the Heavy Eyebrows had steadily infiltrated their numbers to marry the Osage women, especially when the Osage were then seen as people of property. This dilution of the pure Osage blood would eventually lead to the mixed bloods outnumbering the full bloods and would add to the general disintegration of the old bonds and ancient traditions.[10]

By 1874, they had moved atop one of the as-yet-undiscovered major oil fields in Oklahoma and the United States. The reservation measured 2,350 square miles, 57 miles long north to south and 60 miles across east to west. It bordered the Cherokee Nation on the east at the 96th meridian, the Creeks Indians on the south, the Kaw Indians and the Arkansas River on the west. The northern border is the Kansas-Oklahoma state line.[11] The Indian agent reported with both hope and despair that some of the tribes "were civilizing," but that "the Osage as yet are most of them wild, blanket, scalping Indians, far from civilized, many of them hardly ready to give up the war dance and the scalping knife."[12]

The Osage arrived at their new reservation 3,956 strong, with twelve thousand horses.[13] The 1870s proved to be a rocky decade for the tribe. In 1874, they hunted buffalo and came back with "great loads of meat and tallow and 10,800 buffalo robes," but in 1876 they hunted buffalo for the last time.[14] The white hunters had reduced the buffalo herds to negligible numbers. Their Indian agent urged them to become farmers in the Euro-American fashion with men at the plow. The Osage men, however, saw themselves as warriors and farming as tending "squaw patches." They attempted it half-heartedly, but readily gave in to the grasshopper plagues and the drought of that decade.[15] In 1877, half of their tribe died from disease: small pox, tuberculosis and cholera.[16]

The Congress under President Grant supported legislation "for the purpose of inducing Indians to labor and become self-supporting." Indian agents were to see that all able-bodied men from ages 18-45 were to "perform manual labor" in exchange for the annuities they had been receiving. The Indians protested working for what the government already owed them by treaty for land cessions.[17] They understood quid pro quo.

In the view of their oppressors/conquerors, their lack of "acculturation" even as late as the 1880s indicated how far removed they still were from integration. They had neither understanding nor even comparisons in their experience for the white man's ways and mechanisms. They did not understand the concept of a brake on a wagon, for instance, and routinely ran down a hill throwing out passengers and goods as the team ran full tilt for a cliff or a wreck.

Their children at school climbed the stairs on their hands and knees and came downstairs scooting from one step to the next on their bottoms. A group of grown Osage men who had slept inside a white man's house one frigid night, did not understand the idea of a door knob when smoke began to fill the room and they badly wanted out. Their children continually tried to escape the boarding school and were hunted down by white men on horseback and roped and tied in a wagon or dragged back through the dirt.[18] Keenly self-educated in the intricacies of thriving in the open forest and prairie, their frame of reference had no room for the built environment and mores of the Euro-Americans.

In tandem with these negative events, the tribes merged the Great Osage and Little Osage to become "the Osage Nation." They created a constitution in 1881 that divided the nation into five districts, with a national council made up of three members of each of the five districts. The council could "tax, make treaties and impeach officials."[19] This change in power/political structure meant they walked the "ever narrowing path" the white man wanted,[20] diminishing the powers of the council of elders, tribal identities and clan lodges.

Nation with a Capital "N"

Pressure from the outside had succeeded in forcing the Osage to take up ways by which the white man could understand and deal with them. While sublimating their tribal distinctions, they melded into a single tribe, the easier for the white man to address. In losing their identities they became a nation with a capital "N," strong enough together to stand against the white intruders. To the Great Father who lived far away in the East, however, they were a nation with a small "n." In the eyes of the United States government, the tribes were "domestic dependent nations . . . in a state of pupilage . . . whose relationship "resembles that of a ward to his guardian."[21] This paternalistic approach gave the United States government the attitude of "doing what is good for them," in a way that was good for the government.

This Native American Indian family has adopted modern dress, part of an exchange of Wood Age, low-energy-system garments, for the high-energy, Coal Age woven clothing.

On the reservation, these once-mighty warriors and hunters were daily demeaned and corralled by their white plunderers. Horse stealing, whiskey peddling, wife hunting and those bribing their way onto the tribal rolls kept the Indians in a defensive position. The local lawmen arrested "thousands" of Indians for possessing whiskey but not the white man for selling it.[22] Alcoholism was a common problem as the Indians attempted to numb themselves from the confusion of oil derricks, railroad tracks, leases, dubious schemes proposed by white men, and constant negotiation over sovereignty that appeared in ink but nowhere else. "They were afflicted with a nagging certainty that they were not active participants in the capitalistic bustle of the surrounding and pervasive majority culture."[23] In their long struggle for sovereignty to become an independent nation, the Osage were pummeled and pelted with the white man's values and his high-energy system.

In 1897, large amounts of oil were discovered under the reservation.[24] Because the Osage had chosen to share their wealth communally by "headright," each full blood or half blood on the rolls of the tribe, they fared better than other tribes. The Cherokees, Creeks and others had chosen allotments of acreage and only those under whose land oil was found grew rich. Because of the Osage decision the whole tribe became "the richest tribe in the world."[25] Then schemers descended on them en masse to swindle, cheat, rob and even murder them for their wealth in a period known as the "Reign of Terror" that finally ended in 1932 with the falling oil prices of the Depression.[26]

Trading Horses for Horsepower

By 1904, high-grade petroleum was being pumped from 155 producing oil wells on the reservation. Eighteen gas wells also produced a steady stream. With that kind of production their Kansas City connection came into play. In 1904 the entire Kansas-Indian Territory produced 5,602,963 barrels. The Prairie Oil and Gas Company that developed the field increased their production to about 15,000,000 per annum. This production represents a good deal of both oil and money for the day and fueled a metro of over 220,000 with buying power.[27] While it is easy to imagine what the city was doing with such fuel—increases in manufacturing, material goods, conveniences, everything an upwardly mobile city population yearned for, it is also easy to imagine the bustle, noise and pollution that accompanied its production on the Osage reservation. They daily witnessed the disintegration of the remnants of their former world.

Between 1906-1916, a blanket lease for oil production covered 68,000 acres and over a thousand producing wells.[28] In 1907, the Osage nation became part of the state of Oklahoma and the reservation became Osage County. This period of overnight oil wealth for the Osage was called "the Frenzy." White society's wealth pushed the Osage into bizarre behaviors of buying cars they did not know how to drive, hiring chauffeurs to drive them two blocks on the reservation, taking lavish vacations and inviting less fortunate tribes in for days of dancing at which they would give away extravagant gifts. At one point it was said more Pierce Arrow touring cars could be found on the Osage reservation than any other county in the country.[29] They had traded in their once-prized horses for horsepower.

By 1917, the Osage Nation's royalties amounted to $2,719 per person. For a family of five or six "headrights," that became a fortune. Many of the Osage left the reservation for extended vacations in Colorado, Texas and California.[30]

The Kansas City economy felt the wave of money from the oil fields, and, indeed, helped to supply the capital. The *Kansas City Star*, March 11, 1917, corroborated the connection to the Osage oil fields in Oklahoma:

Already the golden backwash is beating closer and closer to Kansas City. The actual, tangible wealth from the Kansas and Oklahoma fields is affecting the financial life of the city. Kansas City capital goes out and oil field capital comes in. The tide swings back and forth, but each day the waves lap nearer. Being in the midst of it, or on the edge rather, it is difficult to realize that something is happening nearby that is as romantic as the days of '49, the Cripple Creek madness or the rush to the Klondike. Yet some day there will surely arise a Bret Harte or a Rex Beach to set it all down that the world may know. Today he may be a driller or a tankie.

In keeping with their warrior tradition, a number of the young Native Americans volunteered for service in World War I. Against the wishes of the Indian agent, all the young tribal men joined one company in the Army known as the "millionaire company" comprised of wealthy Creeks, Choctaws and Osage. The agent felt the young Osage men would not be trainable since they had no discipline and did no work, but when they came home on leave their demeanor had changed. They were able to pass the training and serve in the Oklahoma National Guard.[31] In spite of this exposure to the outside world, the tribe's naiveté invited more big-and small-time swindlers, oil companies that did not pay their royalties, cattlemen who leased pasture and got away without paying for it. One writer said, "Oil merely gave the Osages more money for white men to grab."[32]

By 1925, the Osage reached their peak of $13,200 per headright, an envious amount of money even in the gay '20s. The Osage had come a long way from the pedestrian tribe frightened by the "elk dog" and being king of their Midwestern domain. Some critics compared them to the Germans that the Roman emperor Tacitus described in the second century A.D. in their "incredulous ineptitude of being face to face with the simplest of mechanisms." Journalists enjoyed writing about the "Neolithic tribe" who had become bizarrely rich.[33]

With the original steel knife European traders had opened the Osage world to one of material possession from knives to land. For two centuries the Osage had modified their behaviors to include knives, blankets, guns and horses. They obediently moved from one assigned piece of land to another. They sipped from the cup of the white man but did not dine at his table. Yet after two centuries of association amazingly little of the white man's world rubbed off on them until their food source--their energy source--disappeared. With the loss of the buffalo came the loss of their identity. That great, grand creature defined who they were and how they lived. Wood may have been their fuel source, but the buffalo supplied their energy.

As white farmers organized around the field and the mill, the Osage organized themselves around the buffalo. No longer warriors and hunters, the men disdained farm work. The women no longer had buffalo robes to process and garden plots to plant in the forest. They wept for more than the graves of their family members left behind; they wept for their lost traditions. The children reacted with terror at the white man's ways.

Fueling Change

By the end of the 19th century, the Osage no longer sipped from the cup of the other world, they drowned in it.

The 20th century would find the Osage rich by Euro-American's standards but in poverty by their own. In their original belief system those warriors who died in battle lived on in a lush village with plenty of game and horses. Those who died from other causes struggled endlessly in a poor village.[34] Unfortunately, the reality of the white man's definition of riches did not fulfill their dream, but instead fed their nightmares.

The Osage populations hunting and living in Missouri and Arkansas before Euro-American contact had no yearnings for the white man's things, nor did his grandchildren in Oklahoma conjure up California vacations or touring cars. Those were not in their lexicon, their experience, or on their wish list. Stripped of their energy source and the whole belief system that supported it, the next generation had to find new religion, new food and new ways of being in the white man's world.

"OUT WEST UP TO DATE"

Chapter 26

Oil Expands Against Coal

A growing rivalry between the two fuels carried us throughout the 20th century.

We now live so far removed from handling chunks of coal that only the older generation can remember its personality. A list of instructions from "Hints on the Storage of Coal" from *Coal Age* suggests that both producers and customers used to know a great deal more about coal than any of us can now imagine. (See Appendix D for a complete list of instructions.) Coal could ignite spontaneously in large piles, needed to be handled carefully to reduce coal dust and breakdown of the chunks, and oxidation more common in freshly mined coal.

Such was coal's individual characteristics that underlay the industrial use of coal. Industrial coal users had known these factors for centuries, had learned which coal to use for which task, if a choice was available, and how to get the most out of it. In the Wood Age people knew the kinds of wood that worked best in each kind of use. It is reasonable to assume that as the many coal types became known that their use would also be distinctive and a subject of trial and error. A similar lesson came with oil that flowed from the ground in various qualities from sweet crude to sludge.

Petroleum as Fuel for Steamers is Hopeless

During the first two decades of the 20th century, the baton passed from coal to oil on the high seas as fuel for shipping. In the 1860s oil had been burned in steamships, had proven that it could work, and that ships did not have to refuel nearly as often as with coal. But crude oil had its drawbacks. The level of refinement at that time left the fuel with a bad odor, and the intensity of heat generated by the boilers was more than the crew could endure. A fear of instant explosion should the ship be hit by a torpedo or have an accident discouraged the shipping industry from taking it on. The Secretary of the Navy concluded: "It appears that the use of petroleum as fuel for steamers is hopeless; convenience is against it, and safety is against it. Opposed to these the advantages of the probably very important reduction in bulk and weight, with their attending economies, cannot prevail."[1]

It would be another forty years before the Navy seriously considered using oil again. In the meantime, the illuminant period had passed for oil. That role had been taken over by electricity, and fuel oil had become the dominant motive power in the West where both railroads and shipping ran on California crude. Anywhere from half to four-fifths of crude was refined for fuel oil. Railroads were using 20,000,000 barrels, about 25% of the fuel oil produced in 1909, and nearly that much was used by industry. By then the Navy had changed its mind:

The introduction of fuel oil into the United States Navy has been quite rapid and with fully as good results as were anticipated . . .. The engineering and military advantages of the use of fuel oil are clearly recognized by the Navy Department, as a result of experiment and experience. In the new construction fuel oil is being more and more extensively used.[2] The *Oil and Gas Journal* in 1911 concurred:

> The uniformly good results obtained whenever oil fuel has been given a properly arranged test on an ocean-going steamship have made it certain that someday, and not so very far in the future, oil will take the place of coal as the fuel of the great trans-Atlantic steamships. One remarkable fact in favor of the oil fuel is that in spite of the unusual number of advantages to be derived from the change, there is practically no serious disadvantage.[3]

The United States Navy had been coaling at sea since 1899 and knew the danger involved in the process. The coaling of ships was a challenge even in port though refueling was easiest between dock and moored ship. Winches were set upon the warships to haul bags of coal on board. Crew members moved the bags on small carts to the coal chutes that went from the upper deck to the bunkers below. Re-coaling at sea from ship to ship, i.e., collier (coal carrier) to warship, depended on the weather and the height of the waves. Swells that caused the ships to roll more than three or four degrees made the transfer prohibitive. Colliers carrying a full load of coal were equipped with bumpers made of cotton bales to keep the two ships from touching metal to metal. Some transfers happened quickly with about half the crew participating filling bags of coal of 100 kilograms or 222 pounds each. With enough man power as much as 57 tons per hour could be transferred. The bags were transferred by way of a wire between the two ships, full ones dumped, empties returned. It took about twenty seconds for a bag to make it from one ship to another.[4]

In 1899, the United States Navy carried out their first under-way coaling. The USS Massachusetts towed the collier 300-400 feet astern while the tramway shuttled the bags of coal from one to the other. By 1903, the USS Alabama lashed the collier alongside while coaling. The seas were high enough that one sailor said it was "about the roughest proposition I ever stood up to. At one time the collier rolled so heavily that I was afraid she would stave in against our armor belt and she literally raised right up into the air on each swell and looked as though she would come down on our decks." In over twelve hours the ship took in seven hundred tons using this form of transfer. Further evolutionary steps increased to a ton of coal per minute using better methods.

Bag size increased to eight hundred pounds by 1914. In spite of these improvements, oil would take over the shipping lanes by the end of World War I.[5]

Loading Coal on Ships Before the naval fleet adopted oil, the ships took on coal by this process at the New York Navy Yard, Brooklyn, New York circa 1909.

Bags of coal are being hoisted from the collier, the coal barge, to the hold of the *New Hampshire*. Crew members shovel coal into the bags from the coal pile while sailors on the receiving end wait. This process was very difficult on the high seas. Oil in barrels soon proved to be a much more efficient process.

Most navies switched to oil by 1911, except for Britain. It was a country rich with coal and coal stockpiles but had no oil. For that reason, First Lord of the Admiralty Winston Churchill and others felt uneasy about leaving coal behind and depending totally on oil. They were uncertain about the supply chain at a moment when they would need it most, and a ship once switched from coal to oil would not be able to pinch hit with coal. The grate would be gone, the engine would change, the bags of coal unavailable. The country also had a worldwide network of coaling stations available from their vast number of colonies that stood ready to replenish any British ship that came by.

However, this could be called a "twilight of technology" much like the horse to the streetcar, or kerosene to electricity. Another advantage of coal was that below the water line, a chamber filled with coal bags acted as an added protection should a torpedo hit, an advantage not easily dismissed.

As Winston Churchill himself noted, however, "the ordeal of coaling a ship exhausted the whole ship's company. In wartime it robbed them of their brief period of rest; it subjected everyone to extreme discomfort." The logistics were a nightmare. It was virtually impossible to refuel at sea with coal, which meant that a quarter of the fleet had to be in port at any given time to refuel at dockside. Another disadvantage was the dark plume of coal smoke that made the ships so visible.

Arguments for oil included needing fewer hands to process the fuel: "Oil fuel settles half our manning difficulties! We should require 50 percent less stokers," said one of Churchill's most influential proponents, Admiral Sir John Fisher. Once Churchill started putting together the new fuel chain, he had to find a steady supply of oil. This led him to the Middle East where he eventually made long-term deals with oil companies on which he could rely.

The United States had also moved to oil, and the Italians had crossed over as well so that by 1912 much of the world had left coal behind. Germany did not adopt oil until after World War I, but sometimes used a combination of fuels where possible. One technique was to spray coal with oil to increase its intensity, a half-way step that showed a lack of willingness to jump into oil all at once.

By the end of World War I, the world had switched to oil. The competitive fear between Britain and Germany helped to "fuel" that transition.[6]

Coal-fired ships of World War I take to the seas leaving a trail of black smoke

Chapter 27

Coal Makes Itself Scarce

The coal industry endured difficulties as their fragile delivery system fell apart during the cold winters of 1917-1918, as war raged in Europe. A war of a different kind waged at home among the railroads as a delivery system, the coal industry, and the public who needed fuel.

The Wood Age had endured because it was the basis for life. The suite of landscape and ecosystem in which human beings learned to live and prosper was primary resource to them. Only in the 19th century did people move past that context through increased fuel use and technology to give up wood and domesticated animals and move on to other sources of heat and man-made power. No sooner had they done so, in fact, were in the process of doing so, than the new systems failed them, and they were forced to return willy-nilly to the Wood Age for fuel. A confluence of weather, politics and economics created a bottleneck of enormous proportions in coal delivery in the winters of 1917 and 1918.

A Problem That Was Literally Staggering

World War I had begun in 1914 in Europe with a pledge by the American government to remain neutral. Over the course of the next three years, however, the German submarines began to attack American shipping. These U-boats, *unterseeboots* or "undersea boats," sank a number of American merchant ships as well as the famous British luxury liner *Lusitania* off the Irish coast in 1915. Besides passengers that ship had also carried munitions to which the Germans objected. Over twelve hundred passengers lost their lives, including 128 Americans.

Negotiations for reparations and for security of non-military ships, which had some effect on protecting shipping lanes, occupied the governments for the next two years. But in February of 1917, Germany changed its tactics and sank 500 ships of various nationalities in the first two months, including the American liner U. S. S. *Housatonic*. A month later, Germany sank four more American merchant ships. Though poorly prepared to field an army, President Woodrow Wilson declared war against Germany and Austria-Hungary.[1] "It was apparent to all that we were confronted with a tremendous task," observed one local fuel administrator later," that we must not only furnish men with munitions, and everything that is necessary for conducting the war, but there was the still greater necessity that they should be delivered with the greatest possible speed."[2]

Fueling Change

The weather had already been uncooperative during the winter of 1916-17 causing hardship among the citizens, but more so in Europe where the war broke down food delivery. Germans called it "the turnip winter," since the interruption in shipping left them without foodstuffs and they were forced to turn to turnips to survive. Over 750,000 Germans died of malnutrition that winter.[3] In the United States, communities suffered fuel shortages. Some in the northern states were forced to buy coal only in 500-pound lots, a price beyond the reach of low-income residents.[4]

A country gone to war, high demand for coal, a severe winter, and a shortage of coal cars required national management. The newly created Federal Fuel Administration (FFA) faced such challenges as increased demand for coal for manufacture of war materials for the Allied powers of Britain, France, Italy, Russia and the United States while American citizens suffered fuel shortages.

The Federal Fuel Administration was face to face "with a problem that was literally staggering." The draft for the Army took their quota from the mine rolls so that the mines were immediately shorthanded in the face of the heaviest demand for fuel during a time of frigid weather.[5] The "old-fashioned winter" of 1917-1918 was one of the most severe on record. In the autumn, the unripe corn froze on the stalk and the severe cold stunted winter wheat. Field hands picking cotton found it too cold to work; truck crops of fruits and vegetables were damaged. Railroad tracks were blocked by snow, or their steam engines were barely able to make steam in sub-zero winds. Rivers and harbors were locked in ice. A bridge of ice connected Nantucket Island to the mainland.[6]

In Kansas City, January 16, 1918, the city sent a telegram to *Coal Age* reporting that twelve of the local companies were short 225 cars of coal that day. That was a 7,550-ton loss. "Thirteen mines are idle all day, four idle part of the day. This shortage situation is not improving," the *Coal Age* reporter added.

Desperate Measures

A woman climbs the side of a coal car to join others in gathering enough to take home in the severe winter of 1917-18. This mob scene was not uncommon throughout the nation as the bitter cold exceeded the nation's ability to keep warm.

At the first of the week, he continued, "wealthy people were going around with buckets and wheelbarrows to get a few pounds of coal. It wasn't a question of tons in Detroit; it had got down to pounds."[7]

The reporter said the Fuel Administration had done all it could do—eleven days before Garfield gave the close-down order on January 16th. The country would experience a coal shortage when in reality they were experiencing a coal car shortage. Coal could not be had even if people lived within a few miles of a mine with an abundance of coal. Railroad officials had a habit of assigning cars to all other customers before assigning to the mine to move coal and now the mines had coal but no cars. The railroads received the blame.[8]

In a March edition of *Coal Age,* a letter to the editor suggested the "small wagon mine is a blessing to the country and should be encouraged. The product of these mines is generally consumed in the neighboring locality with the result that freight charges and profits of the middleman are eliminated, and the farmer and local consumer pay less for their fuel supply."[9] Where railroads could not do the job, teams of horses and teamsters have the advantage. The Wood Age energy component stood in reserve to trump the Coal Age when necessary.

The Most Cold-blooded and Heartless Bunch that Ever Went Unhung

With coal at a premium, price gouging became epidemic on all sides. In August 1917 the Food and Fuel Act gave President Wilson the authority to set coal prices nationally. Two national coal organizations were born out of the need and desire to defend the coal-mining industry, the National Retail Coal Merchant's Association (NRCMA) and the National Coal Association (NCA), a group of producers. Their approach was a balancing act between patriotism and defense against "foolish federal intervention."[10]

The public complained bitterly about coal prices rising to more than $2 more than they had paid in 1916. One woman from Kansas City wrote she felt as though she were being "held up," as if the coal industry acted like thieves, while another resident wrote that the "coal dealers were the most cold-blooded and heartless bunch of speculative sharks that ever went unhung."[11]

The symbiotic relationship of coal to railroad meant that railroads favored coal mines and vice versa. Railroads rated mines according to the mine's daily capacity and assigned cars to new mines that were likely to have a good yield before servicing other customers. In May 1917 coal prices rose even though the off-season approached. Citizens wrote to their congressional representatives, to the newspapers and to the Federal Trade Commission threatening and predicting riots when they began to suffer from the cold the following winter. Some called for government possessions of mines.

Soldiers in training camps were freezing from lack of fuel and one official called for the coal operators not to "coin the blood of soldiers into dollars" by extorting high prices. Eventually a price of $3 per ton was agreed on though the Wilson administration thought it high. By August an agreed price of $2.40 was set though the coal associations said that price would discourage production and further complicate the war effort. By October 1917, the FFA issued its first price schedule, an average of 30 to 50 cents per ton above the $2.40 set by President Wilson. In 1916 coal profits were at 8%, but in 1917 they had risen to 29%, in spite of the government's best efforts. Profits declined in 1918 to 18%.[12]

Even though industries bought coal on contract, the railroads frequently let these plants get down to a supply of a day or two. Such impending shortages forced the factories to buy coal from the open market at higher prices. Investigations showed the railroads took care of their own by reassigning coal cars in violation of contracts already held. One railroad had confiscated 1,782 loaded coal cars for preferred customers over a six-month period in the winter of 1916-17.

During that same winter, coal prices in Kansas City rose to $6.50 and $7.00 a ton. Those who bought in the largest quantities paid the least of the inflated prices, while those who could afford it the least and bought it by the bucket or 100-pound bag paid a 100% more than the previous year. The arguments over the coal shortage spiraled along with prices. Was it the railroad's fault they had insufficient cars or was it the coal producers who were inefficient in loading and distributing? Nervous and frightened publics blamed the government for its lack of power over the problem.[13]

In spite of the government's best efforts loaded coal cars sat on sidings with "coal frozen solid in the gondolas." After considerable pressure from officials, President Wilson nationalized the railroads by establishing the United States Railroad Administration (USRA) at the end of 1917. Their purpose was to move the 145,000 loaded cars west of Chicago and increased efficiency in meeting demands.[14]

Heatless, Meatless and Wheatless . . . and Then Lightless, Too!

The coal shortage became acute in the winter of 1917-18. By January The FFA mandated a five–day shutdown called "The Closing Order" of industries east of the Mississippi River from Friday, January 18, through Tuesday, January 22nd. Those industries necessary to the war effort such as railroads and public utilities were exempted. This move would conserve coal and give mines and railroads an opportunity to build domestic coal supplies. To bolster this slowdown, the administration proclaimed that the next ten Mondays would be heatless from January 21 through March 25, 1918. Stores, schools, saloons, theaters and office buildings would be closed. Newspapers and street car lines were to adopt a "Sunday schedule."

The calendar swelled with sacrifice. Tuesday would be "Meatless Day," and Wednesdays would be "Wheatless." One meal of the other days should be meatless and wheatless. Saturday would be a "Porkless Day" for good measure. *The New York Times* called heatless Mondays "workless" Mondays, since many establishments were too cold to tolerate. The public was outraged since their wages were cut accordingly and some could not suffer the loss of even a few days' wages. At the same time merchants suffered the loss of income.[15] These rules were made to reduce traffic on the railroad and save coal at the same time. They were cancelled after four weeks.[16]

The Kansas City *Journal* on January 18, 1918, announced to its public the agenda for the city: Until the nationwide coal shortage could be relieved the following closings would save an estimated 1,500 tons of coal each day by closing the saloons, theaters, dance halls, pool and billiard halls, bowling alleys, restaurants and amusement centers early. Coal dealers estimated that theaters burned as much as two tons of coal each daily. All these places must close on Mondays and Thursdays and must close at 10:00 each night on days they were opened.[17]

In addition, all electricity for advertising purposes and streetlights not needed for public protection would be turned off permanently until the ban was lifted. The coal orders to be filled were household consumers first, public utilities second, factories filling government war contracts third and manufacturing plants producing foodstuffs for immediate consumption came last. Violators of these orders were threatened with immediate action: "Persistent violation will lead to cutting all feed wires to the establishment."[18]

A "Lightless Night" order was added in July of 1918 and was expected to save even more coal. Every effort would be made to reduce the fuel consumption in office buildings, apartment houses and hotels. It was expected to save a considerable amount of fuel. Along with lightless nights, only 50% of coal was to be furnished to breweries during the next year, the average to be based on the last three years' deliveries.[19]

I Have a Boy in France

In January 1918, at the height of this miserable time the editor of the *Coal Age*, Floyd W. Parsons, traveled to Washington, D. C. to visit with the Fuel Administrator, Dr. Harry A. Garfield, to discuss closing down the Nation's industries to relieve the critical fuel situation. Full of belief that alternatives actions were the better solution, he left Doctor Garfield believing that "he took the wisest course possible."[20]

Garfield explained his reasons: The main purpose was to break the snarl on the nation's railroad tracks and to allow the multitudes of cars—up to 50% of the cars were loaded with coal--to get to their destinations even before food and other vitals could be delivered. He also shut down mills and factories operated by waterpower to avoid a pile up of manufactured products and create more congestion. He closed munitions plants that had produced "more war material than transportation could handle." He did not consider the economic effect on the nation. "It simply had to be—there was no other way." Why couldn't industry continue on as it had been, doubling its energies in transportation? A shortage of locomotives made that impossible. Dr. Garfield responded with these statistics:

At least 5,000 new locomotives were needed each year by the railroads of the United States, but they were receiving roughly half that number. Though the American manufacturing produced that many, more than half were shipped to France forcing the American railroad system into a crippling shortage of coal deliveries. Different gauges of rails and heights of engines further made exchanges of engines problematic.[21]

WITHOUT COAL OUR SOLDIERS CANNOT CROSS THE SEA

A Popular Sentiment. Patriotism and coal supply challenges.

Any lengthy warning of the closing rule would have pushed manufacturers into greater production and congestion as they tried to get their goods out before the deadline. "The railroads would have been swamped with freight" and chaos would have followed. Further plans were to create municipal storage yards of coal, government control of important coal-loading piers, better use of water ways and the long talked of zoning system to eliminate cross-hauling. "I have a boy in France and another here in the army. Thousands of other parents are in the same situation. If we, as a people are not big enough to do this most necessary thing, then indeed we are a sorry lot," said Dr. Garfield, in referring to his now famous closing-down order.[22]

The next step of the government's supervisory role was the zoning program that reorganized railroad distribution of coal and cut long shipments of anthracite to western cities besides depending on the Midwest for greater self-sufficiency. After the war was over, one politician quipped "the inefficiency of the American railroads was the greatest ally of the imperial German Government."[23] The system eliminated cross hauls by encouraging users to purchase from nearby sources rather than from across the country. Kansas City and Missouri were in Coal Zone A, one of the 13 bituminous zones, with Iowa, Kansas, Arkansas and Oklahoma. This massive reorganization solved the problems of the eastern industries for which their supply had been the object, but others west of the Mississippi came up short of fuel or had to create alternative plans for development.[24]

One casualty of progress in Kansas City was that of the Kansas City Power and Light Company.[25] On April 8, 1918, the *Kansas City Star* announced that the steam turbines for the $5 million dollar power plant would not arrive any time soon. The explanation was "due to a lack of capacity of the combined turbine industry to meet the present war and near future requirements of the marine and the war situation in general." The news meant that the city would rely on the street railway power plant at Second Street and Grand Avenue for their electric current. Plans were described as "makeshift," though the plant had been improved the previous winter. The shortage of steam turbines remained acute and sources were dubious that they would arrive "even next year."[26]

Sacking coal for easier movement to market via. water

The country continued suffering, sacrificing and swearing at the coal and railroad combination until the Armistice was signed on November 11, 1918. By March 1, 1919, the Fuel Committee was disbanded. As an arm of the government it had done its work. It had secured a certain solution for the nation in that it simplified the shipping across country by eliminating much of the cross shipping. It maintained the coal prices within "reasonable limits" that kept the prices from rising to intolerable heights. It paved the way for more equal distribution of fuel to consumers and saved fuel from waste through stringent economies.[27] The coal crisis was not over, however. A new one would arise in the early 1920s.

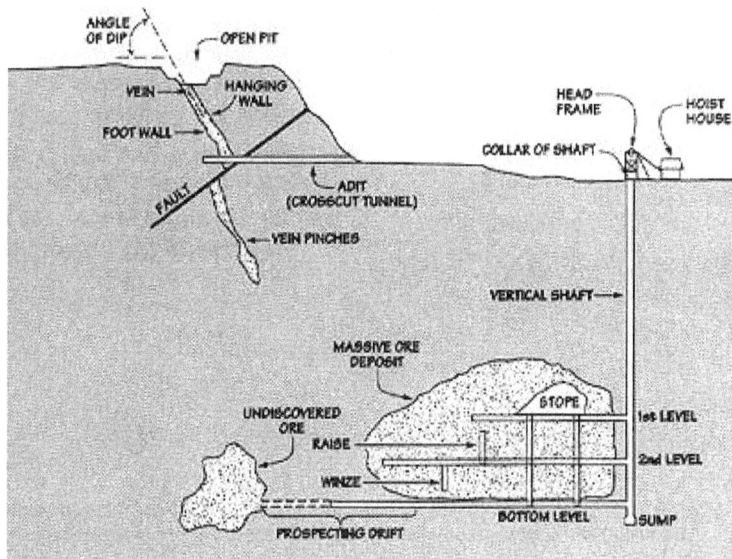

241

Fueling Change

A Open cast mine

Open cast mines are simply a large hole in the ground. The desired material can be hauled out on an inclined plane (a) or dug out with a grab or drag-line excavator (b) to be dumped into rail wagons (c)

Open cast mines are associated with sand, gravel, clay (for brick works), coal and iron ore. See also Fig __

B Quarries

Quarries are open cast mines where the depth of the hole, or the height of the working face is more than ninety feet. The material (usually stone) can be hauled away in light tipper trucks (d) and tipped direct into railway wagons via a chute (e), for the deep hole type you need either an inclined plane or a crane (f) to lift the material to ground level. Quarries are normally associated with stone.

C Drift Mine

Drift mines consist of a tunnel into the ground, usually into a hill-side. The tunnel (called an Adit) might be horizontal or slope up or downwards. Drift mines are the smallest and cheapest way to get at underground deposits, many small coal mines are of this type.

D Shaft mine

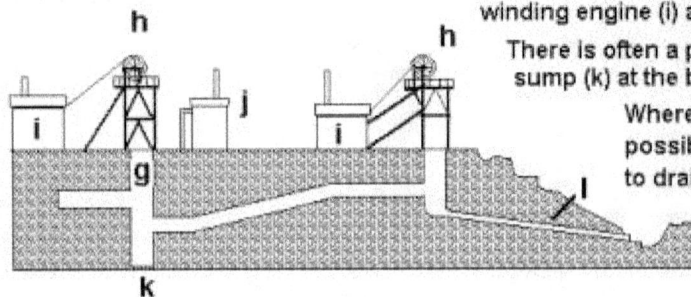

Shaft type mines are used where the material lies deep in the earth. The Shaft (g) can be thousands of feet deep. The winding towers or 'headgear' (h) and the associated winding engine (i) are a characteristic feature.

There is often a pump house (j) to draw water up from the sump (k) at the bottom of the deepest shaft.

Where the lie of the land allows it is sometimes possible to gig a drainage tunnel or 'sough' (l) to drain the water from the mine.

Chapter 28

Wood to The Rescue

Wood's long-term worth remains a standby fuel in emergencies.

The unintended consequence of the whole event was to change the role of coal for the American public and to open opportunity for oil and gas to show their advantages through new markets. Looking back, the most unexpected but, in the end, predictable alternative fuel was wood. When coal is unavailable, when the infrastructure for fuel oil and natural gas cannot meet the demands, the population falls back on wood. Having watched the nation agonize over fuel availability and a certain amount of wood cutting injudiciously and even illegally done, the United States Department of Agriculture published a forty-page booklet called "The Use of Wood for Fuel" in March 1919. Its publication may have been after the fact, but it addressed the subject of wood gathering 20th-century style to a generation who had grown up with coal.

The manual begins with this statement: "Wood has always been of considerable importance as fuel in this country, and the present emergency has greatly increased its comparative value for this purpose." Clearly, the first part of the sentence is an understatement while the second part acknowledges its revival as a fuel. The shortcoming of wood has always been difficulty in moving its bulk great distances; and certainly, from the middle of the 19th century onward the coal industry excoriated wood as being bulky and difficult, but here its weight has been compared against the difficulties of getting coal and found desirable because wood can be found locally. "The use of wood for fuel saves transportation, it utilizes wood that would otherwise go to waste, and it releases coal for ships and railroads and munitions plants."[1] Very much a product of the fuel milieu of 1919, the author says, "preparing wood for fuel involves slightly more labor than is required to produce coal." He must have been thinking of the use of electricity in coal mining that had made it easier than chopping and sawing wood, or the relative ease with which oil came from the ground.[2]

The real purpose of the bulletin was to encourage a rural population of twenty million people to tap into local resources to substitute for the eighteen million tons of coal they normally use. Such a move would reduce the use of coal by nearly three million tons or between 65,000 and 70,000 carloads.[3]

The coal squeeze of the previous two years had increased the price of wood 24% in 1917 to an estimated value of $43.13 per farm. Missouri was estimated to have 275,000 farms with an average of 13 cords per farm. (Tennessee had the highest at nineteen, and North and South Dakota and Nebraska had the fewest at three.)[4]

Fueling Change

The bulletin advocates using wood in factories to keep them running until replaced by coal, and to stockpile wood for future fuel shortages as had already been done by the cotton mills in South Carolina and throughout the South. It further describes how to stack and measure a cord, how to cut with a gasoline- or kerosene-powered saw, how to split the wood, skid and haul it at no more than $1 a cord, what kinds of wood split easily (birch, maple and conifers), what woods are hard to split (sycamore, gum, apple) and how long to season (nine to twelve months) each kind of wood when stacked in the manner prescribed, plus a relatively small loss of heat if the unseasoned wood had to be burned immediately.[5]

Although readers are discouraged from shipping wood farther than five to ten miles from production point, "because its great bulk makes it expensive to ship," the bulletin nevertheless gives detailed directions and costs for shipping by rail, $1.50 a cord per hundred miles.[6] Municipalities are encouraged to "get in a reserve of wood for the winter, sufficient to insure its members against a fuel famine" with the estimated cost of sawing it (again) into stove wood lengths to be fifty cents per cord."[7]

Not leaving the most basic part to chance, the bulletin describes "how to use wood fuel." Grates, as always have been the difference between wood and coal. "Coal has been so generally used lately and furnaces and stoves have become so adapted to its use that it seems impractical too many to burn wood without going to great expense."

Coal grates hold small chunks with a small firebox of brick, while wood grates are larger for pieces of wood and lie several inches below. The bulletin suggests that the firebox can be modified to create more space to burn pieces of wood and that it was not necessary to cut wood into "very small blocks."[8]

The bulletin closes with the encouraging statement that by using wood that is freely available on local landscapes "there is no excuse for suffering because of inability to get coal" but the possibility of hauling wood by rail "is not economical," and any wood should be "wagon-hauled" instead.[9] It is doubtful whether country people without coal had to read a booklet before cutting down a tree, since they were the last ones to have gone to coal in the first place, but the government had pointed out the obvious to some and the necessary details to a new generation shivering for lack of coal.

Thus ended the first 100 years of the fuel and energy story of the site known as Kansas City. From dense forest to dense humanity and industry, such was the growth of an "instant city," of the kind that could only proliferate within the context of a swift fuel increase.

In 1873, the young coal industry put forth the requisites that create a fuel in harmony with its consumers. Within this deceptively simple list can be felt all of the pain and hard-earned lessons of the decades to come, particularly in the first decades of the 20th century:
1) A good quality of coal, 2) a sufficient quantity, 3) cheapness and regularity of production, 4) cheapness of transportation, 5) a sufficiency of transportation, and 6) a good market.[10]

Each one of these items speaks volumes from the experience of coal through the next 50 years as it peaked and tried to maintain its spot atop the fuel pyramid. It was easy to expand against wood because it had been tried and found wanting for century upon century to move humankind beyond its current limitations. But the emergence of oil and other fuels like natural gas, manufactured gas, even its own creation, electricity, crowded the field and gave the public many points of comparison that showed both the up- and downsides of coal as the fuel for all occasions. Too harsh, messy, and undependable in terms of delivery for home fuel (See Appendix D), it retired to its niche as an industrial fuel and has been there ever since. After reading the list of coal characteristics in the appendix, it would be hard to imagine today's home-fire builder digging into a pile of coal, attempting to judge the individual chunks for their qualities and throwing it into a furnace or fireplace. Coal has its place, but it is definitely not in the hearth. Like oil it has found its best use removed from personal contact making industrial fires and internal combustion engines do the bidding of a highly fueled population. Ironically, it is the wood fire that people still enjoy though natural gas has found its place as a steady fuel for decorative fireplaces and displays. Coal and oil, however, offer romance in the way of massive capital, huge profits and international shipping. Face to face, there is no way for us to enjoy a fire from these fuels. They belong to furnaces and tanks, engines and motors. Coal and oil do the dirty work of our lives while the more elegant electricity, natural gas and wood keep us in touch with our fascination with and need for fire up close.

245

OIL

Essential Requisites	Stage I: Discovery and Development	Stage II: Systems Organization	Stage III: Expansion and Defense	Stage IV: Niche and Decline
Dates:	1859-1869	1869-1955	1955-	2100
1. Good Quality of Fuel for Use	Liquid fuel split into illuminant, lubricant and fuel oils	Per-well quality and type varied	Overtakes coal; increased BTUs	Oil shale still available
2. Sufficient Quantity of Fuel	Production of 150,000 bbl in 1860 suggested an endless supply	Pipelines and barrel systems capture and carry liquid fuel quickly	United States imported fuel as of 1947. Rise of tanker fleets	Military niche market may absorb much of oil supply.
3. Cheapness and Regularity of Production	Prices at first higher than coal or wood. Wells drilled as fast as possible as prices dropped	By 1889 fuel oils accounted for 35% of crude production	Plastics increased oil products; Gasoline/ diesel markets increased with more roads	New fields within U.S. borders continue to replace foreign oil
4. Cheapness of Transportation	Wagon, then railroads and pipelines. Tankers crossed the ocean in 1861, wood barrels, ship	Railroad transportation vital as bulk tank technology evolved to handle quantities of oil	Like coal, diesel took over RR fuel to pull long trains of tank cars	New forms of transportation change marketplace for oil
5. Sufficiency of Transportation	A big scramble for containers, RR spurs, pipelines laid	RRs overrule wagons; Coal-fired, external combustion engines carried new fuel	Fuel oil and natural gas replaced coal for home heating	More mass transit and more electronic cottages change oil demands
6. Good Market, (i.e., End-Users)	Consumers used oil for lighting. Stoves were designed for coal and wood. Industry used oil for lubrication.	Natural gas stoves made their debut in the early years of the 20th century. Heating still done by coal.	Natural gas = clean, low-CO2 fuel for homes; Gas takes up to half share of oil use; Air pollution	Difficulty in keeping highways repaired changes transportation of goods for end users.

Chapter 29

Gasoline: A Love Story Headed for Divorce
The *discovery and development* of gasoline

Timing is everything. Four-and-a-half billion years and we discovered gasoline in the 1850s—fifty years before anyone could find a way to unleash its explosive power on our lives. In those 50 years a Civil War had to be fought to change the energy structure of the nation. An engine had to be built, a chassis had to be designed, and roads had to be built. City infrastructure had to be built with boulevards and landscaping. Then, the fuel that would rule our lives in the 20th century could find its place and become the sculptress of our ways and means.

As a technology, and, yes, it is a technology as sure as the cars, trucks, air planes and other engines it powers. Gasoline is a man-made product derived of raw material and designed to perform a particular task. Unlike wood and coal that are what they are--dense carbon-based fuels for heat and light, gasoline was created, distilled by man, separated by and for its exotic possibilities before its use was even known. In finding those uses, gasoline has given us our future selves. Without it we would be untraveled, unaware of so many things to which we have been exposed, we would be ignorant of the world, of the many sciences and engineering specialties like automobile and freeway design, yes, rocket science, that grew up with gasoline as powerhouse, of passions, unable to fulfill urgencies of love and hate and heroism, and we would still be in the horse and buggy days, caught between the Wood Age and the Coal Age. The Oil Age would await its birthing.

It is no accident that the word "travail" and the word "travel" share the same root as well as, er, route. For most of humanity's history, travel has been very difficult. The lack of movement among human groups throughout the world, their isolation from one another except for threads of trade allowed the development of unique languages, and the many different cultures we enjoy today. The effect of being awash in oil and especially gasoline is that we break down these barriers and look and act more and more alike as we blend ways and means.

In the long epic of travel evolution, an engine, not a horse, and a fuel to fill it, has become the greatest boon to civilization the world has ever known. The engine so long evolving had an appointment with a fuel so long to gain recognition. That meeting in the 1870s turned travail (agony, torment, pain) into bearable travel and then luxury travel and exploded out of the prosaic world of the 19th century. An automobile is a lovely thing, but without gasoline, it becomes a very uncomfortable living space. A can of gasoline needs an engine to show off its combustion capabilities. The two are made for each other. Gasoline made the car!

The long task of getting from one place to another overland is satisfied, expanded and celebrated with the use of gasoline. The fuel demands a container. We made a tank for it. A container of gasoline bristles with unspent energy; we made an engine for it. Its explosive character propelled us to give it running space. We made roads for it. Its liquid complexity sucked us into a chemical world of which we were unaware. We gave it identity as it gave us new identities. Its variants challenged the sky. We made air planes fly with it. The sheer volume of gasoline, the combustibility of it demanded these machines to burn it. Gasoline made the car, made the air plane, created our way of life. The whole 20th century is about renaming human activity based on this fuel.

The human psyche has been explored, exploited and fulfilled with the joy of vehicles that use gasoline. Thousands of miles of roads have been built to give people well-designed routes for driving. The story of the 20th century follows gasoline as a great river flowing through and supporting human accomplishment, expansion and triumph though historians seem unaware of it.

"Gasoline: A Love Story Headed for Divorce" is structured as an abstracted timeline and interjects the story of gasoline's growth around the globe, including how it affected Kansas City, Jackson County, Missouri. It follows gasoline's use as a fuel to its rise and expansion through today (2018) and onto the not-too-distant-future of 2050.

Gasoline flows through this story. It is the unacknowledged force that expanded the city, built the freeway system, created the far-flung shopping centers, pushed the bi-state tax for Kansans to enjoy Missouri's sports and arts. Like cities everywhere, gasoline is the love story behind the scenes delivering both life and death and every kind of wish fulfillment. Gasoline is the sculptress of our ways and means.

Gasoline, like all addictive products, offers both pleasure and pain. The convenience it brings to our transportation needs carries the heavy price of CO_2 as waste product. We have burned it for over a hundred years and arranged our very lives and identities around it. There is so much of it, using it for all its possibilities, for all our ego satisfactions is very hard to ignore.

We have, until now, been willing to pay the price of highway deaths, reduced air quality, miles of concrete bisecting our neighborhoods delivered by the flood of gasoline, but now, climate change dictates we decrease this river of fuel, certainly not yet exhausted, but reluctantly deferred to operate our lives with electricity instead. To the extent that we are willing to understand the simple but profound statement below, we are dialing back our use of gasoline and substituting another force in its place.

"We can evade reality, but we cannot ignore the consequences of evading reality."
Ayn Rand

The Birth of Gasoline: The First Test-Tube Baby, 1855

Gasoline, a test-tube baby? Unlike wood so easily visible and coal so identifiable, oil emerged as a mystery liquid with several personalities within even a small sample. Underground and unidentified except for its ferociously flammable qualities used by the ancients in warfare, both oil's quantities and qualities kept their secrets.

What could it be used for other than a medicinal liquid in small bottles?

Did oil have a larger future? In evolutionary terms, each piece of the puzzle that makes a 20th century automobile run goes back a long way. Each developed and existed in separate worlds of use, or lack of use, until the right combination of pieces came together at once.

This timeline reveals the long overlap as one link after another of the fuel chain adapted to all the components of the Wood and Coal Age energy suites and the new Oil Age being born, adapting, replacing, inventing, growing its way to the 20th century and its possibilities.

To travel by car, one must have a drivable machine, a fuel to propel it and roads on which to run it! These three elements tell us much about the design and success of the 20th century: car, fuel, road.

1852   Eli Whitney Blake, nephew of the inventor of the cotton gin Eli Whitney, invents a steam-powered, cast-iron stone crusher that reduces cost and time of crushing stone. This method boosts macadam road production 7 cubic yards in an hour.[1] Farmers pay their taxes by working on the roads that run by their property, a certain form of enslavement. Before this machine takes over crushing stone, children and old people are employed to cut small pieces of stone for roads. It takes an adult working hard two man-days to create a cubic yard of stone. The stones can be no larger than what can "fit in your mouth!" When the railroad becomes a carrier, road building falls behind.

1853   George Bissell visits oil springs in western Pennsylvania and engages in much discussion as to its value and potential.[2]

1854   Here is an overlap between the Wood Age and the Coal Age in which iron rails for trains, the new form of technology for travel made with coal—convey metal trains powered by wood. In other words, chopped wood more than coal is being thrown into the firebox.

At this time, no organized coal mining and railroad transportation exist en masse to supply this new type of transportation with the fuel it needs. Hence the combination—made with coal, powered by wood. An effect of the Kansas Nebraska Act is to open the West to settlers by way of the railroad. No greater overlap than coal-fired engines and tracks propelled by wood-fired trains send men to slay buffalo by the thousands to wipe out both Native Americans and food source to destroy the inhabitants of the Wood Age as abruptly as possible.

CERTIFICATE OF BIRTH
Gasoline
April 16, 1855

This is Silliman's context . . . his 1855 world view.

After a long-wait, Yale University laboratory made the announcement.

George Bissell has presented his samples: Do I have a winner or not, he asks. The fuel is midwifed by Benjamin Silliman, Jr, a renowned Yale University chemist and son of a renowned Yale chemist. As he separates the higher volatility fuels from less-volatile ones, out falls what will become known as gasoline. Like a litter of puppies, the different strains of the fuel that will rule the world begin to separate themselves in his laboratory. Silliman numbers them "product 1-8." What will eventually be named gasoline is product no. 2. Product No. 1 is "almost entirely water, with a few drops of colorless oil." Third from the top are the ones that will be known as kerosene in great demand for lighting, while toward the bottom of the spectrum are the heavier oils for lubrication and finally paraffin for candles. This is the first inquiry into oil scientifically, the first time the question is asked, "What have we here? Is this any good for anything?"

We must wait for the engine to develop, though it has been for centuries—pieces of it, ideas of it—but a few more years and the world changes forever!

Silliman does not name any of these newborns. His task is to analyze them chemically, and history does not record when and how gasoline is named. Silliman's analysis without doubt has been seen as "the most epochal report in petroleum history." The report is so enthusiastically received that its power enrolls wary shareholders to focus on the production of rock oil, meaning coming from rocks or below ground, so named to differentiate it from whale oil, the prevailing and increasingly pricey lubricant of the time.

Why does Silliman fail to jump on that lightweight fuel at the top of the spectrum and say, "Eureka! This liquid will power the vehicles of the 20th century!"? He is not looking for it because the world is not ready for it.

This is the context into which gasoline was born:

• The United States opens the Panama Railroad to facilitate travel to the gold fields of California. It shortens the traveling distance from six months overland to one month by water.

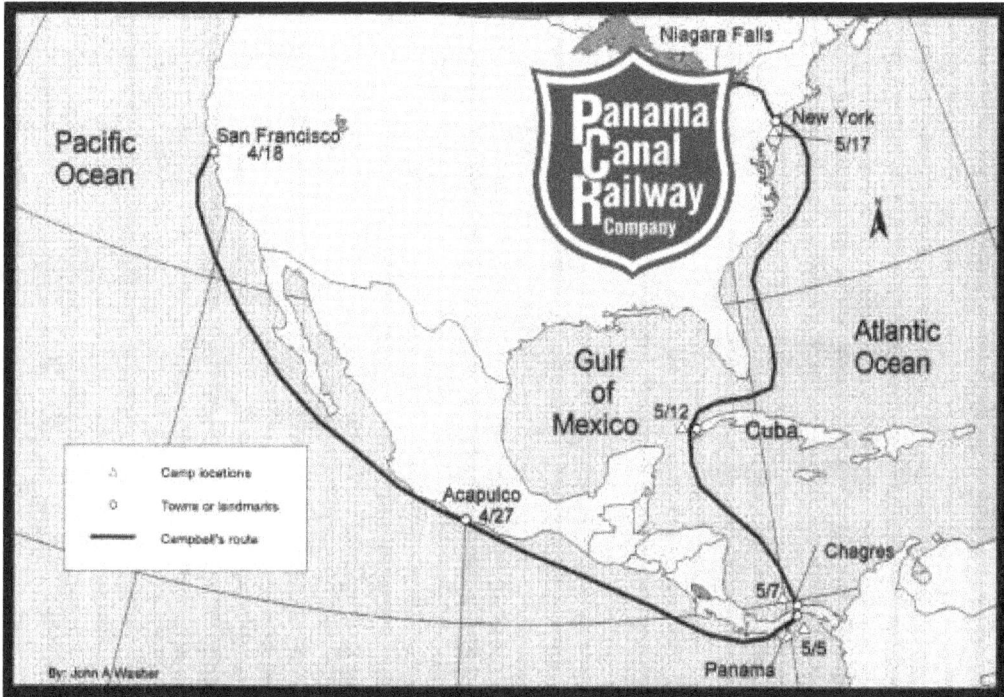

• Congress sets aside $30,000 to start a camel corps to take goods across the southern desert to California. Secretary of War, Jefferson Davis, sends men to Africa to bring back a load of camels to try them out.

251

Fueling Change

- John D. Rockefeller is 16-years-old and is hired as an assistant bookkeeper in a local establishment. In another 15 years, the astute young businessman will create Standard Oil to transform the kerosene trade worldwide.

- Henry Bessemer files his patent in the United Kingdom for the Bessemer process of steelmaking in 1855.[3]

- Whale oil remains the best oil for lubricating such fine works as clocks, and used for lighthouse beacons, railroad train lights and candles for upper class homes. Never cheap, sperm oil, the finest of the whale oils begins to cost dearly. Sperm whale oil—think Moby Dick and the great white whale—creates the best and brightest candles, but their days as supplier of lighting and lubricating are numbered.

- 90,000 Native Americans from assorted tribes like the Fox, Sac, Shawnee, Wyandotte, Huron, Osage, and others encamp across the Missouri River in a territory set aside for them. The two cultures look at each other across the river contemplating their futures.

- The steamboat Arabia sinks in the Missouri River within sight of the limestone pier, leaving 130 passengers muddy on the river bank. Resurrected more than 100 years later, it becomes one of Kansas City's most unique tourist attractions in the City Market area, a testimony to life in the 1850s, and one to private enterprise in the 1980s.

The California Gold Rush is in full-swing; Civil War begins to brew on the western border. Skirmishes over slavery on the Missouri-Kansas border begin to escalate exponentially. John Brown moves to Kansas to lead the anti-slavery movement.

Some 4 million slaves work in this country as forced labor with no real hope of ever being free, though the Underground Railroad is operational, and abolitionists are vociferous.

Abraham Gesner's patented kerosene from bitumen—a natural substance like asphalt found in surface pools—is being produced by the North American Gas Light Company in New York, producing three different grades of what he names, "kerosene," to distribute what will commonly become known as, "coal oil." Gesner boasts having saved whales from further plunder. He shows it is possible to use bitumen products for illumination; but, his kerosene loses to an oil-based formula soon available, cheaper, and in greater quantity.

George Bissell   **Benjamin Silliman, Jr.**   **Edwin L. Drake**
Three men who combined talents to create the oil industry.

It isn't Silliman's fault that he pays little attention to the high volatility end of the oil spectrum. What would it be used for? The internal combustion engine lies so far in the future that perhaps only three or four people in the world fantasize it as a possibility, and a fuel like gasoline cannot have been imagined, though gun powder has been used as a charge, as a fuel in early prototype engines, and cannon are seen by some as the first internal combustion engine.

By analyzing the liquid, Silliman confirms that at least 50% of the oil is usable for illuminants, the primary use. Remember, before this they had only candles and animal oil lamps. He can predict paraffin being extracted and used for candles, but his grasp of the light end of the distillates is beyond his scope of understanding. He assures his clients optimistically—would-be investors in this liquid—that the first fifty percent of the crude oil can be distilled as an illuminant immediately, and that ninety per cent of the samples are commercially viable in one form or another.[4]

Silliman's report pronounces that "there was much ground for encouragement . . . that nearly the whole of the raw product may be manufactured without waste, and this solely by a well-directed process which is in practice one of the simplest of all chemical processes."[5] Ahead lies the invention of wicks that work and lamps that are safe and attractive for kerosene to make its mark as an illuminant.

1857 The Coates House in Kansas City is planned and started but stopped by the Civil War. It becomes a part of a union encampment at the 10th and Broadway site. After the War, construction resumes. The building still stands today.

Steamboats run day and night. A speed of 10 miles per hour is not unusual. A voyage from St. Louis to Kansas City takes about 4 days. Some 729 steamboats arrive this season with 300 passengers, horses, mules, and wagons on the main deck. Furniture, including all those saloon pianos, is piled on the hurricane deck.

1859 Whalers slaughter tens of thousands of whales for three million gallons of sperm oil to light American lamps. Still, only the rich can afford whale oil candles. Bees' wax and animal fat are still used for lamps as they have been for millennia.

E. L. Drake, a street car conductor with unimpressive credentials, brings in the world's first oil well that gushes at Titusville, PA.

Oil prices vary wildly, a feverish business subject to violent fluctuations between sudden overproduction and the eager and highly speculative search for new wells.

Technology for bringing in the well is to drive a pipe from the surface of the earth to cope with water seepage and cave-ins instead of digging down to bedrock and then starting to drill, as was practiced in salt wells.[6]

Slave cabins line the streets of Main and Westport Road in Kansas City. There is still a slave block for sales of slaves within a mile of the free-state Kansas border as the age of slavery nears an end.[7]

Slave traders send the last shipment of slaves from Kansas City to the Deep South. Many Missourians will sell their slaves rather than lose them in the war. A network known as the Underground Railroad carries escaping slaves to freedom. The young leave, while the elders stay with their families, both black and white.[8]

1860s During the Civil War, a liquor tax is placed on ethanol whisky, also called moonshine, to raise money for the war.[9]

1860 Kansas City's population is 4,418. It operates as a town with kerosene for lamps and home lighting. Though the railroad has arrived, oil is manufactured far away in the growing Coal Age facilities in the East while Kansas City uses it in its Wood Age context. Somewhere in the annals of Kansas City memorabilia exists a photo of a whale jaw bone propped up against someone's fence. It is being used as a gate. Two large baleen jaws stretch up and up and meet overhead. This was scrimshaw material had anyone been tempted. The proverbial Jonah could easily stand tall and still have a couple of feet to go standing in this arch. How the jawbone got here is a mystery and where it went as well, but it indicates that whale oil had made its way to this town in the center of the country far from either shore. It may have been delivered in small glass bottles, a couple, three or four ounces for oiling clocks, those big bonging granddaddy clocks of the 19th century. Candles of whale oil probably did not reach to Kansas City as heat and distance would have been quite unkind to them.

U. S. kerosene is exported to St. Petersburg, Russia.[10]

The price of a barrel of crude oil is $19.25 in January.

Oil production is a half-million barrels from Pennsylvania.[11]

1861   The American Civil War ignites on April 12 at Fort Sumter in Charleston Harbor. Three days later, President Lincoln calls for 75,000 volunteers to serve three months in the Union army. The conflict that ensues is fought over fuel and energy, and the manner in which it is to be delivered. Slaves or machines? This is the beginning of the Coal Age as machines replace slaves as working capital.

First oil gusher in Pennsylvania explodes, killing 19.[12]

First full cargo of oil crosses the Atlantic shipped in wooden barrels in the hold of a wooden ship sailing from Philadelphia to London.[13]

Assassination of U.S. President Abraham Lincoln
April 14, 1865

1862 Price of a barrel of oil is 10 cents in January as supply and demand bounce wildly.

1863 British sail an iron sailing vessel and transport oil in a subdivided cargo space using the hull of the ship as container and doing away with expensive barrels or tins. Forerunner of modern tanker.

A building at 14th and Grand in Kansas City, is being used by the Union army as a temporary jail; it collapses on August 14 killing several women who are related to William Quantrill's pro-slavery raiders. Quantrill retaliates 7 days later with his attack on Lawrence, KS, where 150 people are killed, and Lawrence is destroyed.

1864 The Battle of Westport, October 21-23, that progresses through Jackson County and Kansas City, Missouri, is said to be the largest and most decisive Union-Confederate clash in Missouri. It is at Westport, in sight of the slave market and quarters, that the Union army routs the Confederates and breaks their power as an army in the Kansas City region.[14]

Price of a barrel of oil is $11.00 in December.[15]

Chapter 30

Gasoline: The Orphaned Child, 1865-1901
The *organization of systems* to bring gasoline to market

Finally named "gasolene" (yes, that spelling) after 10 years of knocking around and being ignored and thrown out as an unfortunate waste product, technology caught up with this beautiful fuel, but not before it acquired a quarrelsome reputation for an explosive temper and danger in handling. Every kind of use failed from lamp to stove until the right moment presented itself. This most promising of fuels spent decades homeless until other systems organized themselves to meet its potential.

1865 The word "gasolene" first in print, a combination of gas and benzene.[1] "Many refiners (of petroleum) separate first of all the lightest naphtha . . . to this the name of gasoline has been given."[2] The word "gasoline" itself comes from a combination of gas + oil from benzol "ol" + ene, from camphene and kerosene. The word was variously spelled gasoleine, gaxoline, and gasolene.[3] Its reputation had no doubt been established by then as well. Many experiments in using gasoline for lighting would be found to be explosive, besides kerosene is readily available and cheaper, and it is volatile enough. Cooking with it will also have been difficult. No need there either as both wood and coal are plentiful. The liquid is used to kill lice in people's hair. It is certainly used in lamps, but smell, smoke, and volatility prevent much indoor use. Lacking its eventual home in the internal combustion engine, it is useless.[4]

Oil wells are "washed" with benzine to remove sediments and mud, but it has not been ascertained if gasoline is ever used for that purpose, though it may have been tried. Gasoline and benzine are close cousins. What happened as often as not is that the 10 per cent of gasoline that was unavoidably distilled in the kerosene distillation process was thrown into the nearest stream. Resulting fish, vegetation kills, and fires pushed the disposal of gasoline to be thrown out on the ground.[5] None of these disposal methods was satisfactory to anyone, and many intelligent men and women must have wondered what to do with that useless liquid.

It is demonstrated oil can be pumped in pipelines; a five-mile-long wrought iron line moves oil to the railroad station at a charge of $1.00 per barrel.[6]

A gas company is organized, and first gas house built in Kansas City. Great excitement when Louis Hammerslough, a Kansas City merchant, receives goods by rail from New York in eight days![7]

President Lincoln, assassinated on April 14; his funeral train traveling through seven states and 180 cities burns wood; coal is unable to supply needed fuel for the homage.[8]

1866 Work begins on the first railroad bridge to cross the Missouri River, the Hannibal Bridge, under the direction of architect and engineer, Octave Chanute.

1867 The United States Navy reports that "use of petroleum for steamers is hopeless; convenience is against it, comfort is against it, health is against it, economy is against it and safety is against it. Opposed to these the advantages of probably not very important reduction in bulk and weight, with their attending economies cannot prevail."[9]

Octave Chanute

1869 The Hannibal Bridge at Kansas City is completed in the summer of 1869. It provides a connection between the eastern and western markets. Kansas City is soon fully committed to the railroad.[10] The demise of the Pony Express had already been achieved by the coast-to-coast connection of the telegraph in 1861.

Oil's first 10 years produces from 500,000 barrels to 4,215,000 barrels—equivalent in energy content to nearly a million tons of coal.[11] A ten-fold increase.

Catherine Beecher's popular *Principles of Domestic Science* recommends kerosene as an illuminant.[12]

1870s A century of road-building equipment takes off in this decade. The move from wooden to metal tools and from hand labor and teams of horses and mules to mechanized inventions. The three elements take shape—no car is here yet, but roads are.

As the internal combustion engine begins to take shape, people also begin to look at gasoline as a fuel, the second element.

1870 Portable stone crusher invented that requires steam boiler and engine to make gravel for roads.[13]

Population of Kansas City 32,260.

John D. Rockefeller forms Standard Oil Co.[14] Rockefeller launches "Our Plan," in which the firm tries to buy up every refinery around, if they don't sell he then begins to depress the market and starve them out of business.[15]

1872 Kansas City, Kansas, is incorporated.

1873 Baku oil fields open to development in Azerbaijan, a Russian governorate on the Caspian Sea.[16]

Swedish Nobel family enters Russian oil business.

1874 Many gathering lines are merged in a Standard Oil, subsidiary United Pipe Lines.[17]

1876 Otto Cycle is the first combustion engine designed to use alcohol and gasoline.[18]
Portland cement appears for the first time.[19]

1878 Nobel Company launches first oil tanker, *Zoroaster.*[20]
First steam tanker built in Sweden burns oil as fuel.[21]
Kansas City's Union Depot opens in the West Bottoms near the stockyards. The 1903 flood overcomes the area, forcing plans for the current Union Station that opens in 1914.

Union Depot, Kansas City's West Bottoms

1879 First big pipeline—the six-inch Tide-Water line, 110 miles long—is built across the Appalachian Mountains. Within "another few years," more than 75% of all crude oil produced is carried by pipelines to railroad stations or refineries.[22]

1880s "A day on the roads" to pay taxes is still the only way to maintain the roads. Property owners whose property abuts the road must work on their stretch of road or hire others to do it. Roads are worse than two generations ago.[23]
Gasoline is sold as a cleaning fluid in small bottles or buckets. It can be mixed with paint as a thinner. It is tried as stove fuel bought in pharmacies. Overall, it is still found to be dangerous in these experimental uses. It is a fuel looking for a place in the sun.[24]

Tens of thousands of American Bison (buffalo) are exterminated on the Great Plains to destroy the food source of the Native Americans. At the same time, the buffalo serve as a steady food supply for men laying the western railroads. Without buffalo, their way of life cannot survive.

A building boom in Kansas City launches the city into a first-class metropolis. Desirable business addresses move away from the river and center on 9th Street.

Oil is discovered in Ohio and Indiana.[25]

1880 10.3% gasoline is produced to 75.2% kerosene with 12.4% losses.[26] Kerosene production has also generated a river of gasoline volatile, dangerous, useless and badly disposed of.

Hydropower and direct current electricity combine and become popular.[27]

Population of Kansas City is 55,785. Streets are narrow, unpaved with plank sidewalks downtown. Streets illuminated with gas light at night.

League of American Wheelmen organized (LAW) to push for better roads. Bicyclists cannot use country roads.[28]

By 1880, kerosene production has created a river of unused gasoline. Ten per cent of the refined process is gasoline. Could our forebears really have spilled over three million barrels of gasoline a year into streams and onto scrub land? They must have been desperate to use this smelly, smoky byproduct, but, "how?"[29] What use they do make of gasoline burns negligible amounts.

1881 G. Y. Smith and Louis Hammerslough are two of the leading proponents of electric light in Kansas City. His obituary includes a worthy tribute: "Mr. Hammerslough at all times had the best interests of Kansas City at heart. In every worthy enterprise that promised advancement to the city, he took a prominent part."[30]

Harper's Magazine reports that, "street hawkers, with gasoline torches," cried their wares.[31] Some gasoline is distilled again into an even lighter liquid named "rigolene" that is used as an anesthetic and "several hundred gallons (out of over 3 million) were made for "surgical purposes."[32]

1882 Newly formed Standard Oil Trust controls 90 % of the U.S. market.[33]

Thomas Edison demonstrates electricity.[34]

1884 Gillis Opera House in Kansas City is illuminated by "Electric Light," for its June 27 showing of Evans, Bryant and Hoey's, "The Meteors."

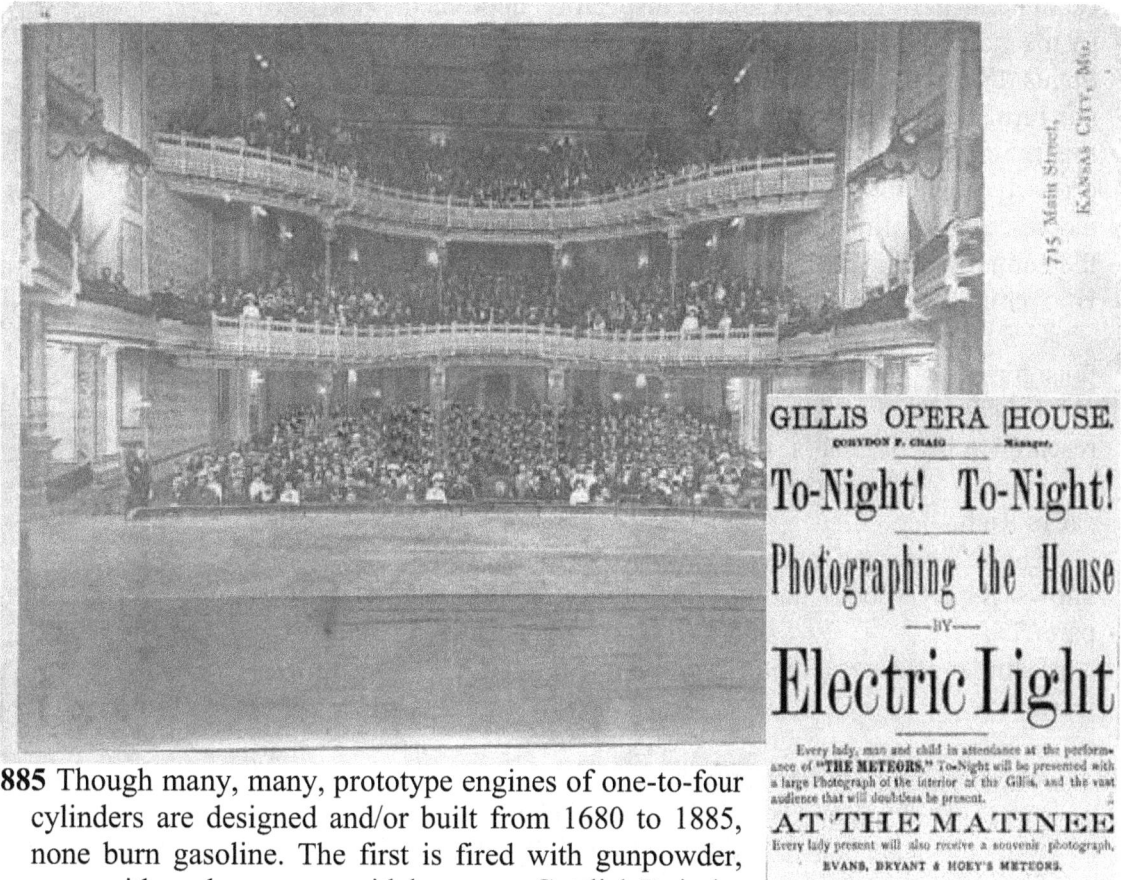

GILLIS OPERA [HOUSE.

CORYDON F. CRAIG   Manager.

To-Night! To-Night!

Photographing the House

—BY—

Electric Light

Every lady, man and child in attendance at the performance of "THE METEORS," To-Night will be presented with
a large Photograph of the interior of the Gillis, and the vast
audience that will doubtless be present.

AT THE MATINEE

Every lady present will also receive a souvenir photograph.

EVANS, BRYANT & HOEY'S METEORS.

1885 Though many, many, prototype engines of one-to-four cylinders are designed and/or built from 1680 to 1885, none burn gasoline. The first is fired with gunpowder, some with coal gas, some with kerosene. Gottlieb Daimler invents the first prototype gasoline-burning engine in 1885.

First catalytic converter is invented by Sylvanus Browner in Fort Wayne, IN.[35] The gasoline pump tank has marble valves and wooden plungers and a capacity of one barrel (52 gallons).

Rothschilds enter the Russian oil business.[36]

Royal Dutch discovers oil in Sumatra.[37]

1886 Modern prototype tanker is built in Germany and launched in England.

Karl Benz receives the first patent for a 3-wheeled, gas-fueled car. Benz's gasoline-injected carburetor with a vertical cylinder burns gasoline efficiently and gives enough speed that he outfits a stagecoach with it, and then introduces the first 4-wheeled automobile to the world. Benz creates the basic engine for cars whose design is fundamentally the same today. Patent no. 37435 is the "birth certificate" for the gasoline-powered engine.[38]

Armand Peugot begins to manufacture bicycles and builds his first car, a steamer.[39]

261

1887 At a meeting of the Kansas City Council an ordinance is introduced, "providing for the establishment of the office of gas inspector," appointed by the mayor for a one-year term paying $1,800. "It shall be his duty to at all times inquire into the quality of the gas furnished in the city, the price charged for the same, the time whenever any of the street lamps are not properly lighted and kept burning and whether the electric and gasoline lights furnished the city are such as the contracts with the Electric Light Company and S. H. Hoover calls for, or such as they should be." [40]

U.S. medical authorities diagnose childhood lead poisoning. [41]

Ransom Olds constructs a steam car but abandons research at his neighbors' insistence. [42]

Frank J. Sprague demonstrates a successful trolley car in Richmond, VA. [43]

Elihu Thompson perfects electric welding, which allows higher speeds and greater ability in machine parts. [44]

Daimler operates a motorized taxi in Stuttgart, Germany. [45]

1888 Windmills supply electricity. [46]

First U.S. steam tanker built by the Standard Oil Company. [47]

Benz cars get their first splash of publicity at a Munich exposition. [48] Benz has three working models of 3-wheeled cars. His wife Bertha, who has underwritten his experiments throughout their marriage and is intimately familiar with the development of his engine, takes one of the models out for a 65-mile drive in Germany to see her mother. She takes her two adolescent sons with her. Her ride has become so famous that it is now a national memorial drive in Germany. Along the way, she has to stop at a pharmacy to buy fuel and buys a small amount of rhigolene to get her on her way. From this small beginning, the internal combustion engine gains international attention. [49]

Meanwhile, Standard Oil is awash with unusable gasoline. In their New Jersey facility alone, 142,000 barrels of gasoline awaited their destiny. By then, gasoline had found some use. It had been added to varnish, paint, and cleaning solvents, and cities used it for lighting gasoline lamps. "Naptha launches," or early motor boats used some as did a small number of autos, but they used "pints," not gallons. Their trips were short and experimental.

Standard Oil executives decide to create a new market for their unstable fuel: They will market kitchen stoves! The stove is developed, and because of gasoline's reputation, has to pass inspection with insurance companies. Those companies require better design of the

stove and better refining of the fuel before underwriting "vapor stoves." They have wisely positioned the gas tank far away from the flame.

The sales force instructs customers how to carefully use these stoves that are particularly popular in the hot summer in the West and Southwest. (These stoves are often located on the back porch and used for canning summer produce, while the real wood-fired or coal-fired range in the kitchen is used in the cooler months.)[50]

These "insurance stoves," named by the market to assure safety, sell well, enthusiastically presented in a massive ad campaign in 20,000 newspapers, 7,000 trolley car signs and 30 million circulars. They focus on the fuel itself under two different brands and promise that they are "guaranteed not to smoke, smell or gum the burner." They cost less than a penny an hour to operate using such branded fuel as "Red Crown Stove Gasoline," and "Pratt's Deodorized Stove Gasoline." Sales in gasoline rise from over two million to over three million barrels a year in 1899, and Standard Oil learn how to sell to the consumer market in a new way.[51]

"Vapor Stoves" burning gasoline become a common feature in hardware stores. Four burner stoves for $18. Fire departments are busy putting out fires from these stoves. Gasoline stoves or "vapor stoves" are for sale in Ypsilanti in 1888. The stoves burn "stove gasoline," a "heavy" or crude form of the fuel. (Vapor stoves can burn multiple fuels that also include kerosene, a type of oil, or a fuel called "distillate"). Gasoline stoves offer a quicker cooking time and, unlike wood or coal stoves, don't make the kitchen unbearably hot in the summer. They also aren't sooty, like coal stoves. They are a blessing to homemakers who are tired of sweltering at every summer meal and that are not connected to a city natural gas system. Gasoline-burning stoves are so short-lived that there simply isn't a lot of information out there that's readily available, aside from mentions in numerous obituaries. Vapor stoves, such as those produced by the nearby Detroit Vapor Stove Company can burn multiple fuels. These gasoline stoves can produce carbon monoxide just as a car can. Perhaps the relative draftiness of old houses—and their usual installation on the screened-in back porch—is the saving ventilation grace for many families cooking over these monsters.[52]

1889 Pneumatic tires are invented.

1890 Tenfold increase in oil production from 1870--50 million barrels.[53]
Population of Kansas City is 132,716.

1891 *Good Roads* magazine published. Members became active in local politics. Depicted horrible state of roads in America.[54]

1890s Teddy Roosevelt becomes a champion of conservation along with such powerful men as John Muir, founder of the Sierra Club and Gifford Pinchot who organizes the Forest Service though Muir wants nature preserved for its own sake and Pinchot wants to make the forest productive for generations to come.[55] The contest between conservation and preservation continues to this day. Gasoline will soon make remote forests accessible and harder to preserve.

Gasoline's reputation continues to be "explosive" in the United States. "Explosive," "dangerous," "volatile," "smelly," this fuel is still the stepchild of a growing kerosene lighting industry. In 1891, the Harris wagon, patented in 1893, takes to the streets of Baltimore with a large tank for the fuel fastened to the front of the wagon. Noisy, smelly and sluggish, it cannot travel far. The axles heat up and the gears will not change in order. The exploding gasoline in the engine sounds like a railroad locomotive, and the "combustion was so imperfect that the odor filled the street."[56]

First gasoline-powered tractor works for two months in South Dakota; it has a vertical single-cylinder motor mounted on wooden beams.[57]

1891 London Shell dealer Marcus Samuels sends the first oceanic tanker, the Murex, from the Black Sea to Singapore to export Russian oil for the Rothschilds.[58]

1892 Hiram Percy Maxim, a young engineer and inventor in Maryland, decides to build a gasoline-powered car. In a paint shop he buys a pint of gasoline. The clerk tells him that everyone "who had experimented with gasoline had blown himself up." Maxim tries a few experiments with the fuel, and sure enough, he creates some resounding explosions with just a few drops, but he is determined to master the fuel and works to create a real auto. He does, and goes to work for Colonel Albert Pope, manufacturer of the Columbia brand, who is building both electric and steamer cars. After a satisfactory ride in Maxim's gasoline-powered jitney, he can see building some of those as well. Shops building two and three different kinds of engines—steam, electric and gasoline—are common. Pope speculates that the gasoline car will be for the adventurous who want to go out of town.[59] National league of Good Roads founded. Picks up where LAW left off to promote good roads for farmers.[60]

Marcus Samuel sends his ship, the Murex, through The Suez Canal; beginning of Shell Oil.[61]

1893 Elwood Hayne's wife throws her husband out of the kitchen after he nearly sets it on fire experimenting with a gas engine.[62]

1894 Only four gasoline automobiles exist in the United States. The first is built by Frank and Charles Duryea in 1892, in Springfield, Massachusetts. Henry Ford, in 1893, builds his first car in his now-famous stone garage in Highland Park, Michigan, and Elwood Haynes builds his car in Kokomo, Indiana, in 1894. The fourth car is imported from Germany for the 1893 Chicago World's Fair. It is a Benz. No automotive industry exists since each inventor produces perhaps a car a year and those are experimental. Communication among the inventors is nil and the whole nascent industry proceeds under "the handicap of ignorance."[63]

1895   First patent for gasoline-powered car in America issued to Charles Duryea from Springfield, MA.[64] Forty years, seven months and some days have passed since Joseph Silliman, Jr., identifies "product no. 2" as a light naptha in his laboratory at Yale University. As fragile a validation of gasoline as this small victory is by the Duryeas in 1895, it is only a matter of time until the gasoline engine will be perfected.

Standard Oil and Nobel-Rothschild groups form a cartel to divide the European oil market. Prices soar.[65]

E. P. Ingersoll publishes his first edition of "The Horseless Age," in November 1895, just before the first big American race. (Europe had been holding races for several years). In his "Salutatory," he admits that the industry, "was as yet embryonic," but those who have "taken the pains to search below the surface for the great tendencies of the age, know what a giant industry is struggling into being there."[66] He is feeling optimistic and expectant in the absence of real proof and decides to publish his first issue just before America's first auto race.

He must have contacted the patent office to discover that in 1895 some 300 patents are waiting for approval on different types of automobiles, improvements in some and radical, new, and unworkable ideas in others. Ingersoll continues on his first page to say:

> "All over this country mechanics and inventors are wrestling with the problems of 'trackless traction.' (Streetcars had traction on tracks; cars would not.) Much of their work is in an unfinished state; many of their theories lack demonstration; but, enough has already been achieved to prove absolutely the practicability of the motor vehicle. What is here presented, however, is merely an earnest guess of what is to come."[67]

The race is held in Chicago and sponsored by the *Chicago Times-Herald*. The 55-mile, round-trip event, scheduled for July 4th, is delayed twice due to the field failing to show or once at the starting line unable to start! Finally, on Thanksgiving Day, November 28, the race is set to go with 16 entrants despite a heavy snowfall the night before that leaves six inches of snow on the ground. Several electrics enter sponsored by department stores that have already started using them for deliveries, one called the Electrobat (made by a storage battery company in Philadelphia.) Most are gasoline-powered, however, including the Duryea car and the Benz. The steamers require 20 minutes to heat up, and the gasoline cars have to be cranked to start. The Electrobat driver has arranged to exchange batteries along the way beforehand but runs out of juice before the first exchange. Of the gasoline-powered field only two cars finish—the Duryea and the Benz. Since the Benz has crashed into a streetcar and fallen into a ditch—the American roads are terrible—the Duryea is declared the winner. The Duryeas wins a $2000 prize, but it is back to the garage for all of the gasoline-powered rigs. That fuel-and-engine combination is far from perfected.[68] The results of that race in 1895 mean that not just producers of gasoline who dedicate themselves to the discovery, development and delivery of that fuel will love that fuel and enjoy the profits, but the drivers of gasoline-powered automobiles will be able to enjoy the fruits of their labors as well. The two sides of that endeavor come together that day and forecast the 20th century.

1896   Henry Ford builds his first automobile, his quadracycle, to run on pure ethanol.[69]

Britain repeals the Red Flag Law. Parliamentary laughter greets assertions that the horseless carriage might someday rival the trolley.[70]

The Kansas City Star reports, January 14, 1896: "The Wayne Avenue Street Railway adopts the T. D. Hoskins gasoline motor as a means of power. This will be the first practical test of that system, though magnates from other cities are considering the new invention, which, it is claimed, is 50 percent cheaper than electricity and equally efficient. The gasoline engine is concealed beneath the car, thus dispensing with overhead and underground wires, conduits, or a central powerhouse. It is predicted it will thoroughly revolutionize methods of mass transit, and that vehicles in general will finally be propelled by the new mechanical arrangement." [71]

Frank Duryea wins the London car race to celebrate repeal.[72]

Henry Ford builds his first car.[73]

Rothschild-controlled Shell Oil Company now holds the Russian oil concession.[74]

On November 13, 1896, *The Kansas City Star* reports 50 new street lights.

1897   First gasoline-powered lawn mower.[75]

Brewer August Busch buys the U.S. rights to the diesel engine.[76]

Stanley twins form a steam car company.[77]

1898   Alexander Winton builds four gasoline cars and sells one per year. The first such sale of the decade. Henry Ford follows.[78]

Duryea gives his car the unfortunate name of "Buggyaut" (Why not "Autobuggy" instead?) and sells it to the Barnum & Bailey circus to lead their parade down the Main Streets of America. Who but the circus can appreciate a name like that?[79] The Duryea brothers go on to make a dozen cars and sell them, which make them the first auto dealers in America.

FAIRBANKS STANDARD SCALES. All Styles and Sizes. Write for Catalogue.

FAIRBANKS·MORSE GASOLINE ENGINES ADAPTED FOR THRESHING, GRINDING OR PUMPING, and GENERAL POWER PURPOSES. ESTIMATES FURNISHED ON APPLICATION.

FAIRBANKS, MORSE & CO., 1217-1219 Union Ave., Kansas City, Mo.

In the midst of this decade bursting with explosive gasoline, gurgling steamers and silent electrics, the "first monthly journal devoted to the interest of the motor vehicle industry" is born. E. P. Ingersoll, editor and proprietor of this New York-based magazine has the prophetic insight and enthusiasm of a futurist, and yet calls it for what it was "The Horseless Age." "The Motor Age," a rival publication, will begin publication in 1899.

1899   "Kansas City's renowned parks and boulevards are provided electric light by the Kansas City Electric Lighting Company…at least temporarily…so that attendees may enjoy lighting at concerts. F. K. Hoover, who provides the city's gasoline lamps and E. R. Weeks with the electric company pledge to work together. "The darkness that has heretofore prevailed at the concerts has been remarked by many persons who attended them. The lights are needed, not only that persons may see the landscape beauties that surround them, but it is comforting to see one's next neighbor in a public gathering and the lights were deemed as an immediate necessity."[80] It would befall the City's Board of Parks and Recreation Commissioners to keep this phenomenon afloat into the future.

THE AUTOMOBILE IS HERE.

A Horseless Delivery Wagon Attracts Attention on the Downtown Streets.

The first automobile to be used in Kansas City for business made its appearance to-day. It belongs to Swift & Co. and is used as an order wagon and to deliver small packages of meat to customers. Swift & Co. use automobiles in Chicago to take orders, but the topography of Chicago is more favorable to automobiles than Kansas City's. The one brought here is for an experiment. If it shall succeed the firm will use others.

The automobile was run through the principal business streets this morning and was the object of considerable curiosity. It is an Edison machine, run by storage battery electricity. It will run thirty miles without going to the power house for recharging. The wagon weighs 2,000 pounds and will carry 1,000 pounds. It has a square box like a laundry wagon for packages and a seat in front. It will be used as much to advertise the firm as for ordinary business until automobiles have come into more frequent use in Kansas City.

It stood to-day on Eleventh street, near Walnut, while a dozen men were examining its machinery. One of the curious was a negro hod carrier. He looked at it soberly, then turned to a companion and said: "De hoss done lost his job now, fo' sho'."

John S. Thurman invents his gasoline-powered vacuum cleaner.[81] Requires horse and wagon and two men to carry and clean a room. Short lived.

The first American popular song about cars is, "Love in an Automobile."[82]

The first driver's license for a woman is granted in Chicago.[83]

Scientific American forecasts that the auto will "eliminate a greater part of the nervousness, distraction and strain of modern metropolitan life."[84]

The Kansas City Star reports, "The Automobile is Here. A Horseless Delivery Wagon Attracts Attention on the Downtown Streets!" An Edison battery-powered car hits the streets on November 13. It is Swift and Company's order wagon that can go 30 miles before recharging![85]

There are auto parades among the rich in Central Park and prizes to the "most beautifully decorated car." Most cars are electric; one even has two footmen in uniform mounted in the front. Society pages love this kind of news. One entry has this to say about the dependability of the automobile: "Owing to several unfortunate mishaps to the mechanism of their machine, Mr. and Mrs. Davis, who left New York City several weeks ago on a trip across the continent, have at last gotten out of the state of New York!"[86]

Transcontinental trips become popular as both men and women attempt them. Their journeys rival Odysseus's as they encounter breakdowns too many to count, primitive roads, no roads, mud, lack of available gasoline—yes, only gasoline-powered cars make the trips—waiting for parts to be delivered by railroad, no maps, bad directions, but eventual, jubilant success.

Kansas City's "rumblings that keep the city going" are driven by massive underground machinery, "whence come the forces that furnish the requirements of modern civilization—places that thousands of us never see…behind it all is some leviathan that gathers power from dormant coal, and grinding, revolving, whirling, sends forth the energy, the power that forces everything before it," from streetcars, to lighting and elevators, from printing presses to the water that coursed through fire hydrants and every kitchen sink.

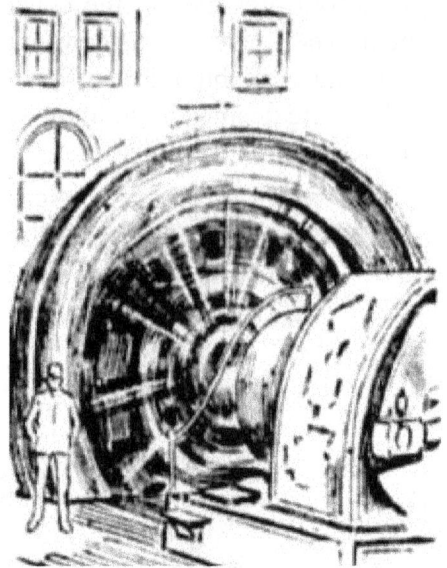

Massive electric motors, a part of Kansas City's underground machinery

1900 Some hold the turn of the century to be the end of the horseless carriage age and the beginning of the automobile. Those who drive cars in the early years of the 20th century are called "automobilists" to differentiate themselves from the very popular "bicyclists."

Those who drive gasoline-powered cars and their cars are called "gasoliners."

Only the truly affluent can afford the cars in the early years. Early autos have price tags in the $1250 range, roughly a $25,000 to $30,000 amount today. Given that factory workers earn not even a tenth of that, sales go to the rich. Auto clubs form in every major city of the rich few who can afford to buy a car. The "Horseless Carriage" magazine shows a photo of at least 80 gentlemen in tuxedos enjoying such a meeting in a grand hotel ballroom.

Thomas Edison film short, "Automobile Parade", and first European auto movie, "How It Feels to Be Run Over" entertain audiences on both sides of the Atlantic.

British engineer Sir John Wolfe Barry estimates that 900,000 suburban commuters enter London daily. Congestion delays cost the owners of the 40,000 horse-operated vehicles in London 880,000 pounds (£) annually. Barry believes that motor cars will relieve this because they occupy half as much street space as horse-operated vehicles.[87]

Population of Kansas City is 163,752.

109 ocean going tankers of more than 2,000 gross tons in operation, 3 under US flag.

Kansas City Star, December 8, 1901

269

Fueling Change

1901   Spindletop, a gusher, comes in near Beaumont, Texas on January 10. It shoots 150-feet in the air and produces 100,000 barrels a day. The price of crude oil drops to less than five cents a barrel. Two new companies based in the Southwest, Gulf, Texaco, will break into Standard Oil's monopoly. Shell buys Spindletop to enter the U.S. market.[88]

Daimler Motors builds a car named after Mercedes Jellinek, the 11-year-old daughter of its agent in France. It is the first production car to break away from carriage design by placing the engine under a hood in front and to have an all-steel frame. American car makers will adopt it after its appearance at the 1902 New York auto show.[89]

Shell turns down a merger offer from Rockefeller and joins Royal Dutch.[90]

Miners receive $.85/ton for lump coal. Day wages are from $1.25 to $2.15.[91]

Joseph Stalin enjoys his first revolutionary success, leading a strike against the Rothschilds' oil wells in Baku.[92]

First film with a car used for courtship is a brief silent film in which a couple elopes. The bride's father gives chase, but his limousine breaks down. He arrives too late to stop the ceremony. "Runaway Match, or Marriage by Motor" is the first filmed car chase.[93]

Kansas City's Peck Dry Goods Company begins using an automobile for regular delivery service. It "was designed and built in Kansas City by the Day Automobile Company at 1407 East 12th Street. W. T. Irvin draws the plans. It is handsomely painted in light yellow and Brewster green, the colors used in all the wagons for the Peck Company. It is capable of 30 miles-per-hour and averages 15 miles over any part of the streets in the city. It is what is known as a 12-horse power automobile and carries a 50-gallon tank for water and 12-gallon tank for gasoline."[94]

Chapter 31

Gasoline: The Young Romantic, 1902-1913
Finally, gasoline *expands and defends* itself in the marketplace

Once people have the chance to drive around "horseless" and give themselves over to "horsepower" in the tank, life would never be the same. Roads are unprepared for the gay and daring combination of early autos, a tank full of gasoline, and intrepid drivers swathed in coats, goggles, hats and scarves pressing on the gas pedal. Movies ware made and songs composed to share the glee of gasoline.

1902 American Automobile Association founded.

The Grand Avenue Power Station is constructed using Wood Age horse-drawn wagons and mules to create a 20th century coal-fired power station.

The ratios of cars begin to change. "Gasoliners" began to take market share from steamers and electrics. On Decoration Day, a *New York Times* article entitled "Automobile's History a Stirring Romance" reports a parade of 39 gasoline cars, 14 steam cars and 1 electric—54 in all—drive in the parade in New York City. That is how quickly the gasoline engine speeds ahead of the others.[1]

Kansas City Council and President Corrigan of the Kansas City Electric Light Company begins bargaining to regulate pricing for lighting to the city and to private customers.[2]

1902-1904 Ida Tarbell's *History of Standard Oil Company* is serialized in *McClure's*.[3]

1903 Kansas City Electric Light Company begins operation on May 29 of a new power plant near the Kaw River on Central Avenue. Five days later a flood covers the engine and boiler room with 20 feet of water and mud. It takes 3 months to clean up and get the station back into operation.[4]

Kansas City's "automobile ordinance has been before the Council for three years and has made very little progress. It requires as much tinkering, apparently, as the automobile itself."[5]

Detroit produces 8,000 gasoliners that year.

Wright Brothers first flight.

Mercedes introduces the gas pedal.[6]

Detroit is in the gasoline-powered automobile business and reports that "the year had been most satisfactory" with 8,000 automobiles being turned out from their factories from the little Olds (Ransome Olds has switched from steamers to gasoliners in 1899) to the big Packard.[7]

1904   Kansas City's "Automobile Ordinance," is passed, "regulating the operation of automobiles," as, "reasonable, and the enforcement of the law should greatly reduce the danger that exists from excessive speed and careless driving. In the first place, no one will be permitted to operate a machine until he has qualified before the Superintendent of Streets and two expert chauffeurs. This should eliminate the danger from inexperienced or unreliable drivers—one of the greatest of the existing menaces. As to the speed limits, they would seem to be fair and safe. Eight miles in the business district and 12 miles in the outlying sections, considering the quickness with which automobiles may be brought to a standstill, should remove the dangers of collision. On the other hand, this speed is sufficient for all reasonable purposes of making time and of pleasant driving. The other terms are rational and easily complied with. The ordinance covers the ground as completely as could be expected, considering the fact that only two years have been consumed in its preparation."[8] The following year, the ordinance will be declared invalid, and a replacement proposed in its place.

Songsters immediately find inspiration in cars, drivers and romance of the road.

Child lead poisoning linked to lead-based paints.[9]

Studebaker sells its first gasoline-powered vehicle.[10]

Kansas City's Board of Examiners of Automobile Operators includes W. C. Brooks, Superintendent of Streets; Louis Curtiss, one of Kansas City's preeminent architects and "an auto enthusiast," who has the purported distinction of owning the first motor car in Kansas City; and, John C. Caps. By the end of September, they announce the first sitting for the examination. Applicants for the license to drive would pay the City Treasurer $1, and once they passed the exam and be "found to have the capacity, skill, experience and habits of sobriety requisite to perform the duties of automobile operator," would have a one-year license granted. [11]

1905   The word "smog" coined to describe smoke and fog in cities and not found in the open country. Dr. Henry Antoine Des combination of Voeux in London: "Smokey fog" equals "smog."[12]

Britain imposes a gasoline tax informally ear-marked for road improvements.[13]

British Army Service Corps Journal: "The selection of a car is a grave matter, and similar in more than one way to the selection of a wife."[14]

In June, the Kansas City Automobile Club and the Kansas City Driving Club are considering joining efforts in a clubhouse, grounds, and track. In 1975, Mrs. John P. Hanback found her 1905 copy of the Kansas City Driving Club's publication, "Drives in and About Kansas City." Reporter Hugh Hadley writes:

"A Kansas City activity which was brought to an untimely end by the advent of the horseless carriage could conceivably gain a new lease on life if the energy crisis becomes a calamity. Mrs. John P. Hanback recently came across her copy of *Drives in and About Kansas City*, published in 1905 and dedicated to the Kansas City Driving Club. It was arranged and compiled by the Studebaker Bros. Mfg. Co., and any motor car buff knows that the Studebakers were into buggies and hansom cabs long before they got into those newfangled automobiles. The handsomely mounted book contains elegant pictures of Kansas City's new and famed boulevard and park system, with an eye to its use by the gentry and their ladies. The preface hailed the "beauty, grandeur and extent of its park and boulevard system" and closed with the earnest hope "that the reader's interest will be awakened thereby, causing a desire for a more perfect knowledge of this, the grandest driving system possessed by any American city." The pictures are fine, showing the new drives, walks, bridges, the "absolutely fireproof" Hotel Baltimore, Penn Valley Park, Gladstone, Armour and Benton boulevards, some famous Percherons imported by McLaughlin Bros., many scenes of the new Paseo, and the George B. Peck Dry Goods Co. . . . . B. Howard Smith, father of the late Mayor Bryce B. Smith, was president of the Driving Club and some of the town's brightest young scions were members. Saturday afternoons were set aside for racing their phaetons on their track at 46th and the Paseo, where they built a comfortable clubhouse. The tract later became Electric Park and now is occupied by the Village Green apartment development. Fabulous dinners with steak, lobster and champagne helped the drivers and their families to savor the delights of the race. But those gentlemen and ladies had not been paying attention. Mr. Ford and the Brothers Dodge and Durant and Fisher and all the others had been busy in their workshops and factories and very soon the horse became a thing almost of the past, supplanted by the popular automobile. The club, founded in 1896 with 25 members, sold its 24-acres, purchased in 1899, seven years later to J. J. Heim and his associates, who built Electric Park."[15]

The most popular song in America is, "Come away with me Lucille . . . You can go as far as you like wit me in your merry Oldsmobile."

Glenn Pool (oil) discovered in Oklahoma. It becomes the nation's largest producing oil field, brought an influx of thousands of settlers and built Oklahoma. Before Glenn Pool Tulsa's population is about 1,500 people. After the well came in in truly classic fashion with a high plume of oil reaching toward the sky, 20 years later Tulsa had grown to 150,000 residents. The discovery influences everything in the new state admitted to the Union in 1907.[16]

Half the American motor vehicles are in New York and New Jersey. The New York Auto show has become the largest industrial exhibit in the U.S.[17]

Kansas City's "Automobile Ordinance," after passing in August 1904 and being invalidated in October 1905, is replaced on December 8. Clarifications to the ordinance include an eight-mile speed limit in the district between the Missouri River, 18th Street, Troost Avenue and State Line. Elsewhere in the city limits, and in parks and boulevards, the speed is limited to 12-miles-per-hour. The ordinance required a lighted lamp on the front of each vehicle that can be seen from a distance of 100 feet, and lamps at the sides and rear that can be seen at 50-feet. The registered automobile would have a plate with the letters "K.C." below the number in white on a black background. Penalties for not yielding to other aspects of the ordinance is a fine not less than $10, nor more than $300.[18]

An early automobile traversing Kansas City's sometimes steep streets (like 9th Street here).

1906 It is announced in January that G. W. Curtiss and W. L. Bell open shops at 1st and Main Streets in Kansas City where they set out to manufacture two styles of automobile: a touring car and a runabout. The touring car is a four-cylinder machine and "will have many things about it to attract attention. There will be no brass trimmings. Lamps and other exposed parts will be silver plated. Much of the material used is imported from Paris. The 2,300-pound touring car is 40-horse-power and sells for $4,000. The runabout is 22-horse power. [19]

A new, six-ton truck for Swift and Company is turned out by the Kansas City Motor Car Company, which hits the streets of Kansas City around New Year's Day and is put into operation in Chicago. [20]

The Kansas City-Belton Railway Line, which filed its articles of incorporation in Jefferson City on March 24, announces plans to build a railway for the operation of gasoline motor cars, to do a general passenger business, and handle the lighter classes of weight. The line connects with the Rockhill or Troost Avenue lines of the Metropolitan Street Railway Company and runs close to Dallas (southeast of Brookside and Waldo) and Santa Fe, run through Grandview and terminate in Belton.[21]

Ford introduces the Model N, a reversion to the cheap gas buggy type, and produces over 100 per day, as Oldsmobile abandons the gas buggy style, curved dash Olds for a Mercedes-style car.[22]

In April 1906, the *Kansas City Star* syndicates a *Pearson's Magazine* article reporting, "Though practically no more than six years old, our American automobile industry has become the champion of the world. We began this year ahead of England, Germany and Italy, and even France, in the number of machines produced…. Here, at last, are the exact figures: In the year 1904, we made 26,601 automobiles [as reported from 100 manufactures and verified by Bradstreet's in a comparison of the amounts paid in royalties], worth $34,650,500. We have $21,313,000 invested in the business.... The new machines are whizzing out of our factories at a rate of one every five minutes.... Twenty-four thousand machines are registered in New York state. In France, where the automobile is born, there are not more than 17,000. And, in the whole United States, if we took an automobile census, we would find about 70,000 now in use."[23]

Automobile accidents and ticketing for recklessness and/or speeding becomes commonplace in daily newspapers. Occasionally, an attempt is made to report statistics, such as this "Automobile Death Record," syndicated in the *Kansas City Star* from the *New York World*: "Excessive speeding and careless handling of automobiles have been responsible for 99 deaths within a period of one year. The number of injured is far in excess of this, yet many owners of motor cars continue to run them with slight regard to the danger to themselves and to others. The record of deaths from automobile accidents this year bids fair to exceed the gruesome record of last year. Within the period from August 3, 1905, to August 9, 1906, no fewer than 94 persons were killed in such accidents, and in the two days following five more fatalities were added to the list." [24]

1907   First drive-in gasoline station opens in St. Louis.[25]
Shell and Royal Dutch combine under Henri Deterding.[26]

1908   The Model T, Henry Ford's first car, burns ethanol corn-alcohol gasoline for fuel energy (gasoline.)[27]
Oil discovered in Persia at the site of a Zoroastrian temple.[28]
Not only is the first decade in automobile construction enough of a time frame to "look back," motorists and members of the Kansas City Driving Club begins campaigning for better roads, and motor reforms. They also promote motor tours, races, and leisurely driving routes for day trip outings. In March 1908, there is a reported 200 miles of rock road in Jackson County, Missouri, outside of Kansas City city limits.[29]

1909   Anglo-Persian, Oil Company (later British Petroleum) forms.[30]
France, Belgium and Austria ban white-lead interior paints.[31]

1910   Friedrich Berjius, a German chemist, discovers the hydrogenation process to convert coal into gasoline, a process that will later allow war transport in petroleum-short Germany.[32]
Mexican oil found "Golden Lane".[33]
The world tanker fleet doubles, the number of U.S. tankers rises to 31 and accounts for 109,000 out of a total of 845,000 gross tons.
Kansas City population is 248,381.

When equipped with regular rear seat, a light, four-passenger touring car, rear seat removed can be done in a moment; and rumble seat substituted, a smart runabout; without rear or rumble seat, a combination passenger and baggage car.

A NECESSARY ADJUNCT TO EVERY SUBURBAN OR COUNTRY HOME

The Studebaker "SUBURBAN" is a car you will use in half a dozen different ways.

The Studebaker "SUBURBAN" Chassis is identical with that of the regular Studebaker "30" Touring Car, which is a sufficient guarantee that from a mechanical standpoint the car will give satisfactory service.

ELECTRIC AND GASOLINE MODELS ON EXHIBITION AT

Studebaker

13th and Hickory.

This January 20, 1910, article could have been written easily 100 years later in 2010:

"The garage of the business man—no matter how many cars he has—is not complete unless he has an electric car for his own use and another for his wife and daughter," said C. H. Tyler, manager of the electric pleasure vehicle department of the Studebaker Automobile Company, at the [Kansas City] motor show this morning. Tyler went on to say that electrics are in a different class than gas cars and are not considered as competitors by the trade.

"A dealer that sells an electric on the representation that it is a car for Sunday touring makes an untrue statement. The electric has a different purpose. It is for city and suburban use, for social outings, for doctors and business men who want to make short trips in a car with the confidence that they are sure to get there. Lots of times, you know, a lawyer, for instance, cranks up his car to make a quick run to a client and the engine won't respond. Mr. Lawyer doesn't know anything about machinery and so it's him for a street car in a hurry. But as long as there is current in an electric and the current is turned on, that car is bound to go—has to go—if the wheels are shy of bearings or whatever is wrong. And there is no excuse for a currentless car, because a dial is ever before the driver showing just the supply of power in storage.

"It was hard to get the sale of electrics started because there were so few charging stations and so few garages catering to owners. But in all big cities now, in Kansas City especially, there are numbers of central charging stations where power is sold so cheaply that the electric is really more economical than a horse and buggy."

"The electrics will figure prominently at the show tonight, insomuch as it's society night and society folk are so interested in the battery-driven, trim type of car. A number of the dealers will give flowers to women visitors tonight...." [See this timeline for an eye-opening article published by the *Kansas City Star* on October 16, 2015.]

1911 U.S. Supreme Court breaks up Standard Oil in an antitrust action. Three major oil Companies without capital: Exxon (nee Esso), Mobile (formerly Standard Oil of NY), and Socal (formerly Standard Oil of California).[34]

Gasoline sales surpass kerosene sales in the U.S.[35]

U.S. Supreme Court orders dissolution of Standard Oil Trust.[36]

The Horseless Age and *The Motor Age*, rival publications, merge into the latter. The psychic impact of cars had already caused the leap to motors and away from horselessness.

1912   First offshore oil wells (in Southern CA.)[37]

Kansas City's first "drive-in filling station" is installed at 1720 Grand Avenue. Alex A. Smith first took the gasoline business away from the curb, "and his idea and subsequent expansion in the new field netted him a fortune. Smith's 'drive in' gasoline station succeeds a coal business his brother-in-law had conducted in the middle of the block on the west side of Grand Avenue between 17th and 18th Streets. He saw motorists lined up at 16th and McGee Streets and 12th and Harrison Streets, driving across tracks to have gasoline brought to their cars.

"Motor cars...were multiplying rapidly on the streets of Kansas City. There were nearly 7,000 cars [in Kansas City] in 1912. And Smith thought nearly all of them passed 1720 Grand Avenue some time during the day.

"A six-hour count revealed 4,820 "pleasure cars," 98 trucks and 453 motor cycles passing by 1720 Grand Avenue. The same vehicle, of course, often passed the point a number of times. And Mr. Smith cut away the curb, invited motorists across the sidewalk, and soon he and his wife were serving customers.

"The profit, in those days, did not come from gasoline, but from the lubricating oils and in servicing the lights. The tank wagon and the retail price of gasoline was the same, 13 cents. Some who carried it to the curb charged 2 cents a gallon for the short trip.

"Mr. Smith's subsequent business history is familiar. His rapidly expanding business was incorporated in 1920 as the Monarch Gasoline and Oil Company. When he sold out in 1920 to the Manhattan Oil Company he had 66 filling stations, had 200 employees, and was handling 20 million gallons of gasoline, distillate, and fuel oil. The Manhattan Corporation...was absorbed into the Independent Oil and Gas Company [in 1929].

"The Independent corporation renewed the 1720 Grand Avenue lease for a trial year, but not finding the middle of the block operation profitable, elected to abandon the pioneer station and to clear the property by November 1 [1929], in compliance with the original lease."[38]

1912-1917 The "Keystone Cops (Kops)" appear on screen for the next five years in silent movies. They satirize both police and traffic with early cars, the first such effort to have fun with the new technology.

Britain decides to switch its naval fuel from coal to oil and starts to buy a majority share of British Petroleum.

Dependable self-starters elude the models until Charles Kittering develops it for General Motors.

The idea of gasoline and romance becomes trendy. By 1912, the vocabulary about gasoline has changed. Instead of "explosive" the word has turned to "romance." The many trips across the continent on gasoline--many by women--and written up in nail-biting memoirs certainly validates the idea of the adventurous open road being conquered by a gasoline-powered car. A series of six adventure stories for girls is published between 1909 and 1913 by Laura Dent Crane. Like Nancy Drew on wheels they drive into one adventure after another: *The Automobile Girls Along the Hudson, The Automobile Girls at Newport,* etc., show that young women can drive, accompanied by an auntie as chaperone and protector, not to mention financier, and be quite independent.[39]

1913   A song called "Gasoline" is published. "What is the precious thing for which we're blowing each blessed dollar of our weekly pay? Gasoline!"[40] The lyrics might have been written by a driver today and the necessity of gasoline in our lives. The song asks a series of questions:

> "What is it keeps this world of ours a going?
> What makes us happy night and day?
> What is the precious thing for which we're
> blowing each blessed dollar of our weekly pay?
>
> Chorus: Gasoline! Gasoline!
> Everywhere you go you smell it,
> Every motor seems to yell it.
> Gasoline! Gasoline!
> That's the cry that echoes thro your dreams.
> Gasoline! Gasoline!
> In this land of milk and honey 'Tisn't love—isn't money
> Rules the world, now ain't that funny? Gasoline! Gasoline!"[41]

Not to be outdone, the following year the new motion picture industry brought out a short romantic comedy called, "Love, Luck and Gasoline," about a father who tries to keep his daughter from eloping with a boy he doesn't approve of. Of course, that boy has a gasoline-powered vehicle at his disposal to whisk away the beloved girl. It's a silent movie and full of pratfalls but it's about gasoline—a character all its own!

William Merton Burton received a patent for cracking process to convert oil to gasoline. Until then the oil companies used a simple distillation process.[42]

The Kansas City Automobile Club announces plans to build a "handsome clubhouse" in the country at Hickman Mills on 40-acres that it purchased three years prior and owned outright. The club also had $8,500 in its treasury, and an income of $9,000 a year. Designed by Louis Curtiss, "It is planned to make the clubhouse as attractive and with as many accommodations as any in the country."[43]

Chapter 32

Gasoline: The Soldier, 1914-1945
Gasoline *expands and defends* itself at war

Gasoline powered machines in two wars. World War I saw the "demise of the equine" once more as a war machine. It had suddenly become obsolete and unable to supply the strength and endurance of a motor vehicle. War had become mechanized and would demand far more horsepower than could have been imagined. Battles were won and lost depending on fuel supply. Nations with newly discovered oil deposits became players on the world stage without ever having to "grow up" as governing bodies. The activity and growth of the oil industry raised all boats and over time fortunes of unimaginable levels would become common and surpass John Rockefeller's original title as "wealthiest man."

1914-1918 WWI mechanization of the battlefield include the popular machine gun, the tank, armored cars and other mass-produced iron products made with coal.[1]

Pediatric lead-paint poisoning death from eating crib paint is described.[2]

1916 As gasoline engines improve and fuel delivery systems mature, drivers prefer gas-powered cars to electrics. Interest drops off. For a time, duel engine—gas and electric engines are offered.[3]

A vehicle, propelled by a gasoline motor, an electric motor, or both at the same time, appears on Kansas City's streets today. The new car, a Woods Dual Fuel, is classed as a '1916 motor sensation' by the motor journals and is said to be the beginning of a new era in motor construction.

"The power plant of the car consists of a small, 4-cylinder gasoline motor and an electric motor generator combined into one unit. The movement of a finger lever on the steering wheel connects the gasoline motor to the electric generator, which cranks the engine. Power is transmitted through the armature shaft of the electric motor and propeller shaft direct to the rear axle.

"There are two levers on the steering wheel, corresponding to the spark and throttle on the ordinary car. One controls the speed of the gasoline motor and the other the electric motor...." The H. A. Dougherty Motor Company, 17th and McGee Streets, will handle the new car. The price of the car is $2,650."[4]

1917 *The Kansas City Sun,* September 1, features an article about "the gasoline horse, (a tractor) rapidly revolutionizing American agriculture." "The farmer took to the automobile as he does to the circus. Old Dobbins has long since been smothered by the exhaust from the 4-cylinder automobile and now is being ousted from his old and arduous vocation of plowing and harvesting."[5]

Studebaker in Kansas City at 13th and Hickory, offers both electric and gasoline models as "a necessary adjunct to every suburban or country home."[6]

A 2-hole "junior gasoline stove" is for sale for $2.48 for a two-burner, light-weight "summer stove" in the *Kansas City Sun.*[7]

The U.S. enters World War I. Woodrow Wilson is the last president to use a horse and carriage in his inaugural parade.[8]

World oil productions tops 500 billion barrels, 60 % from the U.S.[9]

Mexico is the first third world economy to nationalize some U.S. oil holdings.[10]

U-Boat offensive reduces Britain to two months' oil supply.[11]

British soldiers sabotage the Rumanian oil fields, cutting off German supplies for six months.[12]

The Bolshevik Revolution in Russia led to the establishment of the USSR by 1922. Royalty were replaced by uprising peasants who organized the soviet (community assemblies) and socialist democracy which eventually became the Communist party.

1918 Major oil shortages plague the German economy, contributing to home front unrest.[13]

Germany deploys tanks for the first time, too little, too late.[14]

First gasoline pipeline laid in WY, from Salt Creek to Casper and carrying gasoline in a three-inch pipeline.[15]

Scientific American reports alcohol-blend can be used as motor fuel.[16]

Thomas Midgley patents benzene/gasoline blend as anti-knock additive. Increases engine power and efficiency by raising fuel anti-knock quality—what is today called the "octane rating" based on iso-octane reference fuel.[17]

The comic strip, "Gasoline Alley," appears…and, is still running! Its characters have aged out and died off at octogenarian ages. The comic strip further defines and evolves the idea of man vs. liquid fuel. Now in the second decade of the 21st century, our lives are enwrapped and entrapped

Introducing "Walt" and "Skeezix" of "Gasoline Alley."

"Gasoline Alley," introducing to readers of The Star big, good natured "Walt" and "Skeezix," will start in The Star this afternoon. Frank O. King, the artist creator of "Gasoline Alley," writes The Star expressing his appreciation and takes time to draw the accompanying picture of "Walt" and "Skeezix."

Readers of The Star will find "Gasoline Alley" daily in the want ad section, and if your new year resolutions hold out you won't be able to keep from smiling. That's the one and only mission in life of "Walt" and "Skeezix," to make you smile awhile.

In The Star today.

by the very fuel that is ignored for so long in its first 50 years of life. The cartoon strip's first appearance in *The Kansas City Star* is January 1, 1923.

1919 British Lord Curzon comments that the Allies floated to victory on "a sea of oil."[18]

Ned Jordan, playboy, plugs his Playboy car: "It's a car for a man's man . . . or a girl who loves the out of doors."[19]

Oregon imposes the first state gasoline tax.[20]

A young Dwight D. Eisenhower joins a military convoy that drives from Washington, D.C. to San Francisco in 1919. Roads are nonexistent, and many days are spent pulling every truck out of mud and ditches. Sometimes bridges are too fragile to cross or too small. The lieutenant colonel at 28 meets his destiny on that trip and in World War II as he sees how the German autobahns speed trucks and troops on their way. As President from 1953 to 1961, he initiates a modern highway system. The American interstate highway system is named after him in 1990.[21]

1920s By the second decade of the 20th century, Americans love gasoline, aspire to own a car powered by that formerly useless and dreaded fuel, and declare their love in song, on screen and from their pocketbooks.

Standard Oil-New Jersey (Exxon) buys the rights to Soviet oil fields from czarist exiles.[22]

1920   Amendment to the Minnesota state constitution compels earmarking of gasoline taxes for road building.[23]

U.S. Naval Committee approves alcohol-gasoline blend.[24]

DuPont now owns more than 35% of General Motors.[25]

17 workers die of lead poisoning working at Ethyl Corporation creating leaded gasoline.[26]

Coal provides three-fourths of global energy and choking smog shrouds London and Pittsburgh.[27]

Standard Oil begins adding ethanol to gasoline to increase octane and reduce engine knocking.[28]

Steam-powered concrete mixers phased out. Coal and water have to be brought to mixer several times daily over long distances. They begin to use gasoline-powered mixers as more workmen became familiar with gasoline engines.[29]

Kansas City population is 324,410. The city can accurately be called an "instant city," much like more western cities like Phoenix and Denver to grow from 0 population to this size in a hundred years. Francois Chouteau could not have imagined his fur trading post turning into such a place.

In 1927, the Grand Avenue Power Station it is purchased by Kansas City Power and Light Company and extensively rebuilt. That station is the only one of the early day plants still surviving. Today (2019), it provides steam heat to many downtown Kansas City buildings.[30]

There are 15,000 filling stations.[31] Sometimes called "comfort stations," but most often either "petrol stations" or "gas stations." A new lexicon enters into the American dialect. Ordinances in Kansas City propose limiting further construction of new stations, containing them into a 'zone.' Garage owners and operators of filling stations even seek restrictions and standardization on the hours of operation. On the Kansas side of State Line, operators propose no sale of gasoline after 6 p.m., or on Sundays or holidays. [32]

1921 Chouteau 100 years ago landed at the limestone pier and invited trappers to sell their furs to him. He would buy them and market them in St. Louis, and east as far as Europe.

National Lead Company admits lead is a poison.[33]

Midgley demonstrates car powered by 30 percent alcohol-gasoline blend[34]

TEL (tetra ethyl lead) found to be effective antiknock agent by Thomas Midgley who works for Charles Kettering at General Motors Corp. Research.[35]

U.S. Geological Survey predicts the exhaustion of domestic oil reserves within 5 years, starting an early energy crisis.[36]

DODGE BROTHERS ROADSTER

You rarely hear the price of the car mentioned.

Remarks about its low cost and long service are much more frequent.

The gasoline consumption is unusually low.
The tire mileage is unusually high.

BUTLER MOTOR COMPANY

Grand Ave., 26th and Walnut
Kansas City, Mo.
812 Minnesota Ave., Kansas City, Kas.
BUTLER-SANDERSON MOTOR CO.,
Lawrence, Kas.
*See Our Exhibit, Automobile Show,
February 12th to 19th.*

The Kansas City Star
February 9, 1921

1922 Kansas City Mayor Cromwell gets the idea from Jefferson City mayor, Paul Hunt, to propose a tax of $.01/gallon on the price of gasoline, the proceeds to go to a fund for keeping the streets in repair. "About 100,000 gallons of gasoline are consumed here each day," the mayor said. The said fund would produce $365,000/year. The city's legal department arranged for the preparation of an ordinance by mid-December. Immediately, there is a pushback from the Kansas City Motor Car Dealers' Association, and a resolution against the tax as "class legislation," by the Chamber of Commerce. By year's end, city and state levies were being discussed.[37]

The Kansas City Automobile Club makes an offer to the Jackson County Court (predecessor to the Jackson County Legislature), which is accepted by the Court, to install danger signals, direction signs and road markers on the main county highways leading into Kansas City. Mayor Cromwell, President of the Automobile Club, said the expense would be borne by the club."[38]

Prado Motors (NYC) imitates aircraft with the propeller-driven Reese Aerocar.[39]

League of Nations bans white-lead interior paint. U.S. declines to adopt.[40]

Public Health Service (PHS) warns of dangers of lead production, leaded fuel. Scientists express concern to Midgley over TEL (tetra ethyl lead) in gas.[41]

Midgley repairs to Miami to recover from lead poisoning. GM contracts with DuPont to supply TEL.[42]

GM patents the use of TEL (tetra ethyl lead) as anti-knocking agent called "Ethyl" in its marketing to avoid use of the word "lead," and begins to be sold to the public.[43]

First TEL-poisoning deaths occur in Deepwater, NJ. Newly opened plant sells TEL to selected markets.[44]

1922-1928 Negotiation on the Turkish (Iraq) Petroleum Company, leading to the "Red Line Agreement," a cartel of oil companies dividing up the previous Ottoman Empire. This agreement precedes OPEC by 30 years.[45]

1923 Almer McDuffee McAfee develops the first commercially viable cracking process. This process can triple the amount of gasoline yield over the distillation process.[46]

GM contracts with Bureau of Mines to test TEL (tetra ethyl lead). Dr. Robert Kehoe hired to study hazards at plant.[47]

World oil production tops a trillion barrels, 73% in the United States.[48]

Winston Churchill accepts a 50,000£ fee to lobby for Shell.[49]

GM forms medical committee to examine lead threat. Becomes GM's foremost lead apologist.[50]

1924 The first, quarterly, gasoline tax installment on July 16, since Kansas City's Mayor Beach's administration takes office on April 1, garnering $60,000 for street repairs exclusively.[51]

3,666,000 cars are produced in the U.S. this year. Such capital outlay changes the face of America: Financially, consumer credit is born to ensure buyers can buy the cars produced. Roadside restaurants expand. Motor courts for the weary traveler are built. Suburban living becomes possible, separating people socially and economically. Car racing begins to flourish. NASCAR is eventually born from this sport. Russia produces zero cars this year.[52]

Anti-knock ethyl gasoline marketed; high-compression engines come in.[53]

Teapot Dome Scandal erupts. Oil industrialists had bribed the Harding administration to lease oil reserves set aside for military emergencies.[54]

Standard Oil of New Jersey (ESSO/EXXON) and General Motors create the Ethyl Gasoline Corporation, a separate corporation to create and market TEL.[55]

Five workers die of lead poisoning at Bayway plant in port of New York. GM medical committee delivers negative report on TEL. Irene DuPont is "not disturbed."[56]

Five workers die in October and 30 are hospitalized after breathing fumes in a plant making leaded gas. *The Nation* notes: "They died in straitjackets. They died stark mad, grinning and gritting their teeth."[57]

Low cost continuous flow process becomes the norm in refining.[58]

NY Board of Health ban sales of TEL-enhanced gasoline. Standard Oil suspends sale of leaded gasoline in NJ. Bureau of Mines gives TEL clean bill of health.[59]

Sales of TEL is suspended for one year.[60] Hazard assessment by U.S. Public Health Service.

Gasoline is 40-60 octane, increasing power in engines.[61]

1925 Public Health Service holds conference to find alternative. Kettering and Midgley say there is no alternative.[62]

Oil and auto industries pack a committee appointed by the surgeon general to investigate the hazards of leaded gasoline. They wrongly, but profitably, decide it is harmless.[63]

DuPont opens second TEL (tetra ethyl lead) plant.[64] Surgeon General's committee calls for further study funded by Congress; but, it is never funded.

One alternative named is ethanol.[65] Not cheap enough to use.

The *Los Angeles Times* runs a series of twelve weekly articles from July 4th to the end of September under the title, "The Romance of Gasoline." The series begins with the earliest oil history and covers that subject up to 1925. No production figures appear and very little mention of gasoline itself, but the title of the articles clearly indicate that gasoline with a car wrapped around it is the most romantic element in their lives.[66]

1926 "Ethyl is back!" say signs in stations.[67] Deepwater TEL (tetra ethyl lead) plant reopens. GM's Sloan expresses concern about valve corrosion with Ethyl.[68]

1927 GM quells rebellion of dealers against leaded fuel.[69]

In 1912, 100 gallons of crude oil yielded about 12-gallons of gasoline. In 1926, that average has been increased to 37 gallons. That means a barrel of crude in 1926 is equivalent for gasoline production to three in 1912. "Federal government reports indicate motorists in the United States waste at least 1/3 of their gasoline by failing to set the carburetor for as "lean" a mixture as the excellent new gasolines will permit. To ensure easy starting, a richer mixture than necessary is used. The experts advise a happy medium for the sake of fuel economy."[70]

1928 Lead Industries Association formed to combat "undesirable publicity." Surgeon General tells NYC there are "no good grounds" to ban TEL.[71]

Achnacarry Agreement (signed in Achnacarry, Scotland): The seven largest oil companies in the world (Exxon, Socal, Mobil, Gulf, Texaco, British Petroleum and Royal Dutch Shell—the "Seven Sisters") fix world prices resulting in "As-Is Agreement."[72]

Fueling Change

1929   All 48 American states have gasoline taxes reserved for road improvements.[73]
American Petroleum Institute proposes measures to limit oil glut.[74]
Standard Oil-California gets concession in Bahrain, the first U.S. penetration of the Middle East.[75]
British Petroleum decides not to seek oil in Saudi Arabia.[76]
Ellery Queen's *Roman Hat Mystery*. Mystery writer picks up the "death by tetraethyllead" theme.[77]

1930s   Industry stops using kerosene in cars.[78]

1930   The population of Kansas City is 399,746.
Ethyl Export is founded in England to sell leaded gas overseas.[79]
"Dad" Joiner's discovery of oil in East Texas is found to be the largest discovery in the contiguous United States.[80]
East Texas oil field opens.[81]
White Eagle Oil Company in KS becomes Exxon.

1931   The 33-story Kansas City Power & Light building at 14th and Baltimore is built, then the tallest building west of the Mississippi River.[82]
Morris Minor, the first British car to cost less than 100 pounds, now advertises as having 100 mph (160 kph) speed and 100 mpg (42.7 kpl) gas efficiency.
Gasoline prices take a drop in Albia, IA. Two cents a gallon is lopped-off to bring the price to 12 cents a gallon.[83]

1932   Britain puts a 40% tax on gasoline.[84]
British Medical Journal cites "insidious saturation" of lead poisoning.[85]
Texas Railroad Commission rations oil production to stabilize prices. This alleged conservation measure favors the large producers.[86]
Oil discovered in Bahrain.[87]
King Saud sells Arabian oil concession to Standard Oil-CA to counterbalance the British dominance of the Middle East.[88]
Smoot-Hawley Tariff taxes imported oil at 32 cents a barrel.[89]
Franklin Roosevelt becomes president.
Adolph Hitler becomes Chancellor of Germany.
Standard Oil of California wins concession in Saudi Arabia.
Venezuela becomes Britain's largest oil supplier.

As the Great Depression deepens across the globe, Jackson County, Missouri, boasts the accomplishments of two bond issues totaling $10 million, passed by voters in 1928 and 1931, as a major capital and civil improvements, public works project. Included are a major, first-class, modern, road system to accommodate the exponential popularity of the automobile:

"Jackson County as it was eight years ago, the new present Jackson County that has resulted from a definite county plan, and the Jackson County of the future, all are pictured today by Harry S Truman, presiding judge of the Jackson County Court [predecessor of the Jackson County Executive of the Jackson County Legislature], to the Chamber of Commerce.

It was, Judge Truman said, an accounting he was making to the taxpayers of his administration as presiding judge in the five and one-half years since January 1, 1927. Judge Truman spoke at the Chamber of Commerce luncheon at the Kansas City Athletic Club.

"In 1927, there are 360 miles of oiled dirt roads, 200 miles of old water-bound, scandal-built, pie-crust roads constructed out of dramshop funds, and a few miles of state roads under construction. There is an old courthouse in Kansas City and an older one in Independence.

"There are homes for the aged, a home for boys, a home for girls and an empty building constructed for Negro boys. The county also has a grand deficit."

Then Judge Truman gives the other picture—that of Jackson County in 1933:

* 300-miles of concrete highways costing $10 Million
* 800-miles of oiled road
* A nearly completed apportionment of state highways
* Plans and bonds for a great courthouse building in Kansas City
* Plans and bonds for remodeling the Independence courthouse
* The home for Negro boys in operation [Hiram Young Home]
* A home for Negro girls
* A hospital at the Home for the Aged
* An enlarged McCune Home for white boys
* A fully equipped home for white girls [Hilltop]
* A definitely planned park and recreation system
* A regional plan for six adjoining counties
* A planned reorganization and appraisement for tax reform
* A greatly reduced deficit with a good chance of complete elimination.

"We have a goal," Judge Truman said, "that may take a generation to reach. We have passed one in eight years that we all thought would take two generations to reach. I believe this depression we are going through is not a permanent condition. I believe it is a passing difficulty. I believe Jackson County is destined to be the heart of the nation—the center of food production for this country; that Kansas City will continue to be the corn, wheat, oats, hay, and livestock center of the United States; the air center of the country; the cross-roads of the national highway system; and, the railroad center of the country.

"We must finish our job as planned. Let us construct our courthouse and the city building son a plan equal to any in the United States. We don't want to be a hick town. We should build these structures, so we can be as proud of them as we are of our boulevards, our roads, our art gallery [the Nelson Atkins Gallery of Art, completed in 1933], and our war memorial [The Liberty Memorial, which has since become the nation's officially recognized memorial to The Great War, or World War I]. We should complete our county park plan.

"The park plan takes land of small value and gives it a value for public use—for lakes, flood protection, game preserves, and recreation grounds in the front yard of ½ million people.

"Let us solve our financial difficulties by a just and equitable assessment and the elimination of useless and unnecessary offices, by the consolidation of some of the county and municipal offices. Do these things and we'll be turning home seekers away from our gates."[90]

While campaigning successfully for the U.S. Senate in 1934, Truman sits up one evening at the Pickwick Hotel in Kansas City and pens a short autobiographical sketch that covers his early political career: "The most distressing thing in the county at the time was its road system," he wrote. "There were miles and miles of water-bound macadam roads and they were being pounded to pieces much faster than they could be repaired."

Professional engineers Thomas Veatch and Edward M. Stayton are hired to design the new road system. Veatch in a 1961 interview said of Truman, "He had an unusual grasp, for a layman, of things necessary to get good roads." Veatch termed Truman, "a road scholar, not a Rhodes scholar."[91]

1933   USDA, naval researchers find Ethyl and 20% ethanol blend equal in performance.[92]

U. S. Congress passes the Hayden-Cartwright Act which requires states to segregate gasoline taxes for road-building if they want federal highway aid.[93]

Ethyl and I. G. Farben form Ethyl GmbH to make leaded airplane fuel. Ninety percent of gasoline sold in U.S. contains ethyl.[94]

1934   First diesel bus in the United States.[95]

Emir of Kuwait gives the concession for newly discovered oil resources to Kuwait Oil (50% Gulf, 50% British Petroleum.)[96]

1935   Mussolini invades Ethiopia; League of Nations fails to impose oil embargo.[97]

1936   Hitler remilitarizes Rhineland and begins preparations for war, including a major synthetic fuels program. [98]

1937   Eugene Houdry invents the catalytic cracking of low-grade fuel into high-test gasoline. The traditional, thermal cracking process yields an octane of 60 or so. Houdry's mixture turns out a 'gas' that tests around 80 or 81. Then, too, he is able to extract more gallons of gasoline from a barrel of crude.[99]

Japan begins war in China.

1938   Oil company boycott ends exports of newly nationalized Mexican oil. Mexico will not fully regain its international trade until the 1970s.[100]

Oil discovered in Kuwait and Saudi Arabia.

Mexico nationalizes foreign oil companies.

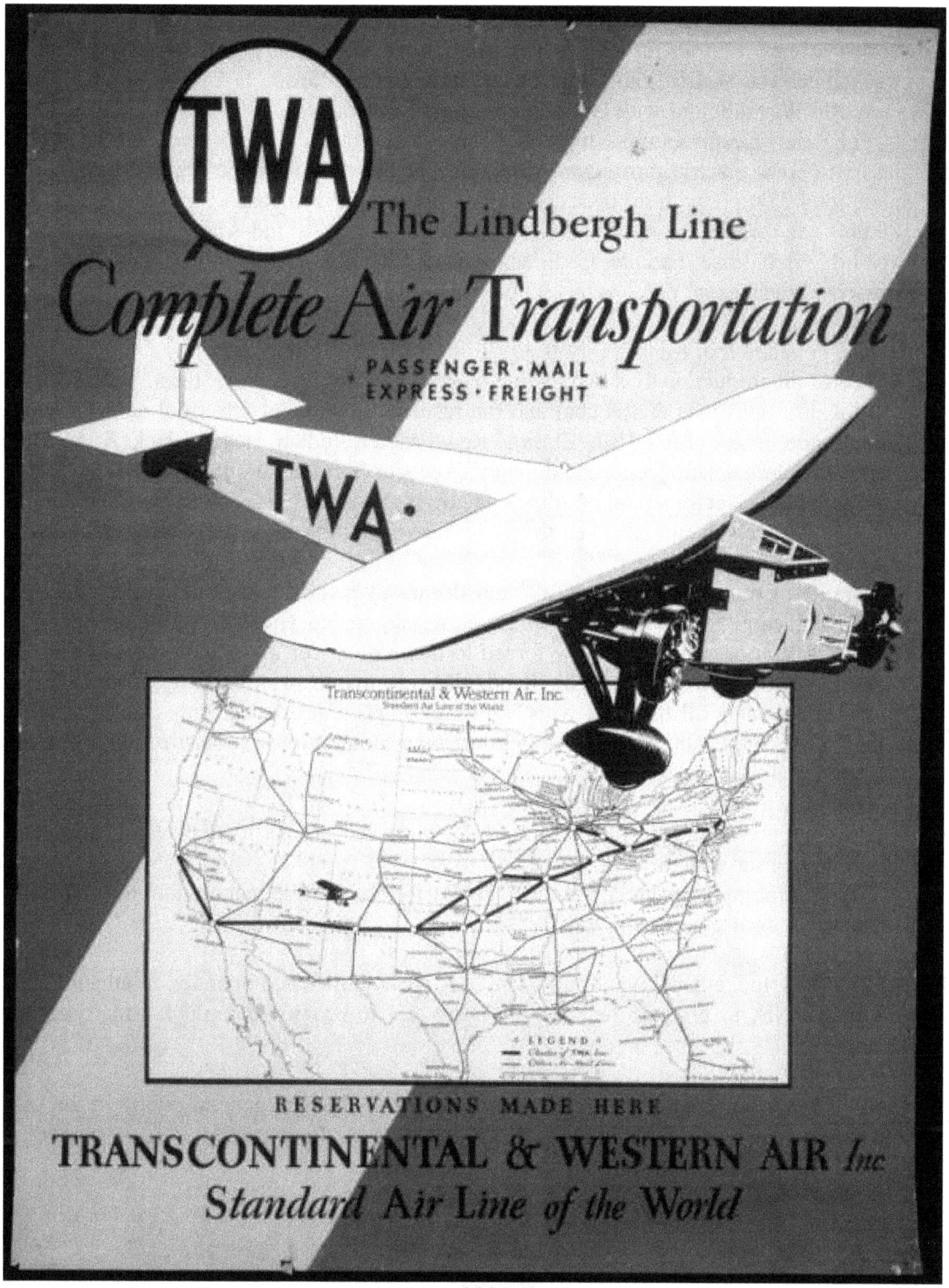
TWA
The Lindbergh Line
Complete Air Transportation
PASSENGER · MAIL
EXPRESS · FREIGHT
TWA
Transcontinental & Western Air, Inc.
LEGEND
RESERVATIONS MADE HERE
TRANSCONTINENTAL & WESTERN AIR Inc
Standard Air Line of the World

1939   Howard Hughes, and American investor and renowned filmmaker, acquires Trans World Airlines; TWA is formed in 1930 to run transcontinental flights from New York to Los Angeles via. St. Louis and Kanas City, among other stops.

World War II begins with German invasion of Poland.

The Safety Fair in Kansas City reduces auto deaths by 54%. Reinforced frames, safety-glass windows, electric turn signals are some of the improvements. Speed limits are a unanimous 25 mph, with an occasional 35 mph on the outer roads.[101] The city now has 100,000 car owners, many bought in the vicinity of 28th and Main from Reid-Ward Packard, Greenlease LaSalle Cadillac, Allied Chrysler Plymouth, Lawler Nash and Armacost Studebaker. You can buy a new Packard coupe for $867. [102]

1940   The population of Kansas City is 399,178.

World oil production tops two trillion barrels, 65% in the United States.[103]

In Kansas City, the fuel is coal and the result is smoke and ash. Coal names include Paris, Eagle, Tiger, Rich Hill, Elmira, Red Feather, Indian Head, Black Rose, Blue Diamond, Acorn, Cherokee Red and Fancy Excelsior Springs Lump! Coal is burned in apartment houses, commercial buildings, factories and railway locomotives. Dense smoke and ash filter the sun and fall to earth as soot fall. Soot falls on statues and shirts, laundry lines and is breathed in lungs.[104]

The Red Crown gas station at 13th and Broadway stands next to the Grace and Holy Trinity Cathedral. The sacredness of gasoline has cozied cheek by jowl up against a competing icon of civilization now forced to make room for it. A motorist can sing the theme song, "Let's swing along with Standard!" get a free map, air in the tires, buy different grades of fuel and fill the tank with "anti-knock gasoline loaded with carefree, thrifty miles."[105] And go to church, go to confession, take communion, get married, be sent to the afterlife . . . all in the same block!

Germany overruns Western Europe.

Prospect streetcars are replaced with trolley buses in Kansas City. Fairyland Park seems 20 minutes closer with the new system.[106]

The federal government constructed a plant for North American Aviation to build the B25 bomber for use in World War II.[107]

1940s   First U.S. fuel ethanol plant built. The U.S. Army builds and operates an ethanol plant in Omaha, NB, to produce fuel for the army and to provide ethanol for regional fuel blending.

1940s-1970s   Virtually no commercial fuel ethanol is sold to the general public in the U.S. due to low price of gasoline fuel.[108]

1941   Germany invades Soviet Union.

Japan invades Southern Indochina.

Hundred octane is the super fuel that American chemists are the first to develop. Octane is the yardstick of gasoline power. The new fuel at a rating of 115 goes into production the following year and is used for warplanes. [109]

Japanese attack the United States at Pearl Harbor, Hawaii, on Sunday, December 7.

The Kansas City Star runs an article with this title/artwork on December 12, five days after the surprise attack on America at Pearl Harbor in Hawaii.

1942   Gasoline stamps used as rationing device beginning on May 15 on the east coast, and nationwide that December.

"Part relief for Kansas City and the Middle West from stringent fuel oil and gasoline rationing was recommended today by the Truman investigating committee after an exhaustive study into the whole broad field of gasoline and oil supplies, rubber conservation and transportation. The Truman report emphasized the need for gasoline rationing on a national basis as a rubber saving measure but urged government agencies to encourage additional production in oil producing states and that special consideration be given homeowners who heat with oil as well as motorists in sections adjacent to pipelines and refineries. When Senator Harry S Truman of Missouri and his fellow committee members returned from their meeting in Kansas City to investigate the Midwestern situation, it was indicated that the committee might recommend a relaxation of fuel oil rationing in the oil producing states. But, the report dodged any such outright recommendation, going only so far as to hold out the hope that with increased production Midwest consumers might obtain increased allotments."

For the next three years, rationing takes hold of the nation and is cancelled after war. [110]

1943   Germany switches most domestic vehicles (and a few tanks) to wood, charcoal or peat fuel in Imbert generators.[111]

Venezuela gets the first "50%-50% oil deal."[112]

1944   On the verge of encircling a German army, General George Patton's tanks run out of gasoline.[113]

1945   Because Allied bombing reduces German fuel production by 95% between March and September, Panzer units run out of gas during the Battle of the Bulge.[114]

World War II ends with defeat of Germany and Japan.

Much of old-growth forest in Europe is cut to provide fuel to survive World War II.[115]

Soviets begin to develop Trans-Ural oil fields.[116]

Aramco (a largely American-owned consortium) brings in the giant Ghawar (Saudi Arabia) oil deposits, which cost 50 cents a barrel to produce, compared with $1 for Texas oil.[117]

"The Great Acceleration" begins, according to John Robert McNeill in his 2015 book, *The Anthropocene.* He explains that humanity has overtaken the systems of the Earth without trying to manage them and the result is a chaotic response from the systems themselves.[118]

General Motors leases the plant from the government and converts it for automobile production.[119]

Downtown Airport

The Kaw River flowing in on top left and the Missouri River turning north at the top right are the geographic outlines of the original Wood Age site of the Town of Kansas. The Hannibal Bridge barely visible on the right introduced the Coal Age, while the wetlands, also in the upper right, have been taken over with airport runways so vital in the Oil Age.

Chapter 33

Gasoline: The Citizen, 1946-1975
Gasoline *expands and defends* itself to create the suburbs

Expanding suburbs became possible, in part, because gasoline expanded for the individual driver so they could join the party in a way streetcars never made possible. A whole new set of "business harmonics" emerges around this liquid fuel with the worship of the individual automobile and plenty of low-cost liquid fuel to propel it. Satellite shopping centers draw people away from downtown by offering free parking and closed, air-conditioned retail experiences. One of gasoline's many gifts to its unquestioning population is convenience with a capital C. At the same time, its many byproducts like CO_2 create smog and its chemistry threatens groundwater.

1946-1964   These were the years in which gasoline spend time in laboratories to meet the standards of a public more aware of the tradeoffs of using it. Born in a test tube it returns there again and again as lead stalks an innocent public.

Smog is the reward for cars, cars and more cars. To add insult to injury, they beef up their engines, become "muscle cars."

1946   Charles Kettering (GM) develops high octane gasoline that allows a doubling of compression ratios.[1]

General Motors plant in Kansas City produces the first car, a black Pontiac two-door, on June 3.[2]

1947   Marshall Plan for Western Europe. Construction begins on Tapline for Saudi Arabia.[3]

Echoing Hitler's synthetic fuel program, a decade prior, Dr. Scott W. Walker, a research scientist for the Standard Oil and Gas Company, forecasts that there will be liquid gasoline and other fuels available for cars, trucks, busses, and planes, "for at least the next 1,000 years." Two plants focusing on synthetic gasoline are under construction in the U.S., including one on the northeastern edge of Tulsa, OK, and an $80 million plant in western Kansas utilizing "gas from the Hugoton field."[4]

1948   Standard of New Jersey (Exxon) and Socony Vacuum (Mobil) join Standard of California (Chevron) and Texaco in Aramco.[5]

U.S. files antitrust suit against Du Pont to break up "largest single concentration of power in the United States." Main target is Du Pont's $560 million investment in GM.[6]

Israel declares independence.

After a series of oil spills the U.S. Coast Guard orders 288 tankers strengthened.[7]

Neutral Zone concession to Amin-oil and J. Paul Getty.[8]
J. Paul Getty acquires the Neutral Zone (between Kuwait and Iraq) oil concession.[9]
Texaco Star Theater with Milton Berle is the first big television hit.[10]

1949 U. S. oil production declines for the first time. Middle Eastern and Venezuelan oil is cheaper.[11]

1950s Photochemical smog first described by California chemist Dr. Arrie Haagen-Smit. Contains VOCs (volatile organic compounds) as well as nitrous dioxide in a chemical reaction to sunlight.[12]
Automakers stifle development of emissions-control devices.[13]

> In Kansas City, "what is perhaps the strangest sewing circle anywhere meets daily in the rear yard of the Midwest Research Institute, just outside the smog chamber. This group of 10 housewives, accomplishes a great deal of sewing, knitting, doll making, reading and chattering. In addition, and more important, the "circle" is contributing significantly to a study of the baffling smog problem.
>
> For the last two years, Midwest Research, under contract with the Southern California Air Pollution foundation, has conducted a smog research study with expenditures of more than $120,000. An integral part of this activity is a panel of "smog testers" who go into the chamber and record their physical reactions---eye and nasal irritation—to simulated smog atmospheres.
>
> Until recently college students had been used as smog testers. But because students had to be concerned with examinations and other school chores, the Institute decided to switch to housewives who, presumably, had less on their mind. Mothers with children in school and whose morning and afternoon hours were relatively free, were selected....
>
> The work consists mainly of spending three hours a day (an hour and a half mornings and afternoons) at the chamber. For brief periods of two to four minutes the housewife panelists enter the chamber, then record on special printed forms their reactions to the smog atmospheres prepared there. They receive $20 a week for this duty....
>
> Smog inquiry previously conducted at the Institute indicated that motor car exhaust was a principal factor creating the Los Angeles air pollution problem. The current work has to do with simulating atmospheres which would result by the installation of "smog-curbing" devices on motor cars. None of these devices is in use at the Institute, but scientists there can produce the kind of atmospheres which would result if they were used."
>
> We're trying to find out if these devices will do the job they are intended to do," Dr. John Goodwin, [manager of the chemistry division at the Institute] in charge of smog experiments, explained.

Essentially, they are injecting hydrocarbons into the chamber for the women referenced in the above article as, "guinea pigs." "Hydrocarbons are among constituents of automotive exhaust." [14]

A PANEL OF MIDWEST SMOG TESTERS—These women, all housewives, have unique jobs at the Midwest Research Institute here. They enter the smog chamber at the Institute to record reactions to smog atmospheres. Seated (left to right) are Mrs. Doris Glenn; Mrs. Dorothy Epps, Mrs. Nan Gholson, Mrs. Lucille Fisher, Mrs. Ann Rose, Mrs. Sedley Shuyler. Standing (left to right) are Mrs. Helen Menn, Mrs. Paula Fiebig and Mrs. Ivy Cartwright. The smog chamber is in the background.

SIT AND SEW AS SMOG IS TESTED

1950 The population of Kansas City is 456,622.

Britain ends gasoline rationing in place since 1939.[15]

Three major refineries are built in Western Europe to process Middle Eastern oil.[16]

Japan still derives more energy from fire wood than from oil.[17]

Saudis get a "50%- 50% deal from Aramco."[18]

After the start of hostilities in Korea, the Kansas City Plant is selected to manufacture the F84F Thunderstreak fighter plane in Kansas City.[19]

1951 *Bulletin of Atomic Scientists* favors decentralized cities for civil defense.[20]

Prime Minister Mohammad Mossadegh, democratically elected premier of Iran, nationalizes Anglo-Iranian oil in Iran. Afraid of the oil reserves falling "behind the Iron Curtain," both British intelligence and the U.S.'s CIA stage a coup and have him removed from office during the Eisenhower administration.[21]

New Jersey Turnpike opens to serve Delaware, New Jersey and Pennsylvania.

The Great Flood of Kansas City in June and July results in adjusted for inflation over $8 billion in damages. It is one of four floods; 1844, 1903 and 1993 to hit the area. The stockyards are heavily damaged, and the new airport is built as a result of the low-lying position of the downtown airport.[22]

1951-1953 Korean War: North Korea invades South Korea. North backed by China and Soviet Union and South by United States and allies.

1952 Top drag racers exceed 288 kph, up from 208 in 1948 and 160 in 1930. They are no longer "street legal," burning nitromethane and driven by professional drivers.[23]

Mercedes introduces the 300SL with gull wing doors, the first production of a fuel-injection car.[24]

Justice Department antitrust suit against DuPont.[25] Focuses on anticompetitive association between it, GM, Standard Oil, and Ethyl Corp.

The Kansas City Fairfax Plant is the first industrial plant in the nation to operate as a dual-purpose facility producing automobiles and jet fighter planes in the same building.[26]

1953 Shah of Iran, with CIA help overthrows the socialist prime minister, Mossadegh. The Shah does not return control of Iranian oil to British Petroleum but turns it over to an American dominated consortium.[27]

1954 Octel begins TEL (tetraethyl lead) production in England to produce anti-knock compounds for aircraft fuel.[28]

The US becomes a net oil importer for the first time.

1955 Soviet oil export campaign begins. Export three million tons of oil to Western Europe.

Admiral Lewis Strauss, USN, predicts that by the 1970s nuclear energy costs will be so cheap that electricity will be unmetered. "Too cheap to meter" becomes the watchword for nuclear power.

13 US service station chains begin to offer premium gasoline.

1956 Oil discovered in Algeria and Nigeria.[29]

Suez Crisis: Egypt nationalizes Suez Canal company owned by French and British since 1869.

After the first Arab oil boycott, broken by US and Russian exports, European car makers seek to increase fuel economy. This search ultimately leads to front wheel drive cars.

Occidental Petroleum breaks the Aramco monopoly on Arab oil by signing contract with Libya. Oil found in Nigeria and Algeria.

1957 European Economic Community established.

Japan's Arabian Oil Company wins Neutral Zone offshore concession.[30]

About 40 members of the Central Electric Railfans Association with headquarters in Chicago, visit Kansas City on June 22 to "mourn the passing of the Kansas City street car system." The last street car rides run that day:

The street cars are going, not because they provide an obsolete ride, but because their maintenance costs are high and because they are inflexible. The Public Service Company, its patronage dwindling year after year and month after month, has had to cut costs. The use of busses instead of street cars is one way to do it.

Streetcar history in Kansas City goes back 88 years to the incorporation of the Kansas City and Westport Railway, a horse car line. Later came the cable cars and finally the general conversion to electricity. Kansas City's electric cars were among the first in the United States.

The bus made its first appearance in 1924, and in those days, it must have seemed a feeble competitor. But, by 1934, the streetcars were gone from the Intercity Viaduct, and by World War II, they had vanished from Prospect, 9th and Independence Avenue. The tire conquered Brooklyn, Woodland, and other lines after the war and the trend quickened. Thirty-first Street was changed in 1953. Next came 12th Street and Troost Avenue.

"A quarter of a century ago, Kansas City had 800 street cars. For the rest of this week it will have 41. Next Sunday, all will be gone. This is the week to say good-bye to Kansas City's street cars.[31]

THE LAST RIDE FOR THE 5:26 "REGULARS"— At 5:26 o'clock this morning the 10 to 15 regular week-day commuters on the Country Club street car line took their last ride with Robert C. Altis (right), 84, who will retire with the last run of the street cars in Kansas City. Left to right, they are: Kenny Marsteller, Mrs. June Marsteller, Edward Collins, William Nowkirk and (seated) Henry A. Merrick.

1958   ENL, the Italian national oil company, already a large purchaser of Soviet oil, further undercuts the major oil companies by offering royalties of 75% of profits to Middle Eastern countries.

President Eisenhower imposes an oil import quota of 15%. The quota will protect domestic producers whose oil is too expensive to compete in world markets until Nixon revokes the quota in 1973.

1959   Arab Petroleum Congress meets in Cairo. Occidental strikes oil in Libya. These are precursors of the energy crisis since the other Arab producers are envious of the high price that Occidental pays Libya.

Dutch natural gas fields (largest outside Soviet Union discovered). Eisenhower imposes import quotas. Groningen natural gas field discovered in The Netherlands.[32] Zelten field discovered in Libya.[33]

1960   The population of Kansas City is 475,539.
U.S. Public Health Survey begins an urban air monitoring program.
OPEC, Organization of Petroleum Exporting Countries, is founded in Baghdad.[34]
India forces oil companies to drop prices by threatening to buy Soviet oil.
Japanese oil consumption doubles 1957 levels; now equals coal consumption.
Albert Camus, French novelist, dies in car crash.

1961   Nigeria begins to export oil.
Iraq attempts to swallow Kuwait.
Ethyl and Associated Octel compete for overseas trade.[35]

1962   Biologist Rachel Carson writes *Silent Spring,* warning of the damage being done to our environment by pesticides, particularly, DDT.
Ethyl sold to Albermarle Paper Co. $200 million leveraged buyout partly financed by sellers GM and Standard Oil.[36]

1964   Exxon's worldwide slogan: "Put a tiger in your tank."

1965   Clair Patterson's study "Contaminated and Natural Lead Environment of Man." Offers first hard proof that high levels in industrial nation are manmade and endemic. Vietnam War buildup.[37]

1966   Senate Public Works Committee holds first hearings on air pollution.[38] A specific clause is added to the regular Highway Act to the effect that no trust funds can be used for beautification, i.e., for controlling outdoor advertising, screening junkyards, or scenic enhancement. Legislation establishes traffic and motor vehicle safety programs, also not to be funded from the Highway Trust Fund.[39]
Oil passes coal as the primary fuel in Western Europe; signals increasing automobility.

1967   Six Day War; Suez Canal closed.[40]
North Slope, Alaska, oil strike-largest oil finds in U.S. history.
Japan begins to buy Soviet oil.
Grounded supertanker Torrey Canyon spills 119,000 tons of oil into the English Channel.

1968   Oil discovered on Alaska's North Slope.
Ba'thists seize power in Iraq.[41]

1969   Automakers settle suit by Justice Dept.[42] Suit is for conspiracy to delay the development of pollution-control devices.
Soviets export 40 million tons of oil to Western Europe.
In real dollars, US energy costs are at the lowest point since the outbreak of WWII.
After 40 years of dry holes, oil found under the North Sea.

1970   The population of Kansas City is 507,330.

Passage of Clean Air Act by Richard Nixon. Put through Congress by Edmund Muskey Reformulated gasoline required by Clean Air Act.[43]

Senator Gaylord Nelson proposes to ban the internal combustion engine by 1975 because of pollution.

Clean Air Act passes Congress, requiring a 90% reduction in emissions by 1976, a goal largely attained.

Methanol-powered car wins a trans-U.S. clean-air race (i.e., produces fewer emissions in a cross-country run than its competition.)

Environmental Protection Agency formed to enforce new environmental laws.[44]

Santa Barbara oil spill.

Libya "squeezes" oil companies. Libya successfully negotiates a better oil deal than other countries.

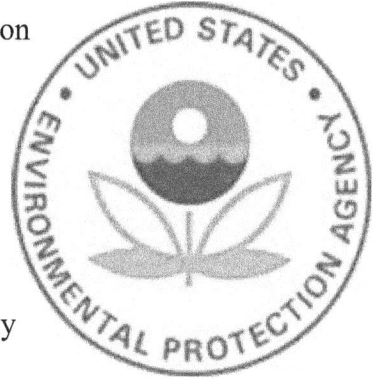

"In early 1970, as a result of heightened public concerns about deteriorating city air, natural areas littered with debris, and urban water supplies contaminated with dangerous impurities, President Richard Nixon presents the House and Senate a groundbreaking, 37-point message on the environment. These points include:

- requesting four billion dollars for the improvement of water treatment facilities
- asking for national air quality standards and stringent guidelines to lower motor vehicle emissions
- launching federally-funded research to reduce automobile pollution
- ordering a clean-up of federal facilities that had fouled air and water
- seeking legislation to end the dumping of wastes into the Great Lakes
- proposing a tax on lead additives in gasoline
- forwarding to Congress a plan to tighten safeguards on the seaborne transportation of oil, and
- approving a National Contingency Plan for the treatment of oil spills."

First Earth Day organized by Senator Gaylord Nelson (inset), Democrat from Wisconsin, April 22, 1970

1971   Robert A. Olson, CEO of Kansas City Power & Light, ". . . electricity has become 'the growth vitamin of the good life' as man's inventive genius capitalized on the wonders of this versatile energy source, new thresholds have been reached in science, industry communications, entertainment and comfort."[45]

Lead-based Paint Poisoning Prevention Act passed.[46]

Tehran Agreement is a strategy meeting of Joseph Stalin, Franklin D. Roosevelt, and Winston Churchill from 28 November to 1 December 1943, after the Anglo-Soviet Invasion of Iran. It is held in the Soviet Union's embassy in Tehran, Iran.

Britain withdraws military force from Gulf.

Texas Railroad Commission ends its quota system, marking the end of surplus American oil production capacity.

1972   Club of Rome study, *The Limits to Growth*. The message of this book still holds today: The earth's interlocking resources—the global system of nature in which we all live—probably cannot support present rates of economic and population growth much beyond the year 2100, if that long, even with advanced technology.[47]

EPA gives notice of proposed phaseout of lead in gasoline. In first use of Freedom of Information Act, Ethyl Corp. sues EPA.[48]

President Richard Nixon and first EPA administrator William Ruckleshaus

Standard of New Jersey changes its brand from Esso to Exxon at a cost of $71 million.

Supertanker *Sea Star* grounds, spilling 115,000 tons of oil into the Gulf of Oman.

Arab oil ministers at an OPEC meeting include graduates of Harvard, NYU, Cornell, Washington and Wisconsin.

1973   Arab oil producers impose a ban on exports of oil to the US, because of US aid to Israel in the Yom Kippur War.

Brazil promotes ethanol, a sugar cane by-product, for fuel.

Yom Kippur War; Arab Oil embargo. Shortages at the pump were noticeable by May 17, 1973, when Kansas City dealers announce having to deal with cuts in supply.[49]

Twenty-years later in 1993, the energy crisis offers retrospective lessons from this memorable era:

Motorists fumed, even fought, in service station lines.

Thermostats are twisted down, leaving a chill on living rooms and offices. Sweaters became the uniform of the day.

Christmas lights are dimmed. Airline schedules are slashed.

Big-car sales and the stock market plunge, rail travel and long underwear sales shoot up. A recession ensues.

Twenty years ago, this month, America was shocked out of a decades-long era of cheap energy and unshakable prosperity when Middle Eastern oil powers shut off their spigots.

It was called the "energy crisis" or the "great oil embargo. " It sowed seeds of panic during the fall of 1973 and the following winter.

"I can remember those lines of cars going up Mission Road for several blocks," said Rocky Hill, who was pumping gas at 95th Street and Mission Road in Prairie Village when the embargo hit.

It also forever changed the way we see the world and our place in it.

"It ended the era of unbridled optimism," said Douglass North, an economics and history professor at Washington University who recently shared the Nobel Prize in economic science. "We no longer were confident we had all the big economic problems solved. " We learned some lessons from the experience. We now have more fuel-efficient cars and planes, better insulated houses and a strategic reserve of oil.

But our dependence on foreign oil has never been higher. And experts continue to argue passionately over whether to limit that dependence, which is growing.

The exact causes of the 1973 crisis are still debated.

The catalyst was a petroleum embargo begun by Arab oil-producing countries in mid-October 1973, in retaliation for U.S. support for Israel in the Yom Kippur War. But the oil war would last longer—and have greater impact—than the shooting war.

The energy crisis hit our pocketbooks with higher prices, not just for fuel but countless related items.

We were warned that the world would run dangerously low on oil. Gasoline rationing was expected, or rather dreaded. *Time* magazine reported that Mafia dons had lined up printing companies to produce counterfeit ration coupons.

There were wild rumors—oil companies were keeping tankers full of crude off the coast to jack up prices.

There were wild predictions—we'd all be riding bicycles to work by the end of the century.

And there were wild solutions. An Indiana farmer burned manure to power his refrigerator and pickup truck, while New England School of Art students rigged up a plastic tent to warm their nude model.

Such stories amused us as the crisis paved the way for the 1974-75 recession, at that time the worst economic downturn since the Great Depression.

The crisis permeated daily life in Kansas City.

Service stations kept shorter hours or went out of business.

The Country Club Plaza Christmas light display was shortened.

Harrisonville limited electric power use. Overland Park extinguished an eternal flame at a servicemen's memorial.

Ride-sharing came into vogue. At Farmland Industries Inc., employees who car-pooled got guaranteed parking spots near the company office.

301

Hill, 38, recalled a mini-oil war that broke out when a motorist broke into line at the 95th and Mission service station.

"We ran out of gas pumping gas into his car," said Hill, now the shipping manager of a Kansas City lithograph company. "The man next in line became angry. He physically pulled the guy out of his car and they went to fist city right there in the parking lot. " Norm Williams, 67, was Kansas City district manager for a service station equipment supplier. He and 24 other district managers were laid off at the end of October.

"I was shocked," said Williams, who found another job.

Nobody had any inclination they were going to do anything that drastic.

After 20 years, different people remember the crisis differently.

"Our gas lines were never very long," said Charles Wheeler, Kansas City's mayor at the time. "We didn't get very alarmed or think we were running out of gasoline. I think the mood was that President Nixon had the situation well in hand." In fact, Kansas City didn't suffer as much as more heavily populated parts of the country, such as the Northeast.

There was even some good news. Business boomed for the only surviving retail coal dealer in Kansas City, Kan., and Kansas oilmen got a boost when price controls were taken off oil from low-yield wells.

A Menninger psychiatrist predicted at the time that the crisis might bring psychological benefits. "Maybe it will shake us out of continuing to deny such things can happen here," said Herbert Modlin.

Yet even Wheeler expressed concern during that dark autumn.

Speaking to the Northeast Community Council in November 1973, the mayor said apathy toward a group of bond proposals was a "product of the frustration, anger and general tensions of the times. " Others remember fear.

"It scared us to realize that something that we had little or no ability to control could have such a devastating effect on our financial health," said Jerry Cosley, Kansas City-based spokesman for Trans World Airlines then and now.

Hill worried about how he would gas up his 1965 Chevrolet Impala Supersport with the 327-cubic-inch engine. "I was pretty much terrified," he said. "I figured that all of a sudden gasoline would become like gold, that I wouldn't be able to buy any. " Other memories are bitter.

B.J. Roney, longtime owner of Prairie Village Standard Service, said he was cut to half his normal allocation of gasoline during the embargo. He asked customers to limit themselves to 10 gallons per purchase, but he would still run out by 11 in the morning. Profits dwindled along with his supplies.

"At the time, I was duped," he said. "If there was a shortage 20 years ago, we should certainly be having a shortage 20 years later, but we're having an oil glut. They're producing so much the world market can't absorb it all. " Where did the fault lie?

Were we duped? There's no clear answer, but plenty of opinions.

Free-market proponents insist that the fuel shortages were caused by government-mandated price controls and allocation systems that later were thrown out.

"It was really the price controls that caused the lines," said Charles DiBona, president of the American Petroleum Institute, who was a special energy consultant to President Nixon when the embargo broke out. "In other parts of the world there were no lines, because they let the price rise."

"But Roney remains convinced that the shortage was "contrived" by the Organization of Petroleum Exporting Countries and the "foreign interests of the major oil companies. " "I think the whole thing was a real sham on the world of consumers," he said.

Contrived or not, the crisis took on mammoth proportions and a warlike urgency.

In a speech on Nov. 7, 1973, Nixon asked Congress to give him emergency powers to combat the growing fuel shortage.

The president asked for lower speed limits, year-round daylight-saving time, exemption from anti-pollution laws, the authority to reduce business hours, curtailment of outside lighting and other measures.

Recalling the country's achievements in developing the atomic bomb in World War II and putting a man on the moon before 1970, Nixon urged the country to develop new sources of energy and free itself from dependency on foreign oil.

"Let us pledge that by 1980, under Project Independence, we shall be able to meet America's energy needs from America's own energy resources," he said.

Kansas Gov. Robert Docking warned the state to cooperate with Nixon on voluntary energy conservation or face the possibility of government regulation.

The embargo ended in March 1974, with the most dire predictions not coming true. We suffer another oil shock after the Iranian revolution of 1979, but it too plays itself out. Fuel prices spike during the Persian Gulf crisis of 1990-91 but quickly retreat.

Still heavily dependent we've made many improvements in the last 20 years that make us less vulnerable to an oil embargo. Our cars, planes, homes, appliances and factories are more fuel-efficient. We've decontrolled energy prices, eliminating layers of bureaucracy. And we have emergency oil supplies in the Strategic Petroleum Reserve.

Fragmentation from within and competition from other parts of the world have weakened OPEC's power in the last 20 years.

But 13 years after Nixon's deadline, we're still not energy self-sufficient. Nuclear power stalled because of environmental concerns, and the viability of synthetic fuels is undermined when oil prices plummet in the 1980s.

"In the future, our dependence on foreign oil, and in particular Middle Eastern oil, will only grow," said Christopher Dyson, energy policy analyst with Public Citizen, a Ralph Nader-affiliated consumer group.

Such groups warn that the United States is running out of economically recoverable oil. They advocate stronger automobile fuel efficiency standards, higher fuel taxes, lower oil industry subsidies and greater efforts to develop renewable energy resources, such as alcohol fuels derived from such sources as trees.

But the American Petroleum Institute says those groups are off base.

"We're not running out of energy," said API spokesman Joseph Lastelic. "The government does not permit new drilling in the best prospects, which are offshore of California and off Florida and in Alaska, such as the Arctic National Wildlife Preserve." Lastelic said auto companies already are turning out fuel-efficient cars, and he pointed out widespread opposition to higher fuel taxes. He disputed the contention that oil companies receive large subsidies, saying the industry pays enormous taxes.

"We're not opposed to alternative fuels or renewable fuels, but you don't have solar cars or electric cars that are affordable to most people," he said.

That could change. It was reported recently that General Motors Corp. is building 50 electric cars to be ready for road testing by spring.

Embargo veterans like [Charles] Wheeler, the former mayor, hope to see more such innovations. He said the energy crisis spurred his interest in mass transit, making him an advocate of such things as high-speed rail.

"I have a bunch of sweaters," he said. "I'm prepared for the next embargo." [50]

EPA creates lead phaseout in gasoline but delays setting standards. When standards are set, EPA is sued by Ethyl. [51] Including the Clean Air Act and Clean Water Act and the formation of the US Environmental Protection Agency itself, OPEC oil crisis causes shortages in gasoline for citizen drivers. Long lines at service stations. Twyla Dell, co-author of *Fueling Change*, sits in a gasoline line at a service station with her 4-year-old son with pneumonia waiting to get enough gasoline to take him to the emergency room.

Oil price rises from $2.90 per barrel (Sept) to $11.65 (December).[52]

United States government bans lead in gasoline.

Alaskan pipeline approved.

OPEC shocks the world raising prices in response to the Yom Kippur War. (See 1979).

55-mph speed-limit in response to Arab oil embargo.

The La Cygne, Kansas, plant opened as a joint ownership between Kansas City Power & Light Company and Kansas Gas and Electric Company of Wichita. It uses coal from surface mines near the plant.[53]

1974   Arab Embargo ends.

Watergate scandal widens. Nixon resigns.

International Energy Agency (IEA) founded.

Price of crude oil is four times 1972 levels. The recession blamed on oil price shock leads to a 5% decline in US incomes.

First quarter profits up 52% (Shell) to 123% (Texaco) for the major oil companies. On "60 Minutes," the Shah of Iran accuses the oil companies of creating an artificial gas shortage.

Soviet Union becomes the world's largest producer and refiner of crude oil.

1975   Automobile fuel efficiency standards established in the U.S.

First oil comes ashore from North Sea.

South Vietnam falls to communists.

EPA restricts the amounts of hydrocarbon nitrogen oxide, and carbon dioxide emitted by industrial production and transportation.

U. S. begins to phase out lead in gasoline; MTBE eventually replaces lead. MTBE (Methyl Tertiary Butyl Ether)—a fuel additive to raise octane—later found to be contaminating ground water and banned in 2006.[54]

Saudi, Kuwaiti, and Venezuelan concession come to an end.[55]

Chapter 34

Gasoline: The Sculptress
of Our Ways and Means, 1976-2030
Gasoline *expands and defends* itself against all new forms of energy

Still expanding, we have no ready replacement for gasoline, nor any sign of its abatement. Over the last fifty years our lives have become so dependent on this fuel that we must consciously wrestle with our way of life to recognize its grip on us. Finally pronounced as "an addiction" by President George Bush" in 2006 and recognized as the power player on the world stage it truly is, the general population must now grapple with both their collective and individual dependency and begin the painful task of becoming "gasoline free." Gasoline has made us traveling sitters in a way nothing else could. Sitting to drive, flexing only our right foot on the gas and hands on wheel . . . . We are now a sitting society with only a few steps a day to take us where we must go.

1976   EPA standards upheld by U.S. Court of Appeals. Supreme Court refuses to hear appeal.[1]
  Catalytic converters are installed in new vehicles to reduce the emission of toxic air pollutants. Such vehicles could not operate on leaded gasoline; leaded gasoline is phased out of the U.S. fuel system by 1996.
  Passenger vehicles are required to have emissions control devices installed.

1977   Alaska pipeline finished. Workers are making as much as $60,000 or more a year.
  MMT banned in US by the Clean Air Act until Ethyl Corporation can prove it did not lead to failure of new car emission-control systems. Ethyl Corp begins a legal battle with the EPA, presenting evidence that MMT is harmless to auto emissions-control systems.[2]
  North Slope Alaskan oil comes to market.
  Buildup of Mexican production.
  Anwar Sadat, third President of Egypt, goes to Israel.

1978   Energy Tax Act creates ethanol tax incentive expands use of ethanol in U. S.[3]
  Gas gets tight again.
  Amoco (Standard Oil and British Petroleum) *Cadiz* tanker sinks, spilling 253,000 tons of oil and fouling 160 km of Brittany coastline.
  Strikes by oil workers in Iran.[4]
  Shah goes into exile. Ayatollah Khomeini takes power.[5]

1979-1981   Panic sends oil from $13 to $34 a barrel.[6]

1979   Iran takes hostages at U.S. Embassy.

Between 1976 and 1980 EPA reports amount of lead consumed in gasoline dropd 50%. Blood-lead levels drop 37%. Benefits of phaseout exceed costs by $700 million.[7]

OPEC raises oil prices, a response to the Iranian Islamic Revolution.

Three Mile Island, Harrisburg, Pennsylvania, partial meltdown allows radioactive nuclear coolant to escape.

Another gasoline crisis forces drivers into gas lines. The first gasoline riot ensues in Levittown, PA.

Livermore Lab, CA, tests solar cars.

1980   The population of Kansas City is 448,078.

Iraq launches war against Iran.

Iran-Iraq war breaks the OPEC cartel. Both sides will sell petroleum at a reduced price to pay for the war.

National Academy of Sciences calls leaded gas greatest source of atmospheric lead.[8]

National Security Act mandates all gasoline be blended with a minimum of 10% grain alcohol--"gasohol." Later scuttled by Reagan administration.[9]

Gasohol Competition Act passed by Congress. To stop oil companies' discrimination against sales of gasohol at their pumps.[10]

Ethyl reports it has expanded its overseas diversification. Profits help fund business tenfold between 1964-1981.[11]

Oxygenates added to gasoline included MTBE (Methyl Tertiary Butyl Ether) made from natural gas and petroleum and ETBE (Ethyl Tertiary Butyl Ether) made from ethanol and petroleum.[12]

1981 Vice President George Bush's Task Force on Regulatory Relief. Proposes to relax or eliminate U.S. leaded gas phaseout.[13]

Iran-Iraq war breaks out over oil prices, supplies and market control.

US Steel buys Marathon Oil, a financial error, because oil prices plunge in the 1980s.

1982-1986 David Hasselhoff stars on TV in "Knight Rider," the story of a hunky crime fighter and his butler-like talking car, "Kitt," a 1981 Pontiac Trans Am. This show wins the People's Choice Award in 1983 for humanizing the car and forecasting features that may appear in the 21st century, many of which do, but Kitt's personality is still missing.

1982 Reagan Administration reverses opposition to lead phaseout.[14]

Surface Transportation Act forces states to accept federally mandated truck weight and size limits larger than many states desire, a response to more expensive fuels.

OPEC's first quotas. A world oil glut causes prices to fall. OPEC loses control of prices.

Non-OPEC oil production surpasses OPEC which begins to cut prices to keep market share and revenue level.

Reagan administration ends alternative energy programs and oil price controls as the U.S. reduces its dependence on imported oil to 28% of its needs, largely because of more fuel-efficient cars.

Exxon (nee Standard Oil of NJ) centennial 65,000 stations worldwide, six million customers daily, over $62 billion assets.

Occidental buys Citgo, becomes the 8th largest US oil company.

1983 OPEC cuts price of oil per barrel to $29.

Nymex, the New York Mercantile Exchange, the world's largest physical commodities futures, launch the crude oil futures contract.

Preservationists save a huge, flashing Citgo gas neon billboard along US Route 1 at Kenmore Square, Boston.

Norwuz well blowout spills 600,000 tons of oil into the Persian Gulf.

Tanker *Castillo de Bellver* catches fire, releases 250,000 tons of oil near Capetown, S Africa.

British Petroleum drops $2 billion on the Mubrak offshore (Alaska) oil well, the most expensive dry well in history.

Texaco doubles its crude oil reserves by purchasing Getty Oil for $10.1 billion.

Standard Oil of CA (SOCAL) takes over Gulf Oil for $13.2 billion, creating the third largest corporation in the US.

Soviets export 70 million tons of oil to Western Europe (20% of its imports.)

Fueling Change

1984   Subtitle I is added to the Solid Waste Disposal Act through the Hazardous and Solid Waste Amendments creates a federal program to regulate USTs (underground storage tanks) containing petroleum and requirements and technical hazardous chemicals to limit corrosion and structural defects and thus minimize future tank leaks. Directed EPA to set operating standards for tank design and installation, leak detection, spill and overfill control, corrective and tank closure.[15]

1985   Kansas City Power and Light's Wolf Creek Generating Station, a nuclear power plant located near Burlington, KS, comes on line. It has one Westinghouse pressurized water reactor rated at 1,170 MW(e).[16]

OPEC cartel no longer can keep its members in line on oil production quotas and Saudi Arabia abandons buttressing prices.

Saudis decide to flood world oil markets, dropping prices to a half of 1983 levels.

World oil consumption down to 52 million barrels per day, a 30% decline in six years.

OPEC share of world oil production is 28% down from over 50% in 1979.

1986   Primary phaseout of leaded gas in U.S. completed.[17] U.S. lead emissions are down 94% from peak; but, only 5% of the gas sold in Western Europe is unleaded.

US government collects $147 million in gas guzzler taxes of at least $500 on cars getting less than 22.5 mpg (9.6 kpl).

OPEC falls apart.

Oil prices collapse.

More than 85% of new cars in the US have air conditioning and automotive transmissions. Over 40% have stereos. All reduce fuel efficiency.

Western European oil consumption down to 75% of 1972 levels.

Crude oil prices fall by a third—not reflected at the gas pump.

1987   The old Fairfax plant ceases production of the Chevrolet Caprice, Buick Le Sabre and the Pontiac Parisiene ending 41 years of production of over 7 million cars, including more than 2 million Buicks, 2 million Pontiacs, 2 million Oldsmobiles and nearly 500,000 Chevrolets.[18]

1988   Alternative Motor Fuels Act rule in favor of alternative fuels made and used as often as possible.

Ceasefire in Iran-Iraq War.

Denver, CO, mandated ethanol oxygenate fuels for winter use to control carbon monoxide emissions. Other cities followed.[19]

Explosion of an Occidental Petroleum North Sea rig kills 166 workers.

Chernobyl nuclear plant in Ukraine, USSR, explodes contaminating large area of the country with radioactive clouds drifting into Sweden, Finland and other nearby European countries. The plant and a large area of the blast are permanently shut-down.

1989 Berlin Wall falls; communism collapses in Eastern Europe.

Bush administration announces that methanol will be at the heart of its fuel/air pollution policies.

Exxon Valdez tanker accident off Alaska Exxon Valdez Ship spills 11.2 million gallons of oil into Prince William Sound, AK. Exxon claims that its ineffective clean-up cost $2.6 billion.

1990 The population of Kansas City is 435,146.

Clean Air Act renewal from 1970 mandated the winter use of oxygenated fuels in 39 major carbon monoxide non-attainment areas (based on EPA emissions standards for carbon dioxide not being met) and requires year-round use of oxygenates in 9 severe ozone non-attainment areas in 1995.[20]

Iraq invades Kuwait, its small oil-rich neighbor, accusing them of stealing their oil by drilling at a slant underground. The First Gulf War follows. Iraq occupies Kuwait for 7 months. Operation Desert Shield/Storm is the result with American forces rescuing its ally Kuwait. George Bush, Sr., is President. Iraqi soldiers set fire to over 650 oil wells, lakes and trenches filled with oil that burns for over 10 months to create one of the 20th century's worst environmental disasters.

UN imposes embargo on Iraq; multi-national force dispatched to Middle East.[21]

Consumers now pump 80% of the gasoline sold in the US.

By midsummer the US is importing over 50% of its oil needs, exceeding even early 1970s import rates.

Iraqi overthrow of the Kuwait government leads to another oil crisis. President Bush defends the dispatch of American troops because clean oil is "essential to the American way of life."

All underground storage tanks have to be replaced by tanks with double lining to avoid and prevent leaks.

1991 First Gulf War. Kuwaiti oil fields set afire.

The US and the allies defeat Iraq. Huge oil spills in the Persian Gulf are a byproduct of the war. Kuwait faces massive air pollution from oil wells set afire by the retreating Iraqis.

Collapse of Soviet Union.

Maastricht Treaty provides for single European currency.

Mean blood lead level drops 13 points in general public, down from 1976. U.S. Center for Disease Control considered blood lead levels above 10 dangerous.[22]

U.S. Congress approves North America Free Trade Agreement (NAFTA).

Fueling Change

1992   Energy Policy Act requires the Energy Information Agency to collect data per year on alternative vehicles.

> "With Missouri poised to increase its gasoline tax for highway and bridge repairs, the critics say, non-highway forms of transportation such as buses, railroads and rivers receive little notice.... Advocates of public transit, like city bus systems, hoped this year to earmark part of the higher gasoline tax for transit programs. So far, they haven't rounded up the necessary support in Jefferson City. Other programs, like development of river ports, rail subsidies, scheduled bus and van service between cities, transit for the elderly and high-speed trains, didn't grab the limelight in the gasoline tax debate. Such programs consume only a fraction of the money the Highway and Transportation Department plans to spend on road construction and maintenance. "Building highways is not the whole ballgame," said Becky Rawlings, lobbyist for the Sierra Club in Jefferson City. "Unfortunately, it is the status quo and nobody wants to change that. Building highways is not a total transportation plan. " Environmental lobbyists, she said, haven't been able to raise enough votes in the General Assembly to bring about change. At the Highway and Transportation Commission meeting Friday, the Chamber of Commerce of Greater Kansas City called for inclusion of alternative forms of transportation in long-range state planning." Mexico City, which had 192 smog alert days in 1991, experiences its worst smog alert with ozone levels four times the dangerous level. The city closes all schools and factories for the duration of the crisis and bans half of its motor vehicles daily. Energy Star program initiated by EPA and E-commerce begins. The turning point of EPA to add positive reinforcement to the regulatory purpose of the agency."[23]

1994   Study shows that U.S. blood lead levels declines by 78% from 1978 to 1991. American Academy of Pediatrics study shows direct relationship between lead exposure and IQ deficits in children.[24]

1995   US. Court of Appeals rule that the EPA has exceeded its authority. MMT, a gasoline enhancer, becomes a legal fuel additive in the U.S. and is now legally manufactured by Afton Chemical Corporation division of Newmarket Corp.[25]

World Bank calls for phaseout worldwide of leaded gasoline.[26]

The EPA begins requiring the use of reformulated gasoline year around in metro areas with the most smog.

The *Kansas City Star* reported on October 11:

> The state of Missouri will have to toughen its anti-pollution efforts under an Environmental Protection Agency plan aimed at reducing the amount of drifting smog that has bedeviled Northeastern states.
>
> Missouri, which would have to reduce emissions of smog-causing nitrogen oxides by 43 percent, is one of 22 states that the agency wants to crack down on power plant pollution - one of the main sources of wind-borne smog.
>
> The steepest reductions would occur in the Midwest and the Ohio Valley. In addition to Missouri, states that will have to reduce nitrogen oxides emissions by 40 percent or more are Indiana, Kentucky, Ohio and West Virginia.[27]

1998   Oil collapses to $10-barrel range.[28]

Consolidation among oil majors that create "super majors": British Petroleum buys Amoco Corp and becomes Britain's biggest company and third largest oil company in the world. It is now known as BP Plc. Deal consummated in 2005.

1999   MTBE (Methyl tertiary butyl ether) production is 200,000 barrels a day This additive is a fossil fuel--natural gas and isobutylene mix. Substance is found in underground aquifers and use is stopped. Cleanup is $1 billion.[29]

French oil groups TotalFina and Elf merge and is now Total SA.

Exxon takes over Mobil and becomes Exxon Mobil Corp, the largest publicly traded oil company in the world.

PetroChina first Chinese oil company initial public offering (IPO) on the stock exchange.

European Union bans leaded gasoline.[30]

A federal appeals court has blocked Kansas City's plan to curb air pollution from traffic, raising concerns among some environmental officials of higher smog levels this summer.

The ruling Tuesday in Washington barred the metropolitan area—including Johnson County suburbs—from introducing reformulated gasoline to local pumps.

"We're looking at another summer of bad air for Kansas City," Roger Randolph, Missouri's director of air pollution control, said Wednesday. "This court decision has set us back pretty severely as far as the quality of air people will breathe in Kansas City."

Kansas and Missouri governors had supported using reformulated gasoline to reduce pollution and to comply with federal orders to improve air quality. But refiners fought the move in court, arguing that the U.S. Environmental Protection Agency wasn't following rules Congress had established for the fuel's use.[31]

2000   The population of Kansas City is 441,545.

BP Amoco Plc takes over Atlantic Richfield or Arco.

2001-2002   Chevron buys Texaco.

2002   Strikes and political conflict disrupt Venezuela oil output.

2003   Ethanol has grown rapidly as oxygenating factor for gasoline. Ethanol replaces MTBE for oxygenating fuel, since almost all states now have banned MTBE, due to groundwater contamination, health and environmental concerns.[32]

California begins switching from MTBE to ethanol to make reformulated gasoline.[33]

War in Iraq begins—Iraqi oil disrupted.

2004   World oil demand jumps on strong global economic growth, tightening market.[34]

Refiners are required to supply gasoline with 97% less sulfur content than the gasoline made in 2004. Gasoline with lower sulfur content reduces emissions from old and new vehicles and is necessary for advanced vehicle emission control devices to work properly.

311

National oil companies (NOCs) move to the fore.[35]

California is first state to completely ban MTBE, a toxic additive to reduce knocking, effective January 1.[36]

U.S. mandates ethanol in gasoline.

2005 Mayor Kay Barnes initiates the first citizen's committee called the Climate Action Plan to study air quality, recommend initiatives and monitor progress.

Aku-Tbilisi-Ceyhan pipeline begins Operations, linking Caspian and Mediterranean Seas.[37]

Energy Policy Act of 2005 amends Subtitle I of the Solid Waste Disposal Act Added new leak detection and enforcement provisions to the program. Requires that all regulated USTs (Underground Storage Tanks) be inspected every three years; expands the use of the LUST Trust (leaking USTs) Fund; requires EPA to develop grant guidelines regarding operator training, inspections, delivery prohibition, secondary containment, financial responsibility, public record, and state compliance reports on government USTs require EPA to develop a strategy and publish a report regarding USTs in Indian Country.[38]

Bombardier Recreational Products (BRP-OMC) is the first marine manufacturer to receive the EPA's "Clean Air Excellence" Award for their newly redesigned outboard engine called the Evinrude ETec, specifically designed to run on E10 ethanol gas in April. Almost all marine engines manufactured prior to 2000 prohibited use of alcohol fuel.[39]

2006 President George W. Bush calls for end to "addiction to oil." The secret is revealed and called for what it is, an addiction.

"Tupi"—first major discovery in new Brazilian offshore oil province.

Renewable Fuel Standard Program (RFS), signed by Bush in September. Designed to encourage the blending of renewable fuels (ethanol) into our nation's motor vehicle fuel. The nationwide RFS will double the use of ethanol and Biodiesel by 2012.[40]

First UN sanctions aimed at Iranian nuclear program.

Kansas City Power and Light's Wolf Creek Generating Station applied to the Nuclear Regulatory Commission (NRC) for a renewal and extension of the plant's operating license. The renewal is granted, extending the license 20 years from 40 to 60 years from the original opening date of 1985.[41]

"Kansas City is dirty brown," announces the *Kansas City Star* in 2006. Not known for any environmental leadership, city manager Wayne Couthen suggests just such a role for the city. A new chief environmental officer, Dennis Murphey, is hired, and Mayor Kay Barnes signs on with the U.S. Mayors Climate Protection Agreement. She appoints an 11-member committee to oversee new programs. At the time, Kansas City is the only midwestern city to take such leadership. Their goal is to achieve the same 7% GHG reduction below 1990 by 2012 as the Kyoto Agreement had championed.[42]

2006+ Many marine and auto engine owners report marine damage and severe engine failure caused by ethanol blend fuels. Investigations reveal gas sold contains over the legal limit of 10% for E10. Some E10 contaminated with water or is used in an engine not designed for Gasohol and all types of alcohol-blends of gas.[43]

2007 Energy Independence and Security Act signed by Congress and President Bush, which requires the use of 15 billion gallons of renewable (ethanol) fuel by 2015. In 2007, about 6.5 billion gallons are produced.[44]

Kansas City adopts a Green Solutions Resolution to integrate green infrastructure into the city's long-term overflow control plan (OCP) to mitigate sewer overflows. This is one of the mayor's and city council's actions to promote sustainability. They also question proposed ordinances and resolutions to answer, "How does this contribute to a sustainable Kansas City?"

A tornado nearly destroys the town of Greensburg, KS, home to 900 residents and more than a four-and-a-half-hour drive southwest of Kansas City in Kiowa County. Greensburg is the county seat. In rebuilding both the courthouse and the town, residents vow to choose a green building program that soon sees the town as a leader in creating solar and wind power, water efficiency, and LEED based construction (Leadership in Energy and Environmental Design) that makes it a national model.

2008 NASCAR switches to unleaded fuel. Last to change as unleaded gas is available throughout the world in 2007.[45]

Oil hits $147.77—U.S. gasoline sells for over $4 a gallon.

"Peak Oil" theory bites the dust having been held as true since proposed by Shell Oil geologist M. King Hubbard in 1956. He forecast the world would run out of oil by 1970. Hubbert's Pimple, or Peak, spreads a timeline to 2050. New approaches to drilling release many gas and oil fields that re-set forecasts. Still, the Energy Information Agency (eia.gov) presently only forecasts to 2050, as Hubbert did in 1956. The idea that the world would run out of oil by 2005 is abandoned as hydraulic fracturing replaces vertical drilling.

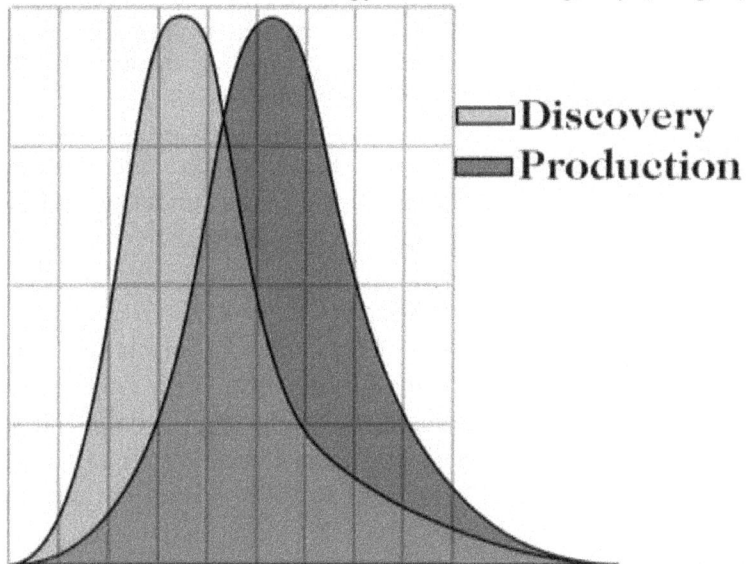

Discovery
Production

Fueling Change

"Speculation" and oil prices become major political issue.

"Worst financial crisis since the Great Depression." World recession, demand weakens, oil falls to $32.40/barrel.

The city manager convenes a "Green Solutions Policy" adopted by the City Council that will among other things adopt "Energy Star" standards for new construction and integrate sustainable materials and processes throughout city government.

Rock Port, Missouri, a city of some 1300 residents 115 miles north of Kansas City, describes itself as the first 100% wind-powered community in the United States. Four wind turbines are installed to supply all the electricity needed for this small town. The turbines are located within the city limits which uses 13 MKH (million kilowatt hours) per year with a capacity of 16 MKH.

Kansas City brings forth its first *Climate Protection Plan* under mayor Mark Funkhouser, according to the *Kansas City Business Journal,* July 22:

> The Kansas City Climate Protection Plan Steering Committee, which includes city staff and community leaders and volunteers, has been working on the plan for a year and a half, according to a Tuesday release from the city.
>
> The plan includes these goals:
>
> • Making climate issues a consideration in all city decisions.
>
> • Lowering greenhouse gas emissions from the community and from city government operations 30 percent below 2000 levels by 2020.
>
> • Acting on 55 measures to meet the 2020 goals.
>
> • Dropping communitywide greenhouse gas emissions 80 percent below 2000 levels by 2050.
>
> "Addressing climate change is a defining issue for our time," City Manager Wayne Cauthen said in the release. "Completing the Kansas City Climate Protection Plan is a significant milestone for the city as we strive to be a national leader among local governments dealing with climate protection, sustainability and environmental quality."

2009   American Recovery and Reinvestment Act. Provides a one-time supplement of $200 million to clean up leaks from USTs (underground storage tanks). $190m allocated to "shovel-ready" sites supervised by states.[46]

2010   The population of Kansas City is 459,787.

Deepwater Horizon oil rig in the Gulf of Mexico becomes the largest marine petroleum spill in the history of the oil industry. Beginning April 20, it goes on for 87 days before being capped and includes the deaths of 11 people, and an oil spill of about 5 million barrels (210 million U.S. gallons)—and a toxic dispersant—into the waters of the Gulf. In 2015, British Petroleum agrees to pay $18.5 billion in fines, the largest corporate fine in history.

Energy Works KC is a $20 Million Grant Award to Kansas City, Missouri, from the U.S. Department of Energy. Partnering with Mid-America Regional Council, the city retrofits buildings throughout several districts to increase efficiency in generating electricity.

2012 Kansas City's 76-year-old City Hall receives ENERGY STAR certification.

2013 Kansas City's *Climate Action Plan* is a success beyond what its architects had hoped. Having created, monitored and wielded their 55 strategies to reduce greenhouse gas emissions in energy and transportation beginning in 2008, they see a 25% reduction in municipal operations by 2013 and a 4% reduction citywide at the end of 2013. [2018 figures will be published in 2019.]

The Communications Office for Kansas City issues a 21-page booklet, "Sustainability in Kansas City," to promote five years of efforts on energy savings; transportation; air quality; water and waste management; and land use . . . all through outreach and collaboration.

The Weather Channel Climate Disruption Index ranks Kansas City fifth of 25 cities to be most impacted by climate change. Because the city has fewer green spaces and open land, and the most freeway lane miles per capita than any other large metropolitan area in the U.S., according to the *Public Purpose* journal in a 1999 report, the city is ranked higher than Miami in terms of global warming threats. The "heat island effect" will cause more human suffering and casualties. Fewer cold snaps, less snow and ice, and heavier rains and flooding are predicted weather changes. Energy, water, heat with temperatures 20 or more days above 90 degrees, local food systems vulnerability and public health will be the biggest issues that will stress the metro area as weather extremes increase. (The top city is New Orleans. 2. Minneapolis. 3. Las Vegas. 4. New York. 5. Kansas City, MO. 17. St Louis. 19. Miami. Los Angeles is not on the list.)[47]

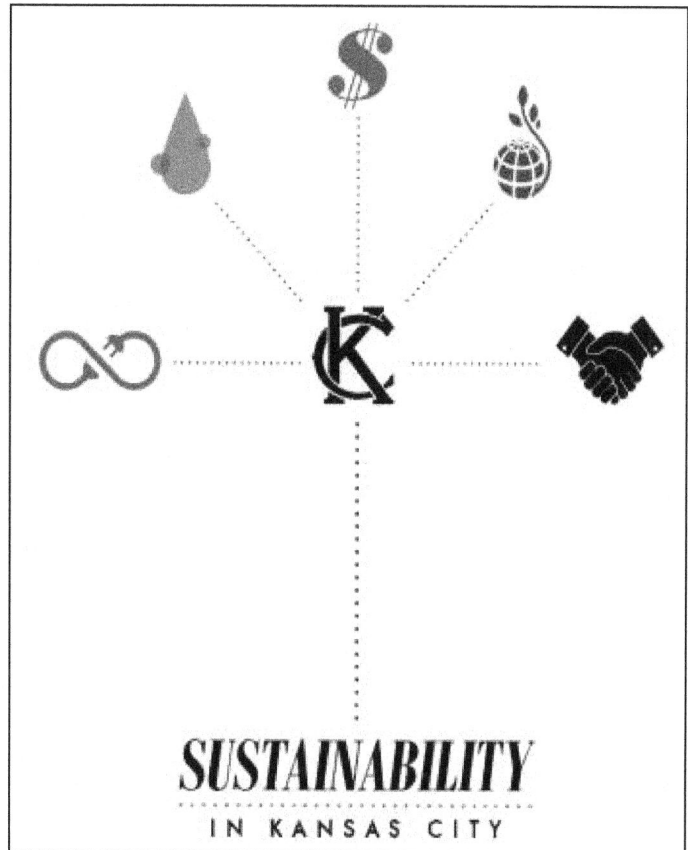

SUSTAINABILITY
IN KANSAS CITY

2015   Revised Underground Storage Tank Regulations require better trained personnel, much more stringent monitoring, replacement of entire system if 50% is replaced and much more testing and monitoring.[48]

Volkswagen found to have lied about carbon emissions since at least 2008. Since that time, it is estimated that their cars may have emitted as much as a million tons/year of NOx, nitrogen Oxide. CEO Martin Winterkorn resigns with a $66.9 million separation package.[49] Volkswagen sells more cars this year than any other company, including GM or Toyota.[50] "Dieselgate" does little to impact VW's bottom line.

Kansas City Power and Light announces in January that it will "make the area one of the best places in the nation to drive an electric car."

> The utility said it plans to install 1,001 public electric chargers in its Missouri and Kansas service territories—a 2,400 percent boost from the roughly 40 units now available. Each charger will be able to charge two cars at a time.
>
> Public chargers are crucial to the success of electric cars because of "range anxiety," the fear that a car's battery power will be exhausted before reaching a destination. The chargers resemble a gasoline fuel pump but instead of hoses and nozzles, they have a cord and plug on each side.
>
> It will cost about $20 million to build the system, to be called the Clean Charge Network. KCP&L will ask state regulators to let it recover the cost through its rates. If regulators agree, residential customers would pay an extra $1 to $2 a year.
>
> But KCP&L noted that the extra revenue it would get from selling electricity for cars, which is also typically done when demand is off-peak, could eventually put downward pressure on rates.
>
> A few of the chargers have already been installed in the Kansas City area, and the ambitious plan calls for the entire network to be deployed by summer.
>
> The Clean Energy Network will have three to five chargers at each location — enough to fuel 6 to 10 cars — to help ensure one will be available when needed. Many locations have already been selected, although most have not been publicly disclosed.
>
> At the news conference, there were hints that Harrah's Casino, Starbucks and the Kansas City Chief will be partners in the project. It was confirmed that four Hy-Vee food stores in the Kansas City area will host chargers.
>
> Some are already mulling the overall impact that Clean Charge will have on the area. Bob Marcusse, president and CEO of the Kansas City Area Development Council, said it is huge and as important as Google's decision to bring its high-speed Internet service here.
>
> "This sends the signal that Kansas City is on the cutting edge of technology," he said.
> 51

A new study touts the economic feasibility of electric cars, harkening back to similar argument proffered more than 100-years-before (see 1910 in this timeline):

> The electric car is known for being environmentally friendly. Jeffrey Chu, an analyst at personal finance information service NerdWallet, also found that owning an electric car can save thousands of dollars.
>
> Chu released his study in mid-September during National Drive Electric Week.
>
> "The objective of the study was to find a comparison of a gas car, a hybrid car and an electric car," Chu said in a telephone interview. "We wanted to see the economic feasibility of having an electric car, having a hybrid car and having a gas car."

Kansas City was one of 27 cities where Chu decided to compare costs.

"During my research, Kansas City really stood out to me because Kansas City Power and Light has a $20 million initiative to install 1,000 car charging stations. That is huge in terms of electric car infrastructure," Chu said. "I wanted to focus on areas that are booming with that kind of project. The three places that stood out to me were Kansas City, Atlanta and Indianapolis."

The three cars Chu selected to compare were the Nissan Leaf (electric), Toyota Prius (hybrid) and the Toyota Camry (gasoline). The reason those three cars were selected because they were similar in price.

Chu used edmunds.com as the source for the costs of the vehicle.

In Kansas City, Chu listed the price of a Camry at $21,376, the Prius at $24,843 and the Leaf at $23,179. Over a five-year period, Chu factored in the cost of maintenance, repairs, insurance, fuel and any federal tax credits.

In that period, the total cost for the Camry was $39,407, the Prius was $40,058 and the Leaf was $29,079. It should be noted that Chu credited the Leaf with a $7,500 federal tax credit that's available for plug-in electric drive motor vehicles, which the other two cars didn't receive.

But the fuel cost was significantly different. The five-year cost for fuel for a Camry was $7,000, the Prius, $4,000 and the Leaf, $2,500.

"The main thing to take away from that is the Nissan Leaf was the cheapest to own even without the tax credit and that is mainly due to fuel savings," Chu said. "What stood out to me was the overall gas savings. Over a one-year span it is a few hundred dollars, but if you were to blow it out over five years, that would lead to huge savings if you were to drive an electric car. That was the biggest thing for me.

"There are state incentives and federal incentives to drive an electric car, but even without those, the Nissan Leaf or electric cars in general are fairly economical."

Chu wasn't paid by a car manufacturer to do this study. NerdWallet, based in San Francisco, provides answers for life's financial questions like credit cards, life insurance, auto insurance and investing, Chu said.

"Our mission is to provide that clarity and empower people to make smart money decisions," he said.

Chu said the study wasn't done to advocate electric car use. It was put together simply to compare cost of hybrids, gas and electric cars.

"In a very unbiased way, we are giving people a financial landscape of electric vehicle purchases," Chu said. "It wasn't done to tell people you should buy electric cars. We are not trying to push that.

There is some intrinsic value in having a gas car that an electric car doesn't provide. We want to give visibility that you can save a lot of money if you buy an electric car. [52]

Chu's key findings are explained below:

Driving an electric car can save 36% or $10,538 over five years. In all 27 cities we examined, the Nissan Leaf was by far the cheapest to own. Although all three car models we analyzed are similarly priced, on average, Nissan Leaf owners will spend $10,538 less than Camry drivers and $9,609 less than Prius owners over five years. The savings are mainly due to the $7,500 federal tax credit provided to Leaf and all electric car owners, but even without the credit, the Leaf is cheaper to own. Prius owners don't receive a credit.

The Leaf costs much less to operate. Over five years, Leaf drivers can expect to spend $4,691 less than Camry owners and $1,707 less than Prius drivers. Much of this difference comes from not buying gas. [In 2019, Leaf's range will be over 200 miles.]

Fueling Change

Owning a Leaf is cheapest in Charlotte, North Carolina, and most expensive in Detroit, Michigan. Leaf drivers in Charlotte enjoy the lowest cost of ownership at $26,491 over five years. On the other hand, Leaf owners in Detroit spend about $47,196, or 78% more, primarily due to high auto insurance premiums for all vehicles in that city.

About Kansas City, Chu's report stated:

Kansas City is taking charge in making its streets friendlier for electric cars. Kansas City Power & Light is spearheading a $20 million initiative to install 1,000 electric-car charging stations, which will span Kansas City and rural areas in western Missouri and eastern Kansas. This new charging infrastructure is aimed at promoting electric-car sales, allowing drivers to travel with greater range and providing an inexpensive means of recharging. The charging stations will be free for electric-car drivers for the first two years of operation.[53]

2016   On February 26, the *Kansas City Star* announces that streetcars will return to Kansas City's streets after more than a 60-year-silence (see 1957):

The praising of—and caterwauling about—the new downtown streetcar system won't end May 6.

But Kansas Citians sure will have a better idea of which side of this debate they're going to choose going forward.

The long-scheduled service on the 2.2-mile line starts that day, highlighted by a giant celebration. Street parties up and down the route from the River Market to Union Station are being scheduled, featuring food trucks and entertainment.

The hoopla is well earned. It also will mark a major turning point, giving the streetcar system the opportunity to prove its value as a public transit service and redevelopment catalyst to help further revive downtown. We disagree with skeptics who think it will be an embarrassing and costly flop.

2017   Kansas City's street cars are crowded enough that the system plans to buy two more vehicles, at a cost of nearly $12 million, although they have to be custom built and likely won't be delivered for two years.

Planning is underway to possibly extend the streetcar route south to the University of Missouri-Kansas City and north to Berkley Riverfront Park, but many more steps would be required to make those projects a reality."[54]

2018   Kansas City's *Climate Action Plan* has reduced the CO_2 emissions by more than the 30% originally stated as the goal leaving the committee to set new goals to reduce further emissions. Recommendations for electric cars awaits the required infrastructure to service them.

Kansas City Power and Light completes its merger with Westar to form Great Plains Energy dedicated to eliminating coal use and working toward efficiency and new approaches to supplying energy to its customers.

The green-building market is anticipated to be among the fastest growing industries worldwide. The number of LEED-certified projects (Leadership in Energy and Environmental Design) in the U.S. rose from 296 certifications in 2006 to over 65,000.[55]

Renewable energy sources account for about 11% of total U.S. energy consumption and about 17% of electricity generation.[56]

The Osage Nation in Oklahoma has the Osage Nation Campus Master Plan which is a building plan that uses passive solar design techniques. Native American governments are leaders in energy innovation.[57]

China puts 20 million new cars and trucks on their highways every year. The United States manufactures over 17 million cars. World total is 73 million. EV global sales 1%.

Greensburg, KS, nearly destroyed by a tornado in 2007, now boasts it has the most LEED (Leadership in Energy and Environmental Design) certified buildings per capita in the world.[58]

BP.com (British Petroleum) tells us we will be out of oil by 2053.

BP reports: Global energy demand is up 35% because of global prosperity. Industrial demand accounts for ½ of the increase. China and India account for one half of the current energy demand. The population will be 9.2 billion, with 2.5 billion lifted out of poverty. Two billion more live in urban areas than before.[59]

GM has invested $265 million into the Fairfax plant to produce the Cadillac XT4, the brand's first compact SUV. Offers 34 mpg on the highway. Buyers can "build their own" with many choices.[60]

"The Fourth National Climate Assessment issued November 23, 2018, by 13 federal agencies has issued warnings about our future quality of life as global warming continues unabated.

"Health, economy and infrastructure warnings give us an unwelcomed look at the future. Organized by regions of the country, the report shows the Midwest will see lower crop yields and drought. Crop yields will reach only 75% of previous highs. Cattle will have a difficult time thriving, either dairy or beef. Food and water-borne diseases will flourish.

"The South will suffer higher temperatures, lower productivity among workers, stress on roads and highway structures due to increased storms, rain and hurricanes. Floods will be more frequent. Asthma from increased humidity and mold will be a great health problem.

"The West will see more forest fires that could burn up to six times more area by 2050. Some areas will become too hot to cultivate almonds and walnuts.

"The East Coast will see infrastructure problems due to coastal flooding. Some 13,000 archaeological sites along the coast will disappear.

"Good quality and quantity of drinking water will be harder to come by. Warmer climates bring out more insects, more mold, more snakes.

"This unhappy news does not offer solutions, only the facts and projections based on present scenarios already in play."

Climate Change Report: 15 big takeaways, CNN.com

2019 Much progress has been made to clean up the air of Kansas City, to manage the environmental problems of a city of a half a million people set within the environs of 9 counties and many cities.

A revolutionary realization has been shared among the many governmental and not-for-profit entities that much could and must be done. Literally thousands of citizens in Kansas City and surrounding counties on both sides of the state line have enthusiastically helped achieve environmental milestones great and small from the LEED building program to more parks, cleaned up abandoned lots, litter pickups, gasoline monitoring and other efforts unrecorded but enthusiastically carried out in the name of sustainability and resilience.

Kansas City environmental officers Dennis Murphey and Gerald Schecter, citizen activist Bob Berkebile, and Climate Protection Plan chair Joann Collins, have devoted countless hours to promoting a better climate for their city. Speaking for the Climate Protection Plan Steering Committee, Joanne Collins has issued this statement:

> I thank our mayors and city councils for their foresight and leadership since 2006. KCMO Climate Protection Plan Steering Committee and the city's environmental staff with so many stakeholders have labored to reduce our greenhouse gas emissions. We set a reasonable goal, only to discover that in city operations we would surpass it. A healthy environment is paramount to our citizens' quality of life. We aim to achieve a goal of 100% renewable energy citywide. Our challenge is how to make renewable energy available, accessible and affordable for low/moderate income households. I believe that is an essential investment in our future generations.

A hundred years before in 1919, one of Kansas City's early residents lived to see the transformation of the early town:

> *"Here in one period of some eighty years, residents viewed from their front doors transportation by river skiff, steamboat, oxen, the first railroads over the Hannibal Bridge, the motor car and finally the airplane. And all in the span of a lifetime!"*[61]

2021 Two hundred years will have passed since Chouteau and his entourage worked their way up the Missouri River by keel boat traveling upstream hand over hand, the Wood Age's only choice to travel by water against the current.

Gasoline 2050: The Matriarch
Gasoline becomes a *niche* fuel and eventually *declines*

This addiction will be a long time leaving us. Like its introduction in the 1850s with no infrastructure to use it, no real infrastructure has yet been created to replace it. As it is an orphan for want of use, we must now make gasoline an orphan by designing its declining use. Can we replace weekly gatherings, for instance, to which we all drive and rub shoulders with each other? Get and give hugs and smiles, perhaps the only ones we exchange all week? Or sporting events? Or work? Or shopping? We have started down this "replacement road" by shopping on line, but humans love crowds. Can we replace that experience on line? If we collectively count up the gallons of gasoline used to assemble a crowd and disperse it, we will discover 20 pounds of CO_2 has been deposited for every gallon burned getting to and from that event. Can we, should we allow ourselves the luxury of this choice? Is there a way to minimize without "minus-ing?"

Let's say we gather together an even 100 people and say many came together so we have 50 cars that burned an average of 2 gallons to arrive and return. So that's 100 gallons of gasoline burned to get together. Multiplied by 20 lbs that is 2000 pounds of CO_2 released into the atmosphere. OK. That's not much. We can do that, right? Once? 52 times? Maybe we don't all come all the time. Say, although we have 100 people, they're not the same hundred people. Doesn't matter. You stayed home; he and she and kids came. So, whether you're there or not, 2,000 pounds of CO_2 will float into the atmosphere EVERY Sunday. 2000 x 52 divided by 104,000 equals 52 tons, or 1 ton per gathering.

If we delivered a ton of toxic particulates to the parking lot by bulldozer and watched it blow away into the air (and into our lungs), would we stop meeting, or drastically change the way we continue to meet?

2050 Two-hundred-years will have passed since the Town of Kansas that became Kansas City, Missouri, is incorporated. The 2006 goal set by community officials in their initial *Climate Action Plan* declares that by the year 2050 greenhouse gas emissions will be reduced by 80% from 1990 levels.

Part 3
Conclusion

The timeline comprising gasoline's first biography wrapped within a city history tells us a great deal about our values as we embrace "gasoline empowerment" as a reality in our lives. We are powerless against it. If we're mobile, we're empowered. Singular mobility in a car is the highest, most cushy form of mobility, whereas basic mobility is public transport by bus, train, subway or streetcar. The more mobile we are, the more richer, healthier, better educated, more worldly. Mobility—upper, lateral or downward—is all done with gasoline, or a variety thereof.

This story of a place defined by its fuel use leads to at least one conclusion: History is simpler than we think. It's all about fuel all the time. FUELS-R-US. Gasoline is the most sophisticated of fuels—versatile, available in unending quantities, democratic, affordable, both volatile and latent, powers any variety of vehicles for any need or desire, combusts on command into potent results at the flash of a spark. It needs merely to be channeled to the right spot and moment. Gasoline is a combination of technology that has taken humanity eons to perfect.

When fire found its way into the hands of hominids a million years ago—give or take—this species began a long trek of improving quality of life. What but fire can do so much more than the basic food, water, cover? Once discovered and manipulated, fire became the center of life, and is to this day. It became the single tool that changed our way of being, eating, cooking, growing, defending, communicating. We became human. At that moment, we humans began to participate in our "fuelture™" because there is no future for humanity without fuel manipulation—discovery, development, systems organization, expansion and defense, niche and decline. We are always in one or another of these stages, sometimes several at once when different fuels burn at the same time. We are all about fuel all the time.

Do you argue over the thermostat? Do you cook or microwave meals? Open the refrigerator to a perfectly cooled container of fresh food? Jump in the car for something at the store? Drive to work? Church? School? Receive Amazon deliveries? Drive, drive, drive? Fill up. Fill up. Fill up. We are all about fuel all the time. That car is useless if the tank is empty!

The use of fuel to make fire can be small, tidy and careful with individual, feminine hands, as with the Osage women. Or, it can be fed to vast furnaces by enormous chains of fuel, machines, and men as in "modern civilization." In whatever quantity, however delivered and used, for whatever expansion—always in search of superior means of light, heat and power—*fuel is our daily, hourly companion, moment by moment purveyor upon which we play out all our purposes, hopes and dreams.* We may not see an open flame for years, but somewhere a flame is burning, consuming fuel from somewhere underground and piping the resultant energy to each of us. Combustion creates the power to turn the wheels of our lives.

Is it possible for the highly fuel-infused lives we lead today to be decelerated? Tamped down? Can we go backward? Or, is it a different way of going forward? We stand at a very important point in the life of our species...our planet. Shall we continue to expand fuel use, population, manipulation and obliteration of our natural ecosystems? Or, shall we dial back our lives to a slower tempo, a smaller footprint? Momentum is a very hard force to decelerate, yet it is our task to do so.

Gasoline use is a deep addiction. It is so appealing, so unconscious, such a basic part of our human right to convenience. What is civilization, after all, but the building of greater kinds of convenience? It seems only a natural progression of evolutionary steps that has brought us to this fuel-enriched existence. If we define human evolution in any other way for the last million or so years when fuel became part of our lives, we overlook the greatest factor in our evolution. Yet we barely mention fuel and fire for our phenomenal climb up the ladder to the convenience-driven, overweight existence in which we find ourselves.

Gasoline is the sculptress of our ways and means. NOTHING has quite left its mark on our way of life like this fuel. The fuel itself—the abandoned child—would have its way. And what were the lyrics of that song? In 1913, they had figured out gasoline even as they followed down that road to what we now see as perdition: "In this land of milk and honey 'Tisn't love— isn't money rules the world, now ain't that funny? Gasoline! Gasoline!"

Yes, gasoline does rule the world, and certainly rules our world. But at what cost? Look at the overall health of humankind, and the health of the planet, polluted with petroleum based products, CO_2-created smog catapulting global climate change.

What is the end game? From now on our future is our "fuelture™."

In the process of mending, protecting, treating a hierarchy of emergencies, a triage of imperatives, how may we become "gasoline free?" Mankind learned to fly in the 20th century. Within one lifetime, Kansas Citians had seen the transition from steamboat powered by wood, railroads with coal, and finally the automobile and airplane fueled by oil to supply motive power.

We have been flying high with oil and gasoline ever since. The question for the 21st century is how high shall we fly without it?

Fueling Change

Part 4

Entering the Solar Age: The Fuelture™ of the City

Once upon a time—200-years-ago—European-American pioneers, ignorant of the future, arrived at the western edge of the United States where the Missouri River takes a decided course northward. Settlers could not possibly have imagined that remote bend of the river would turn out to be one of the hottest geographic spots in the country. They could not have foreseen in 1820 that gold fields in a far-off place that became known as California would lure fortune-seekers through their little hamlet clinging to the edge of the riverbank.

Early settlers drew on the past to lay out their town. First, they built a string of buildings against the cliffs in the Wood Age, then grids of streets and later removed the cliffs, filled in the "gullies," laid out the boulevards and beautified the city in the Coal Age. Ever expanding they then built suburbs and freeways in the Oil Age. Transportation changed from horse to trolley to streetcar to busses to fleets of automobiles individually driven their separate ways, all powered by gasoline.

And here we are. Unlike the pioneers of 1820, we are not ignorant of what lies ahead and can create a 'fuelture™" the best way we know how. The city will need a redesign, the basics of which are in play now. We will need a "transition economy." Renewables and their infrastructure sculpt the coming Solar Age.

Cities, not states are becoming the engines of change. Here are some:
- Austin: Net-Zero Austin Community Climate Plan
- Chicago: Chicago Climate Action Plan
- Kansas City: Climate Action Plan
- Los Angeles: Sustainable City pLAn
- Philadelphia: Greenworks
- Portland: 2015 Climate Action Plan
- Seattle: Seattle Climate Action Plan

Kansas City is 36th in population of the 50 largest cities in the United States, just under Sacramento, and just above San Diego, California.

The unfortunate fate for Kansas City, however, is that it is number five (5) on the list of cities to be most affected by climate change (see pages 315 and 329) a fact that motivates city leaders to get ahead of that forecast and do their best to change it.

Kansas City leaders—mayor, city council, environmental officers, Climate Action Committee members, and others—have joined in the national effort among cities to reduce greenhouse gases in their city buildings and vehicle operations.

Fueling Change

Kansas City's leaders achieved a 30% reduction of CO_2 emissions below 2000 levels by 2020, three years ahead of their first goal. They plan to cut emissions again to be "climate-neutral" by 2030. We can be grateful for their vision, leadership and discipline. They made the tough choice: global warming or reduced fossil fuel use, and then created a plan to do it…and carried it out.

New words to describe our future sound like this: "retrofitting housing, resiliency measures, decarbonizing the electric grid, optimizing energy alternatives to private cars."

Now it is time for a full-scale citizen support system to take fossil fuel off our streets and highways.

Kansas City is earnestly doing its part supported by a network of other cities. It is this last goal—alternatives to private cars—which we must all address. This is the way we get to the Solar Age, the Age of Renewables.

We cannot continue our current fuel use if we are to enter the Solar Age.

Our frenzied guzzling of fossil fuel in the 20th century must be cut in half in the first half of the 21st century. Renewables will not take us to the heights, the speeds, or the distances provided by the Oil Age. We will live in combination with fossil fuels. If we reduce fossil fuel use by 50% we should be very clear about how we use that 50% of fossil fuel. It cannot be burning gasoline.

Glib forecasts for the year 2050 show that fossil fuel use will be reduced by 50%. Are we going to fold up the automotive industry? The shipping industry? Which fossil fuel users will disappear as we make the heavy cuts to 50%? How shall we make these choices? Will the public do it? Who will cut the pie?

Automobile wheels are already being replaced by bicycle and scooter wheels! Shall we let our youth decide our choices? They very well may do so.

We will re-engineer our communities for walking and for telecommuting. In the 21st century we will digitize our lives the way we added fuel to our lives in the 20th century.

We may decide that all our shopping will be online and delivered to our doors.

We may gather together on Sundays to worship and celebrate our beliefs via mobile device. It won't be the same, but it may become the new norm. We will be able to attend in our pajamas if we so desire or we may make it a rule in that group that we have to dress-up, at least from the waist up!

First, We Must Stop Burning Gasoline

Any intelligent fool can make things bigger, more complex and more violent. It takes a touch of genius . . . and a lot of courage . . . to move in the opposite direction.

—Albert Einstein

We all want to stop climate change, even climate deniers wish the whole thing would just go away. We would like to reduce the atmospheric temperature and ultimately reverse it, but are we actually doing it?

Have we pulled all the levers of reduced fuel use that we can to stop the rise in atmospheric temperature?

Not yet. In spite of more and more city-led programs to reduce greenhouse gas emissions, more corporations joining in support, and more anguished pleas from nonprofit officials, there is little sign of reversal of the rising temperature of the earth's atmosphere. We are marching steadily toward the dreaded 2° Celsius ceiling (see page 338) that will tell us we have failed to curb our enthusiasm for all fossil fuels.

Somehow, we have overlooked a very powerful lever to do so. It is before our eyes. We use it every day. In fact, we love it. We are completely and hopelessly addicted to it, cannot live without it in our current life design. To relinquish our use of it has not yet been contemplated.

If we want to stop global warming, stop burning gasoline. **Yes, stopping global warming may be as simple as stopping burning gasoline.**

Not an abrupt stop. Not jumping on the brakes and screeching to a stop, but a, "slow to a stop." A phased-out approach over ten years just might work.

327

What If?

- What if we could slow our individual, community and national use of gasoline to a stop 10% a year over the next ten years?

- What if we as citizens organized at a grass-roots level? Instead of waiting for the government to move us away from fossil fuels, what if we took the lead?

- What if we could enroll our city to sponsor the effort so that citizens could compare and communicate with others doing the same thing?

- What if we enrolled cities around the world to stop global warming in this 10-year period?

- What if over the course of that 10 years we reduced the amount of CO_2 from car exhausts so that the temperature of the Earth's atmosphere showed signs of cooling?

- What if we didn't?

Many cities' air quality looks like this. To fly into a large city is to lower the plane into a soup of brown air. The mountains on the horizon disappear—on a clear day you can see them—the landscape below begins to emerge, the freeways are clogged with cars and trucks emitting the greenhouse gases we need to eliminate if we are to stop global warming.

How the Weather Will Change Our City

Here are some weather changes expected in Kansas City due to global warming:

- The average annual precipitation will increase from 38.8" to 44.6" per year.
- Maximum 1-day precipitation will increase from 3.4 to 4.0 inches while 5-day and, 15-day precipitation will increase from 5.5 to 7.0 inches and 7.5 to 10.4 inches respectively.
- The number of days with more than 1.5" of precipitation will increase from 5.0 to 9.3.
- The maximum number of consecutive dry days will increase from 30.9 to 39.5 days.
- Average annual temperatures will increase from 56.5° to 64.4° F.
- The number of days per year in which the temperature exceeds 105° F will increase from 0.7 to 21.9.
- The number of cooling degree days, a reflection of the demand for energy needed to cool a building, will nearly double. Conversely, energy demand for heating will decline by 27%.
- The last spring frost is projected to occur 2 weeks earlier, whereas the first fall frost will occur about 11 days later.
- More cooling in summer and degraded local air quality will place additional stress on water supply systems, wastewater and storm water management systems and flood control efforts.

Top 10 of 25 American Cities Most at Risk for Climate Change

1.	New Orleans, Louisiana	Vulnerable to sea-level rise
2.	Minneapolis, Minnesota	Increase of both precipitation, drought
3.	Las Vegas, Nevada	Hotter, dryer, drought
4.	New York City, New York	Sea levels rising 18 to 75 inches
5.	**Kansas City, Missouri**	**Heat island, heavy rains, drought**
6.	Boston, Massachusetts	Rising sea levels, future storms
7.	Denver, Colorado	23 degrees hotter than rural areas
8.	St. Paul, Minnesota	Rain and heat extremes
9.	Washington, D.C.	Heat island, flooding
10.	Philadelphia, Pennsylvania	Extreme drought and sea-level rise[1]

To be in fifth place on the list above might look and feel like this:

- The growing season comes earlier and stays later.
- Local eco-systems are stressed. Warmer temperatures mean more tropical invasion of foreign species and insects.
- Summer nights will be hotter. Air-conditioning may become inadequate.
- Hotter, drier climate dries out the soil and reduces farm production.[2]

329

"Risky Business:"
The Economic Impact on Climate Change in The United States

The "Risky Business" report by co-chairs Michael R. Bloomberg, Henry Paulson and Tom Steyer, suggests increased heat will lead to an increase of 5.3% in violent crime due to hotter temperatures—unrelieved heat creates frustration and people outside after dark, contributes to decreased labor productivity of 2.3 percent and increased energy demand of 8 to 19%. Many reports predict that the impacts of changes in extreme weather will likely affect disadvantaged communities in a disproportionate manner.

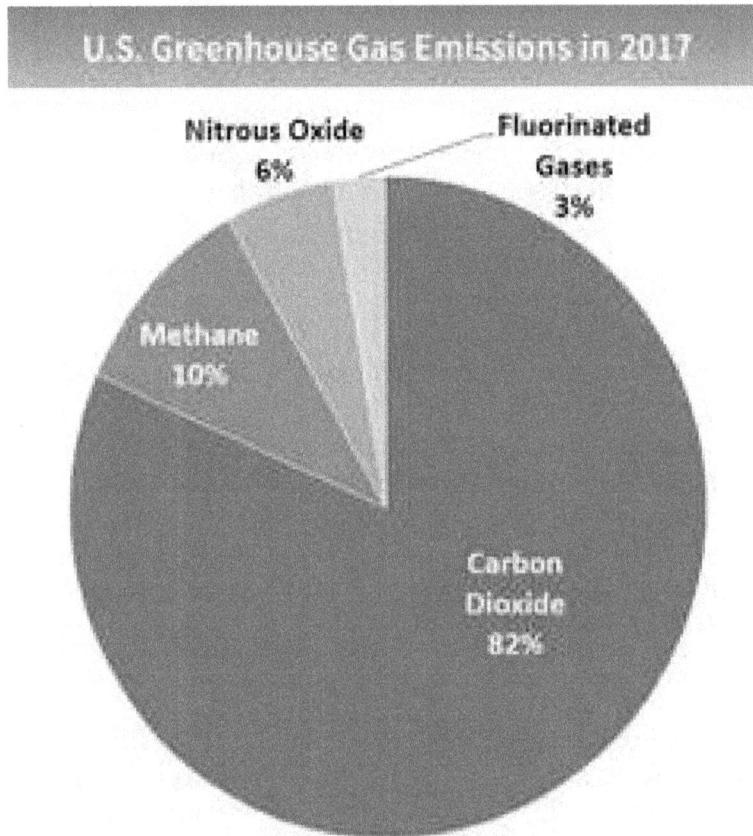

U.S. Greenhouse Gas Emissions in 2017

Nitrous Oxide 6%

Fluorinated Gases 3%

Methane 10%

Carbon Dioxide 82%

Source: Environmental Protection Agency

Carbon dioxide is by far the biggest contributor to global warming at 81%. Nitrous oxide is the gas that Volkswagen allowed to be released from their cars as they attempted to squeeze past regulations. Volkswagen admitted their cars were programmed to cheat on the testing of their emissions. Their cars were not able to pass the EPA standards so were programmed only to meet the requirements during testing. About 11 million cars were affected worldwide.

Methane gas is a biproduct of oil production among other sources. Oil companies are beginning to concentrate on eliminating methane in that industry.

Sources of Greenhouse Gas Emissions in 2016

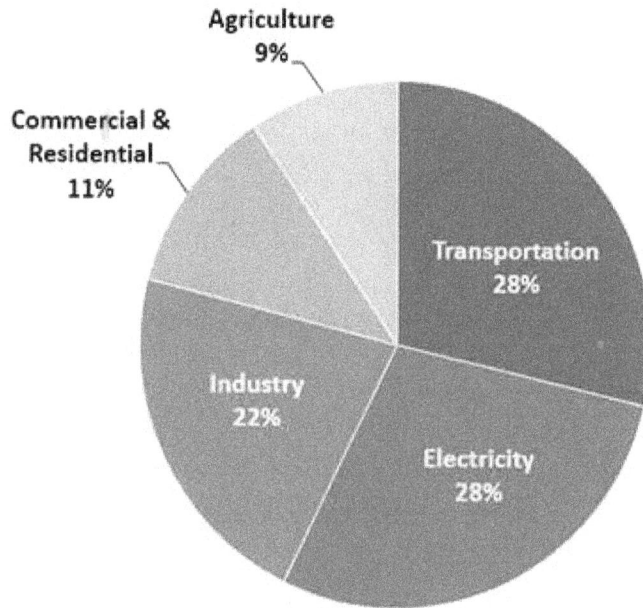

Agriculture 9%

Commercial & Residential 11%

Transportation 28%

Industry 22%

Electricity 28%

Source: Environmental Protection Agency

If you look at the other sectors in this graph you will see that all the electricity we burn, fired by either coal or natural gas, is also 28%. We have taken seriously the idea of using LED lights instead of incandescent along with the other myriad efficiencies that have become common to the electrical system. All of the industrial might of the United States is less than the transportation sector. All of agriculture is only 9%. All the houses in the country and buildings are only 11%. That puts transportation in a new perspective. That is you and me driving, our goods moving around the country—movement. Who says we can drive past forest fires and trees dead from insects because the temperature doesn't get cold enough in the winter to kill the pests and not feel our CO_2 is connected to such damage to nature? Who says we can't do something about it?

331

Source: Environmental Protection Agency

Global Carbon Emissions from Fossil Fuels, 1900-2014

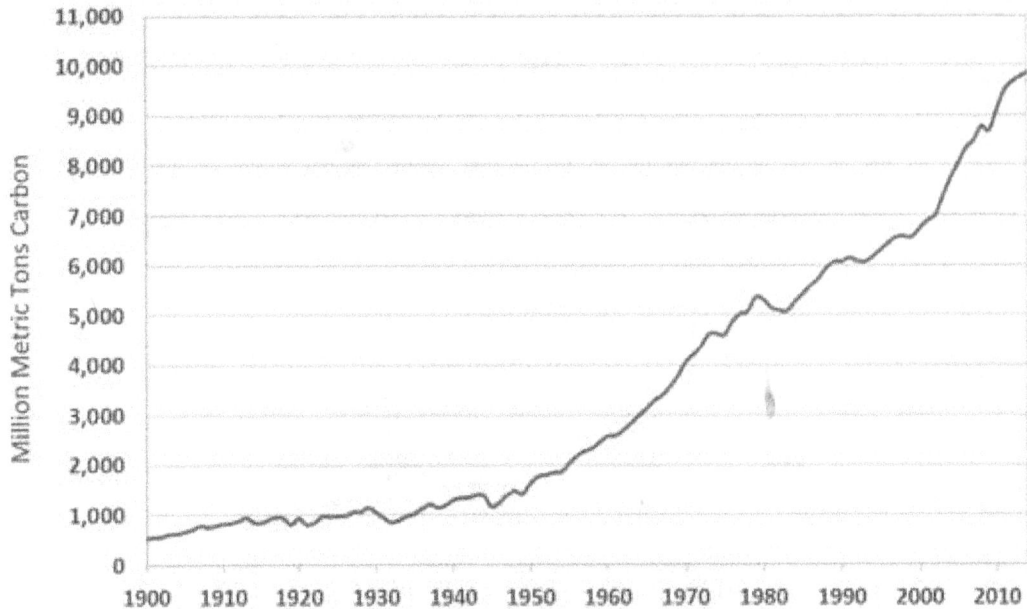

How High? How Long?

This upward line (above) must peak and begin to decline by 2020, according to scientists worldwide, if we are to reverse climate change. Even though it has steadily risen ever upward, all eyes focus on the data to 2020. Will that line level off and begin to decline? If not, deep and harsh cuts may be in order around the world to reverse its upward climb. If so, we will know we are doing enough things right that we can continue to repeat successful mitigating programs.

This graph from 2014 shows the climb upward. The graph on the next page shows a slight decline to 2016. If that trend continues, we can rejoice at the turn of events. It is still too early to know whether the line will continue to decline to 2020.

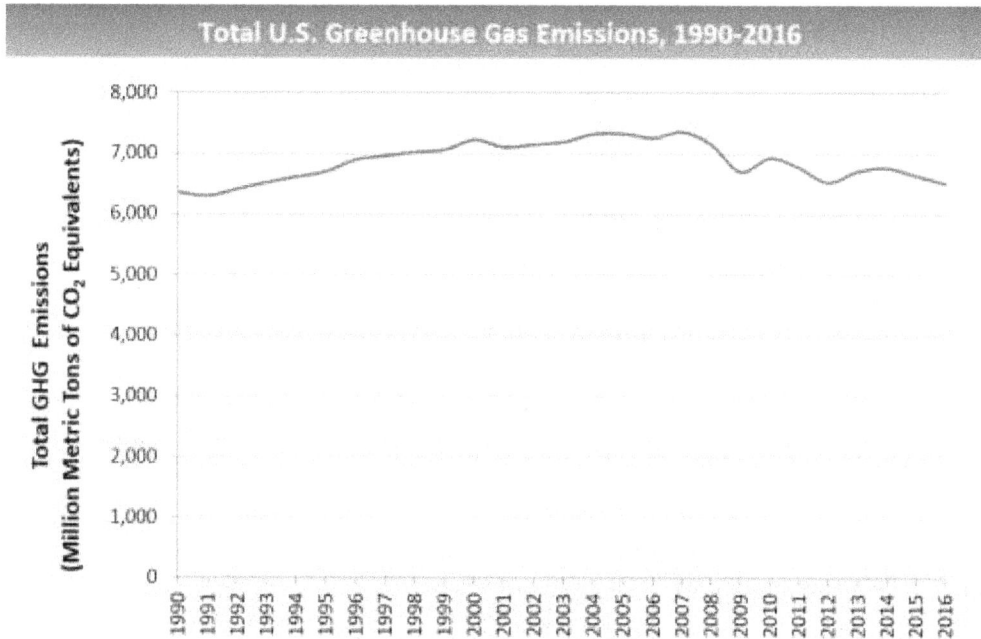

Total U.S. Greenhouse Gas Emissions, 1990-2016

U.S. Environmental Protection Agency (2018). Inventory of U.S. Greenhouse Gas Emissions and Sinks: 1990-2016

How Many? How Much?

How many cars are on American roads? 10 million? 20 million? 100 million?

Would you believe 253 million cars and trucks fill their tanks and run on U.S. roads every day?

In 2017, about **142.98 billion** gallons (or about **3.40 billion** barrels[1]) of finished motor gasoline were consumed in the United States, a daily average of about **391.71 million** gallons (or about 9.33 million barrels per day. See eia.gov).

That number looks like this: 391,000,000 gallons burned per day. Every gallon of gasoline burned leaves 20 pounds of CO_2 behind. That would mean 7,820,000,000 pounds of CO_2 left behind every day as air pollution to go to the store, work, school, movie, visit people, pick up the child from the babysitter, sit on the freeway while waiting for traffic to ease, the light to turn green . . . . In other words our way of life floats on a sea of gasoline.

What can we do? We are locked into a transportation system designed for gasoline use. Can we break away from that slowly and safely? Safe for the economy and for us?

Here's OUR Plan
What Can Be Measured Can Be Achieved

1 THE FIRST YEAR, drivers will record their fuel use:

- How much gasoline we use: 20 lbs of CO_2 for every gallon burned
- How much carbon dioxide we each leave behind
- What alternative travel choices are available to decrease our use of gasoline
- What groups may be doing this in which a driver may participate

Here is the real difference between asking people to do this on their own and seeing that they have a way to participate in a group effort citywide to show real results.

Keeping it local brings home our own global warming climate changes.
Drivers may be able to combine trips with others to car pool, bike ride,
walk to the store and so on.

Kansas City will enroll other cities in creating the same program:

Rule # 1:   Keep it local.
Rule # 2:   Make it measurable.
Rule # 3:   Make it competitive and connect with other cities.

Yes! There will be an app for this adventure. Drivers will be asked to input their mileage and gasoline purchases. The app will help find a way to choose an alternative, shorten distance, and try any of the following choices:

- Delay, combine or eliminate the trip.
- Ride a bicycle.
- Walk.
- Ride share.
- Telecommute—telephone, Facebook, Instagram, Skype, etc.
- Move closer to work.

In your car:

- Drive within the speed limits.
- Inflate your tires properly.
- Empty your trunk. Don't pay in gasoline the weight of unnecessary baggage.
- Help us design an easy way to reduce your use on a daily or weekly basis.
    We need to celebrate small victories, feel progress and pride.

2 The second-year drivers and passengers will begin to choose new ways of meeting transportation needs, communicating with each other, digitizing various meetings. The infrastructure of communication begins to change. A certain number of people will buy electric cars. Some 750,000 already run the roads of America.(1.2 million China, 90,000 in the United Kingdom.) A refitting industry may spring up to replace internal combustion engines with electric models.

3 The third-year life will have changed, not just for the driver and family but for our buying patterns, our working patterns. More walking in the neighborhoods will create more neighborly relationships but also dangers of being on the street. Many of the frustrations of the first two years have been resolved, and people know how to handle a certain level of transportation needs. More electric cars will require more electric grids and off-hour recharging.

4 The fourth year a major change will be underway, depending on the number of drivers participating in the campaign. Many more electric cars will become available. Ride sharing will have become attractive. Employers rethink large parking lots full of cars. The automotive industry feels the pain and grapples with reworking its whole role as creator of automobiles. (Actually, this has already happened at General Motors. Their post-Thanksgiving 2018 announcement of factory closings is a sign of the times.) A "scooter invasion" may throw the auto industry off balance.

5 The next six years will be about rearranging the travel patterns we created for ourselves in the 20th century that do not work in the 21st century. Long-term questions about the ratio of cars to population, the need for working closer to jobs, jobs changing because cars are less available, new kinds of transportation and fuels like hydrogen-powered cars, new definitions of travel vs. staying in one place and traveling by electronic device.

New habits are hard to create. There will be much failure and starting over, but the cause is so imperative that restarts are worth it. If you travel an average of 20,000 miles a year burning over a thousand gallons of gasoline at 20 lbs of CO_2 per gallon, you would be leaving 400,000 pounds of CO_2 or 200 tons of particulates in the air.

Get together with friends and neighbors, family, community group and co-workers. We have work to do!

Fueling Change

> *The people who are crazy enough to think they can change the world are the ones who do.* –Steve Jobs

Discuss your travel options. Make choices. Keep a record. At some point we will have an app on which to record this information, but we should not wait for that app to appear. Start now.

Create and/or become a member of a small group of thoughtful, committed citizens willing to change the world.

On November 22, 2018, the **National Climate Assessment Report** was issued by the U.S. federal government. This statement below was part of that report.

Surely you and I can do something to impact this. Individually we can cut back; in a small group we can discuss strategies and test out new ideas. But we can and must do something to impact this statement below:

EACH YEAR, 214 MILLION AMERICAN DRIVERS WILL RELEASE ABOUT 2.4 TRILLION POUNDS OF CO_2.

How do we begin to withdraw from this problem and become part of the solution?

The following mathematical explanation may not be easy to understand, but it is the simplest explanation available on the chemistry of gasoline exploding into CO_2.

If the shaded diagram's calculations elude you, comprehend the last three sentences at the bottom of the next page.

How can a gallon of gasoline produce 20 pounds of carbon dioxide?

It seems impossible that a gallon of gasoline, which weighs about 6.3 pounds, could produce 20 pounds of carbon dioxide (CO_2) when burned. However, most of the weight of the CO_2 doesn't come from the gasoline itself, but the oxygen in the air.

When gasoline burns, the carbon and hydrogen separate. The hydrogen combines with oxygen to form water (H^2O), and carbon combines with oxygen to form carbon dioxide (CO_2).

A carbon atom has a weight of 12, and each oxygen atom has a weight of 16, giving each single molecule of CO_2 an atomic weight of 44 (12 from carbon and 32 from oxygen).

Therefore, to calculate the amount of CO_2 produced from a gallon of gasoline, the weight of the carbon in the gasoline is multiplied by 44/12 or 3.7.

Since gasoline is about 87% carbon and 13% hydrogen by weight, the carbon in a gallon of gasoline weighs 5.5 pounds (6.3 lbs. x .87).

We can then multiply the weight of the carbon (5.5 pounds) by 3.7, which equals 20 pounds of CO_2.

For every gallon of gasoline your car burns, you add 20 pounds of CO_2 into the atmosphere.

Each time you fill your tank with 15 gallons of gasoline, you will leave behind 300 pounds of fine CO_2 particulates.

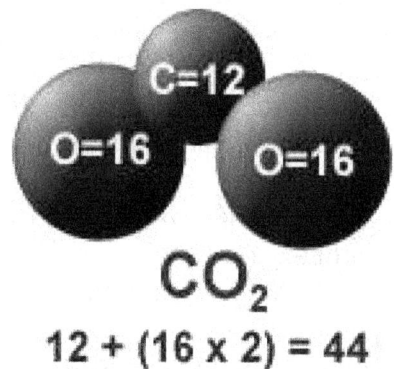

C=12

O=16   **O=16**

$$CO_2$$

12 + (16 x 2) = 44

Data provided by eia.gov

15 gallons x 20 pounds CO₂ = 300 pounds of CO₂

If you, individually, burn 15 gallons of gas each month for 12 months, you will have emitted as exhaust <u>3,600 pounds</u> of CO₂.

A family with two vehicles burning this amount of gas or more, adds over <u>10,000 pounds</u> of CO₂ into the atmosphere <u>each year</u>.

The Dreaded 2° Celsius

We know it! We hate it! We are threatened by it. What is it exactly?

Before the Industrial Revolution that sprang to life in the mid-1800s, the atmosphere was pretty clear. Except for an occasional volcanic explosion that might affect the atmosphere and last for several years, the skies eventually cleared. Cities contended with wood smoke and the beginnings of coal smoke, but that was seen as a necessary tradeoff for staying warm, cooking food, and producing goods like iron and glass.

Once industry began burning coal, however, creating iron and steel in factories and mass-producing goods, the air turned murky and sour. Darkness at noon by way of factory smoke was not unusual. Cities had become hot messes of exuberant exhaust. People were actually proud of the smoke on which they choked. "That means jobs," they said, and were glad to have one.

By the 1950s scientists had become aware of the "greenhouse effect," (though proposed and defined in 1824, no one took it seriously until a century of pollution began to choke populations). The idea that man-made smoke could create such a noxious cloud of particles in the air was new. Thick smoke could block out the rays of the sun. The sun's rays would bounce off the clouds of smoke and back to the edge of the atmosphere creating a "greenhouse" effect, warming the air and changing the temperature at ground level.

Scientists now understand that this window of temperature whose ceiling is 2°C above where we started in the pre-industrial period is the outside limit of what we and the planet can experience without great hardship, drought, poverty, loss of ecosystems and general breakdown of the quality of life on this planet humankind has enjoyed for the past 10,000 years.

Atmospheric carbon dioxide rose at record rate in 2015 and 2016 as measured by national oceanic and atmospheric administration (NOAA) at the Mauna Loa observatory in Hawaii.

The global temperature has increased about 0.85°C (1.5F) since 1880, setting off the alarm bells we are responding to today.

And the addition of carbon dioxide from such fuels as oil, coal and gasoline is part of the reason.

Much scrambling to reverse that trend toward the ceiling of 2° is now underway. It is way too little effort to make the kind of turnaround needed so far. We are like the Titanic. We can see the iceberg. Can we somehow reverse course and miss it? History will tell.

One thing is certain, however: We cannot reverse global warming, we cannot miss that ceiling, we cannot save the world for our grandchildren <u>if we do not stop burning gasoline</u>. We just cannot.

Now that the problem has been brought to our attention, do we really think we can all continue to drive around in our gasoline-burning cars like they are *not* spewing 20 pounds of CO_2 out of the tailpipe with each gallon burned?

Really?

IF we as citizens realize what is at stake, what we can choose to do vs. ignoring the obvious, using our cars as delivery vehicles of CO_2, waiting for a new technology to save us or a new governmental program to force us to do something else we don't like, we may just be able to stop ourselves from touching that ceiling.

In 10 years, 10% a year so that we can cooperatively and with realization of the most important collective action humankind can ever take, we can pull that lever of turning off gasoline. We can save our planet for ourselves and our children.

Replacement for Gasoline

Amount of Electricity from Solar Power Today (2019)

About 11% of our energy is generated by solar power and other renewables.

A projected 50% of power will be generated by renewables by 2050.

What will the other half be?

Gasoline. Oil. Natural Gas. Coal.

No matter how hard the renewable energy industries work at increasing market share and reducing CO_2 emissions from fossil fuels, at least half of the fuel basket will be made up of fossil fuels.

That means perhaps 50% less greenhouse gas will be getting loose into the atmosphere, but loose it will be.

Maybe it is time to stage a requiem for gasoline. Great fuel on the upswing, bad on the downswing. In fact, gasoline has always been bad. Even though it satisfies everything we want in the short term, it asks too high a price in the long term. The seductress of our ways and means drives a hard bargain.

Gasoline has been fun, no doubt about it, but now we are in the hangover stage.

Now it's time to give up the liquid that has dominated our lives. Time to realize how deep and strong our addiction has been that we discount traffic deaths and traffic jams, suburban sprawl and disappearance of buses and streetcars as just the inevitable byproduct of being able to travel in the greatest luxury humankind has ever known. We can do better.

Bumper to bumper traffic is not a necessity; it is a choice. We don't have to accept that way of travel. The pressure to stop burning gasoline means we change our strategies, tactics, goals and values.

We need a 21st century solution to a 20th century problem. Let's get to work!

The Digital Village in Our Future

There is no real replacement for gasoline. Its very plenitude makes it hard to match. Look back on its early history in Part 3 of this book. There was so much gasoline it was thrown out. The internal combustion engine saved it and us from drowning in gasoline.

The problem of its unused quantities was only solved by legions of automobiles using it. The hydrogen car in our future may keep us in individual transportation. The electric car will certainly provide a sleek fleet of silent salons on wheels. Perhaps today's gasoline infrastructure will be adapted to meet the needs of both. A station may offer both electric recharge and hydro recharge services. Gasoline is not going to go away without a fight and a mighty effort to replace it.

Ultimately, we may have to learn to travel differently, arrange our neighborhoods and cities differently. There will be a reorganization of priorities, values, lifestyles, imperatives. Over time, we may steer toward the electronic village where physically we walk and technically, we talk. Digitizing distance will be the order of the day while a stroll to the store is considered not only good form but the only way you'll get there. If that is our vision for the future, it is a worthy goal.

What is the future but the past dressed up in new clothes?

These predictions promise hard choices and hard work. We should do our individual work of helping a group reduce its use of this wonderful, dynamic and ultimately destructive fuel. If we don't . . .

What do we say to these young people? They know "climate change" will forever be a part of their lives, or do they? Have we educated them enough to prepare for the lifelong task of caring for an ailing planet? Have we done all we could to create solutions to problems whose long-term resolutions exceed our lifetimes? Did we act by example enough to inspire and instruct them? Have we taught them to love the planet more than we have?

Their ancestors created the beginnings of Kansas City on the banks of the Missouri River. Generations of pioneers have left their mark. This new generation of pioneers have a new city to build, new ways of work and life to invent. Unless we make massive changes now, the future Kansas City will be the capital of an increasingly drought-prone city state that requires more and more care and resources to stabilize the effects of global warming. Mitigation, resilience, sustainability are already watchwords of this condition.

So much good work has already been done. Let's build on that.

Transportation will be replaced by telecommunication. This will be our building block for the future. Our goal is a world in 2050 that we will be proud we created. Fueling change means changing fuel.

Fueling Change Means Changing Fuels

The beginnings of the conservation movement in the 19th century saved places like Yellowstone and Yosemite for generations. We couldn't be more grateful to those who exerted will and political might to preserve and deliver such places for today's pleasure. Past citizens did what they could to save jewels like that for us. Now it is our turn to protect and deliver our remaining living systems to the generations ahead.

The past has delivered its gifts and its challenges. The future is ready to receive what we are willing to do, must do, to deliver to our youth and their future youth the best of planet Earth.

The Earth cannot endure another period of time like the Industrial Revolution and the Fuel Revolution—virtually one in the same—without losing what remains of its living systems.

The story of Kansas City's fuel use is artifact if it does not carry that story forward to today and beyond. If it does not point out the heroic work of many, many citizens and city officials who do their best to pay forward a legacy of preservation, then it has taught us little.

We will share our focused message of both the joy and burden of gasoline and clarify the steps needed to evolve beyond its use.

To the youth who look at us in Part 4, we will do what it takes to remove gasoline from our lives. It may be only 30% of our fuel uses, but it stretches into the far corners of every surface. We have the momentary leisure to expand and share ideas, learn from one another and adapt to our own needs. The duty is to share our successes and warn of our failures so that we may all reach new successes together.

The Year is 2050

Our descendants stand on hillsides and city streets, mountain tops, beaches, riversides and in parks throughout Kansas City. Together at some appointed time, they will all say in their many languages, "We did it! We reversed climate change! We will continue to preserve, restore and protect the world for our children."

That effort will be humanity's grandest accomplishment.

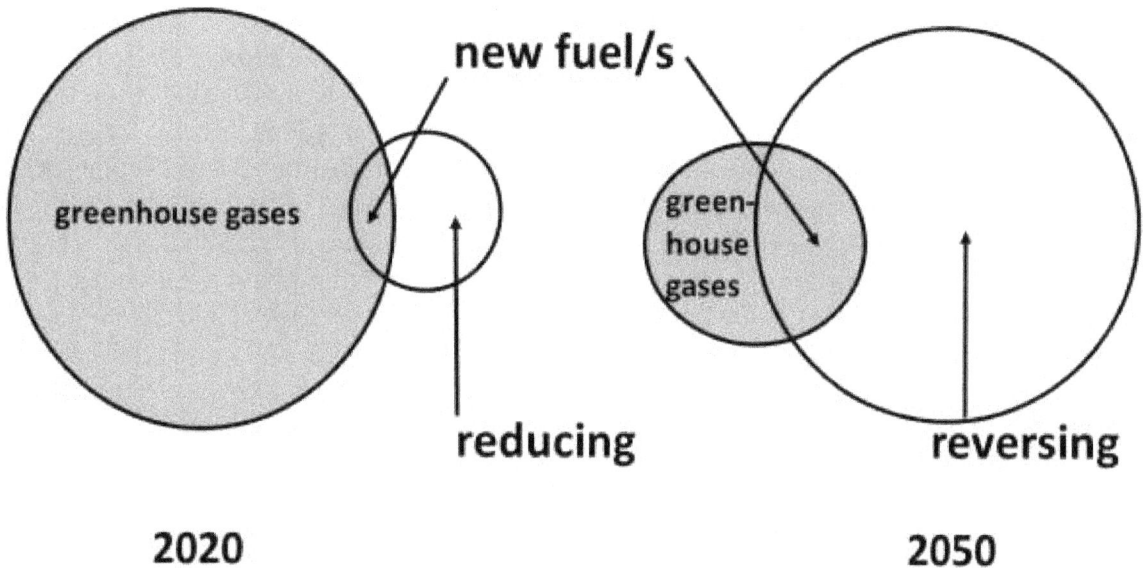

new fuel/s

greenhouse gases

reducing

2020

green-house gases

reversing

2050

"We must REDUCE the greenhouse gases to REVERSE global warming."

— Paul Hawken, *Drawdown: The Most Comprehensive Plan Ever Proposed to Reverse Global Warming*

For a condensed action plan to reduce our consumption of gasoline, refer to the booklet, *The Gasoline Diet*, by Twyla Dell, Ph.D.

For the most up-to-date information on this subject, consult fuelingchange.org.

Five Last Key Points

1. Our city's future is in all our hands, individually and collectively.
2. Our lives are designed by and for gasoline use. We can change that.
3. The CO_2 emissions we create are a choice, not a necessity.
4. A retreating fuel system opens new markets. We can push for those.
5. When we reduce fossil fuel use by over 50%, the Solar Age can begin.

As this book goes to press in March 2020, the best, formalized proposal at the Federal level in the United States is the **Green New Deal (GND)**, "a set of proposed economic stimulus programs in the United States that aims to address climate change and economic inequality." It was introduced in February by Sen. Ed Markey (D-MA) and Rep. Alexandria Ocasio-Cortez (D-NY), who tweeted an introduction to the GND in December 2018: "Our goal is to treat climate change like the serious, existential threat it is by drafting an ambitious solution on the scale necessary—aka. a Green New Deal—to get it done."[3]

Included in this groundbreaking legislation with "just transition" is the bright idea to cut current carbon emissions (the largest of which is transportation) by 45% by 2030 and reach net zero by 2050. It CAN be done! "With some decent subsidies, electric cars and buses are now cost-competitive with fossil-fuel vehicles, and they are getting better and cheaper with every passing month."[4] And, infrastructure needed to recharge electric vehicles already exists. That, together with a tax on gas and diesel (like Norway instituted), will propel this plan. We must start somewhere. And, it appears some progressive thinkers and doers have already crossed the starting line. The future is ours. Let us chase it!

U.S. net electricity generation by fuel (1990-2040)
billion kilowatthours

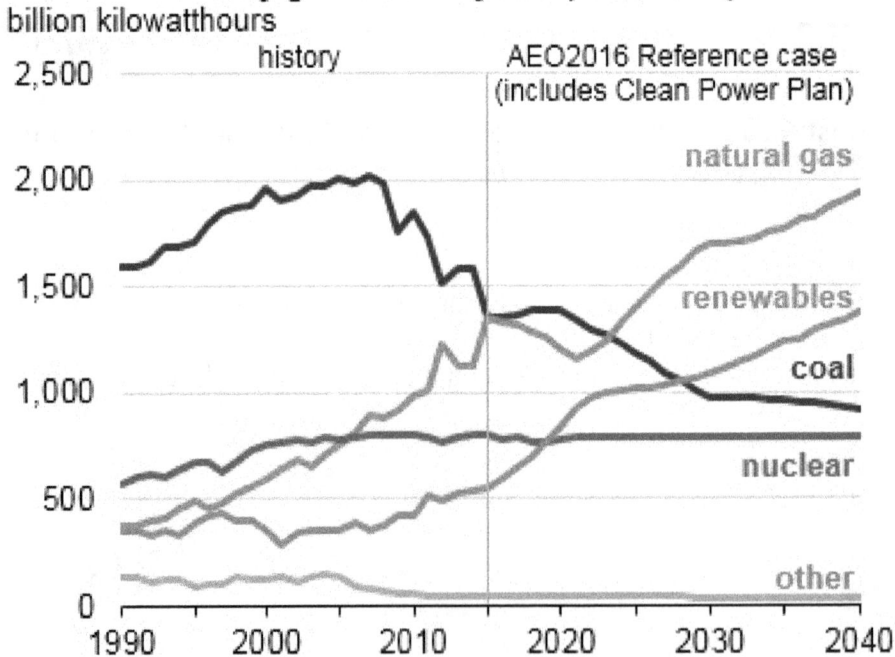

Appendices

A   **Osage Chiefs' Signatures, 1837 Treaty**

B   **Racing Steamboats on the Missouri River**

C   **Duties of Master of the Levee**

D   **Care of Coal**

E   **Care of Mules**

F   **Fuel Savings from Lawrence, Kansas, to Kansas City, Missouri, Commute**

G   **Green New Deal, 2019**

Fueling Change

Appendix A

Osage Chiefs' Signatures
1837 Treaty

Treaty with the Kioway, Ka-ta-ka and Ta-wa-ka-ro, Nations of Indians:

Whereas a treaty of peace and friendship was made and signed on the 24th day of August 1835, between Montfort Stokes and Brigadier General Matthew Arbuckle, commissioners on behalf of the United States on the one part; and the chiefs, and head-men and representatives of the Comanche, Witchetaw, Cherokee Muscogee, Choctaw, Osage, Seneca and Quapaw nations or tribes of Indians on the other part: and whereas the said treaty has been duly ratified by the Government of the United States; now know all whom it may concern, that the President of the United States, by letter of appointment and instructions of the 7th day of April 1837, has authorized Col. A. P. Chouteau to make a convention or treaty between the United States and any of the nations or tribes of Indians of the Great Western Prairie; we the said Montfort Stokes, and A. P. Chouteau, commissioners of Indian treaties, have this day made and concluded a treaty of peace and friendship, between the United States of America, and the chiefs, headmen and representatives of the Kioway, Ka-ta-ka, and Ta-wa-ka-ro nations of Indians....

The chiefs signing their mark (aka. touching the feather) for the Osage were listed as follows:

Clermont, the Principal Chief
Ka-hi-gair-tanga, the Big Chief
Ka-hi-gair-wa-chin-pi-chais, the Mad Chief
Chan-gais-mon-non, the Horse Thief
Wa-cri-cha, the Liberal
Ta-lais, the Going Deer
Chonta-sa-bais, the Black Dog
Wa-clum-pi-chais, the Mad Warrior
Mi-ta-ni-ga, the Crazy Blanket
Hec-ra-ti, the War Eagle
Tan-wan-ga-hais, the Townmaker
Ha-ha-ga-la, the One They Cry For
Chongais-han-ga, the Learned Dog
Man-pa-cha, the Brave Man
Joseph Staidegais, the Tall Joseph
Tais-ha-wa-gra-kim, the Chief Bearer
Sa-wa-the, the Dreadful
Ca-wa-wa-gu, the One Who Gives Horses
U-de-gais-ta-wa-ta-ni-ga, the Crazy Osage[1]

Appendix B

Racing Steamboats James H. Lucas and Polar Star

The energy transition of the steamboat using wood as motive power brought about the need for speed and the joy of winning in a race on the frontier waters. This is the story of a race run in 1858 on the Missouri River, one of the golden years of steam boating, as relayed in Jackson County, Missouri's 1881 history:

The fastest of these [boats] was the *James H. Lucas*, which held the record for the quickest time from St. Louis to St. Joseph. In the early fifties the *Polar Star*, with a bow like a knife, and paddle wheels low set in the water, engines quick in stroke and powerful, a load well bestowed so that the stern sat low, and the bow raised like a bird just starting in flight, had made a phenomenal run from St. Louis to St. Joseph.

So delighted were her St. Louis owners that they had old Jim Bridger, the famous scout, trapper, guide and explorer, to secure for them the finest pair of elk horns to be found in the upper Missouri valley. Bridger delivered the horns and there was a great blow out when these were presented to the proud captain of the *Polar Star*. Tacked on to the horns was a sterling silver tablet, upon which was engraved the record of the *Star's* run, and following that, this couplet:

> The fleetest elk hath shed them from his brow;
> Fit emblem, *Polar Star*, to deck thy prow.

About this time the *James H. Lucas* came into commission and its captain, having in one or two runs arrived at the conclusion that his boat had some speed, made up his mind to try and win those horns. Abiding his time until the stage of water was just right he carefully adjusted his up-stream cargo—for upon a proper loading a boat largely depended its ease of motion—he stored his lower decks with much rich pine, several barrels of rosin, a few tons of fat pork, and started forth.

The swift strokes of the buckets churned the river into foam while the shapely bow cut and turned the water like a plowshare. The *Lucas* made the same stops the *Star* had made and remained as long at each landing. When she pulled in at Kansas City she had gained a little on the *Star's* time, but not enough for safety, so the stokers chucked in more rosin and pork and the black smoke curling in a dense cloud from her lofty funnels told of the lively work going on down below.

As the boat left Atchison the captain took his stand in front of the pilothouse and holding his chronometer in his hand kept the time while he closely watched the river on ahead. Soon the siren signaled St. Joseph, and the captain turned to receive the congratulations of his officers and passengers. He had beaten the *Star's* time, as I remember, by about three hours and 16 minutes. The master of the *Star* was game, and as soon as his successful rival returned to St. Louis the horns were transferred to the hurricane deck of the *Lucas*, which held them as long as it ploughed the muddy waters of the "old Mizzo." (Hickman, 199-201)

349

Appendix C

Duties of Master of the Levee

This description of the master of the levee drawn up by the Town of Kanzas city council in the 1850s indicated how much responsibility he had for the half dozen large boats a day and dozens of smaller, "tramp" boats, cannel coal, wood and keelboats that landed at the limestone pier. Busy as the master of the levee was by this description, the arrival of the railroad trains and the opening of the railroad station on the West Bottoms dwarfed his efforts. The number of trains arriving and departing increased to 200 or more a day by the 1880s. The increase in complexity had as much to do with the efficiencies brought on by greater use of fuel, forced *Systems Organization* built on previous models of steam boating, and the demand for service brought on by sheer numbers of people and vehicles as central to the widening circle of transportation, mail and hotels to be handled daily.

The levee master had the following duties:

To direct the landing and stationing of all water craft arriving or lying at any point on the river bank within the City, and the discharge and removal, and lading of their cargo, so as to prevent interference between different vessels and their repairs on the river bank, so that they shall occupy as little space and cause as little inconvenience as possible; to see that all combustible materials on the river bank are sufficiently protected from fire; to keep the wharf and river along the shore free from all improper obstructions; to keep in repair the ring bolts and posts provided for fastening boats and to vessels; to regulate and control, by proper rules to be established and published, all vehicles traversing the wharf; and to remove thence such as unnecessarily obstruct free passage upon the wharf or street, and generally to exercise complete supervision and control over the wharf, river bank, landing and Front street. (Whitney, I:141)

Appendix D

Care of Coal

Coal was deceptively tricky to keep and burn. It required understanding and respect or the fire would not catch hold. The following instructions were generated to help users understand their coal pile better and to get more from it:

Coal should be stored in small quantities as near to the point of consumption as possible, says a recent statement of the Bureau of Mines about stocking coal in piles. Small coal piles rarely ignite from spontaneous combustion. Coal should be stored near the point of use to avoid rehandling, extra transportation and the degradation of size which follows each rehandling. For these reasons the bureau would advocate storage, so far as possible, in the bins and yards of the ultimate consumer, thus dividing the risk of loss from spontaneous combustion. If large storage piles are necessary, certain general principles must be borne in mind. The generation of heat is the result of slow oxidation of the coal surface. The oxidation is much more rapid from freshly mined coal or from freshly broken surfaces. The oxidation rate increases rapidly with increased temperature. Different coals have different oxidizing rates. These facts led to the following recommendations:

Where there is choice of coal to be stored, that having the lowest oxidizing rate should be chosen, if known.

Between two coals, that which is least friable, and therefore which presents the least total coal surface in the pile, should be selected.

The method of handling should be such as to produce the least freshly broken coal surface.

The coal should be as cool as possible when piled. Piling warm coal on a hot day is more likely to produce spontaneous combustion.

The coal must be kept from any extraneous source of heat.

Alternative wetting and drying of coal during piling is to be avoided if possible.

The fine coal, or slack, which furnishes the larger coal surface in the pile, is the part from which spontaneous combustion is to be expected. Piling of lump coal where possible is therefore desirable.

Fueling Change

In the process of handling, if the lump coal can be stored and the fine coal removed and used immediately, the practice prevents spontaneous combustion in coals which would have otherwise given trouble.

The Sulphur content of coal is believed by many to play an important role in spontaneous combustion. The evidence on this point is still conflicting, but to play safe it is desirable to choose coal having a lower Sulphur content, when choice is possible.

There is a current belief that dissimilar coals stored in one pile are more liable to spontaneous combustion. The evidence on this point is also conflicting, but, to play safe, it is advisable to store only one kind of coal in a pile.

The ground on which a coal pile is built should be dry.

The foregoing recommendations are all derived from the factors affecting the heating of coal.

--*Coal Age,* March 30, 1918, 585.

Appendix E

Care of the Mule

Years went by and still mule care was a concern in the pages of *Coal Age*. A series of instructions was offered in 1917 as a definitive look at mule treatment. "Humane Treatment for the Mule" leaves no harness unexamined. These mules were animate units of energy employed to do the work that men could or would prefer not to do with greater efficiency. It is difficult to think of mules in an industrial setting, but the roots of the Coal Age grew from the Wood Age and carried forward with it certain components of that era until ultimately replaced by inanimate labor:

It seems to me that the mule doesn't receive the proper sort of treatment when he is being broken in for work in the mines, and it has occurred to me that the following "Don'ts" may prove of help to those who are responsible for the care of these animals. A strict compliance with the few warnings set forth below will result in more efficiency from "green" mules.

Fueling Change

Don't take a mule into a mine for the first time and set him to work on a steep grade hauling car that would require the best effort of a practiced animal to draw out.

Don't delegate the work of breaking in a new mule to an extra driver or some mine worker who has never had any experience in driving mules.

Don't let the mule be harnessed by one who doesn't know whether the harness fits or not, or whether the hames (pieces of the harness attached to the collar) are adjusted to throw the draft in the right position on the shoulder.

Don't fix the trail chain so that the weight pulls down on the animal's rump or adjust his collar so that it pinches the top of his neck.

Don't take a mule into a heading where the smoke is so thick you cannot see.

Don't walk alongside a mule while he is drawing a car and belabor him at every step he takes.

Don't put the halter chain around the animal's jaw and stand in front of him and pull on it, while a helper whips him with a belt or a club. *(Is it the position of the handler or the beating of the mule that is in question here?)*

If a mule is balky, have the stable boss adjust his harness and let the mule haul something outside, such as drag rails, or let him haul empties for a few days. It is also a good plan to put a "green" mule in a strong team with an animal that understands the work and let the two mules do the work of one until the new mule becomes accustomed to the work.

A mule lasted from five to ten years in a mine, "some mines use them up faster than this because of specially [sic.] hard and adverse working conditions." The mule, better than the horse, was well suited to this work and displayed "an almost human sagacity in getting about the mine and avoiding the many dangers incident to his precarious life, such as being run down by trips of loaded cats, etc." They responded well to kind treatment, as the article above suggests, but could sulk and become vicious when abused.

--*Coal Age,* September 22, 1917, 451.

Appendix F

Fuel Savings from Lawrence, Kansas, to Kansas City, Missouri Commute

These trips were recorded by participants in the 2017 Green Commute Challenge, sponsored by the Mid-America Regional Council *RideshareKC* program. These participants became conscious users of gasoline, the first step toward reducing its use.

Commute Mode	Entries #	Distance Miles	Money Saved	Money Spent	Calories Burned Cal	Fuel Saved Gal	Fuel Burned Gal	GHG Saved Lbs	GHG Produced Lbs
Drove a carpool	4,388	81,211	$10,543	$8,686		2,087	1,712	41,101	33,708
Passenger in a carpool	4,851	80,584	$10,685	$8,394		2,101	1,668	41,374	32,848
Drove a vanpool	435	9,108	$1,431	$726		276	151	5,427	2,964
Passenger in a vanpool	870	16,118	$2,633	$1,185		505	249	9,943	4,906
Transit - Bus	15,809	177,538	$42,046			8,303		163,534	
Bicycle	5,759	25,647	$6,071		1,361,928	1,199		23,618	
Walking, jogging	12,672	12,701	$3,006		1,534,657	594		11,695	
Telework (work from home)	5,449	111,661	$26,433			5,222		102,847	
Transit - Rail	1,419	4,986	$1,181			233		4,597	
Day Off - Compressed Work Week	627	7,775	$1,841			364		7,161	
Total	52,279	527,329	$105,869	$18,990	2,896,585	20,883	3,779	411,295	74,427

The first column, "entries" means the number of trips recorded by individuals that **replaced** commuting, business, and personal trips they *would* have taken by car. Or, in the case of telecommute, or a compressed work week, trips that were eliminated altogether.

Fueling Change

These stats only reflect commute and business trips, not personal trips such as shopping or errands, which are also captured in this data.

These trips were recorded by participants in the 2017 Green Commute Challenge, sponsored by the Mid-America Regional Council *RideshareKC* program.

There were 681 participants who recorded their trips from June 1-August 31, 2017. This is a somewhat subjective measurement because participants are self-reporting. But, it does give a snapshot of the collective impact that even a small number of people can make.

Below are stats about one, regular carpooler capturing one individual's experience.

Profile of a Power 'Pooler'

Name:	A.R.
Home:	Lawrence, Kansas
Work:	Garment District, Kansas City, Missouri
Daily commute:	76 miles round trip

Estimated savings over **12 years of carpooling**:

- **1,368** hours behind the wheel
- **5,268** gallons of gas
- **$26,400** in driving costs
- **103,512** lbs. of pollutants

Appendix G

Green New Deal, 2019

RESOLUTION
Introduced in House February 7, 2019
by Ms. Ocasio-Cortez, et al.[2]

Recognizing the duty of the Federal Government to create a Green New Deal.

Whereas the October 2018 report entitled "Special Report on Global Warming of 1.5° C" by the Intergovernmental Panel on Climate Change and the November 2018 Fourth National Climate Assessment report found that—

(1) human activity is the dominant cause of observed climate change over the past century;

(2) a changing climate is causing sea levels to rise and an increase in wildfires, severe storms, droughts, and other extreme weather events that threaten human life, healthy communities, and critical infrastructure;

(3) global warming at or above 2 degrees Celsius beyond preindustrialized levels will   cause—
   (A) mass migration from the regions most affected by climate change;
   (B) more than $500,000,000,000 in lost annual economic output in the United States by the year 2100;
   (C) wildfires that, by 2050, will annually burn at least twice as much forest area in the western United States than was typically burned by wildfires in the years preceding 2019;
   (D) a loss of more than 99 percent of all coral reefs on Earth;
   (E) more than 350,000,000 more people to be exposed globally to deadly heat stress by 2050; and
   (F) a risk of damage to $1,000,000,000,000 of public infrastructure and coastal real estate in the United States; and

(4) global temperatures must be kept below 1.5 degrees Celsius above preindustrialized levels to avoid the most severe impacts of a changing climate, which will require—
   (A) global reductions in greenhouse gas emissions from human sources of 40 to 60 percent from 2010 levels by 2030; and
   (B) net-zero global emissions by 2050;

Fueling Change

Whereas, because the United States has historically been responsible for a disproportionate amount of greenhouse gas emissions, having emitted 20 percent of global greenhouse gas emissions through 2014, and has a high technological capacity, the United States must take a leading role in reducing emissions through economic transformation;

Whereas the United States is currently experiencing several related crises, with—

(1) life expectancy declining while basic needs, such as clean air, clean water, healthy food, and adequate health care, housing, transportation, and education, are inaccessible to a significant portion of the United States population;
(2) a 4-decade trend of wage stagnation, deindustrialization, and antilabor policies that has led to—
  (A) hourly wages overall stagnating since the 1970s despite increased worker productivity;
  (B) the third-worst level of socioeconomic mobility in the developed world before the Great Recession;
  (C) the erosion of the earning and bargaining power of workers in the United States; and
  (D) inadequate resources for public sector workers to confront the challenges of climate change at local, State, and Federal levels; and
(3) the greatest income inequality since the 1920s, with—
  (A) the top 1 percent of earners accruing 91 percent of gains in the first few years of economic recovery after the Great Recession;
  (B) a large racial wealth divide amounting to a difference of 20 times more wealth between the average white family and the average black family; and
  (C) a gender earnings gap that results in women earning approximately 80 percent as much as men, at the median;

Whereas climate change, pollution, and environmental destruction have exacerbated systemic racial, regional, social, environmental, and economic injustices (referred to in this preamble as "systemic injustices") by disproportionately affecting indigenous peoples, communities of color, migrant communities, deindustrialized communities, depopulated rural communities, the poor, low-income workers, women, the elderly, the unhoused, people with disabilities, and youth (referred to in this preamble as "frontline and vulnerable communities");

Whereas, climate change constitutes a direct threat to the national security of the United States—

(1) by impacting the economic, environmental, and social stability of countries and communities around the world; and
(2) by acting as a threat multiplier;

Whereas the Federal Government-led mobilizations during World War II and the New Deal created the greatest middle class that the United States has ever seen, but many members of frontline and vulnerable communities were excluded from many of the economic and societal benefits of those mobilizations; and

Whereas the House of Representatives recognizes that a new national, social, industrial, and economic mobilization on a scale not seen since World War II and the New Deal era is a historic opportunity—

(1) to create millions of good, high-wage jobs in the United States;

(2) to provide unprecedented levels of prosperity and economic security for all people of the United States; and

(3) to counteract systemic injustices: Now, therefore, be it

Resolved, **That it is the sense of the House of Representatives that—**

(1) **it is the duty of the Federal Government to create a Green New Deal—**
   (A) to achieve net-zero greenhouse gas emissions through a fair and just transition for all communities and workers;
   (B) to create millions of good, high-wage jobs and ensure prosperity and economic security for all people of the United States;
   (C) to invest in the infrastructure and industry of the United States to sustainably meet the challenges of the 21st century;
   (D) to secure for all people of the United States for generations to come—
      (i)   clean air and water;
      (ii) climate and community resiliency;
      (iii) healthy food;
      (iv) access to nature; and
      (v)   a sustainable environment; and
   (E) to promote justice and equity by stopping current, preventing future, and repairing historic oppression of indigenous peoples, communities of color, migrant communities, deindustrialized communities, depopulated rural communities, the poor, low-income workers, women, the elderly, the unhoused, people with disabilities, and youth (referred to in this resolution as "frontline and vulnerable communities");

(2) the goals described in subparagraphs (A) through (E) of paragraph (1) (referred to in this resolution as the "Green New Deal goals") should be accomplished through **a 10-year national mobilization** (referred to in this resolution as the "Green New Deal mobilization") that will require the following goals and projects—

(A) building resiliency against climate change-related disasters, such as extreme weather, including by leveraging funding and providing investments for community-defined projects and strategies;

(B) repairing and upgrading the infrastructure in the United States, including—

    (i) **by eliminating pollution and greenhouse gas emissions as much as technologically feasible;**

    (ii) by guaranteeing universal access to clean water;

    (iii) by reducing the risks posed by climate impacts; and

    (iv) by ensuring that any infrastructure bill considered by Congress addresses climate change;

(C) **meeting 100 percent of the power demand in the United States through clean, renewable, and zero-emission energy sources, including—**

    (i) by dramatically expanding and upgrading renewable power sources; and

    (ii) by deploying new capacity;

(D) building or upgrading to energy-efficient, distributed, and "smart" power grids, and ensuring affordable access to electricity;

(E) upgrading all existing buildings in the United States and building new buildings to achieve maximum energy efficiency, water efficiency, safety, affordability, comfort, and durability, including through electrification;

(F) spurring massive growth in clean manufacturing in the United States and removing pollution and greenhouse gas emissions from manufacturing and industry as much as is technologically feasible, including by expanding renewable energy manufacturing and investing in existing manufacturing and industry;

(G) working collaboratively with farmers and ranchers in the United States to remove pollution and greenhouse gas emissions from the agricultural sector as much as is technologically feasible, including—

    (i) by supporting family farming;

    (ii) by investing in sustainable farming and land use practices that increase soil health; and

    (iii) by building a more sustainable food system that ensures universal access to healthy food;

(H) **overhauling transportation systems in the United States to remove pollution and greenhouse gas emissions from the transportation sector as much as is technologically feasible, including through investment in—**

    (i) zero-emission vehicle infrastructure and manufacturing;

    (ii) clean, affordable, and accessible public transit; and

    (iii) high-speed rail;

(I) mitigating and managing the long-term adverse health, economic, and other effects of pollution and climate change, including by providing funding for community-defined projects and strategies;

(J) removing greenhouse gases from the atmosphere and reducing pollution by restoring natural ecosystems through proven low-tech solutions that increase soil carbon storage, such as land preservation and afforestation;

(K) restoring and protecting threatened, endangered, and fragile ecosystems through locally appropriate and science-based projects that enhance biodiversity and support climate resiliency;

(L) cleaning up existing hazardous waste and abandoned sites, ensuring economic development and sustainability on those sites;

(M) identifying other emission and pollution sources and creating solutions to remove them; and

(N) promoting the international exchange of technology, expertise, products, funding, and services, with the aim of making the United States the international leader on climate action, and to help other countries achieve a Green New Deal;

(3) a Green New Deal must be developed through transparent and inclusive consultation, collaboration, and partnership with frontline and vulnerable communities, labor unions, worker cooperatives, civil society groups, academia, and businesses; and

(4) to achieve the Green New Deal goals and mobilization, a Green New Deal will require the following **goals and projects**—

(A) providing and leveraging, in a way that ensures that the public receives appropriate ownership stakes and returns on investment, adequate capital (including through community grants, public banks, and other public financing), technical expertise, supporting policies, and other forms of assistance to communities, organizations, Federal, State, and local government agencies, and businesses working on the Green New Deal mobilization;

(B) ensuring that the Federal Government takes into account the complete environmental and social costs and impacts of emissions through—

(i) existing laws;

(ii) new policies and programs; and

(iii) ensuring that frontline and vulnerable communities shall not be adversely affected;

(C) providing resources, training, and high-quality education, including higher education, to all people of the United States, with a focus on frontline and vulnerable communities, so that all people of the United States may be full and equal participants in the Green New Deal mobilization;

(D) making public investments in the research and development of new clean and renewable energy technologies and industries;

(E) directing investments to spur economic development, deepen and diversify industry and business in local and regional economies, and build wealth and community ownership, while prioritizing high-quality job creation and economic, social, and environmental benefits in frontline and vulnerable communities, and deindustrialized communities, that may otherwise struggle with the transition away from greenhouse gas intensive industries;

(F) ensuring the use of democratic and participatory processes that are inclusive of and led by frontline and vulnerable communities and workers to plan, implement, and administer the Green New Deal mobilization at the local level;

(G) ensuring that the Green New Deal mobilization creates high-quality union jobs that pay prevailing wages, hires local workers, offers training and advancement opportunities, and guarantees wage and benefit parity for workers affected by the transition;

(H) guaranteeing a job with a family-sustaining wage, adequate family and medical leave, paid vacations, and retirement security to all people of the United States;

(I) strengthening and protecting the right of all workers to organize, unionize, and collectively bargain free of coercion, intimidation, and harassment;

(J) strengthening and enforcing labor, workplace health and safety, antidiscrimination, and wage and hour standards across all employers, industries, and sectors;

(K) enacting and enforcing trade rules, procurement standards, and border adjustments with strong labor and environmental protections—
  (i) to stop the transfer of jobs and pollution overseas; and
  (ii) to grow domestic manufacturing in the United States;

(L) ensuring that public lands, waters, and oceans are protected and that eminent domain is not abused;

(M) obtaining the free, prior, and informed consent of indigenous peoples for all decisions that affect indigenous peoples and their traditional territories, honoring all treaties and agreements with indigenous peoples, and protecting and enforcing the sovereignty and land rights of indigenous peoples;

(N) ensuring a commercial environment where every businessperson is free from unfair competition and domination by domestic or international monopolies; and

(O) providing all people of the United States with—
  (i) high-quality health care;
  (ii) affordable, safe, and adequate housing;
  (iii) economic security; and
  (iv) clean water, clean air, healthy and affordable food, and access to nature.

Notes

Part 1

[1] Fred Cottrell, *Energy and Society: The Relation Between Energy, Social Change, and Economic Development* (Westport, CT: Greenwood Press, Publishers, 1955) vii. The 1607 date for the beginning of this period was a difficult choice. 1607 represents the founding of Jamestown as the date from which to mark the beginning of white settlement in what is now the continental United States.

Chapter 1

[1] Original survey maps of Jackson County, MO, 1818-1843 (containing detailed analyses of natural resources and political boundary surveys relating to the early settlement of the county). Jackson County (MO) Historical Society Archives. Unpublished atlas.

[2] Terry P. Wilson, *The Underground Reservation: The Osage and Oil* (Lincoln: University of Nebraska Press, 1985). Rolf Sieferle, *The Subterranean Forest: Energy Systems and the Industrial Revolution* (Cambridge, UK: White Horse Press, English trans. 2001).

[3] "Pre-commercial" is a term borrowed from Arthur Bright in his classic work, *The Electric Lamp Industry: Technological Change and Economic Development from 1800-1947* (New York: MacMillan, 1949). He divides the development of the electric light between pre-commercial and early commercial.

[4] Energy historian Earl Cook calls these two levels "primitive agricultural man" and "advanced agricultural man," "The Flow of Energy in an Industrial Society," *Scientific American* (Volume 225, Number 0, September 1971), 136.

[5] Gary E. Moulton, ed., *The Definitive Journals of Lewis & Clark from the Ohio to the Vermillion, Volume 2 of the Nebraska Edition* (Lincoln: University of Nebraska Press, 1986), 321.

[6] William Z. Hickman, *History of Jackson County, MO* (Topeka: Historical Publishing Company, 1920), 96.

[7] Hickman, 96-97. All the authors who write on early Kansas City mention the limestone pier that would entice steamboat traffic to move from Independence west to be closer to the river bend. The limestone pier represented a natural hard footing for loading and unloading instead of a river bank that could become a sea of mud in the winter and hard pan in the summer.

[8] Moulton, Volume 2, 320.

[9] Garrick Alan Bailey, *Changes in Osage Social Organization 1673-1906* (University of Oregon Anthropological Papers, No 5, 1973), 109. Dory De Angelo, *What About Kansas City! A Historical Handbook* (Kansas City: Two Lane Press, 1995), 10. Kristie C. Wolferman, *The Osage in Missouri* (Columbia: University of Missouri Press, 1997), 19, John Joseph Mathews, *The Osages: Children of the Middle Waters* (Norman: University of Oklahoma Press, 1961), 46. Louis F. Burns, *A History of the Osage People* (Tuscaloosa: University of Alabama Press, 2004), 243, says their population was highest in 1680 at 17,000. Kansas City evolved from its predecessor, the Town of Kansas, sometimes written Kanza, derived from another Native American population immediately to the west.

[10] Thomas R. Vale. *Fire, Native Peoples, and the Natural Landscape* (Washington, D. C: Island Press, 2002), 17. These figures are an estimate of the population at time of conquest. Boone's story of traveling alone for two months is in Hickman, 251. Paul H. Carlson, *The Plains Indians* (College Station: Texas A & M University Press, 1998), 11, sets the population of the Osage in 1780 as 6,200.

[11] In regard to beliefs of bravery see Kristie C. Wolferman, *The Osage in Missouri* (Columbia: University of Missouri Press, 1997), 16; for bluff war, see Burns, 32.

[12] Wilson (1985), 2.

[13] Ibid., 2-3.

[14] *James Mooney's History, Myths, and Sacred Formulas of the Cherokees* (Asheville, NC: Historical Images, 1992). This expression is used in the National Museum of the American Indian exhibit on the Cherokee in Washington, D.C.

[15] "Missouri at the time was considered the western confines of civilization, and it was believed then that there never would be in the future any white settlements of civilized people existing between the western borders of Missouri and the Pacific Coast, unless it might be the strip between the Sierra Nevada Mountains and the Pacific Ocean, which the people at that time knew but little or nothing about." Speaking of the early decades of the 19th century was Alexander Majors, *Seventy Years on the Frontier: Lifetime on the Border* (Minneapolis: Ross & Haines, Inc., 1965), 30.

[16] Alfred D. Chandler, Jr., "Anthracite Coal and the Beginning of the Industrial Revolution in the United States, *Business History Review* (Summer, 1972, 46), 146. Chandler quotes historian Samuel Batchelder that in machinery "metals were used only where friction was constant, where a cutting edge was needed, or to strengthen areas of stress." Otherwise, the machinery was made of wood with leather belting tied to waterwheels for power.

[17] Mathews (1961), 95.

[18] George C. Sibley, "Indian Mode of Life in Missouri and Kansas," *Missouri Historical Review* (No. 2, January 1910), 44-45. The estimates of Osage numbers vary from author to author with no definitive numbers. Sibley's are probably as accurate as any, lewisandclarktrail.com/section1/mocities/kansascity/fortosage/index.htm, accessed 29 Dec 2008.

[19] Paul Wilhelm, Duke of Wurttemberg, *Travels in North America, 1822-24* (Norman: University of Oklahoma, 1973) "found a four-foot catfish, *Pimelodus catus*, on my set hook" one morning, 275. Many accounts of the passenger pigeon have been written: See. A. W. Schorger, *The Passenger Pigeon* (Madison, University of Wisconsin Press, 1961), E. Fuller, *Extinct Birds* (New York: Facts on File Publications, 1987). The Passenger Pigeon, perhaps the only species for which an exact time of extinction is known—"Martha," the last pigeon died in the Cincinnati Zoo, September 1, 1914--made its home in primary forest that once covered North America east of the Rocky Mountains. Their flocks, a mile wide and up to 300 miles long, were so dense that they darkened the sky for hours and days as the flock passed overhead. When they roosted on trees, their weight often broke down branches. Population estimates from the 19th century ranged from 1 billion to close to 4 billion individual birds. Total populations may have reached 5 billion and comprised up to 40% of the total number of birds in North America. They may have been the most populous species of bird on the planet at one time, 2. "Martha, Passenger Pigeon, Roadside Pet Cemetery," roadsideamerica.com/pet/martha.html, accessed 29 Dec 2008.

[20] James Williams, *Energy and the Making of Modern California* (Akron: Akron University, 1997), 17.

Chapter 2

[1] Burns (1984), 168-169.

[2] Carlson, 52.

[3] Burns, (1984), 168-169.

[4] Robert F. Heizer, "Domestic Fuel in Primitive Society," *The Journal of the Royal Anthropological Institute of Great Britain and Ireland,* Vol. 93, No. 2 (July-Dec. 1963), 190.

[5] Stephen J. Pyne, "Indian Fires: The fire practices of North American Indians transformed large areas from forest to grassland" *Natural History* (Vol. 92, No. 2, 1983) 6-11. William Christie McLeod, "Fuel and Early Civilization," *American Anthropologist* (N. S. Vol 27, 1925), 344-46. Paul Wilhelm, 245, 292.

[6] Wilson (1985), 47.

[7] Milton D. Rafferty, ed., *Rude Pursuits and Rugged Peaks: Schoolcraft's Ozark Journal 1818-1819* (Fayetteville: University of Arkansas Press, 1996), 79.

[8] R. V, Reynolds and Albert H. Pierson, "Lumber Cut in the United States, 1870-1920," Bulletin of the U. S. Department of Agriculture (Issue 1119, 1923), 27-35.

[9] This conclusion is more by inference than outright statement. Sufficient scholarship states that women kept cooking fires going. It seems likely that men managed the larger fires that made their hunting possible.

[10] Bailey, 43.

[11] Paul H. Carlson, *The Plains Indians* (College Station: Texas A & M University Press, 1998), 59.

[12] Francis La Flesche, "War Ceremony and Peace Ceremony of the Osage Indians," *Smithsonian Institution Bureau of American Ethnology, Bulletin 101* (Washington, D.C.: United States Printing Office: 1939), 50. Bailey, 197.

[13] Charles F. Carroll, "The Forest Society of New England," Brooke Hindle, *ed., America's Wooden Age: Aspects of its Early Technology* (Tarrytown, NY: Sleepy Hollow Press, 1976), 13.

Chapter 3

[1] Burns (2004), 306.

[2] Smil, Vaclav, *Energy in World History* (Boulder, CO: Westview Press, 1994), 66. An ox is a castrated male cow of about four years of age from any breed of cattle. Ann Norton Greene, dissertation, "Harnessing Power: Industrializing the Horse in Nineteenth Century America" (University of Pennsylvania, 2004), 70.

[3] Greene, Ibid.

[4] Josiah Gregg, *Commerce of the Prairies: Life on the Great Plains in the 1830s and 1840s* (Santa Barbara: The Narrative Press, 2001, originally published 1844), 21. See also R. Douglas Hurt's treatment of mules and mule breeding in Missouri in *Agriculture and Slavery in Little Dixie* (Columbia; University of Missouri Press, 1992), 140-151.

[5] See Hampton Sides, *Blood and Thunder: An Epic of the American West* (New York: Doubleday, 2006) for a detailed description of the activity along the southern border. Alexander Majors, 105. John Joseph Mathews, (1961), writes that the Osage got their horses from the Kiowa before the end of the 17th century, 127. Burns (2004), 95.

[6] Frank Norall, *Bourgmont: Explorer of the Missouri, 1698-1725* (Lincoln: University of Nebraska Press, 1988), 157-8. Osage author John Mathews estimates that the Osage had horses by 1682, the year they all came under the protection of Louis XIV. Mathews (1961), 126.

[7] thefurtrapper.com/david_thompson.htm#Horses, accessedc15 Jan 2009. Mathews (1961), 129. The most thorough treatment of the Indian horse culture may be found in Pekka Hamalainen, "The Rise and Fall of Plains Indian Horse Cultures," *Journal of American History* (December 2003), 833-862. He covers the intricacies of gains and losses from the horse culture, particularly climatic and environmental conditions such as wintering horses on the northern plains as well as exchange of woodlands for grasslands, increasing incursions into other tribes' territories, raids and wars, creating caste systems and overhunting of buffalo for trade by virtue of being mounted that led to loss of food source.

[8] Alan M. Klein, "Political Economy of the Buffalo Hide Trade: Race and Class on the Plains," *The Political Economy of the North American Indian,* John H. Moore, ed., (Norman: University of Oklahoma Press, 1993), 141.

[9] Carlson, 52-53.

[10] Carlson, 56-57.

[11] Mathews (1961), 128. Terry Wilson says that the French gave the Osage both guns and horses. Wilson, (1985), 2.

Chapter 4

[1] John Bradbury, *Travels in the Interior of America* (Originally published in Liverpool, 1817; Readex Microprint, 1966), 42.

[2] John Bradbury quotes George Sibley, the factor of Fort Osage, as saying that he came upon an Osage camp on the Arkansas River. They had "killed 200 buffalo within a few days." Ibid., 184. He footnotes that in the fall the buffalo have acquired a good deal of fat on their bodies after a summer of grazing and use it to see them through the hard winters, 178. In regard to garden plots and crops see Bailey (1973), 26. Burns (2004), 211.

[3] Mathews (1961), 29. Large fatty animals were favored as targets for hunting over smaller ones. A buffalo could take the place of twenty deer, and the fat was as desirable as the meat.

[4] Buffalo kill, see Carlson, 56. For other food and cooking details see Linda Murray Berzok, *American Indian Food* (Westport: Greenwood Press, 2005), 26, 48, 57-76. Wolferman, 14-15.

[5] Ibid.

[6] Rafferty, Ibid.

Chapter 5

[1] Burns (2004), 488.

[2] Ibid., 493.

[3] Mathews (1961), 341. Burns (2004), 488.

[4] Mathews, (1961), variously calls them half faces and heavy eyebrows, 98.

[5] "Treaties with the Osage," See nanations.com/osage, accessed 15 Jan 2009; for a list of ten Osage Treaties with the federal government.

[6] Wilson, 6.

[7] Wilson, 7. Burns, (2004), 153.

[8] Mathews (1961), 306-7."

[9] Burns (2004),153-156. Bailey, (1973), 53-54.

[10] Burns, (2004), Ibid.,159-60.

[11] Mike Wimmer, *Osage Treaty of 1825*, oklaosf.state.ok.us/~arts/capitolart/permart/paintings/wimmer/osage.html, accessed 15 Jan 2009.

[12] Jedediah Morse, *A Report to the Secretary of War of the United States* (New York: Augustus M. Kelley, 1970, originally published 1822) 206-7.

[13] Christian, 353-354.

[14] "Indian Removal Act spurred intertribal warfare in Kansas," ljworld.com/news/2004/aug/15/indian_removal_act/, accessed 15 Jan 2009.

[15] Cronon, 107.

[16] Richard White, *The Roots of Dependency: Subsistence, Environment, and Social Change among the Choctaws, Pawnees, and Navajos* (Lincoln: University of Nebraska Press, 1983), xix.

Chapter 6

[1] Whitney, Vol. 1, 35.

[2] A. Theodore Brown and Lyle W. Dorsett, *K.C. A History of Kansas City, Missouri* (Boulder, CO: Pruett Publishing Company, 1978), 10.

[3] Perry McCandless, *A History of Missouri: 1820 to 1860* (Columbia: University Press, 2000), 7.

[4] Ibid. 3.

[5] Simon Schama, *Rough Crossings: Britain, the Slaves and the American Revolution* (London: Ecco: 2006), 14.

[6] Harriet C. Frazier, *Slavery and Crime in Missouri*, 1773-1865 (Jefferson, NC: McFarland, 2001), 82.

[7] See Hurt for an in-depth explication of this area.

[8] Jackson, David W. *Winding the Clock on the Independence Square: Jackson County's Historic Truman Courthouse*. (Independence, MO: Jackson County Historical Society, 2013), 11-14. Also, Jackson, David W. *Kansas City Chronicles: An Up-to-Date History*. (Charleston, SC: The History Press, 2010), 23-25.

[9] Salt mines in Pennsylvania at the same time were using coal for fuel. Horse power was soon replaced by steam engines to pump brine from the wells and coal boiled off the residue by the 1830s. Carmen Di Cicchio, *Coal and Coke in Pennsylvania* (Harrisburg, PA: Pennsylvania Historical and Museum Commission, 1996), 22.

[10] Hickman, 235-7. R. V. Reynolds, Albert H. Pierson, "Fuel Wood Used in the United States, 1630-1930" (Washington, D.C., Circular No. 641, January 1942), 1.

[11] Jackson County Missouri, Censuses of 1830, abstracted by Hattie E. Poppino (Kansas City: 1959), State

Historical Society of Missouri-Kansas City Research Center, University of Missouri-Kansas City; hereinafter SHSMO-UMKC.

[12] N. M. Harris, "An Old-fashioned Wedding in the Oldest House in Kansas City," *Kansas City Star*, February 24, 1907. State Historical Society of Missouri-Kansas City Research Center, University of Missouri-Kansas City.

[13] Ibid.

[14] Jackson County Missouri, Censuses of 1830, 1840, 1850 and 1860, abstracted by Hattie E. Poppino (Kansas City: 1959), State Historical Society of Missouri-Kansas City Research Center, University of Missouri-Kansas City.

[15] Poppino, Censuses of 1850 and 1860.

[16] Lyle Wesley Dorsett, "Slaveholding in Jackson County, MO," March 1962, p.19, State Historical Society of Missouri-Kansas City Research Center, University of Missouri-Kansas City.

[17] Dorsett, 22. Another testimony to this practice: "During the Civil War my grandfather Swinney sent fifty Negroes to Texas in the care of a responsible white man, so that in case the South won the war, they would be saved for him." Berenice Morrison-Fuller, "Glimpses of the Past, Missouri Plantation Life," *Missouri Historical Society* (Volume IV, January-March, No. 1-3, St. Louis, 1937), 32.

[18] Burns (2004), 34.

[19] For slaves traded see Bailey, 1973, 34; Fowler 23-4, 183-4; Burns, (2004), 34, 98.

Chapter 7

[1] Moulton, 325, 327.

[2] Hickman, 96; Norall, 23, 82-85.

[3] Everett Dick, *Vanguards of the Frontier: A Social History of the Northern Plains and Rocky Mountains from the Earliest White Contacts to the Coming of the Homemaker* (New York: Appleton-Century, 1941), 156.

[4] Dick, 156.

[5] Leland D. Baldwin, *The Keelboat Age on the Western Waters* (Pittsburgh: University Press, 1941), 40.

[6] Bradbury, 139.

[7] Baldwin, 5.

[8] Dick, 159. Baldwin, 41.

[9] Baldwin, 4.

[10] Michael Allen, *Western Rivermen, 1763-1861: Ohio and Mississippi Boatmen and the Myth of the Alligator Horse* (Baton Rouge: Louisiana State University Press, 1990), 27-34. Pittsburgh began burning coal in 1795 to make glass and iron. It was "located at the head of water navigation in the West." Richard C. Wade, *The Urban Frontier: The Rise of Western Cities, 1790-1930* (Chicago: University of Illinois Press, 1959), 48.

[11] Ted Morgan, *A Shovel of Stars: The Making of the American West, 1800 to the Present* (New York: Simon & Schuster, 1995), 33. Moulton, 318-319.

[12] Wilhelm, 278.

[13] Dick, 163.

[14] Moulton, 318-319.

[15] "Trip to St. Louis from New Orleans," Conard, Howard C., ed., *Encyclopedia of Missouri*, (St. Louis: Southern History Company, 1901).

[16] Mark Twain, *Life on the Mississippi*, (New York: Viking Penguin, 1984, originally published 1883), 50.

[17] Baldwin, 46-52, Dick, 157-8.

[18] Bradbury, 198. Estimates are that from 4,000 to 7,000 flatboats carrying 40 to 75 tons each engaged in Bradbury's time frame in the New Orleans trade. Erik Haites, James Mak and Gary M. Walton, *Western River Transportation: The Era of Early Internal Development, 1810-1860* (Baltimore: Johns Hopkins Press, 1975), 22.

[19] Baldwin, 5.

[20] Christian, 352.

[21] SHSMO--KC.

[22] Allen, 360.

[23] Schurr and Netschert, 46.

[24] Ibid., 54. Thirty-three percent of work was done by wind and water as late as 1870.

[25] Smil (1994), 107.

[26] Louis C. Hunter, *Steamboats on the Western Rivers: An Economic and Technological History* (New York: Dover Publications, 1949), 41.

[27] Ibid., 38.

[28] Priscilla Ann Evans, "Merchant Gristmills and Communities 1820-1880," *Missouri Historical Review* (Columbia MO, vol. 68, April 1974), 323.

[29] Ibid.

[30] Ibid., 323. See Jeffrey Bremer, "Frontier Capitalism: The Market Revolution in the Antebellum Lower Missouri River Valley, 1803-1860" (dissertation, University of Kansas, 2006), 198. Brook Hindle, *America's Wooden Age*, p. 191. Jonas Viles, "Old Franklin: A Frontier Town of the Twenties," *The Mississippi Valley Historical Review* (Vol. IX, No. 4, March 1923), 274. Linda K. Hubaleck, *Trail of Thread: Historical Letters 1854-1855* (Aurora, CO: Butterfield Books, 1995), 7.

[31] Hunter, 40.

[32] Hurt, 8. Viles, 274.

[33] John Calvin McCoy Collection (1811-1889), KC 296, Roll 001, Vol 2, 1871-1950, Western Historical Manuscript Collection--Kansas City.

[34] Thomas R. Vickroy, "Jackson County," *Encyclopedia of Missouri*, Vol X, 407.

[35] James Williams, *Seventy-Five Years on the Border* (Kansas City: Standard Press, 1912), 48-49.

[36] Evans, 319.

[37] The corn hand mill was actually written about by a member of the Lewis and Clark expedition, Whitehouse, in which he said, "Tuesday June 11th We had a clear pleasant morning, about 8 o'clock A. M. Captain Lewis & four Men of our party, set out for the Snowey Mountain, There was put into the holes or Carsh [*erased, illegible*] Yesterday 1 keg of powder, 1 keg barr lead, 1 keg flour, 1 Keg pork, 2 Kegs parched Corn meal, the Blacksmiths bellows & tools, Augers, planes, Saw &ca—. some tin cups, a dutch Oven, a Corn and Mill, packs of beaver, bear Skins, horns of different kinds, Buffalo robes &ca. &ca—." The Gary Moulton 1987 edition of the Lewis and Clark Journals of 11 volumes, does not contain the writings of other men on the expedition, only Lewis and Clark's notes. The above reference "Corn hand Mill" can be found at libtextcenter.unl.edu/examples/servlet/transform/tamino/Library/lewisandclarkjournals?&_xmlsrc=http://libte xtcenter.unl.edu/ lewisandclark/files/xml/1805-06-11.xml&_xslsrc=http://libtextcenter.unl.edu/lewisandclark/ LCstyles.xsl, accessed 15 Jan 2009.

[38] Rafferty, 60.

[39] Rafferty, 69. G. W. Featherstonhaugh, 93.

[40] "Early Settlers," Joseph S. Chick, Native Sons Archives, Vol. II, Folder 1, 19, State Historical Society of Missouri-Kansas City Research Center, University of Missouri-Kansas City.

[41] Joseph Savage, "Recollections of 1854," territorialkansasonline.org, accessed 15 Jan 2009.

[42] William Grant, *The Romantic Past of the Kansas City Region, 1540-1880* (Kansas City, MO: Business Men's Assurance Company of America, 1987), 24. freepages.history.rootsweb.ancestry.com/~vlwest/NewSantaFe/watts.htm, accessed 15 Jan 2009.

[43] *Kansas City Journal*, February 1, 1925. State Historical Society of Missouri-Kansas City Research Center, University of Missouri-Kansas City.

Chapter 8

[1] Perlin, 281-283.

[2] Ibid, 282.

[3] Ibid., 285.

[4] Ibid., 282, 285.

[5] Ibid., 284.

[6] Howard N. Eavenson, *The First Century and a Quarter of American Coal Industry* (Pittsburgh, PA, 1942), 29. Some of the coal was provided by "privateers," i.e. pirates who confiscated a ship and sold its contents, while some came from Nova Scotia, as records show in the 1770s and 1780s. Ibid., 59.

[7] Ibid., 29.

[8] Ibid., 37. Records show vessels cleared to sail from the port of Hampton, VA, in the years beginning 1758 to New York, Philadelphia, New Providence, Rhode Island, New England, Boston, Nantucket, Salem, and Baltimore as well as more exotic ports such as St. Kitts, Bermuda, Bahama (sic), Barbados, St. Augustine, Pensacola, and Antigua to the south and the Caribbean, and Newfoundland and Nova Scotia to the north with loads of from 25 bushels to 2,200 bushels. Eavenson, 32-33, 36.

[9] Ibid., 30.

[10] Ibid., "the production of bituminous coal in Pennsylvania started a few years after that in Virginia," 446.

[11] H. Benjamin Powell, *Philadelphia's First Fuel Crisis: Jacob Cist and the Developing Market for Pennsylvania's Anthracite* (University Park: Pennsylvania State Press, 1978). Jacob's father Charles helped to promote coal use through the magazine *Columbian* he helped found in 1787, an interest to which Jacob was educated and readily took on as an adult. "Hard coal" was being used then in small amounts. The book does not mention exact date of discovery in PA, which varies from source to source from 1762 to 1790. See msha.gov/ District/Dist_01/History/history.htm, 15 Jan 2009.

[12] Eavenson, 138.

[13] Powell, 13-14.

[14] Ibid., 8-9.

[15] Ibid., 334.

[16] Burns, (1984), 10.

[17] Robert Raymond, *Out of the Fiery Furnace: The Impact of Metals on the History of Mankind* (University Park: The Pennsylvania State University Press, 1986), xv.

[18] Ibid.

[19] See Perlin's repeated treatment of this challenge from ancient Troy to London. Powell mentions transportation's effect on the cost of coal: "Since the mine was only four miles from a coal landing [on a river], the partners could conduct business at a lower cost and sell anthracite cheaper." Not only distance but season affected the shipping of coal. Arks of coal had to wait for spring waters to rise to ship coal to market. Autumn's low water presented problems and shipping on winter's ice was fraught with danger. Powell, 78-79.

[20] Ibid.

[21] Ibid., 26. In 1804 Jesse Fell invented a grate to burn anthracite in a fireplace where most fuel was burned. Stoves would come later. Powell, 18-19.

[22] Ibid., 47, 49.

[23] Harold F. Williamson and Arnold R. Daum, *The American Petroleum Industry: The Age of Illumination 1859-1899* (Evanston: Northwestern University Press, 1959), 33.

[24] See Walter R. Borneman, *1812: The War that Forged a Nation* (New York: HarperCollins, 2004) for a complete treatment of the war. One reviewer said Borneman's claim that the war forged the nation may have been exaggerated, but that otherwise the book was a fine popular rendition of the events. Other authors have also made the claim, however, and have termed it "America's second war for independence." Nevertheless, the unexpected consequence was a turn to coal and a turn westward for pioneers to migrate over the mountains and to cross the Mississippi in search of new lands for settlement. See Sean Patrick Adams, *Old Dominion: Industrial Commonwealth: Coal Politics, and Economy in Antebellum America* (Baltimore, MD: Johns Hopkins University Press, 2004). Adams treats the war of 1812 as an impetus to rising interest in coal in Pennsylvania and Virginia's decision to suppress coal in favor of tobacco.

Chapter 9

[1] Hickman, 263.

[2] Bioenergy feedback development; See bioenergy.ornl.gov/papers/misc/energy_conv.html, evworld.com/library/energy_numbers.pdf and generatorjoe.net/html/energy.html, accessed 3 Feb 2009.

Chapter 10

[1] Hindle, 10.

[2] *Native Sons of Kansas City Collection,* SHSMO—UMKC.

[3] Ibid.

[4] *Encyclopedia of Missouri*, Volume III, 404. Hickman, 243. Isaac Moffat, "The Kansas Prairie, Or Eight Days on the Plains (1858)," *Kansas Historical Quarterly*, May 1973, (Vol. VI, No. 2) 148. C. C. Spalding, *Annals of the City of Kansas* (Kansas City: Van Horn & Abeel's Printing House, 1858), 27. Whitney, Vol 1, 88.

[5] *Kansas City Journal*, October 22, 1893, Native Sons Archives, Vol. II, folder I, p. 3 SHSMO-UMKC.

[6] Ibid., 10, SHSMO-UMKC.

[7] Christian, 271, 274-6. Twain, *Life on the Mississippi*, 109.

[8] Christian, 360.

[9] Ibid. Dick, 166.

[10] Hunter, 266.

[11] See Sutcliffe's *Steam* for a full description of early racing between steamboats while still in the experimental stage. At that point racing was more to prove patent rights and simple seaworthiness and durability than to win races.

[12] Stebbens, 183.

[13] In 1819 the *City of Savannah* sailed to London with no passengers and loaded with coal. Engines had been attached to a fully fitted sailing ship that used the engines only within sight of land. uh.edu/engines/epi550.htm, accessed 20 Jan 2009.

[14] Hunter, 265.

[15] Twain, *Life on the Mississippi*,138.

[16] "Before Kansas City's Day," *Kansas City Times*, February 2, 1949.

[17] Native Sons Archives, Volume 2, 102, WHMS—UMKC.

[18] gi.alaska.edu/ScienceForum/ASF3/302.html, 20 Jan 2009.

[19] A bag of coal probably contained a bushel, roughly 76 pounds of coal. The bags made coal easy to handle to load on board quickly. An illustration showing bags of coal being filled on a loading dock is shown in Carmen Di Cicchio, *Coal and Coke in Pennsylvania* (Harrisburg, PA: Pennsylvania Historical and Museum Commission, 1996), 15.

[20] See Hunter, 268, Twain, *Life on the Mississippi,* 51, 152, 158 for more discussion on coal.

[21] Twain, *Life on the Mississippi,* 140.

[22] Ibid., 141-2.

[23] Ibid., 141-2, 198. Dick, 175. David E. Schob, "Woodhawks and Cordwood: Steamboat Fuel on the Ohio and Mississippi Rivers, 1820-1860," *Journal of American History* (July 1977), 124-133.

[24] See Twain's detailed description of this phenomenon of communication and organization in *Life on the Mississippi,* 128-137.

[25] Haites et. al. 142.

[26] Ibid., 143.

[27] Spalding, 72.

[28] Haites, 145.

[29] Ibid.

[30] Ibid., 145-6.

[31] Ibid., 147.

[32] Shurr and Netschert, 48.

[33] Wilhelm, 272.

[34] Morgan, 33. Schob, 127.

[35] Parkman, 10.

[36] George Byron Merrick, *Old Times on the Upper Mississippi: Recollections of a Steamboat Pilot from 1854 to 1863* (Minneapolis: University of Minnesota Press, 2001, originally published 1909), 59-61.

[37] James A. Tharp, "Tumbledown of Gilliss House," *Jackson County Historical Society JOURNAL* (Spring, 2004), 14-17. David W. Jackson collaborated in 2008 with the Kansas City Museum for their *Community*

Curator project. They selected the Gillis House hotel guest register for him to examine, prepare a report, and develop a presentation around.

"Kansas City lost the famous Gilliss House hotel long ago, but its foundations are recoverable in the riverfront *Town of Kansas* archaeological park, slated as one of Kansas City's future re-development attractions. The hotel faced Front Street (originally called Water Street) and stood for many years from the 1840s beyond 1911. Gilliss House Hotel was on lots 133 and the west half of 134, Block 13, a triangular block in the original Old Town of Kansas. On the 1886 atlas of Kansas City, it is shown as being in the C.G. Hopkins and W.A. Hopkins estate.

"Another relevant, preserved artifact harkens to the Gilliss House's past--a guest book that dates from Tuesday, September 7, 1869, through February 4, 1870, preserved at the Kansas City Museum.

"Known at various times as the Claiborne House, the Western, the American, the Eldridge and the Union Hotel, Gilliss House stood majestically beside the Missouri River at Westport Landing since the origin of the Town of Kansas, and through the infancy of Kansas City.

"William Gilliss, who for a number of years was its landlord, constructed the Gilliss House hotel or hostelry in 1846-47 as a two-story brick building of very modest dimensions. The fame of the cuisine and the good cheer of the bar traveled far up and down the River.

"Gillis was assisted at times in the early days of his hotel career by his future brother-in-law, Dr. Benoist Troost. After striking it rich in the California Gold Rush, Troost returned about 1852 and married Gilliss's niece. Gilliss House quickly showed the effect of Troost's newly acquired wealth after the two became partners. The hotel property was greatly enlarged. Another story was added to it and its frontage extended until it became the finest building anywhere on the river west of St. Louis.

"Gilliss House reached the zenith of its fame.

"In 1854, Mr. Eldridge leased the House. Another floor was added, and the hostelry otherwise enlarged and improved. One of the most exciting and thrilling episodes of the Border War occurred at the Gilliss House when Kansas Governor Andrew Reeder, fleeing east for his safety, hid there for 24 hours from his hot-blooded enemies, who were clamoring for his life. Reeder narrowly escaped in a creative disguise with proprietors' help.

"By 1860, Gilliss House was again undergoing renovations that included beautiful carpets and wallpapers, and new, elegant furniture for the ease and comfort guests of the Gilliss House who were passing through on their westward journey.

"Who were those guests? Turn to this fascinating guest register, which was first discovered in 1891 by Fred Hacker, a plumber, who was doing some repair work and found it in a deserted closet of the old hostelry. The register was carelessly placed in Hacker's shop at 400 Delaware (in the City Market) where it became buried beneath a clutter of pipe fittings and tools. He even took the liberty of using the register as his own personal scrapbook by pasting cancelled checks on a few pages.

"In 1912, one of Hacker's workers uncovered the guest book once again. It was donated to the Missouri Valley Historical Society and after that organization ceased operations, the book was donated to the Kansas City Museum between 1940 and 1942.

"The oversized ledger contains autographs of hotel guests from near and far. While some signatures were penned in florid, Spencerian script, others were less elegant. Just image the conversations as guests signed in. On the day this book was first opened, 64 guests registered. The following day 34 signed in. Some guests had their own rooms; up to four guests shared the same room on these first two days. With more time and attention to additional names, it is quite likely that more this guest book will yield more fascinating details."

[38] Ibid, 14.

[39] "Andrew Horatio Reeder," kshs.org/places/capitol/representatives/ reeder_andrew.htm, accessed 3 Feb 2009.

[40] Receipt book of steamboat *Columbian,* 1848-1851, Steamboats and River History Collection, Missouri Historical Society, St. Louis. No further information on this steamboat in terms of tonnage, lifespan, wages paid to the men who wrote the receipts or other interesting facts. Only the receipt book remains but nevertheless tells an interesting story of daily fuel gathering that is impossible to construct otherwise.

[41] Twain, *Life on the Mississippi*, 101.

[42] The bushel was adopted because it was a measurement with which everyone was familiar. The weight of a bushel varied from mine to mine from 72 pounds to 90 pounds, though by the writing of this book in 1939 it was still unsettled and varied from 89 pounds in Kentucky, Illinois and Missouri to 76 pounds in Pennsylvania and Montana, and 70 lbs. in Indiana. Howard N. Eavenson, *The First Century and a Quarter of American Coal Industry* (Baltimore: Waverly Press, 1942.), 11. Government oversight began in Pittsburgh in 1802 to regulate the measurement of coal in full bushels. Coal carts and wagons must be clearly marked with their capacities, DiCiccio, 18.

[43] Twain, *Life on the Mississippi,* 51.

[44] Ibid., 209.

[45] Whitney, Vol. 1, 138.

[46] Ibid., Vol. 1, 95.

[47] *Native Sons of Kansas City Collection (KC0465),* SHSMO--UMKC.

[48] See Appendix C for complete description of the leveemaster's duties as described by the city council.

[49] Wyman, Walker D., "Kansas City, Mo., A Famous Freighter Capital,"*Kansas State Historical Society* (Vol. 6, no. 1, February 1937), 341. Exactly where this figure originates or just what area it covers is not stated, but it surely included what became known as the West Bottoms--part of the original Prudhomme property which would support many a saw mill up to the 1880s and the two thousand acres across the river to the north mentioned by Spalding. Other descriptions of forests like the timber of walnut and oak between the levee and Westport or the "rich and luxuriant woods between Westport and Independence" noted by Parkman, abound but are unmeasured in the descriptions of passing wayfarers.

[50] Gregg, 21.

Chapter 11

[1] Hickman, 160.

[2] George A. Root, "Ferries in Kansas, Part 1 -- Missouri River," February 1933 (Vol. 2, No. 1), transcribed by Gardner Smith; *Kansas Historical Quarterly*, 3-28.

[3] Henry Pickering Walker, *The Wagonmasters; High Plains Freighting from the Earliest Days of the Santa Fe Trail to 1880* (Norman: University of Oklahoma Press, 1966), 53.

[4] Hubaleck, 54,32.

[5] Gregg, 33.

[6] Spalding, 73.

[7] Parkman, 25. They readied themselves to "bid our final adieu to the frontier; or in the phraseology of the region, to 'jump off.'"

[8] "Westport: Where the West Began," westporthistorical.org/history.html, accessed 3 Feb 2009; Williams, *Seventy-Five Years on the Border* (Kansas City: Standard Printing Co., l913), 93.

[9] Hickman, 245. "Westport: Where the West Began." The name of Kanzas was still being used in 1852 in *Ballou's Pictorial*, a magazine issued in Boston, MA. *Kansas City Star*, February 7th, 1907.

[10] Hurt, 125-151.

[11] George Martin, ed., "Westport and the Santa Fe Trade," *Transactions of the Kansas State Historical Society, 1907-1908* (Vol. X), 556.

[12] "Bypaths of Kansas History," "Kansas in 1854," from the New York *Daily Tribune*, New York, June 23, 1854, *Kansas Historical Quarterly*, August 1937 (vol. 6, no. 3), 314-15.

[13] Gregg, 23.

[14] Ibid. Wyman, 3. Jane Hamill Sommer, "Outfitting the West, 1849" (*Missouri Historical Society*, vol. 24, July 1968), 341.

[15] Hickman, 117.

[16] Ibid., 116.

[17] Ibid., 116-117.

[18] Whitney, Vol. 1, 141.

[19] Larry Mahon Beachum, "To the Westward: William Becknell and the Beginning of the Santa Fe Trade," *Journal of the West*, (vol. 28, April 1989), 6-12. Other figures on size of wagon trains from Lass, 7.

[20] See the last signature in Appendix A.

[21] Ibid., 12.

[22] Thomas Becknell, "The Journals of Thomas Becknell from Boone's Lick to Santa Fe, and from Santa Cruz to Green River," *Missouri Historical Review* (Vol. 4, No. 2, January 1910), 71. It appears that this article is a misprint since William Becknell is the name of the founder of the Santa Fe Trail. I suspect the trouble comes from the fact that Thomas H. Benton, senator from Missouri, introduced a bill in Congress to establish a road from Independence, MO, to Santa Fe, NM in 1824. The road became known as the Santa Fe Trail. Whoever titled the above article may have confused Thomas Benton's first name for William Becknell's name. Just a guess, but perhaps a plausible one. Otherwise, the article offers a slightly different approach and sources. See Beachum's article cited above.

[23] Gregg, 38.

[24] firstpeople.us/FP-Html-Treaties/TreatyWithTheKiowaetc1837.html, accessed 20 Jan 2009.

[25] Whitney, Vol.1, 59. Gregg, 210-211. Alexander Majors, *Seventy Years on the Frontier: Lifetime on the Border* (Minneapolis, 1965: Ross & Haines, Inc.), 102.

[26] Hickman, 115.

[27] Ibid., Lass 124.

[28] Ibid., 144.

[29] Ibid., 144-5.

[30] F. A. Wislizenus, M.D., *A Journey to the Rocky Mountains in the Year 1839* (New York: Cosimo Classics, 2005), 27.

[31] Walker D. Wyman, "Kansas City, Mo., A Famous Freighter Capital, "Kansas State Historical Society (Vol. 6, no. 1, February 1937), 4.

[32] Whitney, Vol. 1, 60.

[33] Spalding, 20.

[34] Ibid.

[35] Majors, 30-31.

[36] Parkman, 11.

[37] See Jeffrey Bremer for a thorough treatment on the pre-market economy of Missouri.

[38] Spalding, 22-23.

[39] Ibid., 73.

[40] John D. Unruh, Jr., *The Plains Across: The Overland Emigrants and the Trans-Mississippi West, 1840-1860* (Urbana: University of Illinois Press, 1979), 120.

[41] *Native Sons of Kansas City Collection (KC0465,)* SHSMO—UMKC.

[42] Unruh, 120.

[43] Ibid., 122.

[44] Gregg, 260. Gregg's account ends in 1843 because the road was closed to freighting in 1844 after citizens of the republic of Texas attacked and robbed Mexican wagons with permission from the governor. As a result of these attacks, President Santa Anna of Mexico decreed in August 1843 that the ports of entry at Taos, El Paso del Norte and El Presidio del Norte should be closed. This cut off all overland trade. Trade was resumed the following year but in much smaller amounts. After the Mexican War of 1846-48, the trade was no longer

international, and freighting resumed in large measures. By 1857, the freighters had learned to make two trips per season thus doubling their profits. Walker, 144-45.

[45] Walker, 56. Leavenworth was a rival town to Kansas City as was St. Joseph, MO, and Atchison, KS. The depot of Russell, Majors and Waddell that Greeley observed in Leavenworth moved to Kansas City in 1859, 55. Greeley traveled from New York to California, going by rail from New York City to St. Joseph, then across the river to Atchison. Horace Greeley, *An Overland Journey from New York to San Francisco, in the Summer of 1859* (New York: Alfred A. Knopf, 1964).

[46] Ibid., 19.

[47] Majors, 104.

[48] Ibid., 105.

[49] Walker, 54.

[50] Ibid.

[51] Majors, 186-187. Donald Chaput, *Francois X. Aubry: Trader, Trailmaker and Voyageur in the Southwest, 1846-1854* (Glendale, CA: Arthur H. Clark Co, 1975), 60-70.

[52] Majors describes the ride in *Seventy Years on the Frontier*, 186. Aubry may have used a shorter route he discovered in 1851 that cut off about fifty-two miles. Dary, 222.

[53] Chaput, 67.

[54] Chaput, 67-68, Theodore S. Case, *History of Kansas City* (1888), 45, Majors, 185-186.

[55] Chaput, 60-68, Majors, 185-86. Chaput's book is the only one written to memorialize Aubry's amazing speed which he performed again and again before being killed in a barroom challenge to his reputation August 18, 1854, at the age of 30 in Santa Fe. See Chaput, 155-158.

[56] Chaput, 68.

[57] Ibid., 69, inventors.about.com/library/inventors/bltelegraph.htm, accessed 20 Jan 2009.

[58] Majors, 186.

[59] Kansas City received the telegraph from Jefferson City, December 20th, 1858. Whitney, Vol. 1, 145. Majors 182-184.

[60] Jacqueline Lewin and Marilyn Taylor, *On the Winds of Destiny: A Biographical Look at Pony Express Riders* (St. Joseph: Platte Purchase Publishers, 2002), xii-xxii.

[61] Christopher Corbett *Orphans Preferred: The Twisted Truth and Lasting Legend of the Pony Express* (New York: Broadway, 203) 252. Corbett says no certain origins have been found for this ad, but it has become a choice bit of Western Americana, and no one thinks of questioning its authenticity. Constant usage by such illustrious magazines as *National Geographic* and *Christian Science Monitor* have legitimatized it.

[62] frontiertrails.com/oldwest/ponyexpress.htm, 3 Feb 2009.

[63] Twain, *Roughing It*, 63.

Chapter 12

[1] Albert R. Greene, "The Kansas River--Its Navigation" *Transactions of the Kansas State Historical Society, 1905-1906* (Vol. IX, Geo W. Martin, ed.), 317-358.

[2] Hurt, xii.

[3] Ibid., xiii.

[4] Albert Bushnell Hart, *Slavery and Abolition*, 1831-1841 (New York: Harper Brothers, 1906), 123.

[5] An interesting story has just surfaced that must be included here: In the February 9th, 2018, edition of *The Week*, a United Kingdom weekly news magazine with an American edition, published an article entitled "The dress that drove the slave trade." According to the article Marie Antoinette posed for a painting in 1783 in which she wore a cotton "chemise." This dress was so unlike her previous portraits in satins and silks, opulent jewels and impressive hats, that it caused a sensation. When thousands tried to emulate this simple cotton frock, suppliers turned to American cotton plantations to produce it, a choice which unfortunately devastated the French silk industry. The timing was such that the South was likely about to follow the North and outlaw slavery, then found itself staring at an economic opportunity too good to pass up. While the dress in France caused a political uproar of class, style, political loyalties, Indian suppliers of cotton feeling threatened and so on, the dress eventually became a patriotic symbol--and triggered more abandonment of silks and velvets—of the common man. Technology stepped in to solve a production problem: Eli Whitney invented the cotton gin in 1794 collapsing the time delay of processing cotton. All that was necessary was the work force to pick the cotton and feed the cotton gin mills. Slavery, more cotton for clothing and the cotton gin became a production triangle that led the South into expanding its work force from a little over half a million in 1790 to over four million by the time of the Civil War. Never underestimate the power of a fashionista! *The Week*, February 9, 2018, p. 36.

[6] Bushnell., 147.

[7] Ibid., 322.

[8] Barbara Freese, *Coal: A Human History* (Cambridge, MA: Perseus, 2003), 126-7.

[9] Coal first arrived from nearby Lexington County in 1876, and from Bates County in 1880. It is to be assumed that coal for the railroads was supplied by local mines and supplemented by wood or vice versa before that time. Case, 150.

[10] The Kansas City *City Directory 1870*, 16.

[11] W. B. Knight, "The Street Pavements in Kansas City," *Kansas City Review of Science and Industry 8* (1885), 489.

[12] Case, 80.

[13] William Miller, *History of Kansas City* (Kansas City: Hudson-Kimberly Publishing Co., 1900), 104.

[14] Case, 79.

[15] Ibid. 73. Case's thirteen-page description is the most complete short history of the city during the war. Not much has been written about the city's survival during this period.

[16] Ibid., 72.

[17] John Starret Hughes, "Lafayette County and the Aftermath of Slavery, 1861-1870, *Missouri Historical Review* (Volume LXXV, No. l, October 1920), 58.

[18] The Emancipation Proclamation. See archives.gov/exhibits/featured_documents/emancipation_proclamation/, accessed 20 Jan 2019.

[19] Hughes, 58.

[20] Ibid., 59.

[21] archives.gov/exhibits/featured_documents/emancipation_proclamation/, accessed 20 Jan 2019; Hughes, 63.

[22] Hughes, 54.

[23] Ibid., 53.

[24] Lorenzo J. Greene, et. al., *The Role of the Negro in Missouri History, 1719-1970* (St. Louis: Lincoln University Official Manual, State of Missouri, 1973-1974) 10-11.

[25] Ibid.

[26] Ibid.

[27] Hughes, 62.

[28] Morrison-Fuller, 33.

[29] Hughes, 53.

[30] Jackson, David W. *Born a Slave: Rediscovering Arthur Jackson's African American Heritage*. (Greenwood, MO: The Orderly Pack Rat, 2015).

[31] Hughes, 54.

[32] news.bbc.co.uk/1/hi/sci/tech/3557077.stm, accessed 15 Jan 2009. Scientists estimate fire use may go back into the past as far as 1.5 million years or as little as 230,000. Evidence gathered of late pursues the longer period.

[33] Martin Melosi, *Coping with Abundance: Energy and Abundance in Industrial America* (New York: Alfred A. Knopf, 1985) 10.

[34] Schurr and Netschert, 55.

[35] Ibid., 48.

[36] Schurr and Netschert, 48.

Part 2

[1] See Schurr and Netschert for discussion of changing fuel supplies, 63, that shows a 500% increase in coal use between 1850 and 1900, and 66, showing annual pig iron production smelted with coal and coke. Reference to "fuel revolution" comes from Leslie White, 382.

Chapter 13

[1] Perlin, 23.

[2] Ibid., 241-243. en.wikipedia.org/wiki/The_Iron_Bridge, accessed 20 Jan 2009.

[3] DiCiccio, 25.

[4] Spalding, 95. This document is called "Annals of Kansas" because that was the official name of the city at the time.

[5] Kansas City *City Directory*, 1858.

[6] uwsp.edu/CNR/wcee/keep/Mod1/Whatis/energyresourcetables.htm, accessed 20 Jan 2009. A Btu stands for British thermal unit developed in the 19th century in Britain as a standard of measurement in which one pound of water is heated by a certain amount of fuel to raise the temperature of the water one degree.

[7] Di Ciccio, 22.

[8] Ibid., 25.

[9] Schurr and Netschert, 68. The United States surpassed Britain's iron production in 1890 and pig iron output was 36% of the world's steel production with 28% of the world's coal output.

[10] Judith McGaw, *Early American Technology: Making and Doing Things from the Colonial Era to 1850* (Chapel Hill, NC: University of North Carolina Press, 1994), 246-248.

[11] DiCiccio, 7.

[12] Ibid., 21. Coal was being used as a household fuel in the Monongahela Valley of Pennsylvania by 1790. By 1810 Pittsburgh used it as well, earning for itself the name of the "smoky city." Bituminous has 26.2 million Btu per ton. Schurr and Netschert, 35.

[13] Schurr and Netschert, 519.

[14] Larsen, Lawrence H. *The Urban West at the End of the Frontier* (Lawrence: University of Kansas, 1978), 100.

[15] Ibid., 101.

[16] Ibid.

[17] Ibid., 102.

[18] Case, 81.

[19] Ibid.

[20] Ibid., 82. en.wikipedia.org/wiki/Battle_of_Westport#Fighting_along_Brush_Creek, accessed 20 Jan 2009.

[21] Kansas City *City Directory, 1865-6,* 9.

[22] Larsen, 103.

[23] *City Directory*, 1870, 16.

[24] Ibid. 17.

[25] O. Chanute, *The Kansas City Bridge with an Account of the Regimen of the Missouri River, and a Description of Methods Used for Founding in that River* (New York: Van Nostrand, Publisher, 1876), 9, 15.

[26] Ibid., 16.

[27] Freese, 127.

Chapter 14

[1] Ibid., 84. Also Schurr used the phrase "purposely drilled to obtain petroleum," 84.

[2] Harold F. Williamson, Arnold R. Daum, *The American Petroleum Industry: The Age of Illumination, 1859-1899* (Evanston, Northwestern University Press, 1959), 79-80.

[3] Paul H. Giddens, *The Beginnings of the Petroleum Industry* (Harrisburg: Pennsylvania Historical Commission, 1941) 81. George Bissell was one of four original backers of Edward Drake's oil well through the Seneca Oil Company. The others were Francis Beattie Brewer, Benjamin Silliman, Jr. and James M. Townsend. Williamson and Daum describe the drilling and catching of liquid, 80.

[4] Ibid., 82. Dr. Francis Beattie Brewer, one of the partners in the original well at Titusville, was a physician who had been well acquainted with the oil from the area. He had been given a five-gallon can of the "exudate," i.e., what was caught oozing out of the ground, and had found it to have "remarkable curative qualities" that he used as long as he practiced medicine. That oil was also used as a lubricant. Williamson and

Daum, 64. The oil was called rock oil to differentiate it from whale oil or animal fats like lard. Daniel Yergen, *The Prize: The Epic Quest for Oil, Money and Power* (New York: Simon and Schuster, 1991), 19.

[5] See Williamson and Daum for greater detail on the medicinal trajectory of rock oil, 12-24.

[6] Yergen, 20.

[7] Ibid, 83.

[8] Williamson and Daum, 77, 94.

[9] Ibid., 94-5. Brian Black, *Petrolia: The Landscape of America's First Oil Boom* (Baltimore: Johns Hopkins Press, 2000) 48. This excellent account gives great detail about the discovery and its effect on the surrounding countryside.

[10] Black, 51.

[11] Williamson and Daum, 46-47.

[12] Yergen, 24-25, Williamson and Daum, 46-47.

[13] Yergen 25, Williamson and Daum, 55, 59, 60.

[14] Yergen, 26-27. Black, 54-57, and Williamson and Daum, 82-88.

[15] Black, 55.

[16] Williamson and Daum, 113-114.

[17] Williamson and Daum refer to it as the Region throughout their narrative.

[18] Ibid., 109. Kerosene developer Abraham Gesner surveyed available plants at the end of 1860. He found 56 plants producing coal oil with a dozen more distilling crude coal oil. All were located near wells.

[19] Williamson and Daum, 84-5.

Chapter 15

[1] *Encyclopedia of Missouri*, Volume 1, 35-36.

[2] Energy Information Administration/State Coal Profiles: Missouri, 56-57, 1993. eia.doe.gov/cneaf/coal/st_coal_pdf/0576q.pdf, accessed 1 Apr 2009.

[3] Missouri State Energy Profile, eia.gov.

[4] Kansas City *City Directory,* 1867-8, 70.

[5] Mercantile Illustrating Company, *Imperial Kansas City 1900: Her Wonderful Growth and Resources* (Kansas City, Missouri, 1900), 12.

[6] Freese, 127.

[7] *Imperial Kansas City 1900*, 51.

[8] G. C. Broadhead, Theodore S. Case, "Geology: Jackson County, Missouri" (*Western Review of Science and Industry,* July 1878, Issue 4 Volume 2), 204-11.

[9] John H. Conlin, *Frontier Times*, Feb-March 1979.

[10] *Imperial Kansas City*, 1900. As far as the Midwest was from the bankers of the East Coast, they had become partners long ago in financing growth on the frontier. Kersey Coates, one of Kansas City's most illustrious citizens, came from Philadelphia in the 1850s with strong East-Coast connections, built the Coates Opera House and the Coates Hotel as well as financing and serving on the boards of a number of projects that promoted the city's growth. The Abolitionists settling Kansas were financed by Bostonians through the Emigrant Aid Company, including by one Amos A. Lawrence, for whom Lawrence, Kansas, was named. (See Richard Cordley, D. D., *The History of Lawrence, Kansas, from the Earliest Settlement to the Close of the Rebellion,* (Lawrence: Journal Press, 1895). The hallmark of Kansas City politics in general was to approach eastern businessmen with legitimate opportunities for them to build railroads, bridges, hotels, factories. It is the nature of the frontier to return to the flow of higher energy systems for reinforcing materials and funds. The author of *Imperial Kansas City* mentioned Gould's name as a boast as well as an accepted part of the business scene of Kansas City.

[11] Maury Klein, "Jay Gould: A Revisionist Interpretation," *Business and Economic History,* (Second Series, Vol. 15, 1986) 57, 61, 65.

[12] *Imperial Kansas City*, 70.

[13] Clark, 11.

Chapter 16

[1] William E. Parrish, *History of Missouri, III, 1860-1875* (Columbia: University of Missouri Press, 1973, 2001), 230.

[2] The slope mine followed the land down to the coal seam underground not more than a hundred feet. If the coal seam was deeper, mine operators sank a vertical shaft to the needed depth called a shaft mine. If the coal seam lay open on a cliff or hillside, a drift mine would be excavated directly into it. If the coal lay on or near the top of the ground, workers and horses stripped off the soil creating a strip mine. This and the following description about coal mining was taken from two excellent books, Dorothy Schweider *Black Diamonds: Life and Work in Iowa's Coal Mining Communities, 1895-1925* (Ames: Iowa State University Press, 1983) 27-58, and Price V. Fishback, *Soft Coal, Hard Choices: The Economic Welfare of Bituminous Coal Miners, 1890-1930* (New York: Oxford University Press, 1992) 42-49.

[3] Schwieder, 32.

[4] Fishback, 43. Large chunks were the most desirable for easy handling and price. Small pieces and coal dust had little market value though they might add to the weight of the cart. Slate and dirt were forbidden.

[5] Schwieder, 37.

[6] Fishback, 66. After machine cutting began to speed up the production process less emphasis was placed on chunk coal. Screens to measure size were developed. Markets were found for smaller coal, ways to handle it evolved.

[7] Schwieder, 43.

[8] Fishback, 47.

[9] Ibid., 44.

[10] A. T. Shurick, *The Coal Industry* (Boston: Little, Brown and Co., 1924).

[11] Schwieder, 32.

[12] Fishback, 79-81. Statistics show that miners worked 70 fewer days per year than factory workers. Miners earned more per hour than their manufacturing counterparts, but with fewer days the earnings came out very close. The higher wage helped compensate for the danger of the work and the miner's greater independence made mining attractive to many. Coal miners earned nearly double that which farmhands earned. Coal mining earned 28% more than manufacturing up to 1913. Wages matched manufacturing in the 1920s in most years. Coal wages dropped to 3% less than manufacturing by 1933.

[13] David Alan Corbin, *Life, Work, and Rebellion in the Coal Fields: The Southern West Virginia Miners 1880-1922* (Urbana: University of Illinois Press, 1981), 30-31.

Chapter 17

[1] Mr. Bowen in a speech on "The Superiority of Electricity over other Illuminants for Public Lighting." *Proceedings of the National Electric Light Association at the First Annual Convention,* Chicago, 1885 (Baltimore: The Baltimore Publishing Co., 1886), 130.

[2] See *Proceedings, Baltimore, 1885* (Baltimore: The Baltimore Publishing Co., 1886), Linda Hall Library, Kansas City, Missouri.

[3] James P. Boyd, *Triumphs and Wonders of the 19th Century: The Mirror of a Phenomenal Era* (Philadelphia: A. J. Holman and Co., 1899), 43.

[4] Harold L. Platt, *The Electric City: Energy and Growth of the Chicago Area, 1880-1930* (Chicago: University of Chicago Press, 1991), 4. For a thorough discussion of the development of the arc lamp, see Arthur Bright, 17-36.

[5] Wolfgang Schivelbusch, in *Disenchanted Night: The Industrialization of Light in the Nineteenth Century* (Berkeley, CA: University of California Press, 1995) has explored this phenomenon deeply.

[6] Richard B. Du Boff, *Electric Power in American Manufacturing, 1889-1958* (New York: Arno Press, 1979), 3. Platt, 4. Both authors mention that lighting first, local railway systems second and industrial power third was the order in which electricity expanded in American life, although Du Boff cites communication in the form of the telegraph along with lighting.

[7] *Proceedings, Baltimore*, February 10th, 1885, 6.

[8] *Proceedings*, Union Square Hotel, New York, August 18th, 1885, 164.

[9] Werner Siemens proposed the name "dynamo machine" in a speech in Germany in 1867. By 1876 the dynamo had been developed to power a single-arc lamp. By 1877 Charles F. Brush had created an electric light system with his dynamo with copper-coated carbons for arc lamps. The carbons burned for eight hours before burning out. Brush introduced the first successful electric street lighting system in the United States by 1878 and the arc-lamp industry was born. National Electrical Manufacturers Association, *A Chronological History of Electrical Development from 600 B.C.* (New York, 1946), 36-43.

[10] Bright, 34.

[11] James P. Boyd, 43. The incandescent bulb took longer to create because of the difficulty of finding a substance suitable for the filaments. Edison eventually solved the problem. See the entire story of the invention of the incandescent bulb and lighting system by Edison in Martin V. Melosi *Thomas A. Edison and the Modernization of America* (New York: Longman, 1990), 58-76, and Arthur Bright, 35-70.

[12] Bright, 20-21.

[13] "Electric Light and Power in Kansas City," *Encyclopedia of the History of Missouri,* 362-3.

[14] *Proceedings*, Baltimore*, 1885,* 17.

[15] Edison Institute, *The Electric Industry* (New York: Edison Electric Institute, 1951), 35. Edwin Weeks, the manager of the Kawsmouth and Later Kansas City Electric Company, spoke to the size of engines at the second annual Proceedings of the Electric Light Association in Baltimore in 1886: "With a large engine, for instance a 250 horse-power, running 300 lights, one of the first objections would be, that in case of any disaster, the failure of any one of the hundreds of appliances that go to make up that 300-light lamp, the 300 light would be out unless you had a reserve equal to that number, or a duplicate of that part of the plant. But with a high-speed engine you, of course, do not have so much at stake. In case of stoppage, there is not so much dissatisfaction. These are two of the chief reasons why the high-speed engines have come into favor." Edwin Weeks, *Second Annual Proceedings of the Electric Light Association, Baltimore, February 10, 1886*, 96-7.

[16] *Proceedings,* Detroit, August 31, 1886, 411.

[17] Brian J. Cudahy, *Cash Tokens and Transfers: A History of Urban Mass Transit in North America* (Fordham University Press, New York, 1990), 4.

[18] Bright, 21.

[19] Ibid., 32,33.

[20] Ibid., 43.

[21] Joel Tarr, "Transforming an Energy System," Olivier Coutard ed., *The Governance of Large Technical Systems* (London: Routledge, 1999), 20.

[22] Bright, 31.

[23] Ibid., 33.

[24] Ibid., 31, 32.

[25] *Proceedings*, August 18, 1885, Union Square Hotel, New York, 116.

[26] Bright, 33.

[27] Ibid., 70.

[28] Ibid., 34.

[29] Harry Black, "The Predecessor Companies of the Kansas City Power and Light Company," (Master's Thesis in History, University of Missouri--Kansas City, 1953), 8.

[30] Bright, 43.

[31] Gerald A. Motsinger, "The Development of Main Street, Kansas City, Missouri (Master's thesis in History, University of Missouri, Kansas City, 1986), 67.

[32] Ibid., 64.

[33] Bright, 31. These two high school teachers developed their own systems of electricity generation early on by improving the dynamo and arc lamp and had considerable success in promoting their systems in arc lighting before Edison's incandescent lighting took over.

[34] "Electric Light and Power in Kansas City," *Encyclopedia of the History of Missouri*, Volume II, 363.

[35] Harry Black, 42. Like other electric-light enthusiasts, Weeks had no background in electric lights and no experience running a station but traveled to New Jersey to visit with Edison himself and to learn the means and the ways of running an electric light company. He became one of the leading voices in the National Electrical Lamp Association proceedings and a voice of reason in Kansas City's volatile field for several years. He was eventually elected president of the Association in 1889. *Proceedings*, Baltimore, 1885, 85. Election notice in *Electro-Mechanic*, Volume II, Kansas City, MO, March 1, 1889, No. 5, 81.

[36] *Proceedings,* September 1, 1886, 57.

[37] *Proceedings*, August 18th, 1885, p. 181-2.

[38] Harry Black, 86.

[39] Ibid., 85-86. Joel Tarr also mentions this counter trend (1999), 25.

[40] *Proceedings*, August 1885, 130.

[41] *Electro-Mechanic*, Volume II, No. 4, Kansas City, Missouri, February 15, 1889, 67.

[42] Harry Black, 42.

[43] Motsinger, 71.

[44] *Encyclopedia*, Volume VI, 363.

[45] *Proceedings,* Baltimore, 1885, 147.

[46] "Operating Expenses," *Proceedings*, Baltimore, February 1886, 98.

[47] *Proceedings,* New York, August 18th, 1885, 153.

[48] *Proceedings,* Baltimore, 1886, 96-7.

[49] *Proceedings,* Baltimore, 1885, 130.

[50] Harry Black, 31.

[51] *Journal Post*, September 28, 1924.

[52] Harry Black, 16.

[53] *Encyclopedia,* Volume X, 364.

[54] Ibid., 365.

[55] Harry Black, 5.

[56] Bright, 73.

[57] Harry Black, 76.

[58] *Electro-Mechanic* (Volume II, Kansas City, MO, February 15, 1889, No. 14), 61.

[59] Ibid., 68. Weeks also announced to "all electric workers and thinkers" that the National Electric Light Convention might be held in Kansas City, "but it will be some time before Kansas City will be as convenient a center, owing to the fact that the greater number of enterprises of an electrical nature and those engaged therein lie east of us," 64.

[60] *Encyclopedia, X,* 365.

[61] *Encyclopedia, X,* 366.

[62] *Proceedings*, Baltimore, 1885, 130.

[63] Harry Black, 94-96.

[64] Ibid., 43.

[65] "Edwin Weeks," *Encyclopedia, Volume VI*, 427.

Chapter 18

[1] This document is labeled 1902 and printed in 1905 though it is included in the 1900 census. Thomas Commerford Martin, "Electricity in Mining," Department of Commerce and Labor, Bureau of the Census, Special Reports, *Mines and Quarries, 1902*, (Washington: Government Printing Office, 1905) 145.

[2] Ibid., 145.

[3] Ibid., 146.

[4] Ibid., 149.

[5] Ibid., 153.

[6] Ibid., 153.

[7] Ibid., 155.

[8] Ibid., 150.

[9] Ibid., 150.

[10] Ibid., 151.

[11] Joel Tarr and Clay McShane "Urban Horses and Changing City-Hinterland Relationships in the United States," *Resources of the City: Contributions to an Environmental History of Modern Europe*, Dieter Schott, et. al., eds (Burlington, VT: Ashgate: 2005), 49.

[12] Joel Tarr and Clay McShane, "The decline of the urban horse in American cities," *Journal of Transport History* (September 2003), 17.

[13] McShane, pvonthenet.com/rpv/planning/equestrian/HorseManure CompostingGuidelines.pdf, accessed 26 Jan 2009.

[14] Tarr and McShane (2005), 48-62.

[15] *City Directory 1867-8*, 8.

[16] Motsinger, 62.

[17] Kansas City *City Directory 1870*, 29.

[18] Kansas City *City Directory 1869*, 19.

[19] Case, 423.

[20] Ibid., 407.

[21] *City Directory 1869*: brick works, 324; car builders—street, 343; hoisting machines, 358.

[22] Ibid.

[23] Boyd, 223.

[24] *Proceedings,* Baltimore, February 10, 1886, 55. Local Kansas City representative and vice-president of the Electric Light Association Edwin Weeks attended this meeting. The association was about electric lights because at the time, electric lights were all there was. Lighting had been a big challenge throughout the second half of the 19th century and power in the form of motors had not yet arrived, hence the names of the early utilities were known as "light and power" in the order in which they were developed, though Kansas City's company reversed the name around 1912.

[25] Ibid.

[26] Ibid., 56.

[27] Case, 407.

[28] Ibid., 408.

[29] Ibid.

[30] Ibid.

[31] *Electro-Mechanic*, August 10, 1888, (Vol 1. No. 1), 4.

[32] Ibid.

[33] *The Journal*, August 10, 1888, 5.

[34] *The Railwayan* (Vol. VI, No. 4, 1923, Kansas City, Missouri), 9. Case, 413.

[35] *The Railwayan*, Ibid., 10.

[36] *The Electro-Mechanic* (Vol. 2, No. 2, January 15, 1889), 35.

[37] Ibid.

[38] Ibid., (Vol II, No. 3, February 1, 1889), 48.

[39] Ibid., (Vol. II, No. 14, August 1, 1889), 50.

[40] *The Journal*, January 1, 1896, NSA Commercial Club files, SHSMO--U Missouri, Kansas City.

[41] *The ASPCA*, aspca.org/site/ history, accessed 3 Jan 2009.

[42] Boyd, 82.

Chapter 19

[1] Case, 420.

[2] Ibid.

[3] Ibid.

[4] George C. Hale and T. R. Tinsley, *Souvenir of Kansas City and her Fire Department to the Grand International Fire Congress and Exhibition held at Royal Agricultural Hall* (London, England, June 12th to 17th, 1893).

Chapter 20

[1] Schurr and Netschert, 35.
[2] Ibid., 47. Lumber and building materials came from as far away as Pittsburgh.
[3] From an *Illustrated Historical Atlas of Boone County, MO* (Philadelphia, 1876, 16.) *Missouri Historical Review* (Columbia: State Historical Society, Volume LXXV, Number 1), October 1980, 119.
[4] Va Nee L. Van Vleck, "Reassessing Technological Backwardness: Absolving the 'Silly Little Bobtailed' Coal Car," *The Journal of Economic History*, Vol. 55, No. 2 (June 1995), 383. See Mark Twain's mathematics of coal in *Life on the Mississippi*, 209-10. Klein, 57, tons to a coal car in 1870, 62. Keith's biographical notes from Whitney, Volume II, 15.
[5] Whitney, Volume II, 12, 15.
[6] *Kansas City* (Mo.) *Times*, April 13, 1979. kchistory.org/cdm4/item_viewer.php?CISOROOT= /Mrs&CISOPTR=761&CISOBOX=1&REC=2, accessed, 27 June 2018.
[7] *Imperial Kansas City*, 97.
[8] Whitney, Volume II, 119.
[9] *The Conservationist,* theodoreroosevelt.org/life/conservation.htm, accessed 26 Jan 2009.
[10] Alfred Chandler, "Anthracite Coal and the Beginnings of the Industrial Revolution in The United States, *Business History Review* (pre-1986), Summer 1972, 141-173.
[11] R. V. Reynolds and Albert H. Pierson, "Lumber Cut in the United States, 1870-1920," *Bulletin of the U. S. Department of Agriculture* (Issue 1919, 1923), 27-35.
[12] Kansas City *City Directory 1870*, p. 27.
[13] Schurr and Netschert, 36.
[14] Chandler, 168. Chandler points out that in 1845 the cost of making wrought iron from charcoal was $82 a ton compared with $47 a ton for wrought iron from anthracite coal. The cost of the charcoal as fuel was $20 a ton versus with coal as fuel at $3.25 a ton. Charcoal could no longer compete in either time or cost.

Chapter 21

[1] Philip W. Bishop, *The Beginnings of Cheap Steel* (Washington, D.C.: Smithsonian Institute, 1959), 30.
[2] Ibid., 37.
[3] Robert B. Gordon, *American Iron, 1607-1900* (Baltimore, MD: Johns Hopkins Press, 1996), 223, 227. Peter Temin, *Iron and Steel in the Nineteenth Century: An Economic Inquiry* (Cambridge, MA: MIT Press, 1964), 127.
[4] Bishop, 28.
[5] Temin, 149.
[6] Bishop, 28.
[7] Gordon, 231.

Chapter 22

[1] *Coal Age*, July 19, 1913, 95.
[2] Ibid.
[3] Ibid.
[4] *Coal Age*, January 1, 1913, 53.
[5] *Coal Age*, February 10, 1910, 578.
[6] *Coal Age*, July 5, 1913, 47.
[7] *Coal Age,* April 11, 1914, 617.
[8] *Coal Age,* November 8, 1917, 650.
[9] Schurick, A. T., *The Coal Industry* (Boston: Little, Brown & Co., 1924), 105.

[10] *Coal Age,* July 1, 1920, 8.

[11] Schurr and Netschert, 55. Interview of the author's husband, Carl Blomgren, in Overland Park, Kansas, about his father's coal-mining career in Iowa.

[12] Thirteenth Census of the United States, 1902, "Coal," 225.

[13] Ibid., 225.

[14] Ibid., 226.

[15] Ibid., 230.

[16] Ibid., 184, 188.

[17] *Coal Age,* June 13, 1914.

[18] *Coal Age,* January 16, 1913, 95.

[19] *The Oil and Gas Journal,* May 18, 1911.

[20] *Coal Age,* April 15, 1920, 769; April 22, 1920, 826.

[21] Ibid., 769.

[22] See Brian Black's description of Oil City, Titusville, and environs in *Petrolia.*

Chapter 23

[1] Schurr and Netschert, 57, 84.

[2] Williamson and Daum, 371.

[3] Schruben, xii.

[4] Williamson and Daum, 492-3.

[5] Schruben, xii.

[6] Williamson and Daum, 466-470.

[7] Ibid., 476. "What Ever Happened to Standard Oil?" A highly abridged history of the petroleum companies that have used the 'Standard' brand name," us-highways.com/sohist.htm, accessed 26 Jan 2009.

[8] Ibid. A greater level of detail is available in Williamson and Daum and in Paul Giddens, *Standard Oil Company of Indiana: Oil Pioneer of the Middle West* (New York: Appleton, Century Crofts, 1955).

[9] Ibid.

[10] Cartoon depicting standard oil and J. D. Rockefeller, Library of Congress control number 200961643, Reproduction Number LC-USZ62-84055 (b&w film copy neg.).

[11] Williamson and Daum, 613.

[12] Ibid., 610.

[13] See Governor Reeder's story that follows for more information. "A Hoosier in Kansas-The Diary of Hiram H. Young, 1886-1895, Pioneer of Cloud County," *Kansas Historical Quarterly*, Part Four, 1893, edited by Powell Moore, February 1947 (Vol. 15 No. 1), 42-80. This diary makes repeated mention of bringing home a bucket of coal or taking a bucket of coal to an event or as a guest at someone's home.

[14] The author's uncle was in charge of a cavalry horse unit (as opposed to the cavalry units now made of tanks and trucks) in the early years of World War II. Though the American army did not use horses in battle, the German army was forced to use as much as 80% of their transportation in horses because of fuel shortages. See Paul Louis Johnson, *Horses of the German Army in World War II*, (Gloucester, MA 2006). "German Horse Cavalry and Transport, and lonesentry.com/articles/germanhorse/index.html, accessed 9 Mar 2008.

[15] "The History of Skyscrapers," inventors.about.com/library/inventors/blskyscapers.htm, accessed 2 Feb 2009.

Part 3

[1] Gunther Barth, *Instant Cities: Urbanization and the Rise of San Francisco and Denver* (Albuquerque: University of New Mexico Press, 1975, 1988) speaks to the rise of western cities in contrast to the colonial cities of the east, new fuels of oil and gas being a key factor in their quick growth. Rose, Mark H., *Cities of Light and Heat: Domesticating Gas and Electricity in Urban America,* (University Park, PA: Pennsylvania State University Press, 1995) pairs Kansas City and Denver in a study of the urbanization of gas and electricity systems in both cities.

[2] The entire panoply of the revolution in industry created by great amounts of coal is beyond the scope of this study, however, the Homestead strike as a case in point is covered in the following works: Paul Krause, *The Battle for Homestead, 1880-1892: Politics, Culture, and Steel* (Pittsburgh, PA: University of Pittsburgh Press, 1992) and David P. Demarest and Fannia Weingartner, *"The River Ran Red:" Homestead 1892* (Pittsburgh, PA: The University of Pittsburgh Press, 1992). The intuitive artisanship of making steel in small batches was taken over by factories using the Bessemer process to create the metal in great quantity. The workers tried to retain some dignity and ownership of that process and were ultimately squashed by violence and the power of federal troops brought in by Henry Clay Frick, maker of coke for steel-making, and Dale Carnegie, owner of steel mills, to stop the strikers. See also bgsu.edu/departments/acs/1890s/carnegie/strike.html, accessed 31 Jan 2009.

[3] Schurr and Netschert, 36, 145.

[4] Ibid., 36.

[5] Ibid., 145.

Chapter 24

[1] Craig Miner, *Discovery! Cycles of Change in the Kansas Oil and Gas Industry, 1860-1987* (Wichita: Kioga, 1987), 89.

[2] Clark, 14. Spindletop oil well drilled in 1901 tripled the United States oil production with one well and began the "real petroleum age." priweb.org/ed/pgws/ history/spindletop/lucas_gusher.html, accessed 31 Jan 2009.

[3] Miner, xvii.

[4] Schruben, Francis, *WEA Creek to El Dorado: Oil in Kansas, 1860-1920* (Columbia: University of Missouri Press, 1972), 55-6.

[5] Miner, 234.

[6] Bill Allison, "Sugar Creek Grew Up Around Oil Refinery," *Jackson County Historical Society Journal* (Volume XVII, July 1975, No. 2), 4.

[7] John La Roe, *Kansas City Magazine*, (Volume 12, issue 12), 36-41.

[8] Schruben, 69.

[9] Ibid., 50.

[10] Ibid., 51.

[11] Clark, 16. For the complete story on this event see Steve Weinberg, *Taking on the Trust: The Epic Battle of Ida Tarbell and John D. Rockefeller, How an Investigative Journalist Brought Down Standard Oil* (New York: W. W. Norton, 2008). Also see the incomparable Ida M. Tarbell and David M. Chalmers, editor, *The History of Standard Oil: The Briefer Version* (New York: Dover reprint, 2003).

[12] Williamson and Daum, 6. A clearer subtitle for this volume would have been, in my view, *The Age of Fuel*. Their second volume continues the story in Harold F. Williamson, et. al., *The American Petroleum Industry: 1899-1959, The Age of Energy* (Evanston: Northwestern University Press, 1963).

[13] Ibid. Clark, 15-16.

[14] Pratt, 15.

[15] "Domestication," by Michelle Staples on Equiworld.net, equiworld.net/uk/horsecare/evolution/domestication.htm, accessed 31 Jan 2009.

[16] "Origins of Domestic Horse Revealed" Helen Briggs on BBC News Worldwide, news.bbc.co.uk/1/hi/sci/tech/2129182.stm, accessed 31 Jan 2009.

[17] Jackson, David W. *Kansas City Chronicles: An Up-to-Date History*. (Charleston, SC: The History Press, 2010), 62-64.

[18] "Horseless Carriages Conquer Kansas City's hills after many trials have been overcome by the Locomobile," *Kansas City Manufacturer*, Summer, 1901.

[19] *The Kansas City Manufacturer, a journal devoted to the manufacturing interests of Kansas City* (Vol 3. No. 10, Kansas City, MO, July 1901), 17.

[20] *Kansas City Journal*, Sunday, September 3, 1905.

[21] *Kansas City Annual, 1907*, 110.

22 *Kansas City Annual, 1908*, 175.

23 The oil cup was invented as a lubricant for steam engines by Elijah McCoy in 1872. inventors.about.com/od/mstartinventors/a/Elijah_McCoy.html, accessed 31 Jan 2009.

24 *Kansas City Manufacturer, 1901*, 6, 16.

25 Ibid., 17-18.

26 Ibid., 4, 6, 14.

27 Ibid., 14.

28 Ibid., 4.

29 Ibid., 14, 22.

30 Ibid., 22.

31 Ibid., 15.

32 In the *Greater Kansas City Yearbook 1904-5,* 46, these features were advertised. Whether they existed in 1901 or not, the "ice box" was still evolving and had reached its highest level before true refrigeration set in the 1920s.

33 *The Kansas City Manufacturer, 1901*, 8.

34 Ibid., 2.

35 Ibid., 8.

36 Ibid. Nancy Miller and Colleen Newman, Water Services History, kcmo.org/water. nsf/web/history? Opendocument, accessed 2 Feb 2009.

37 *The Kansas City Manufacturer*, 1901, (Volume 3, No. 11), July, cover.

38 Ibid., 43.

Chapter 25

1 *Greater Kansas City Yearbook, 1904-5*, 9, Kansas City, Missouri.

2 Wilson, 23.

3 Mathews, (1961), 660.

4 Wilson, *Underground Reservation*, 2.

5 Mathews, (1961)*,* 667.

6 Ibid., 670.

7 Ibid., 693. The Osage in this treaty insisted on owning their land communally. They did not want it owned in "severalty," but to own it in common. This decision would allow them to share the wealth of the still-undiscovered oil under the surface of their new reservation.

8 Ibid., 670-672.

9 Ibid., 771. In the Treaty of 1825 they had paid the Cherokees seventy cents an acre for over a million and a half acres. Now they were buying it back and both tribes were relocating along with others to the Indian Territory.

10 Ibid., 772. By 1906 these "intermarried citizens" had had children and together outnumbered the full bloods 1,369 to 360. Terry P. Wilson, "Chief Fred Lookout and the Politics of Osage Oil, 1906-1949," *Journal of the West* (Vol. 23, No. 3, 1984), 48.

11 Kenny A. Franks, *Osage Oil Boom* (Oklahoma City: Western Heritage Books, 1988), 3.

12 Mathews (1961), 719.

13 Ibid., 706. How the internal dynamics of the tribe must have changed and adjusted to having at least three horses per capita. The last two hundred years was a time of increasing materialism in the tribe if only in terms of horses.

14 Ibid.,716, 719.

15 Wilson, 20.

16 Franks, 6.

17 Wilson, 21.

18 Mathews (1961), 725, 731.

[19] Franks, 8.

[20] Wilson,1.

[21] Ibid., So decreed by Chief Justice John Marshall in 1832 in regard to the Osage.

[22] Mathews (1961), 728.

[23] Wilson, 132.

[24] Mathews (Mathews), 772.

[25] Wilson, ix.

[26] Franks, 12, 141. Wilson, *Journal of the West*, 48. Congress passed an act in 1925 to protect the Osage from further plundering. It forbade any but heirs of Indian blood from inheriting from allottees of one half or more Osage blood quantum. This helped to keep the voice of the full bloods alive even after their deaths. See *Killers of the Flower Moon: The Osage Murders and the Birth of the FBI* op. cit. for the full story of murderous havoc visited on this tribe.

[27] No further information is available at this time on whether fuel actually was sent or just the backwash of money from the exploration.

[28] Wilson, 108.

[29] Ibid., 129.

[30] Not far from the Los Angeles International Airport, LAX, is a street called "Osage Street." I had always wondered how it got its name. Now I think some of those vacationing Osages must have visited there if not settled.

[31] Wilson, 131.

[32] Ibid., xii.

[33] Mathews (1961) 723, 777.

[34] Wolferman, 17.

Chapter 26

[1] Schurr and Netschert, 105.

[2] Ibid.

[3] *Oil and Gas Journal,* 18 May 1911, 26.

[4] "Bags of Coal," globalsecurity.org/military/systems/ship/coaling.htm, accessed 3 Feb 2009.

[5] Ibid.

[6] Erik J. Dahl, "Naval Innovation: From Coal to Oil," National Defense University, Institute for National Strategic Studies, 260 Fifth Avenue SW Bg 64 Fort Lesley J. McNair, Washington, D.C., 20319.

Chapter 27

[1] "U-boat," en.wikipedia.org/wiki/U-boat; *Lusitania*," pbs.org/lostliners/lusitania.html; "U. S. Enters World War I," history.sandiego.edu/gen/ww1/submarine.html; history.com/this-day-in-history.do?id=425&action=tdihArticleCategory, accessed 31 Jan 2009.

[2] "Federal Fuel Administration," R. Bruce McPherson, Chairman, Federal Fuel Administration, Livingston County, MI. Each county had an administrator for fuel for that county. memoriallibrary.com/MI/Livingston/WWI/Home/Fuel, accessed 10 Mar 2009.

[3] "History of Germany during World War I," en.wikipedia.org/wiki/WW1, accessed 1 Feb 2009.

[4] Ibid. 2.

[5] Ibid. 3.

[6] Charles F. Brooks, "The 'Old-fashioned' Winter of 1917-18," *Geographic Review*, (Vol. 5, No. 5, May 1918), 405.

[7] *Coal Age*, 5 Jan 1918, 11.

[8] Ibid.

[9] *Coal Age*, 16 Mar 1918, 515.

[10] Clark, 58.

[11] Ibid., 57.

[12] Ibid., 57-63.

[13] Ibid., 51-52.

[14] Ibid., 71.

[15] *The New York Times*, 4 Feb 1918. Also, *New York Times*, 22 Nov 1918: "Hotels in New York City, by the observance of meatless Tuesdays and wheatless Wednesdays and by other self-imposed restrictions, saved more than 116 tons of meat and 60 tons, or about 620 barrels, of flour last week, it was reported."

[16] Jim Blount, "War time of less meat and wheat," *Journal-News*, Hamilton, Ohio, Sunday, February 24, 1991.

[17] Kansas City *Journal*, 18 Jan 1918.

[18] Ibid.

[19] *Coal Age,* 13 July 1918, 67.

[20] *Coal Age*, 26 Jan 1918, 216.

[21] Ibid.

[22] Ibid.

[23] Clark, 71.

[24] Ibid.

[25] Between its beginnings as a light company and the year in question, the company had added power to its offerings to customers and then reversed the words to their current order. Power, virtually unavailable in the beginning won out over lighting in the long run.

[26] *Kansas City Star*, 8 Apr 1918.

[27] McPherson, 4.

Chapter 28

[1] Henry S. Graves, *The Use of Wood for Fuel,* Bulletin No. 753 (Washington, D. C.: United States Department of Agriculture, 10 Mar 1919), 1.

[2] Ibid., 3.

[3] Ibid.

[4] Ibid., 4.

[5] Ibid., 15.

[6] Ibid., 16.

[7] Ibid., 17.

[8] Ibid., 24.

[9] Ibid., 38.

[10] Henry F. Walling and O. W. Gray, New Topographic Atlas of the State of Pennsylvania (Philadelphia: Steadman & Lyon, 1873), 27, as footnoted in Di Cicchio, 29.

Chapter 29

[1] Holley, 19.

[2] Daniel Yergin, *The Prize: The Epic Quest for Oil, Money and Power,* 1991, 782.

[3] Henry Bessemer patented his steelmaking process described as a "carbonization process utilizing a blast of air" in 1855 in Great Britain, inventors.about.com/library/inventors/blsteel.htm, accessed 10 Apr 2011.

[4] Charles A. Whiteshot, *The Oil Well Driller, The History of the Oil Industry of the World*, (Mannington, West Virginia, 1905), p. 33.

[5] Ibid.

[6] Schurr and Netschert, 84 notes.

[7] *Kansas City Star,* February 3, 1935. "History Lurks in Many Old Structures of Westport When Kansas City was a Dream of the Future."

[8] Winch, 18.

9 fuel-testers.com/ethanol_fuel_history.html.

10 McShane, 13.

11 Schurr and Netschert, 87.

12 McShane, 13.

13 Schurr and Netschert, 102.

14 *Kansas City Journal Post*, 2-1-1925, James Anderson Scrapbook—KC Vol 1,

15 Schurr and Netschert, 85.

Chapter 30

1 *Oxford English Dictionary*, Ibid.

2 *Oxford English Dictionary* Second Edition, J. A. Simpson and E. S. C. Weiner, Clarendon Press, Oxford, Volume VI, p. 388

3 Ibid.

4 Oxford English Dictionary. Defined as "one of the first products in the distillation of crude petroleum, employed for purposes of healing and illumination." By 1883 refining procedures had ten substances from petroleum, including "gasoline, used in artificial gas machines."

5 By 1880, 10.3% gasoline is produced to 75.2% kerosene with 12. 4% losses. Sam H. Schurr and Bruce C. Netschert, *Energy in the American economy, 1850-1975* (Baltimore: Johns Hopkins Press, 1960), p. 95.

6 Ibid., 102.

7 *Kansas City Journal Post*, 1 Feb 1925; photo from *Kansas City* (Mo.) *Star,* 18 Sept. 1930.

8 Seen and asked about at Lincoln Library in Illinois. Docent confirmed.

9 Schurr and Netschert, 103.

10 Ehrlich, 19.

11 Ibid.

12 McShane, 15.

13 Ibid., 18.

14 Ibid.

15 Ibid.

16 Ibid.

17 Schurr and Netschert, 102.

18 fuel-testers.com/ethanol_fuel_history.html.

19 Ibid., 19.

20 McShane, 17.

21 Schurr and Netschert, 102.

22 Ibid.

23 Ibid., 5

24 John H. Lienhard, "Bertha Benz's Ride," uh.edu/engines/epi2402.htm, accessed 6 Apr 2017.

25 Schurr and Netschert, 102.

26 Ibid., 95.

27 lead.org.au

28 Ibid., 20.

29 Schurr and Netschert, p. 93

30 *Kansas City* (Mo.) *Star*, 22 June 1903.

31 *Oxford English Dictionary*, Ibid.

32 *Oil Well Driller*, p. 104.

33 McShane, 17.

34 Yergin, 1991, 782.

35 inventors.about.com/od/gstartinventions/a/gasoline_2.htm,

36 McShane,18.

37 Ibid.

[38] McShane, 19; Charles A. Whiteshot, *The Oil Well Driller, The History of the Oil Industry of the World*, (Mannington, West Virginia, 1905), 52.

[39] Ibid.

[40] *Kansas City* (Mo.) *Star,* 13 Jan 1887.

[41] globallleadnet.com/132/timeline-8500-years-of-lead-79-years of leaded gasoline.

[42] McShane, 19.

[43] Ibid.

[44] Ibid.

[45] Ibid.

[46] lead.org.au, accessed 10 Apr 2011.

[47] Schurr and Netschert, 102.

[48] McShane, 19.

[49] uh.edu/engines/epi2402.htm. "Prof. John Lienhard on Bertha Benz's ride." "Engines of Our Ingenuity, Bertha Benz' Ride," John H. Lienhard, University of Houston's College of Engineering, uh.edu, accessed 14 July 2017.

[50] Ralph W. Hidy and Muriel E. Hidy, *History of Standard Oil Company (New Jersey): Pioneering in Big Business 1882-1911* (New York: Harper & Brothers, 1955) p. 298. (Back porches memories from my grandmother born in 1891 in Philadelphia.).

[51] Ibid.

[52] *Dusty Diary*, ypsiarchivesdustydiary.blogspot.com/2009/05/late-19th-century-gasoline-stoves.html, accessed 22 June 2011; *The Rotarian*, December 1958, 30; goantiques.com/vapor-stove,146707.html.

[53] Ibid. 87.

[54] Ibid., 7.

[55] Gifford Pinchot, *Breaking New Ground*, 1947, 32.

[56] "Horseless Age," p. 9.

[57] inventors.about.com/od/gstartinventions/a/gasoline_2.htm, accessed 21 June 2017.

[58] McShane, 21.

[59] youautomobile.com/index.php/automobile-history/the-horseless-carriage/, accessed 10 Apr 2011.

[60] Ibid.

[61] Yergen, 1991, 782.

[62] McShane, 21.

[63] Ibid.

[64] inventors.about.com/od/gstartinventions/a/gasoline_2.htm

[65] McShane, 23.

[66] "The Horseless Age," (Volume 1, No. 1) November 1895, p. 1.

[67] Ibid.

[68] youautomobile.com/index.php/automobile-history/the-horseless-carriage/, accessed 10 Apr 2011, Ibid. *The Horseless Age*, Volume 2, p. 10.

[69] fuel-testers.com/ethanol_fuel_history.html, accessed 16 Aug 2011.

[70] Ibid., 23.

[71] *Kansas City* (Mo.) *Star,* 14 Jan 1896.

[72] Ibid.

[73] Yergin, 1991, 782.

[74] McShane, 24.

[75] Ibid., 25.

[76] Ibid.

[77] Ibid.

[78] *Oil Well Driller*, 33.

[79] Ibid. history.com/this-day-in-history/frank-duryea-wins-first-us-horseless- carriage-race, accessed 10 Apr 2011.

80 *Kansas City* (Mo.) Star, 3 and 4 Aug 1899.
81 ideafinder.com/history/inventions/vacleaner.htm, accessed 22 June 2017.
82 McShane, 26.
83 Ibid.
84 Ibid.
85 Jackson, *Kansas City Chronicles*, 62. *Kansas City* (Mo.) Star, 13 Nov. 1899.
86 Ibid.
87 Ibid., 27.
88 Ibid., 29.
89 McShane, 28.
90 Ibid., 29.
91 *Monroe Country (IA) News*, March 8, 2011, p. 3.
92 Yergin, 782.
93 McShane, 27.
94 *Kansas City (Mo.) Star,* 24 Dec 1901.

Chapter 31

1 "Automobile's History a Stirring Romance," *New York Times*, June 9, 1912. *Motor Ag*e, Volume V, No. 1, January 7, 1904, p. 7.
2 *Kansas City (Mo.) Star,* 16 Nov 1902.
3 McShane, 29.
4 Robert A. Olson, op. cit., *Kansas City Power and light; The First 100 Years* (Newcomen Society in North America: New York, 1972) 5.
5 *Kansas City (Mo.) Star,* 10 Dec 1903.
6 McShane, 31.
7 *Motor Ag*e, Volume V, No. 1, 7 Jan 1904, p. 7.
8 *Kansas City (Mo.) Star,* 30 Aug 1904.
9 *Motor Ag*e, Volume V, No. 1, 7 Jan 1904, 7.
10 McShane, 31.
11 *Kansas City (Mo.) Star,* 26 Sept. 1904; 8 Feb. 1931; 20 June 1982; 16 Sep 1991. Louis Singleton Curtiss, who died June 24, 1924, liked to dress in white suits, and he liked to drive a white car... "a machine remembered as 'the three-eyed-monster' because its headlights were mounted in a triangular array. 'It was an expensive car, and Louie used to run it fast to show what it could do' an old timer recalled in 1927." At the time of his 1924 death, Curtiss owned three cars, including a 1912 Regal valued for estate purposes at $10.
12 en.wikipedia.org/wiki/Smog#Major_incidents_in_the_US.
13 McShane, 34.
14 Ibid., 34.
15 *Kansas City (Mo.) Star,* 18 June 1905, and 21 June 1975.
16 McShane, 34, *Tulsa World*, November 9, 2005.
17 Ibid.
18 *Kansas City (Mo.) Star,* 8 Dec 1905. The section of the ordinance that is proved invalid, which licensed chauffeurs, is stricken and left out of the new ordinance.
19 *Kansas City (Mo.) Star,* 7 Jan 1906.
20 *Kansas City (Mo.) Star,* 7 Jan 1906.
21 *Kansas City* (Mo.) *Star*, 25 Mar 1906.
22 Ibid.
23 *Kansas City* (Mo.) *Star*, 29 Apr 1906.
24 *Kansas City* (Mo.) *Star*, 19 Aug 1906.
25 Yergin, 782.
26 Yergin, 782.

27 fuel-testers.com/ethanol_fuel_history.html.

28 McShane, 40.

29 *Kansas City* (Mo.) *Star,* 15 Mar 1908.

30 Ibid., 41.

31 The Nation.com.

32 McShane., 42.

33 Ibid.

34 Ibid., 44.

35 Ibid.

36 Yergin, 782.

37 McShane, 45.

38 *Kansas City* (Mo.) *Times,* 24 Oct 1929.

39 The remaining titles are *The Automobile Girls at Washington, The Automobile Girls at Palm Beach, The Automobile Girls at Chicago, The Automobile Girls in the Berkshires*, all published by Henry Allemus Company, Philadelphia. Each has a drawing on the hardback cover of a car with four young women and the auntie in an open-air touring car with a grand building in the background.

40 Ibid.

41 The Smithsonian now has this song in its National Museum of American History collection, *America on the Move.*

42 inventors.about.com/od/gstartinventions/a/gasoline_2.htm; McShane, 47.

43 *Kansas City* (Mo.) *Star,* 16 May 1913. According to the *Kansas City* (Mo.) *Star,* 14 Oct 1914, the $12,000 country club house opened on October 14, 1914. Nineteen months prior, the old clubhouse 300 yards east of the present site, was destroyed by fire. They then built a $50,000 downtown clubhouse and garage at 1020 Oak Street. The stone for the building was taken from the farm of A. D. Cottingham, one of the club's directors, adjoining the property of the club. "Not even an architect was employed to draw up the plans. That was done by members." The architect was Kansas City's Louis Curtiss, who was mentioned previously in 1904 with his connection to the Kansas City's Board of Examiners of Automobile Operators. The drive to the club—in the country at that time—took 30-minutes each way, "south on Wornall past the Red Bridge Road, and east on that road to the club grounds, turning back at the junction of the Red Bridge Road and the Grandview Road."

Chapter 32

1 Yergin, 782.

2 inventors.about.com/od/gstartinventions/a/gasoline_2.htm

3 Ibid., 51

4 *Kansas City* (Mo.) *Star,* 29 Jul 1916.

5 *Kansas City Sun,* 1 Sept 1917.

6 McShane, 51.

7 Ibid.

8 Ibid., 52.

9 Ibid. 53.

10 Ibid.

11 Ibid.

12 Ibid.

13 Ibid.

14 Ibid.

15 en.wikipedia.org/wiki/Smog#Major_incidents_in_the_US

16 McShane, 53.

17 radford.edu/--wkovarik/papers/kettering.html.

[18] McShane, 56.

[19] Ibid., 55.

[20] Ibid.

[21] history.com

[22] McShane, 57.

[23] Ibid., 57.

[24] en.wikipedia.org/wiki/Smog#Major_incidents_in_the_US.

[25] Ibid.

[26] en.wikipedia.org/wiki/Tetra-ethyl_lead.

[27] Ausebel, 2.

[28] fuel-testers.com/ethanol_fuel_history.html.

[29] Holley, 139.

[30] Olson, op. cit., 14.

[31] Denison, 16.

[32] *Kansas City* (Mo.) *Star,* 2 Jul 1918 and 26 Jun 1919.

[33] globallleadnet.com/132/timeline-8500-years-of-lead-79-years of leaded gasoline.

[34] Ibid.

[35] en.wikipedia.org/wiki/Tetra-ethyl_lead.

[36] McShane, 59.

[37] *Kansas City* (Mo.) *Star*, 26 Sept., 23 Oct, 11 Dec, 13 Dec, 14 Dec, 16 Dec, 26 Dec 1922; 26 July 1923; 21 Apr 1924.

[38] *Kansas City* (Mo.) *Star*, 30 July 1922.

[39] Ibid.

[40] globallleadnet.com/132/timeline-8500-years-of-lead-79-years of leaded gasoline.

[41] Ibid.

[42] Ibid.

[43] en.wikipedia.org/wiki/Tetra-ethyl_lead.

[44] globallleadnet.com/132/timeline-8500-years-of-lead-79-years of leaded gasoline.

[45] Yergin, 1991, 782.

[46] inventors.about.com/od/gstartinventions/a/gasoline_2.htm.

[47] Ibid.

[48] McShane, 62.

[49] Ibid.

[50] inventors.about.com/od/gstartinventions/a/gasoline_2.htm.

[51] *Kansas City* (Mo.) *Star*, 13 July 1924.

[52] J. Bradford Delong, "XIII. The Roaring Twenties." Slouching Towards Utopia? The Economic History of the Twentieth Century.

[53] Denison, 17.

[54] Yergin, 1991, 783.

[55] Ibid.

[56] Ibid.

[57] McShane, 63.

[58] Ibid.

[59] inventors.about.com/od/gstartinventions/a/gasoline_2.htm.

[60] en.wikipedia.org/wiki/Tetra-ethyl_lead.

[61] inventors.about.com/od/gstartinventions/a/gasoline_2.htm.

[62] globallleadnet.com/132/timeline-8500-years-of-lead-79-years of leaded gasoline.

[63] McShane, 65.

[64] globallleadnet.com/132/timeline-8500-years-of-lead-79-years of leaded gasoline.

[65] Ibid.

[66] *Los Angeles Times*, July 4, 1925 section H, weekly to the end of September; imdb.com/title/tt0004262/, accessed 9 Apr 2011.

[67] Ibid.

[68] Ibid.

[69] Ibid.

[70] *Kansas City* (Mo.) *Star*, 12 Feb 1928.

[71] Ibid.

[72] McShane, 72, Yergin, 1991, 783.

[73] McShane, 73.

[74] McShane, 74.

[75] Ibid.

[76] Ibid.

[77] Ellery Queen, *Roman Hat Mystery*, 1929.

[78] Ibid.

[79] globallleadnet.com/132/timeline-8500-years-of-lead-79-years of leaded gasoline.

[80] Yergin, 1991, 783.

[81] McShane, 75.

[82] Olson, op. cit., 19.

[83] *Monroe Country (IA) News*, March 8, 2011, 3.

[84] McShane, 77.

[85] globallleadnet.com/132/timeline-8500-years-of-lead-79-years of leaded gasoline.

[86] McShane, 78.

[87] Ibid.

[88] Ibid.

[89] Ibid.

[90] "A New Jackson County: Judge Truman Recites Progress and Hope for Chamber of Commerce," *Kansas City* (Mo.) *Star*, 11 May 1932; 30 Nov 1983, Wednesday Extra, North and Central Jackson County Section, 1, 8 (and in the Kansas City-Jackson County edition on 7 Dec 1983, 6); also, 6 May 1984, 2E; Jackson, David, W. "Little Blue Valley holds vistas and history," 26 July 2006, 6; and Jackson, David W. "Bridge over Blue River marks historic crossing," 7 Feb 2007, 12. The 1932 article continued: "The County Court distributed at the Chamber of Commerce luncheon today a booklet of 125-pages showing the Results of County Planning in Jackson County. It reveals in hundreds of photographic reproductions beauties of rural scenes to which the average Kansas Citian is a stranger. Jackson County, with its wooded hills, its rolling farmland, its rugged rock outcroppings, and its winding streams long ago was referred to as a natural park by such men as Thomas Hart Benton and Washington Irving. The camera caught for the booklet and recorded for all time much of the beauty that is Jackson County. The booklet pictures it as Kansas City's front yard, its playground. Here and there, in photographs, are glimpses of sweeping concrete highway, but the highway program of the county is only incidental in the collective picture the booklet presents. Its purpose is to arouse in citizens a sense of appreciation of the unusual natural beauty that surrounds them in this county and to stimulate interest in the remainder of the county plan, the park and recreation system.... Truman states the purpose of the booklet in a cover letter that in Results of County Planning, to officials across the country: "I am sending you this book in the belief that counties in every section of the country are overlooking some organized developments that would add to the health, the pleasure and the prosperity of every citizen.... 'At today's cost, a roads project of the same magnitude would cost more than $50 million—five times the original bond issues...' Truman wrote in his Pickwick Hotel account: 'After the [bond] issue carried my troubles began. The BOSS [Tom Pendergast] wanted me to give a lot of crooked contractors the inside and I couldn't.' Pendergast had financial interests in the concrete business, and his political machine, which Truman had supported Truman, dominated county politics at the time.... 'If I had been a crook or if Veatch and Stayton had been crooks, my career as a public official would have been the usual scandal.'"

[91] Jackson County Court. *Results of County Planning: Jackson County, Missouri.* (1932).

[92] globallleadnet.com/132/timeline-8500-years-of-lead-79-years of leaded gasoline
[93] McShane, 80.
[94] globallleadnet.com/132/timeline-8500-years-of-lead-79-years of leaded gasoline
[95] Ibid., 81.
[96] Ibid.
[97] Ibid.
[98] Ibid., 84.
[99] inventors.about.com/od/gstartinventions/a/gasoline_2.htm; *Kansas City* (Mo.) *Star*, 7 Feb 1939.
[100] McShane, 89.
[101] John Simonton, *Kansas City, 1940, A Watershed Year,* History Press, Charleston, 2013, p. 83.
[102] Ibid.
[103] McShane, 89.
[104] Simonton, 31. (1940 was the year that Tom Pendergast was run out of town and the city began to create the wholesome image it has today.)
[105] Ibid. 81.
[106] Ibid.,129.
[107] *The Fairfax Plant Celebrates 50 Years of Teamwork: 1946-1996.*
[108] fuel-testers.com/ethanol_fuel_history.html, accessed 16 Aug 2011.
[109] *Kansas City* (Mo.) *Star*, 8 Oct 1941.
[110] "Gas rationing during WW2," alumnibhs.com/old geezer photos/gas_rationing_during_ww3.htm, accessed 9 Aug 2017; *Kansas City* (Mo.) *Star,* 1 Dec 1942.
[111] McShane, 92.
[112] Ibid.
[113] Ibid.
[114] Ibid.
[115] Jesse Ausubel, *Daedalus* 125(3):1-17 (Summer 1996), accessed 4 June 2018.
[116] McShane, 93.
[117] Ibid.
[118] J. R. McNeill, Peter Engelke, *The Great Acceleration, An Environmental History of the Anthropocene since 1945.*
[119] *The Fairfax Plant Celebrates 50 Years of Teamwork: 1946-1996.*

Chapter 33

[1] McShane, 96.
[2] *The Fairfax Plant Celebrates 50 Years of Teamwork: 1946-1996.*
[3] Yergin, 783.
[4] *Kansas City* (Mo.) *Star*, 25 June 1947; 25 Jan 1948.
[5] Ibid.
[6] globallleadnet.com/132/timeline-8500-years-of-lead-79-years of leaded gasoline
[7] McShane, 99.
[8] Yergin, 1991, 783.
[9] McShane, 99.
[10] Ibid.
[11] Ibid.
[12] en.wikipedia.org/wiki/Arie_Jan_Haagen-Smit.
[13] Ibid.
[14] *Kansas City* (Mo.) *Star*, 20 Feb and 21 Oct 1956.
[15] McShane, 102.
[16] Ibid.
[17] Ibid.
[18] Ibid.

[19] *The Fairfax Plant Celebrates 50 Years of Teamwork: 1946-1996.*

[20] *Kansas City* (Mo.) *Star*, 20 Feb and 21 Oct 1956.

[21] Yergin, 1991, 783. cnn.com, accessed 4 June 2018.

[22] kshs.org, accessed 4 June 2018.

[23] McShane, 103.

[24] Ibid., 104.

[25] globallleadnet.com/132/timeline-8500-years-of-lead-79-years of leaded gasoline.

[26] *Kansas City* (Mo.) *Star*, 20 Feb and 21 Oct 1956.

[27] McShane, 106.

[28] Ibid.

[29] Yergin, 1991, 783.

[30] Ibid.

[31] *Kansas City* (Mo.) *Star*, 19, 20, and 23 June 1957; 22 Aug 1957.

[32] Yergin, 1991, 783.

[33] Ibid.

[34] Ibid.

[35] globallleadnet.com/132/timeline-8500-years-of-lead-79-years of leaded gasoline

[36] Ibid.

[37] Yergin,1991, 783; globallleadnet.com/132/timeline-8500-years-of-lead-79-years of leaded gasoline

[38] globallleadnet.com/132/timeline-8500-years-of-lead-79-years of leaded gasoline

[39] Helen Leavitt, *Superhighway—or Superhoax* (New York: Doubleday, Inc. 1970) p. 303.

[40] Yergin, 1991, 783.

[41] Ibid.

[42] globallleadnet.com/132/timeline-8500-years-of-lead-79-years of leaded gasoline.

[43] Yergin,1991, 783.

[44] globallleadnet.com/132/timeline-8500-years-of-lead-79-years of leaded gasoline

[45] Olson, op. cit., 24.

[46] globallleadnet.com/132/timeline-8500-years-of-lead-79-years of leaded gasoline

[47] en.wikipedia.org/wiki/Club_of_Rome, accessed 5 Oct 2016.

[48] globallleadnet.com/132/timeline-8500-years-of-lead-79-years of leaded gasoline

[49] Yergin, 1991, 784. *Kansas City* (Mo.) *Star,* 17 May and 31 July 1973.

[50] *Kansas City* (Mo.) *Star,* 31 Oct 1993.

[51] globallleadnet.com/132/timeline-8500-years-of-lead-79-years of leaded gasoline

[52] Yergin, 1991, 784.

[53] Olson, op. cit., 23.

[54] fuel-testers.com/ethanol_fuel_history.html, accessed 16 Aug 2017.

[55] Yergin, 1991, 784.

Chapter 34

[1] globallleadnet.com/132/timeline-8500-years-of-lead-79-years of leaded gasoline.

[2] en.wikipedia.org/wiki/Gasoline. A Quarles 18-20, accessed 22 June 2017.

[3] en.wikipedia.org/wiki/energy tax act.

[4] Yergin, 1991, 784.

[5] Ibid.

[6] Ibid.

[7] Ibid.

[8] globallleadnet.com/132/timeline-8500-years-of-lead-79-years of leaded gasoline.

[9] Ibid.

[10] Ibid.

[11] Ibid.

[12] Ibid.

[13] Ibid.

[14] Ibid.

[15] epa.gov/oust/faqs/genesis1.htm, accessed 11 July 2017.

[16] Wikipedia, Wolf Creek Generating Station.

[17] epa.gov/oust/faqs/genesis1.htm, accessed 11 July 2017.

[18] *The Fairfax Plant Celebrates 50 Years of Teamwork: 1946-1996.*

[19] fuel-testers.com/ethanol_fuel_history.html, accessed 16 Aug 2017.

[20] Ibid.

[21] Yergin, 2009, 777.

[22] wikipedia.org/wiki/Tetra-ethyl_lead.

[23] *Kansas City* (Mo.) *Star,* 17 Feb 1992.

[24] globallleadnet.com/132/timeline-8500-years-of-lead-79-years of leaded gasoline

[25] en.wikipedia.org/wiki/Gasoline, accessed 22 June 2017.

[26] globallleadnet.com/132/timeline-8500-years-of-lead-79-years of leaded gasoline

[27] *Kansas City* (Mo.) *Star,* 11 Oct 1997.

[28] Yergin, 2009, 777.

[29] en.wikipedia.org/wiki/Methyl_tert-butyl_ether, accessed 24 June 2017.

[30] globallleadnet.com/132/timeline-8500-years-of-lead-79-years of leaded gasoline.

[31] *Kansas City* (Mo.) *Star,* 6 Jan 2000.

[32] fuel-testers.com/ethanol_fuel_history.html, accessed 16 Aug 2017.

[33] Ibid.

[34] Yergin, 2009, 777.

[35] Ibid.

[36] fuel-testers.com/ethanol_fuel_history.html, accessed 16 Aug 2017.

[37] Yergin, 2009, 777.

[38] epa.gov/oust/faqs/genesis1.htm, accessed 11 July 2017.

[39] fuel-testers.com/ethanol_fuel_history.html, accessed 16 Aug 2017.

[40] Ibid.

[41] Wikipedia, Wolf Creek Generating Station.

[42] *The Fairfax Plant Celebrates 50 Years of Teamwork: 1946-1996.*

[43] Yergin, 2009, 777.

[44] Ibid.

[45] en.wikipedia.org/wiki/Tetra-ethyl_lead.

[46] epa.gov/oust/faqs/genesis1.htm, accessed 11 Jul 2017.

[47] stories.weather .com, accessed 4 June 2018.

[48] Ibid.

[49] Jamie Lincon Kitman, "Volkswagon Lied and Cheated 11 Million Times, Will Anyone Go to Jail for That?" October 1, 2015, thenation.com.

[50] Ibid.

[51] *Kansas City* (Mo.) *Star,* 26 Jan 2015.

[52] *Kansas City* (Mo.) *Star,* 16 Oct 2015.

[53] nerdwallet.com/blog/loans/electric-hybrid-gas-how-they-compare-costs-2015/, accessed, 19 Sep 2017.

[54] *Kansas City* (Mo.) *Star,* 5 May 2017

[55] statistica.com, accessed 4 June 2018.

[56] eia.gov. accessed 4 June 2018.

[57] Kathryn Hall, *Solar Energy Technologies and the Utilization on Native American Tribal Lands*, University of North Dakota, 2017.

[58] energy.gov, accessed 4 June 2018.

[59] bp.com, accessed 4 June 2018.

[60] *The Fairfax Plant Celebrates 50 Years of Teamwork: 1946-1996.*
[61] *Kansas City Pioneer*, 1920.

Part 4

[1] Climate Disruption Index, weather.com.
[2] Dan Walker, PH.D. A.M. ASCE, Climate Moneys LLC and Christopher Anderson, Ph.D. Iowa State University, climatelook.com. Sponsored by *Risky Business* Co-Chairs, Michael R. Bloomberg, Henry Paulson and Tom Steyer.
[3] In the 116th Congress, The Green New Deal is a pair of resolutions, H. Res. 109/ S. Res. 59, sponsored by Rep. Alexandria Ocasio-Cortez (D-NY) and Sen. Ed Markey (D-MA). "On January 10, 2019, a letter signed by 626 organizations in support of a Green New Deal was sent to all members of Congress. It called for measures such as "an expansion of the Clean Air Act; a ban on crude oil exports; an end to fossil fuel subsidies and fossil fuel leasing; and a phase-out of all gasoline-powered vehicles by 2040." en.wikipedia.org/wiki/Green_New_Deal and congress.gov/bill/116th-congress/house-resolution/109/text, accessed 3 Mar 2019.
[4] theweek.com/articles/815287/green-new-deal-cars-easier-than-think, accessed 3 Mar 2019.

Appendices

[1] firstpeople.us/FP-Html-Treaties/TreatyWithTheKiowaetc1837.html, accessed 9 Dec 2018.
[2] congress.gov/bill/116th-congress/house-resolution/109/text, accessed 3 Mar 2019.

Fueling Change

Illustrations

Unless otherwise noted, all images appear courtesy of and with great appreciation to Missouri Valley Special Collections, Kansas City Public Library, Kansas City, Missouri.

Part 1

Fueling Change

Fueling Change

Part 2

Fueling Change

Part 3

Fueling Change

Part 4

All remaining images in Part 4 and Appendices are anonymous, public domain-sourced images.

References

Books

Adams, Richard N., *Paradoxical Harvest: Energy and explanation in British History, 1870-1914: Energy and Explanation in British History, 1870-1914* (Cambridge: Cambridge University Press 1982).

Adams, Sean Patrick, *Old Dominion: Industrial Commonwealth: Coal Politics, and Economy in Antebellum America* (Baltimore, MD: Johns Hopkins University Press, 2004).

Allen, Michael, *Western Rivermen 1763-1861: Ohio and Mississippi Boatmen and the Myth of the Alligator Horse* (Baton Rouge: Louisiana State University Press, 1990).

Bailey, Garrick Alan, *Changes in Osage Social Organization, 1673-1906* (University of Oregon Anthropological Papers, No 5, 1973).

Bailey, Garrick A., ed., *The Osage and the Invisible World from the Works of Francis La Flesche* (Norman: University of Oklahoma, 1995).

Baldwin, Leland D., *The Keelboat Age on the Western Waters* (Pittsburgh, University Press, 1941).

Barth, Gunther, *Instant Cities: Urbanization and the Rise of San Francisco and Denver* (Albuquerque: University of New Mexico Press, 1975, 1988).

Berzok, Linda Murray, *American Indian Food* (Westport, CT: Greenwood Press, 2005).

Bishop, Philip W., *The Beginnings of Cheap Steel* (Washington, D.C.: Smithsonian Institute, 1959).

Black, Brian, *Petrolia: The Landscape of America's First Oil Boom* (Baltimore, MD: The Johns Hopkins University Press, 2000).

Bloomberg, Michael and Carl Pope, *Climate of Hope: How Cities, Businesses, and Citizens Can Save the Planet* (St Martin's Press, 2017).

Boyd, James P., *Triumphs and Wonders of the 19th Century: The Mirror of a Phenomenal Era* (Philadelphia: A. J. Holman and Co., 1899).

Borneman, Walter R., *1812: The War that Forged a Nation* (New York: HarperCollins, 2004).

Bradbury, John, *Travels in the Interior of America* (University Microfilms, 1966; originally published 1819).

Bright, Arthur, *The Electric Lamp Industry: Technological Change and Economic Development from 1800-1947* (New York: MacMillan, 1949).

Fueling Change

Brown, A. Theodore, *Frontier Community:* Kansas City to 1870 (Columbia, MO: University Press, 1963).
——and Lyle W. Dorsett, *K.C. A History of Kansas City, Missouri* (Boulder, CO: Pruett Publishing Company, 1978).

Burke, Diane Mutti and John Herron, *Kansas City, America's Crossroads: Essays from the Missouri Historical Review, 1906-2006* (State Historical Society of Missouri, Columbia, MO, 2007).

Burns, Louis F., *A History of the Osage People* (Tuscaloosa: University of Alabama Press, 2004).

——*Osage Indian Customs and Myths* (Tuscaloosa: University of Alabama Press, 1984).

Carlson, Paul H. *The Plains Indians* (College Station: A&M University Press, 1998).

Case, Theodore S., *History of Kansas City Missouri* (Kansas City, MO, 1888).

Chamber of Commerce, *Where These Rocky Bluffs Meet* (Kansas City, Missouri, 1938).

Chaput, Donald, *Francois X. Aubry: Trader, Trailmaker and Voyageur in the Southwest, 1846-1854* (Glendale, CA: Arthur H. Clark Co, 1975).

Chanute, O., *The Kansas City Bridge with an Account of the Regimen of the Missouri River, and a Description of Methods Used for Founding in that River* (New York: Van Nostrand, Publisher, 1876).

Catton, William, Jr., *Overshoot: The Ecological Basis of Revolutionary Change* (Urbana: University of Illinois Press (1980).

Christian, Shirley, *Before Lewis and Clark: The Story of the Chouteaus, the French Dynasty That Ruled America's Frontier* (New York: Farrar, Straus and Giroux, 2004).

Clark, John G., *Energy and the Federal Government: Fossil Fuel Policies, 1900-1946* (Urbana, IL: University Press, 1987).

Conard, Howard C., *Encyclopedia of Missouri*, Vol I-X (St. Louis: Southern History Company, 1901).

Connor, Seymour CV., and Jimmy M. Skaggs, *Broadcloth and Britches* (College Station: Texas A & M University Press, 1977).

Corbett, Christopher, *Orphans Preferred: The Twisted Truth and Lasting Legend of the Pony Express* (New York: Broadway, 203).

Corbin, David Alan, *Life, Work, and Rebellion in the Coal Fields: The Southern West Virginia Miners 1880-1922* (Urbana: University of Illinois Press, 1981).

Cordley, Richard, D. D., *The History of Lawrence, Kansas, from the Earliest Settlement to the Close of the Rebellion,* (Lawrence: Journal Press, 1895).

Cottrell, Fred, *Energy and Society: The Relations between Energy, Social Change, and Economic Development* (Westport, CT: Greenwood Press, 1955).

Cudahy, Brian J., *Cash Tokens and Transfers: A History of Urban Mass Transit in North America* (Fordham University Press, New York, 1990).

Cronon, William, *Changes in the Land, Indians, Colonists and the Ecology of New England* (1983 (New York: Hill and Wang, 1983).

Dary, David, *The Santa Fe Trail: Its History, Legends, and Lore* (New York: Alfred A. Knopf, 2000).

De Angelo, Dory, *Voices Across Time: Profiles of Kansas City's Early Residents* (Kansas City, MO: Tapestry Publications, 1987).

——*What About Kansas City! A Historical Handbook* (Kansas City, MO: Two Lane Press, 1995).

Deffeyes, Kenneth S., *Hubbert's Peak: The Impending World Oil Shortage* (New York: W. W. Norton & Co., 2004).

——*Beyond Oil: The View from Hubbert's Peak* (New York: Hill and Wang, 2005).

Demarest, David P., and Fannia Weingartner, *"The River Ran Red:" Homestead 1892* (Pittsburgh, PA: The University of Pittsburgh Press, 1992)

Di Cicchio, Carmen, *Coal and Coke in Pennsylvania* (Harrisburg, PA: Pennsylvania Historical and Museum Commission, 1996).

Dick, Everett, *Vanguards of the Frontier: A Social History of the Northern Plains and Rocky Mountains from the Earliest White Contacts to the Coming of the Homemaker* (New York: Appleton-Century, 1941).

Dolson, Hildegarde, *The Great Oildorado: The Gaudy and Turbulent Years of the First Oil Rush* (New York: Random House, 1959).

Du Boff, Richard B., *Electric Power in American Manufacturing, 1889-1958* (New York: Arno Press, 1979).

Edison Institute, *The Electric Industry* (New York: Edison Electric Institute, 1951).

Eavenson, Harold F., *The First Century and A Quarter of the American Coal Industry* (Pittsburgh, PA, 1942).

Ehrlich, George, Kansas City, Missouri, *An Architectural History, 1826-1976* (Kansas City, MO: Historic Foundation of Kansas City, 1979).

Ellis, William Donohue, *On the Oil Lands with Cities Service* (N.p.: Cities Service Oil and Gas Corporation, 1983).

Ellison, George, *James Mooney's History, Myths, and Sacred Formulas of the Cherokees* (Asheville NC: Historical Images, 1992; originally published 1900).

Featherstonhaugh, G. W., *Excursion through the Slave States, from Washington on the Potomac to the Frontier of Mexico; with Sketches of Popular Manners and Geological Notices* (New York: Negro Universities Press, 1968; originally published New York: Harper and Brothers, 1844).

Fishback, Price V., *Soft Coal, Hard Choices: The Economic Welfare of Bituminous Coal Miners, 1890-1930* (New York: Oxford University Press, 1992).

Fowler, Loretta, *The Columbia Guide to American Indians of the Great Plains* (New York: Columbia University Press, 2003).

Fueling Change

Frazier, Harriet C., *Runaway and Freed Missouri Slaves and Those Who Helped Them, 1763-1865* (Jefferson, North Carolina: McFarland & Co., 2004).

Freese, Barbara, *Coal: A Human History* (Cambridge, MA: Perseus, 2003).

Fuller, E., *Extinct Birds* (New York: Facts on File Publications, 1987).

Giddens, Paul, *Standard Oil Company of Indiana: Oil Pioneer of the Middle West* (New York: Appleton, Century Crofts, 1955).

Gordon, Robert B., *American Iron, 1607-1900* (Baltimore, MD: Johns Hopkins Press, 1996).

Grant, William, *The Romantic Past of the Kansas City Region, 1540-1880* (Kansas City, MO: Business Men's Assurance Company of America, 1987).

Greeley, Horace, *An Overland Journey from New York to San Francisco, in the Summer of 1859* (New York: Alfred A. Knopf, 1964).

Greene, Lorenzo J., et. al., *The Role of the Negro in Missouri History, 1719-1970* (St. Louis: Lincoln University Official Manual, State of Missouri, 1973-1974).

Gregg, Josiah, *Commerce of the Prairies: Life on the Great Plains in the 1830's and 1840's* (Santa Barbara: The Narrative Press, 2001, originally published 1845).

Grossman, Mark, *The ABC-CLIO Companion to The Environmental Movement* (ABC-CLIO, 1994).

Haites, Erik, James Mak and Gary M. Walton, *Western River Transportation: The Era of Early Internal Development, 1810-1860* (Baltimore: Johns Hopkins Press, 1975).

Hart, Albert Bushnell, *Slavery and Abolition, 1831-18*41 (New York: Harper Brothers, 1906).

Hickman, W. Z., *History of Jackson County, Missouri* (Topeka, KS: Historical Publishing Company 1920).

Hindle, Brooke, ed., *America's Wooden Age: Aspects of its Early Technology* (Tarrytown, NY: Sleepy Hollow Press, 1976).

Hubaleck, Linda K., *Trail of Thread: Historical Letters 1854-1855* (Aurora, CO: Butterfield Books, 1995).

Hulbert, Archer B., *Waterways of Westward Expansion: The Ohio River and Its Tributaries* (Cleveland, 1903).

Hunter, Louis C., *Steamboats on the Western Rivers: An Economic and Technological History* (New York: Dover Publications, 1949).

Hurt, R. Douglas, *Agriculture and Slavery in Little Dixie* (Columbia: University of Missouri Press, 1992).

Illustrated Historical Atlas of Boone County, Missouri (Philadelphia, 1876).

Irving, Washington, *A Tour on the Prairies*, John Francis McDermott, ed. (Norman: University of Oklahoma Press, 1956, fourth printing, 1985; originally published 1835).

Jackson, David W. *Born a Slave: Rediscovering Arthur Jackson's African American Heritage* (Greenwood, MO: The Orderly Pack Rat, 2015).

——*Kansas City Chronicles: An Up-to-Date History* (Charleston, SC: The History Press, 2010).

——*Winding the Clock on the Independence Square: Jackson County's Historic Truman Courthouse* (Independence, MO: Jackson County Historical Society, 2013).

Johnson, Paul Louis, *Horses of the German Army in World War II* (Gloucester, MA: 2006).

Krause, Paul, *The Battle for Homestead, 1880-1892: Politics, Culture, and Steel* (Pittsburgh, PA: University of Pittsburgh Press, 1992).

Larsen, Lawrence H., *The Urban West at the End of the Frontier* (Lawrence: University of Kansas, 1978).

Lass, William E., *From the Missouri to the Great Salt Lake: An Account of Overland Freighting* (Nebraska State Historical Society, 1972).

Lewin, Jacqueline and Marilyn Taylor, *On the Winds of Destiny: A Biographical Look at Pony Express Riders* (St. Joseph: Platte Purchase Publishers, 2002).

Majors, Alexander, *Seventy Years on the Frontier: Lifetime on the Border* (Minneapolis: Ross & Haines, Inc., 1965).

Mathews, John Joseph, *The Osages: Children of the Middle Waters* (Norman: University of Oklahoma Press, 1961).

——*Wah'kon-tah: The Osage and the White Man's Road* (Norman: University of Oklahoma Press, 1932).

McCandless, Perry, *A History of Missouri*, Volume II, 1820 to 1860 (Columbia: University of Missouri Press, 1971, 2000).

McGaw, Judith, *Early American Technology: Making and Doing Things from the Colonial Era to 1850* (Chapel Hill, NC: University of North Carolina Press, 1994).

McCutcheon, Marc, *Writers Guide to Everyday life in the 1800s* (Cincinnati: Writers Digest Books, 1993).

Mein, D. W., The *Shaping of America: A Geographical Perspective on 500 Years of History*, Volume 2: Continental America, 1800-1867. New Haven: Yale University Press, 1993).

Melosi, Martin V., *Coping with Abundance: Energy and Abundance in Industrial America* (New York: Alfred A. Knopf, 1985).

——*Thomas A. Edison and the Modernization of America* (New York: Longman, 1990).

Mercantile Illustrating Company, *Imperial Kansas City 1900: Her Wonderful Growth and Resources* (Kansas City, Missouri, 1900).

Merrick, George Byron, *Old Times on the Upper Mississippi: Recollections of a Steamboat Pilot from 1854 to 1863* (Minneapolis: University of Minnesota Press, 2001, originally published 1909).

Fueling Change

Miller, William, *History of Kansas City* (Kansas City: Hudson-Kimberly Publishing Co., 1900).

Miner, Craig, *Discovery! Cycles of Change in the Kansas Oil and Gas Industry, 1860-1987* (Wichita: Kioga, 1987).

Morgan, Ted, *Wilderness at Dawn: The Making of the American West 1800 to the Present* (New York: Simon and Schuster, 1995.

Morse, Jedediah, *A Report to the Secretary of War of the United States* (New York: Augustus M. Kelley, 1970, originally published 1822).

Moulton, Gary E., ed., *The Definitive Journals of Lewis & Clark from the Ohio to the Vermillion, Volume 2 of the Nebraska Edition* (Lincoln: University of Nebraska Press, 1986).

Mumford, Lewis, *Technics and Civilization* (San Diego, CA: Harcourt Brace, 1934).

National Electrical Manufacturers Association, *A Chronological History of Electrical Development from 600 B.C.* (New York, 1946).

Norall, Frank, *Bourgmont: Explorer of the Missouri, 1698-1725* (Lincoln: University of Nebraska Press, 1988).

Nye, David E., *Consuming Power: A Social History of American Energies* (Cambridge, MA: MIT Press, 1998).

——*Electrifying America: Social Meanings of a New Technology, 1880-1940* (Cambridge: The MIT Press, 1995).

Odum, Howard T., and Elisabeth C. Odum, *Energy Basis for Man and Nature* (New York: McGraw Hill, 1976).

Parkman, Francis, *The Oregon Trail* (New York: Literary Classics of America, 1991, originally published 1847).

Parrish, William E., *History of Missouri, III, 1860-1875*, (Columbia: University of Missouri Press, 1973, 2001).

Perlin, John, *A Forest Journey: The Role of Wood in the Development of Civilization* (Cambridge, MA: Harvard University Press, 1989).

Petulla, Joseph M., *American Environmental History* (San Francisco, CA: Boyd and Fraser Publishing, 1977).

Platt, Harold L., *The Electric City: Energy and Growth of the Chicago Area, 1880-1930* (Chicago: University of Chicago Press, 1991).

Pratt, Joe, *The Ascent of Oil*, Lewis Perleman, et. al., eds., *Energy Transitions: Long-term Perspectives* (Boulder, CO: Westview Press, 1981).

Rafferty, Milton D., ed., *Rude Pursuits and Rugged Peaks, Schoolcraft's Ozark Journal 1818-1819* (Little Rock: University of Arkansas Press, 1996).

Raymond, Robert, Out of *the Fiery Furnace: The Impact of Metals on the History of Mankind* (University Park: The Pennsylvania State University Press, 1986).

Reynolds, Terry S., *Stronger than A Hundred Men: A Historical View of the Vertical Water Wheel* (Baltimore, MD: Johns Hopkins University Press, 1983).

Rose, Mark H., *Cities of Light and Heat: Domesticating Gas and Electricity in Urban America*, (University Park, PA: Pennsylvania State University Press, 1995).

Powell, H. Benjamin, *Philadelphia's First Fuel Crisis: Jacob Cist and the Developing Market for Pennsylvania Anthracite* (University Park: Pennsylvania State University Press, 1978).

Schama, Simon, *Rough Crossings: Britain, the Slaves and the American Revolution* (London: Ecco: 2006).

Schivelbusch, Wolfgang, *Disenchanted Night: The Industrialization of Light in the 19th century* (Berkeley, CA: University of California Press, 1995).

Schorger, A. W., *The Passenger Pigeon* (Madison, University of Wisconsin Press, 1961).

Schruben, Francis, *WEA Creek to El Dorado: Oil in Kansas, 1860-1920* (Columbia: University of Missouri Press, 1972).

Schurick, A. T., *The Coal Industry* (Boston: Little, Brown and Company, 1924).

Schurr, Sam H. and Bruce C. Netschert, et. al., *Energy in the American Economy, 1850-1975* (Baltimore, MD: The Johns Hopkins Press, 1960).

Schweider, Dorothy, *Black Diamonds: Life and Work in Iowa's Coal Mining Communities, 1895-1925* (Ames: Iowa State University Press, 1983).

Sieferle, Rolf Peter, The *Subterranean Forest: Energy Systems and the Industrial Revolution* (White Horse Press, Cambridge, UK, 2001; originally published in German in 1982).

Smil, Vaclav, *Energy in World History* (Boulder, CO: Westview Press, 1994).

——*Transforming the 20th Century: Technical Innovations and Their Consequences* (New York: Oxford University Press, 2006).

——*Energy in Nature and Society: General Energetics of Complex Systems* (Cambridge, MA: MIT Press, 2008).
——*Energy and Civilization: A History* (MIT Press) 2017.

Spalding, C. C., *Annals of the City of Kansas* (Kansas City: Van Horn & Abeel's Printing House, 1858).

Stebbins, L. *One Hundred Years' Progress of the United States* (Hartford, CT: By the author, 1872).

Sutcliffe, Andrea, *Steam: The Untold Story of America's First Great Invention* (New York: Macmillan, 2004).

Tarr, Joel "Transforming an Energy System," Olivier Coutard ed., *The Governance of Large Technical Systems* (London: Routledge, 1999).

Tarr, Joel and Clay McShane, "Urban Horses and Changing City-Hinterland Relationships in the United States," *Resources of the City: Contributions to an Environmental History of Modern Europe*, Dieter Schott, et. al., eds (Burlington, VT: Ashgate, 2005).

Fueling Change

Temin, Peter, *Iron and Steel in the 19th century: An Economic Inquiry* (Cambridge, MA: MIT Press, 1964).

Twain, Mark, *Life on the Mississippi* (New York: Viking Penguin, 1984; originally published 1883).

——*Roughing It* (New York: Penguin Books, 1962; originally published 1872.)

Unruh, John D., Jr., *The Plains Across: The Overland Emigrants and the Trans-Mississippi West, 1840-1860* (Urbana: University of Illinois Press, 1979).

Vale, Thomas R., ed., *Fire, Native Peoples, and the Natural Landscape* (Washington, D. C: Island Press, 2002).

Wade, Richard C., *The Urban Frontier: The Rise of Western Cities, 1790-1830* (Urbana: University of Chicago Press, 1959, reissued 1996).

Walker, Henry Pickering, *The Wagonmasters; High Plains Freighting from the Earliest Days of the Santa Fe Trail to 1880* (Norman: University of Oklahoma Press, 1966).

White, Leslie A., *The Science of Culture: A Study of Man and Civilization* (New York: Farrar, Straus and Giroux, 1949, 1969).

White, Richard, *The Roots of Dependency: Subsistence, Environment, and Social Change among the Choctaws, Pawnees, and Navajos* (Lincoln: University of Nebraska Press, 1983).

Whitney, Carrie, *Kansas City, Missouri: Its History and Its People, 1808-1908*, Vol. 1 & 2 (Chicago: The S. J. Clarke Publishing Co., 1908).

Wilhelm, Paul, Duke of Wurttemberg, *Travels in North America, 1822-1824, translated by W. Robert Nitske, ed, Savoie Lottinville* (Norman, University of Oklahoma Press, 1973).

Williams, James, *Energy and the Making of Modern California* (Akron: Akron University, 1997).

Williams, James. *Seventy-Five years on the Border* (Kansas City: Standard Printing Co., 1913).

Williamson, Harold F., and Arnold R. Daum, *The American Petroleum Industry: The Age of Illumination 1859-1899* (Evanston: Northwestern University Press, 1959).

Williamson, Harold F., et. al., *The American Petroleum Industry, 1899-1959: The Age of Energy* (Evanston: Northwestern University Press, 1963).

Wilson, Terry P., *The Underground Reservation: The Osage and Oil* (Lincoln: University of Nebraska Press, 1985).

Wolferman, Kristie C., *The Osage in Missouri* (Columbia: University of Missouri Press, 1997).

Wislizenus, F. A., M.D., *A Journey to the Rocky Mountains in the Year 1839* (New York: Cosimo Classics, 2005).

Yergen, Daniel, *The Prize: The Epic Quest for Oil, Money and Power* (New York: Simon and Schuster, 1991).

Youngquist, W. G., H. O. Fleischer, *Wood in American Life: 1776-2076* (Madison, WI: Forest Products Research Society, 1977).

Archives

Receipt book of steamboat *Columbian*, 1848-1851, Steamboats and River History Collection, Missouri Historical Society, St. Louis.

McCoy, John Calvin Collection (1811-1889), 1871-1950, State Historical Society of Missouri-Kansas City Research Center, University of Missouri--Kansas City.

Native Sons Archives, State Historical Society of Missouri-Kansas City Research Center, University of Missouri--Kansas City.

Original survey maps of Jackson County, MO, 1818-1843 (containing detailed analyses of natural resources and political boundary surveys relating to the early settlement of the county). Jackson County (MO) Historical Society Archives. Unpublished atlas.

Jackson County census reports prepared by Hattie Poppino, 1830, 1840, 1850. 1860, State Historical Society of Missouri-Kansas City Research Center, University of Missouri--Kansas City.

Periodicals

Annual of Kansas City, 1907, 1908.

Allison, Bill, "Sugar Creek Grew Up Around Oil Refinery," *Jackson County Historical Society Journal* (Volume XVII, No. 2, July 1975).

Ausubel, Jesse, 'The Liberation of the Environment," *Daedalus* 125(3):1-17 (Summer 1996) URL: http://phe.rockefeller.edu/Daedalus/Liberation/ accessed 6/4/18.

Beachum, Larry Mahon, "To the Westward: William Becknell and the Beginning of the Santa Fe Trade," *Journal of the West*, (Vol. 28, April 1989).

Becknell, Thomas, "The Journals of Thomas Becknell from Boone's Lick to Santa Fe, and from Santa Cruz to Green River," *Missouri Historical Review* (Vol. 4, No. 2, January 1910).

Broadhead, G. C., and Theodore S. Case, "Geology: Jackson County, Missouri," *Western Review of Science and Industry* (Issue 4 Volume 2, July 1878).

Brooks, Charles F., "The 'Old-fashioned' Winter of 1917-18," *Geographic Review*, (Vol. 5, No. 5, May 1918).

"Bypaths of Kansas History," "Kansas in 1854," from the *New York Daily Tribune*, New York, June 23, 1854, *Kansas Historical Quarterly* (Vol. 6, no. 3, August 1937).

Chandler, Alfred D., Jr., "Anthracite Coal and the Beginning of the Industrial Revolution in the United States," *Business History Review* (Summer, 1972).

Coal Age, 1912-1920.

Fueling Change

Conlin, John H., *Frontier Times* (Feb-March 1979).

Cook, Earl, "The Flow of Energy in an Industrial Society," *Scientific American* (Volume 225, Number 10, September 1971).

Donohue, James, ed. *Secretary Manufacturers and Merchants Association, Greater Kansas City Official Year Book 1904-5* (Made in Kansas City, USA, the Guaranty of Excellence).

Ellis, William Donohue, *On the Oil Lands with Cities Service* (n.p. Cities Service Oil and Gas Corporation, 1983).

Energy Information Administration, *State Coal Profiles: Missouri* (1993).

Evans, Priscilla Ann, "Merchant Gristmills and Communities 1820-1880," *Missouri Historical Review* (Columbia MO, vol. 68, April 1974).

Forbes, Gerald, "History of the Osage Blanket Lease," *The Chronicles of Oklahoma* 19 (March 1941).

Graves, Henry S., *The Use of Wood for Fuel*, Bulletin No. 753 (Washington, D. C.: United States Department of Agriculture, March 10, 1919).

Greene, Albert R., "The Kansas River--Its Navigation" *Transactions of the Kansas State Historical Society*, Geo W. Martin, ed, (Vol. IX, 1905-1906).

Greater Kansas City Yearbook, 1904-5.

Hale, George C. and T. R. Tinsley, *Souvenir of Kansas City and her Fire Department to the Grand International Fire Congress and Exhibition held at Royal Agricultural Hall, London, England,* (June 12th to 17th, 1893).

Hamalainen, Pekka, "The Rise and Fall of Plains Indian Horse Cultures," *Journal of American History* (December 2003).

Heizer, Robert F., "Domestic Fuel in Primitive Society," *The Journal of the Royal Anthropological Institute of Great Britain and Ireland* (Vol. 93, No. 2, July-Dec. 1963).

"Horseless Carriages Conquer Kansas City's hills after many trials have been overcome by the Locomobile," *Kansas City Manufac*turer (Summer, 1901).

Hughes, John Starret, "Lafayette County and the Aftermath of Slavery, 1861-1870," *Missouri Historical Review* (Volume LXXV, No. l, October 1920).

Illustrated Historical Atlas of Boone County, Missouri (Philadelphia, 1876).

Klein, Alan M., "Political Economy of the Buffalo Hide Trade: Race and Class on the Plains," *The Political Economy of the North American Indian*, John H. Moore, ed., (Norman: Univ. of Oklahoma Press, 1993).

Klein, Maury, "Jay Gould: A Revisionist Interpretation," *Business and Economic History*, (Second Series, Vol. 15, 1986).

418

Knight, W. B., "The Street Pavements in Kansas City," *Kansas City Review of Science and Industry,* 8 (1885).

La Flesche, Francis, "War Ceremony and Peace Ceremony of the Osage Indians," *Smithsonian Institution Bureau of American Ethnology, Bulletin 101* (Washington, D.C.: United States Printing Office: 1939).

La Roe, John, *Kansas City Magazine*, (Volume 12, issue 12).

Martin, Geo ed., "Westport and the Santa Fe Trade," *Transactions of the Kansas State Historical Society, 1907-1908* (Vol. X).

McLeod, William Christie, "Fuel and Early Civilization," *American Anthropologist,* (N. S. Vol 27, 1925).

Missouri Historical Review, State Historical Society of Missouri (Columbia: Volume 75, No. l, October 1920).

Moffat, Isaac, "The Kansas Prairie, Or Eight Days on the Plains (1858)," *Kansas Historical Quarterly*, (Vol. VI, No. 2, May 1973).

Moore, Powell, ed., "A Hoosier in Kansas-The Diary of Hiram H. Young, 1886-1895, Pioneer of Cloud County," *Kansas Historical Quarterly*, Part Four, 1893, February 1947 (Vol. 15 No. 1).

Morrison-Fuller, Berenice, "Glimpses of the Past, Missouri Plantation Life," *Missouri Historical Society* (Volume IV, January-March, Numbers 1-3 St. Louis, 1937).

Pyne, Stephen J., "Indian Fires: The fire practices of North American Indians transformed large areas from forest to grassland" *Natural History* (Vol. 92, No. 2, 1983).

Reynolds, R. V., and Albert H. Pierson, "Lumber Cut in the United States, 1870-1920," *Bulletin of the U. S. Department of Agriculture* (Issue 1119, 1923).

Root, George A., "Ferries in Kansas, Part I -- Missouri River," transcribed by Gardner Smith, *Kansas Historical Quarterly*. (Vol. 2, No. 1, February 1933).

Rose, Mark H. and John G. Clark, "Light, Heat, and Power: Energy Choices in Kansas City, Wichita, and Denver, 1900-1935," *Journal of Urban History (*Vol. 5, No. 3, May 1979).

Sanchez, Luis Enrique, ed., "Guidelines and Principles for Social Impact Assessment," *Impact Assessment* (Volume 2, No. 2, Summer, 1994.)

Schob, David E., "Wood hawks and Cordwood: Steamboat Fuel on the Ohio and Mississippi Rivers, 1820-1860," *Journal of American History* (July 1977).

Schmidt, Huburt, "Farming in Illinois a Century Ago as Illustrated in Bond County," *Journal of the Illinois State Historical Society* (31, 1938).

Seabright, Walter V., "Coal Production, Distribution and Consumption in Missouri," Information Circular No. 3, 1949, State of Missouri, Department of Business and Administration, Division of Geological Survey and Water Resources, Edward L. Clarke, State Geologist, Rolla, Missouri.

Sibley, George C., "Indian Mode of Life in Missouri and Kansas" *Missouri Historical Review* (No. 2, January 1910).

Sommer, Jane Hamill, "Outfitting the West, 1849," *Missouri Historical Society* (vol. 24, July 1968).

Tharp, James A., "Tumbledown of Gilliss House," *Jackson County Historical Society Newsletter* (Spring, 2004).

Va Nee L. Van Vleck, "Reassessing Technological Backwardness: Absolving the 'Silly Little Bobtailed' Coal Car," *The Journal of Economic History* (Vol. 55, No. 2, June 1995).

Viles, Jonas, "Old Franklin: A Frontier Town of the Twenties," *The Mississippi Valley Historical Review* (Vol. IX, No. 4, March 1923).

Williams, G. W., "Introduction to Aboriginal Fire Use in North America," *Fire Management Today* (60:3).

Wilson, Terry P., "Chief Fred Lookout and the Politics of Osage Oil, 1906-1949," *Journal of the West* (Vol. 23, No. 3, 1984).

Wyman, Walker D., "Kansas City, MO., A Famous Freighter Capital," *Kansas Historical Quarterly* (February 1937, vol. 6, no. 1).

U. S. Bureau of the Census, 1870, 1880, 1890, 1902, 1910, 1920, Washington, D.C.

Newspapers

Journal Post, Kansas City, Missouri, 1854-1924.

Journal News, Hamilton, OH, 1991.

Kansas City Star, 1907, 1918.

Kansas City Journal, 1893, 1905, 1925.

The Electro-Mechanic, A Journal devoted to Electrical and Mechanical Engineering, Kansas City, Missouri, 1889-1890.

Kansas City *City Directory* 1858, 1865-66, 1867-68, 1869, 1870.

New York Times, 1918.

Oil and Gas Journal, May 18, 1911

Proceedings of the National Electric Light Association at the First Annual Convention, 1885, 1886.

The Railwayan, Kansas City, 1923.

Dissertations

Black, Harry, "The Predecessor Companies of the Kansas City Power and Light Company," (Master's Thesis, University of Missouri--Kansas City, 1953).

Bremer, Jeffrey, "Frontier Capitalism: The Market Revolution in the Antebellum Lower Missouri River Valley, 1803-1860" (diss., University of Kansas, 2006).

Greene, Ann Norton, "Harnessing Power: Industrializing the Horse in 19th century America" (diss., University of Pennsylvania, 2004).

Motsinger, Gerald A., "The Development of Main Street, Kansas City, Missouri (Master's Thesis, University of Missouri, Kansas City, 1986).

Internet Resources

Consult extensive citations for internet resources throughout the endnotes, too voluminous to replicate here.

Fueling Change

Acknowledgements

My original guide to the outlines of Kansas City history was David Boutros before he retired as associate director of the State Historical Society of Missouri, Kansas City Research Center (formerly, Western History Manuscript Collection) at University of Missouri--Kansas City. His introduction was invaluable and directed me toward many primary sources of early Kansas City.

David W. Jackson gave my early dissertation research a great deal of his expert attention before he retired as archives and education director of the Jackson County (Mo.) Historical Society Archives. Jackson, as The Orderly Pack Rat (orderlypackrat.com), has stuck with me for me for nearly a decade to transform my dissertation. Our goal was to present a unique and heretofore unexplored aspect of Kansas City's rich history; yet, present a model for the global scientific and environmental communities needing a format to discuss fuel in historical context. Jackson urged me to develop Part 4. He helped add Kansas City-pertinent data throughout, especially the 20th century gasoline 'love story' bringing the history up to date. Finally, Jackson indexed and designed the book you now hold.

My classmates at Antioch University provided helpful feedback over time and surrounded me with support and enthusiasm. Melissa Laser designed the graphs that crystallized my research and was willing to work with me at length to make them accurate and attractive. Luanne Johnson, Randi Pokladnik and Marian Knapp became good friends as well as good critics. Their companionship made the difference in a long-distance run.

My dear friend and adopted daughter Kelly Ellison provided an excellent sounding board for my ideas from their infancy to their finish. I depend on her clarity, organization and intuitive ear. Other friends who have given their support, written letters of reference and nurtured me throughout this long effort include former classmate Jan Prock who remained interested, attentive and helpful, Jeannine Fox who listened and analyzed as only one author can for another, Charlotte Shelton, whose wisdom and encouragement I prize, Alan Ives, as fine and giving a supporter as anyone could ever ask for, and Ralph Ford, who asked, "What else are you going to do with the next 10 years if you don't do this?"

My thanks to Antioch University New England, the institution itself, a place of learning so much greater than the sum of its parts. It is an optimistic, purposeful place that operates with grace and good humor, forgiveness and willing support of students from around the world. The staff members were unfailingly kind and helpful, always did more than their share to solve problems and never made obstruction of my progress part of their business model. This was particularly true of the environmental studies department headed by Mitch Thomashow, a scholar of great depth, scope and passion. My thanks to Professor Beth Kaplan for understanding there is more than one way to approach the environment.

Fueling Change

I was extremely fortunate to have a fine dissertation committee: Thomas N. Webler of Antioch University listened to the evolving ideas in this work for seven years and gave valuable feedback. Renowned energy and city history scholar Martin V. Melosi of the University of Houston generously gave of his time and deep knowledge of the fields of urban and energy history and traveled twice to Keene, New Hampshire, to hear my proposal and my defense with good will, valuable criticism and steady encouragement. My advisor Alesia Maltz helped me shape this work with patience, insight, and cheerful good faith. She gave me the discipline to produce a good work and the freedom to follow my own instincts. I can ask for no greater gift. My deepest thanks to each of you.

Finally, thanks to my dear family members for accepting my announcement that I was going to begin this work with the unblinking expectation that I could not only start it but that I would finish it. For them I have done so. Sons Brennan and Gavin, daughters-in-law Genevieve and Ronni were my personal fan club. My grandchildren Cameron, Jordan, Austin and Zoe cheered me across the graduation platform. I walked for them.

My deepest thanks and love to my husband, Carl Blomgren, who made it all possible, including the many flights to MHT from MCI, and even when he regretted over the years ever having acquiesced to my desire to undertake this project, he suffered silently, put on a happy face, and listened to my alternating passionate and frustrated outbursts with equanimity. Such longsuffering good cheer made the trek possible. It has taken 10 years for me to transform the dissertation to a narrative fit for public viewing, and to add another, fact-filled 100 years to the story. Without David W. Jackson this piece would not exist. With him I have had the strength and endurance to continue to the end, and he has had the patience through many changes and modifications throughout.

The same thanks from 10 years ago applies today: all those previously enumerated gave me liftoff and confidence to pursue this to new heights.

Thanks again.

Index

About the Author

Twyla Dell arrived in Kansas City in 1978 from northern Virginia with a fresh master's degree in English from George Mason University. She soon joined the public information office of the Environmental Protection Agency, Region VII, then located at 12th and Oak in downtown Kansas City.

In 1990, she published *Call of the Rainbow Warrior: An Environmental Fable.* She also created the Environmental Leadership Program and offered it through her company The Foresight Institute. Business and community leaders, teachers and students attended the two-and-a-half-day weekend program introducing 12 interlocking environmental issues and awakening participants to action. The firm organized The Rainbow Generation for high school students and offered both the weekend retreat followed by after-school programs plus college scholarships for science students in 45 high schools in the area. She also worked to create "Eco-Kansas City" in 1995 and managed the 25th anniversary of Earth Day.

In 1996, Dell published, *The Corporate Environmental Leader: Five Steps to A New Ethic.* In 2001, she returned to graduate school and earned her Ph.D. in environmental studies from Antioch University Graduate School in Keene, New Hampshire, in 2009. Her thesis, *Flame, Furnace, Fuel: Creating Kansas City in the 19th Century,* was a case study of fuel use in Kansas City.

Fueling Change: How We Created Climate Change One Fuel at a Time adds the path of the dominant fuel, gasoline, to the city's 20th century story, and leaves readers with a progressive challenge at the dawn of the 21st century Solar Age. For more, see *Fueling Change's* companion guide booklet, *The Gasoline Diet.*

About the Author

David W. Jackson, a native Kansas Citian, was graduated magna cum laude with a B.S. in Historic Preservation–Archives Studies from Southeast Missouri State University in 1993.

While attending community college he had been a member of the Longview Environmental Group (affectionately called "LEG" by its faculty sponsor), educating students about good stewardship. Earth Day 1991 was the largest turnouts Kansas City had ever seen.

Throughout his 20+year career as an archivist at Jackson County (Mo.) Historical Society and Unity School of Christianity, Jackson served as editor of various publications where he advocated for saving and preserving the past. He also shared practical ways for readers to reduce their impact, or 'carbon footprint,' and to inspire them to up-cycle, pre-cycle, reduce, reuse, donate, and recycle. Jackson volunteered to lead educational workshops with Bridging the Gap community environmental organization for Kansas City's *RecycleFIRST* rollout, its free, curbside recycling program. The photo at the left was taken the day Jackson's Gregory Circle neighbors began recycling at the curb on September 7, 2004. He is also proud of his 2005 Toyota Prius' 50+miles-per-gallon average.

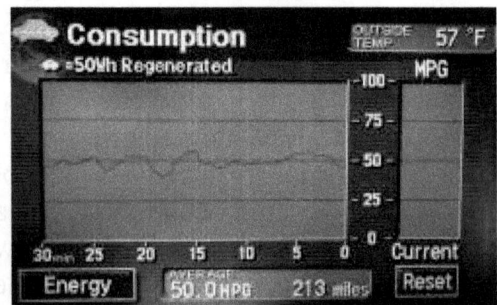

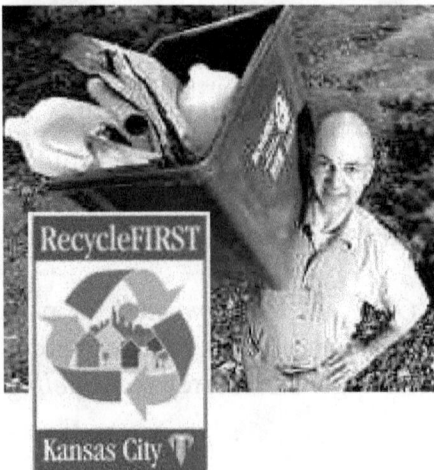

Jackson is director of The Orderly Pack Rat (orderlypackrat.com), an independent historical research, consulting service, and publishing house he founded in 1996. Responsible for adding more than 30 local history titles to bookshelves to date, Jackson continues to consult, research, write, and publish books, newspaper columns, and periodical features. He also delivers presentations related to local history and its preservation.

432

www.ingramcontent.com/pod-product-compliance
Lightning Source LLC
Chambersburg PA
CBHW062032090426
42740CB00016B/2887